Marketing
with AI

by Shiv Singh

A Wiley Brand

Marketing with AI For Dummies®

Published by: **John Wiley & Sons, Inc.,** 111 River Street, Hoboken, NJ 07030-5774, www.wiley.com

Table of Contents

CHAPTER 5: **Making Connections: Machine Learning and Neural Networks**. 77

CHAPTER 6: **Adding Natural Language Processing and Sentiment Analysis** 93

Introduction

Technology can revolutionize our lives in unimaginable ways. Many people don't remember life before e-mail, the World Wide Web, mobile phones, and video streaming. Work routines often rely heavily on laptops, wireless Internet, and search engines. The transformations driven by artificial intelligence (AI) fall into this same category of technological shifts but, arguably, will be more dramatic than any of the other shifts that came before.

When ChatGPT 3.0 launched in November 2022, AI moved to the forefront of everyday technology use. ChatGPT quickly became one of the fastest-growing apps in history, marking a pivotal shift in the use of AI in everyday life.

Every marketing sub-function — annual planning, strategy, research, campaign development, ad production, media planning, analytics, CRM — stands poised for a transformation with the advent of AI. Marketers will copilot every activity with AI, leading to more insightful, creative, personalized, and impactful marketing than ever before.

About This Book

Discussing technological transformations in broad terms can feel abstract. In this book, you can find out how AI's impact on everyday lives is becoming increasingly tangible and personal, and what that means for your work in marketing.

Marketing with AI For Dummies breaks down the implications of using AI for marketing into digestible pieces, making the subject accessible to any marketer. It provides definitions, frameworks, concepts, case studies, and practical guidance to translate AI's vast potential into actionable strategies for your business.

And although the world of AI is changing rapidly, the pace at which it gets incorporated into the marketing ecosystem is slower, meaning that the core concepts, strategies, frameworks, and practical guidance are more timeless than you may initially think.

Here are some conventions that I use throughout this book and what they mean:

>> *Italicized* words or phrases are terms that I define for you in the surrounding text.

>> Web addresses appear in monofont. If you're reading a digital version of this book on a device connected to the Internet, note that you can click the web address to visit that website, like this: www.dummies.com.

>> In several chapters, I point out what I consider to be best marketing practices with the words **Best Marketing Practice** in bold and italics.

To make the content of *Marketing with AI For Dummies* more accessible, I divided it into six parts:

>> **Part 1: Getting Started with AI and Marketing.** This part lays the historical and contextual foundation for AI. It also traces the evolution of AI from its mythological roots to modern-day applications, covering significant milestones such as the development of the Turing test, machine learning, and generative AI.

>> **Part 2: Exploring Fundamental AI Structures and Concepts.** In this part, I identify some of the best use cases for AI in marketing, evaluate various tools, and introduce some of the risks you may face when integrating AI into your workflow.

>> **Part 3: Using AI to Know Customers Better.** This part discusses AI's ability to deliver personalized experiences to customers, tailoring content and advertisements to individual consumers, and enhancing customer engagement. You can examine AI-driven technologies, such as chatbots, and how they can contribute to enhanced customer satisfaction.

>> **Part 4: Transforming Brand Content and Campaign Development.** This part explores the role of AI in generating creative content. It discusses how to prompt the AI tools to create content effectively and identifies which tools can help you produce high-quality content efficiently and at scale. You can read about AI's impact on advertising, including how to run effective A/B testing with the latest AI technologies, develop stronger SEO programs, and localize content using AI.

>> **Part 5: Targeting Growth Marketing and Customer Focus with AI.** This part covers AI's integration into growth marketing, focusing on optimizing campaigns, improving customer experiences, and enhancing operational efficiency. It also emphasizes the importance of ethical guidelines, responsible use, and strategic integration into business operations. Additionally, the part addresses ethical, legal, and privacy concerns, providing principles for responsible AI use in marketing.

>> **Part 6: The Part of Tens.** In this part, you can find a list of ten things to avoid in AI marketing and ten developments that I predict are coming for the marketing world while it begins using AI more commonly.

Foolish Assumptions

Whether you're a chief marketing officer at a Fortune 500 company, a junior marketer in a small business, an agency executive working with marketers, or wearing several hats (including the marketing hat) in your business, this book is for you. The only real assumptions I make about you are that you're interested in AI and how it can be used in marketing, and some best practices for doing so.

Icons Used in This Book

Throughout this book, icons in the margins highlight certain types of valuable information that call out for your attention. Here are the icons that you may encounter and a brief description of each.

TIP

The Tip icon marks tips and shortcuts that you can use to make working with AI in your marketing efforts easier.

REMEMBER

Remember icons mark the information that's especially important to know. To siphon off the most important information in each chapter, just skim through these icons.

TECHNICAL STUFF

The Technical Stuff icon marks information of a highly technical nature that you can normally skip over unless you want to get some nonessential info on the subject.

WARNING

The Warning icon tells you to watch out! It marks important information that may save you headaches, including issues such as ethical missteps to avoid or common mistakes in execution that you can steer clear of.

Beyond the Book

In addition to all the AI-marketing information and guidance that you can find in this book itself, you get access to even more help and information online at Dummies.com. Check out this book's online Cheat Sheet by going to www.dummies.com/ and searching for "Marketing with AI For Dummies Cheat Sheet."

Where to Go from Here

The chapters in this book cover all the critical facets of marketing with AI. Each part builds on the previous one, providing a comprehensive road map for navigating the AI-driven transformation of the marketing landscape. However, you don't have to read the book from cover to cover. You can dip into chapters that address different AI-related questions that you have while you incorporate AI into your marketing efforts. Check out the Table of Contents to identify the subjects most important to you, and dive in!

1

Getting Started with Marketing with AI

IN THIS CHAPTER

» Tracking AI from conception
to fruition

» Watching machines fool people and
beat the experts

» Seeing advanced AI capabilities in
everyday life

Chapter **1**

A Brief History of AI

To fully grasp the role of artificial intelligence (AI) in business, I begin by helping you trace its fascinating history. This background exploration not only illuminates AI's vast advancements, but also highlights its utility in business and marketing.

The earliest conceptions of artificial intelligence date back to Greek mythology, where Talos — an 8-foot-tall giant constructed of bronze — stood guard over the island of Crete to protect it from pirates and other invaders. Talos would throw boulders at ships and patrol the island each day. As the legend goes, Talos was eventually defeated when a plug near his foot was removed, allowing the *ichor* (blood of the gods) to flow out from the single vein in his body.

From that point forward, tales of automated entities flourished in mythology, captivating the minds of scientists, mathematicians, and inventors. Modern science and technology have realized some of these mythological concepts through recent advancements. In this chapter, I introduce you to those advancements, including the Turing test, machine learning, expert systems, and generative AI.

Early Technological Advances

Scientists trace the dawn of automation back to the 17th century and the invention of the *pascaline*, a mechanical calculator. Constructed by French inventor Blaise Pascal between 1642 and 1644, this groundbreaking device featured a *controlled* carry mechanism that facilitated the arithmetic operations of addition and subtraction by effectively carrying the 1 to the next column. This calculator worked especially efficiently when dealing with large numbers. Following in Pascal's footsteps, Wilhelm Leibniz, a German mathematician, invented a calculator in 1694 that expanded upon the concept of the pascaline by enabling all four basic arithmetic operations — addition, subtraction, multiplication, and division (not just addition and subtraction). These devices first offered a glimpse into the potential for mechanical reasoning.

Fast-forward to the early 1800s, and you encounter the Jacquard system, developed by Joseph-Marie Jacquard of France, which used interchangeable punched cards to dictate the weaving of cloth and the design of intricate patterns. These punched cards laid the groundwork for future developments in computing. Near the mid-1800s, British inventor Charles Babbage unveiled the first computational device known as the *analytical engine*. Employing punch cards, this machine could perform a variety of calculations involving multiple variables, and it featured a reset function when it completed its task. Importantly, it also incorporated temporary data storage for more advanced computations — a feature crucial for any artificial intelligence (AI) system.

By the late 1880s, the development of the tabulating machine — designed by American inventor Herman Hollerith specifically to process data for the 1890 U.S. Census — helped the development of AI reach another milestone. This electro-mechanical device utilized punched cards to store and aggregate data, effectively enhancing the analytical engine's storage capabilities through the inclusion of an accumulator. Remarkably, modified iterations of the tabulating machine remained operational until as recently as the 1980s.

Alan Turing and Machine Intelligence

Many people regard Alan Turing, a British mathematician, logician, and computer scientist, as the founding father of theoretical computer science, and he paved the way for further AI breakthroughs. During World War II, he served at Bletchley Park, the United Kingdom's codebreaking establishment; and he played a pivotal role in decrypting messages encoded by the German *Enigma machine* (a code-generating device). Scholars and historians credit his work at Bletchley Park with both shortening the war and saving millions of lives.

Turing's key innovation at Bletchley was the development of the *Bombe*, a machine that significantly accelerated the code-breaking process used to decode messages from the Enigma machine. The Enigma used a series of rotating disks to transform plain text messages into encrypted cipher text. The complexity of this encryption device and the coded messages it generated came in part from the fact that Enigma users changed the machine's settings daily. The United Kingdom and all the Allies found cracking the code within the 24-hour window — before the settings were altered again — exceedingly difficult. The Bombe automated the process of identifying Enigma settings, sorting through various potential combinations far more rapidly than any human could. This automation enabled the British to regularly decode German communications.

REMEMBER

Although the details of this code-breaking device remained classified for many years, the Bombe stands as one of the earliest examples of technology outperforming humans in tasks that traditionally required human intelligence, executing them more efficiently and accurately.

The Turing Test in 1950

Soon after World War II, in a paper published in 1950 titled "Computing Machinery and Intelligence," Turing introduced the idea of defining a standard by which we can call a machine intelligent. He designed the experiment (now called the *Turing test*) to answer the question, "Can machines think?" The fundamental premise of the experiment said that if a computer can participate in a dialogue with a human in such a way that an observer can't tell which participant is human and which is computer, then you can consider that computer intelligent.

Turing's test proposed that a human evaluator assess dialogues between a human and a machine that was designed to generate human-like responses. The evaluator knows that one of the participants is a machine, but not which one. To eliminate any bias from vocal cues, Turing proposed that the test giver limit the interactions to a text-only medium. If the evaluator found it challenging to distinguish between the machine and the human participant, the machine passed the test. The evaluation didn't focus on the correctness of the machine's answers, but on how indistinguishable its responses were from a human's. In fact, the test's criteria didn't make any reference to the accuracy of the answers.

The Turing test: 1960s and beyond

In 1966, well after Alan Turing's death, German-American scientist Joseph Weizenbaum created ELIZA, the first program that some say appeared to pass the Turing test. Many sources refute that it could pass the Turing test, but it was technically capable of making some humans believe that they were talking to human operators. The program worked by studying a user's typed comments for keywords and then executing a rule that transformed the user's comments, resulting in the program returning a new sentence. In effect, the ELIZA, like many programs since then, mimicked an understanding of the world without actually possessing any real-world knowledge.

Taking this development a step further, in 1972, Kenneth Colby, an American psychiatrist, created PARRY, which he described as ELIZA with attitude. Experienced psychiatrists tested PARRY in the early 1970s by using a variation of the Turing test. They analyzed text from real patients and from computers running PARRY. The psychiatrists correctly identified the patients only 52 percent of the time, a statistic consistent with random guessing.

REMEMBER

Even to this day, the Turing test gives the world a concise, easily understandable method of assessing whether a piece of technology has intelligence or not. By limiting the test to text-based interactions that require natural language query (conversational English), anyone could easily understand the nature of the test when Turing first introduced it. And by separating out the accuracy of the response from the question of identification, it focused the test on evaluating what truly makes humans more human.

TIP

Computers have advanced by leaps and bounds since the time that Alan Turing first proposed the Turing test. But consider this timeline regarding the ongoing development of intelligent technology:

>> **As recently as 2021,** chatbots that much of the world had access to struggled to pass the Turing test consistently. Services such as Siri from Apple, Alexa from Amazon, and Google's Assistant could speak to us in natural language but would quickly get stumped with some of the most basic of questions. For example, the question "Describe yourself using only colors and shapes?" may prompt the answer "Okay, I found this on the web for describing colors and shapes. . . ."

>> **As of 2023,** major chat interfaces from the likes of OpenAI, Google, and others, can pass the Turing test. This quick change shows how technological advancements in the field of AI happen in fits and starts, with so much having changed dramatically in just 24 months.

The Dartmouth Conference of 1956

The academic community often considers the Dartmouth Conference of 1956 as the birth of artificial intelligence (AI) as a distinct field of research. Held during the summer of that year at Dartmouth College in Hanover, New Hampshire, the conference brought together luminaries from various disciplines — computer science, cognitive psychology, mathematics, and engineering — under one roof for an extended period of six to eight weeks. Organized by computer scientists John McCarthy, Marvin Minsky, and Nathaniel Rochester, and mathematician Claude Shannon, the conference aimed to explore "every aspect of learning or any other feature of intelligence," as stated in the original proposal for the conference.

The Dartmouth Conference of 1956 was groundbreaking for several reasons. It was more than just a summer gathering of intellectuals; it was a seminal event that shaped the trajectory of AI as we know it today. It provided the name, the initial community, the research directions, and the momentum that have fueled decades of innovation in AI.

Specifically, the conference

>> **Coined the term *artificial intelligence* (AI):** The conference gave a name to a field that had been, up until that point, loosely defined and interdisciplinary across mathematics, computer science, engineering, and related fields. John McCarthy, one of the organizers, was credited with introducing the term, which helped in shaping the future direction of research by providing a focal point around which scholars could rally.

>> **Served as a catalyst for future research:** It set the research agenda for decades to come. During the conference, participants engaged in deep discussions, brainstorming sessions, and even early-stage experiments on foundational topics in the AI field. The participants aimed to discover whether they could program machines to simulate aspects of human intelligence, with research topics such as

- Problem-solving
- Symbolic reasoning
- Neural networks
- Language understanding
- Learning machines

They designed programs to play chess, prove mathematical theorems, and generate rather simplistic sentences.

>> **Provided a collaborative platform for interdisciplinary research:** Researchers who may not have otherwise crossed paths now engaged in meaningful dialogues, forging relationships that would lead to significant collaborations in the years and decades to come. This interdisciplinary nature was crucial for tackling the complex problem of simulating human

intelligence, which requires insights from various fields such as psychology, neuroscience, linguistics, operations research, economics, and more.

>> **Attracted critical funding and attention to the developing field of AI:** The visibility and credibility gained from this event led to increased investment in AI research from both governmental and private sectors. This financial backing was essential for the development of labs, academic programs, and research projects that propelled the field forward.

Machine Learning and Expert Systems Emerge

Following the Dartmouth Conference (see the preceding section), two key sub-fields emerged that became the cornerstones of artificial intelligence — machine learning and expert systems. The *expert systems* were rule-based methods that drew upon predefined sets of instructions established by human beings. *Machine learning* (initially referred to as *self-teaching computers*) represented a radical shift in approach that aimed to build systems that learned from data, rather than by following scripted rules.

Meeting machine learning

Arthur Samuel, an American pioneer in the field of computer gaming and artificial intelligence, officially coined the term *machine learning* in 1959. Unlike traditional computing methods that relied on explicit instructions for every operation, machine learning focused on developing algorithms capable of producing results from existing data. These algorithms use statistical techniques to identify patterns, make decisions, or predict future outcomes based on those patterns.

In the 1960s, the Raytheon Company made a significant contribution to the field by developing an early learning machine system that could analyze various types of data, including sonar signals, electrocardiograms, and speech patterns. The machine used a form of *reinforcement learning*, a subset of machine learning in which the algorithm identifies optimal actions through trial and error. In essence, the system was rewarded for correct decisions and punished for incorrect ones. Humans operated and fine-tuned the system, and those humans pushed a goof button to flag and correct any errors. These corrections enabled the machine to adapt and improve its performance over time.

Critical standout features of machine learning include the following:

>> **Adaptability:** Instead of relying on humans to manually code solutions to problems, machine learning enables computers to come up with their own solutions by examining large sets of data. This freedom has led to groundbreaking applications across various sectors. For example, machine learning algorithms power large language models and computer vision systems that enable computers to identify and understand objects and people in images and videos.

These systems can

- Generate human-like text.

- Recognize thousands of objects and filter spam e-mails with incredible accuracy.

- Transcribe and translate human speech in real time.

I discuss each of these topics in detail in subsequent chapters (Chapters 4 and 5, for example).

>> **Efficient and scalable solutions:** Because developing specific algorithms for each recognition, filtering, or generating task would be both costly and time-consuming, machine learning offers a far more efficient and *scalable solution* (which means that the solution can perform tasks on huge data sets without having a corresponding increase in costs). The data-driven approach to finding solutions has revolutionized the way technologists approach and solve problems, and it has automated complex tasks (such as reviewing social media content for hate speech) that computer scientists once considered beyond the reach of computers.

REMEMBER

Because machine learning continues to evolve, experts expect its impact and relevance across various fields to continue to grow. See Chapter 2 for examples of the effects on areas of business.

Examining expert systems

In the late 1960s, many researchers focused on capturing *domain-specific knowledge*, which laid the foundation for *expert systems*, meaning technology systems or computers that played the role of experts in a specific domain such as drug discovery. Those expert systems were the precursors to modern-day AI systems that now exist. By the 1970s, researchers created some of the first expert systems, including DENDRAL (designed for chemical mass spectrometry) and MYCIN (aimed at diagnosing bacterial infections). These expert systems captured knowledge and reasoning capabilities from human experts to offer advice as diverse as simple medical diagnoses and exploration strategies for mineral mining.

The systems worked well in narrow subject domains, but the cost and difficulty of maintaining and scaling their rule-based knowledge effectively limited their usefulness. Research and development of expert systems went something like this:

>> **In the late 1970s,** a thawing of the AI Winter (see the following section) supported the broader adoption of expert systems in various industries, including healthcare, finance, and manufacturing. During this period, computer scientists developed specific tools to help expand their expert systems while those systems' usefulness grew exponentially.

>> **By the 1990s,** the limitations of expert systems became very evident, particularly their inability to learn from their processing experiences or strengthen their performance without external programming. This shortcoming led to a decline in the development of stand-alone expert systems, and computer scientists began to integrate them into larger, more complex computer systems.

>> **More recently,** ideas at the heart of expert systems have seen a resurgence of sorts, although they often appear in hybrid forms that incorporate machine learning (see the preceding section) and other data-driven techniques. Although not many corporations create and use stand-alone expert systems (after their limitations on explicit knowledge and brittleness became more apparent), the core concepts of capturing and applying human expertise in computational models remains integral to AI. And broader AI solutions incorporate expert systems as a complement to other advanced methods (such as machine learning and natural language processing, or NLP; see the section "More AI Developments in the 1980s" later in the chapter for more).

REMEMBER

The introduction of expert systems was an important moment in the history of artificial intelligence. Expert systems development pioneered knowledge engineering techniques that computer scientists still use to train AI systems today. But most AI tools now depend more on machine learning (which is much more scalable, or easily expanded), rather than explicitly programmed rules that require human involvement.

An AI Winter Sets In

After the hype of artificial intelligence in the 1960s and early 1970s, the limitations of early AI became clear, leading to a period of reduced funding and interest, which was coined the *AI winter*. The Lighthill report, compiled for the British Science Research council and originally published in 1973, helped bring about this AI winter. The report criticized the lack of practical applications and questioned the potential of AI research. These criticisms led to reduced government funding in several countries, including the United Kingdom.

But even during this period of reduced funding, research continued that advanced core technical capabilities such as probabilistic reasoning, neural networks, and intelligent agents. Even in this period of reduced optimism, diligent computer scientists still drove key advancements before machine learning unlocked its next era of rapid progress in the 1980s.

The lessons of the AI winter of the 1970s have continued to inform the ethics debate around realistic versus overhyped claims in the AI world. This debate matters more than ever while differing opinions on the promise and perils of AI collide around the world.

The Stanford Cart: From the '60s to the '80s

You can't have a conversation about the history of artificial intelligence (AI) without discussing the story of the Stanford Cart, a remote controlled four-wheeled cart first developed in the 1960s that later came equipped with a camera and onboard computer for vision and control. This seminal project in the history of AI and robotics was one of the earliest attempts to create a self-driving vehicle. The cart, which was developed over a 20-year period, served as a platform for research into computer vision, path planning, and autonomous navigation.

The evolution of the Stanford Cart project not only mirrored the evolution of AI and robotics over its 20-year time span, but it also shaped the trajectory of AI and robotics, as well. The project remains a testament to the enduring impact of focused research and iterative development in the field of AI.

The stages of the Stanford Cart's evolution include

>> **Remote control:** In the 1960s, the first version of the cart simply allowed for remote control capabilities. Starting the cart's development this way made perfect sense because the cart served as a research platform for investigating the problem of controlling a Moon rover remotely from Earth.

>> **Self-navigation:** The early 1970s saw the cart get a camera and an onboard computer, which allowed it to navigate an obstacle course by taking photographs and then computing the best path forward based on those images. Later in the 1970s, more advanced computer vision algorithms allowed the cart to navigate complex environments more quickly while the image processing capabilities accelerated as well.

>> **Real-time complex navigation:** By the 1980s, the cart could follow roads and avoid obstacles in real time, largely due to improvements in both hardware and software, especially in broad increases of computer processing power. This capability marked a significant milestone in the development of autonomous vehicles, which entered commercial production decades later. Increased processing power allowed for faster and more complex computations, while advanced algorithms enabled the cart to make split-second decisions.

REMEMBER

As one of the first practical applications of AI in robotics, the Stanford Cart demonstrated how computers could interact with the real world. The computer components that allowed visual input and analysis demonstrated the potential benefits of sophisticated image recognition and scene interpretation. And today's robotics and autonomous systems for path planning and obstacle avoidance use various algorithmic techniques that the Stanford Cart first introduced.

More AI Developments in the 1980s

Arguably, the 1980s stand as a critical decade in the development of artificial intelligence, characterized by groundbreaking advancements in various subfields, especially in machine learning, neural networks, and natural language processing. This period saw foundational advancements that set the stage for the AI technologies of today.

This decade's significant developments include

>> **Backpropagation:** The introduction and popularization of the backpropagation algorithm for training neural networks. Before backpropagation, training complex neural networks took a lot of computational power and was less effective. The *backpropagation algorithm* streamlined the training process by efficiently calculating the error between predicted and actual outcomes, and then distributing this error back through the network to adjust the *internal weights* (which effectively transform the input data within the network's hidden layers). This innovation facilitated the training of multi-layer neural networks and paved the way for more complex architectures and applications.

>> **Deep learning:** A subfield of machine learning that uses neural networks that have three or more layers. Researchers such as Geoffrey Hinton, Yann LeCun, and Yoshua Bengio (operating at various universities) were instrumental during this period because they laid the groundwork for this subfield. These layered neural networks found use in a range of applications, from image and voice recognition to natural language understanding, which would later fuel innovations in automating various business processes.

>> **Natural language processing (NLP):** Initially, programmers largely based NLP systems on handcrafted rules. However, the 1980s saw a significant shift toward statistical models, making these systems more robust and scalable. The decade set the stage for machine learning-based approaches that have come to dominate the NLP landscape, enabling more complex applications such as chatbots, translation services, and sentiment analysis tools.

>> **Robotics:** The decade also marked the beginning of significant advancements in robotics, much of which was built on the foundational concepts of AI. The Stanford Cart project, for example (see the preceding section), served as a crucial catalyst for research into autonomous systems.

Rapid Advancements of AI in the 1990s and Beyond

The remarkable journey of artificial intelligence (AI) goes from its mythological inspirations (Talos, the bronze giant in Greek mythology who protected Crete) to groundbreaking inventions such as Pascal's calculator (discussed in the section "Early Technological Advances," earlier in this chapter) and projects such as the Stanford Cart (see the section "The Stanford Cart: From the '60s to the '80s," earlier in this chapter). The progress made since the early 2010s alone transformed the AI landscape and altered the way people think about technology's role in various domains, including business and society at large.

Beginning in the 1990s, rapid advancements in existing branches of AI research brought expansion of capabilities to machine learning and deep learning. Other advancements in AI research brought new depth to the capability of AI to demonstrate seemingly intuitive thinking and to generate human-like original content.

Watching machine learning grow up

Between the 1990s and the early 2000s, machine learning emerged as a dominant force in AI development. (See the section "Meeting machine learning," earlier in this chapter, for an introduction to machine learning.) This field of AI uses algorithms to analyze huge data sets to uncover patterns and make predictions without built-in, explicitly programmed rules. Spurred on by significant increases in computing power and data availability, machine learning delivered new use cases in the realm of *computer vision* (where computers derive information from images, videos, and other input) and *recommender systems* (information filtering systems that suggest items most pertinent to the user).

These AI advancements came about in part because the AI engines had access to large data sets. The models used to analyze these data sets mimicked more human-like pattern recognition and decision making by using statistical relationships between the data objects. These developments illustrated how quickly an AI system could learn (extrapolate) from data on its own, rather than having a programmer code specific and explicit instructions for that system. Machine learning is at the heart of AI to this day.

Playing a pivotal chess match

The 1990s saw a pivotal moment in the history of AI that captured the imagination of people around the world. IBM's Deep Blue, a chess-playing computer, defeated the reigning world chess champion, Garry Kasparov, in 1997. Even though Deep Blue didn't have the benefit of a modern neural network at the time and instead relied on brute-force heuristic search techniques and specialized chess algorithms, it did incorporate basic machine learning techniques to evaluate board positions and enhance its game play. Deep Blue's chess win was another momentous advance for AI and machine learning; it

» Proved that a machine can outperform a human in a task that required complex decision-making over many steps.

» Triggered huge debates about the future of AI and its potential impact on all facets of life. Those debates have only accelerated today with the much more recent introduction of generative artificial intelligence (see the section "Creating content with generative AI," later in the chapter).

» Supported Kasparov's perspective that machines and humans working together can accomplish much more than either of them working alone. He introduced the term, *advanced chess* for a form of chess in which humans partner with computer systems to play chess, emphasizing that human intuition and machine calculations together were an almost unbeatable combination.

REMEMBER

Kasparov's idea of advanced chess had a lasting impact on how we think about AI today, and many AI researchers consider advanced chess a precursor to modern theories around AI serving as an assistant to a human operator in various domains. (Satya Nadella, Microsoft CEO, has referred to this assistance more popularly as AI co-piloting.) In subsequent chapters, I delve into the role of AI as a complementary tool for humans in the realm of business and marketing, and in those discussions, you can clearly trace the philosophical roots of this cooperative approach to Kasparov's insights.

Tracking the deep learning revolution

In recent years, the advent of deep learning has significantly elevated the capabilities and accuracy of AI systems. Building on the foundations laid by traditional machine learning, deep learning employs neural networks that have multiple layers — often referred to as *deep neural networks* — to achieve unprecedented levels of accuracy in tasks such as image classification, speech recognition, and natural language processing.

What sets deep learning apart from earlier AI technologies is the advancement in computational power, the availability of massive data sets, and the use of intricate algorithms that optimize neural networks with more than just a few layers. This multi-layered architecture enables the system to model complex relationships in the data, leading to remarkably precise results.

Deep learning–enabled systems

>> **Stand as the engine powering an extensive range of AI applications in use today.** Deep learning revolutionizes automation by enabling systems to perform complex analytical and predictive tasks entirely autonomously, without any human intervention. Whether you use digital voice assistants such as Siri or Alexa, voice-activated TV remotes, or advanced driver-assistance systems in modern automobiles, deep learning acts as the key technology underpinning many of these innovations.

>> **Promise to offer even more cross-domain intelligence in their next generation.** These future systems will likely require less data for effective learning, operate more efficiently on increasingly sophisticated processors, and employ even more advanced algorithms. People developing AI technologies want to bring artificial intelligence closer to mimicking the complexities and capabilities of the human brain.

REMEMBER

Although scientists and programmers may still be decades away from achieving *artificial general intelligence* — a state where AI possesses reasoning, learning, and common sense akin to human cognition — deep learning undeniably serves as a significant step toward that lofty goal.

Demonstrating intuition in the age of AI

The Turing test raised the seminal question, "Can machines think?" People began to ponder whether humans could distinguish between a machine and a human during a text-based interaction. (See the section "Alan Turing and Machine

Intelligence," earlier in this chapter, for info about the Turing test.) This question appeared to find a definitive answer in the groundbreaking 2016 victory of AlphaGo over Lee Sedol in a game of Go.

AlphaGo was the brainchild of DeepMind, a British AI company that Google later bought. Unlike conventional AI programs, AlphaGo was purpose-built to master the game of Go, an ancient board game that boasts a complexity far surpassing that of chess. Although the game has simple rules, the sheer number of possible moves adds astronomical complexity. Top Go players — such as Lee Sedol, a leading figure in the world of Go — are revered for their intuition, creativity, and analytical skills.

In preparation for its 2016 face-off with Lee Sedol, AlphaGo underwent rigorous training, using a combination of machine learning methodologies, including deep learning, along with other algorithms such as the probability-based Monte Carlo tree search. The program analyzed thousands of historical Go matches and, perhaps more impressively, honed its skills by playing countless matches against itself. This self-play allowed AlphaGo to simulate various strategies and tactics, thereby enhancing its own game-playing capabilities.

When AlphaGo beat Lee Sedol in a five-game series, the global AI community sat up and took notice of two startling realizations:

>> **The unexpected display of AI ingenuity:** AlphaGo's ability to make apparently creative and intuitive strategic choices — qualities that many assumed were the exclusive domain of human cognition. Sergey Brin of Google — whose company acquired DeepMind — was in Seoul for the third game and said, "When you watch really great Go players play, it is like a thing of beauty. So I am very excited that we have been able to instill that kind of beauty in our computers."

>> **The profound capabilities and future potential of AI:** AlphaGo's win provided more than just a technological milestone; it created a paradigm shift that raised the awareness of leaders across various sectors — from scientists and politicians to business leaders and the general public.

REMEMBER

This historical event where AlphaGo beat a consummate human Go player served as an irrefutable testament to the advancements in deep learning, indicating that AI can indeed perform tasks that many people previously thought only human intelligence could do.

Creating content with generative AI

Advancements in AI after 2010 saw dramatic innovation, particularly in the development of *generative models* (which can generate new synthetic data such as text or images). And by the 2020s, generative models found applications in a variety of fields ranging from art and entertainment to scientific research and drug discovery. Two specific developments provided the necessary foundation for generative models' advancement:

>> **Generative adversarial networks (GANs):** Introduced by computer research scientist Ian Goodfellow and his colleagues in 2014, GANs had the capability to generate incredibly realistic images, text, and other types of data. This significant leap forward provided a robust framework for generating intricate, high-quality digital assets. Subsequent advancements in GANs led to models such as StyleGAN, which can generate high-resolution, highly realistic images.

>> **The Transformer architecture:** Initially designed for natural language processing, it was adapted for generative tasks later in the same decade. The adaptation to generative tasks culminated in models such as OpenAI's GPT series that can generate human-like text.

I cover generative AI models extensively in Chapter 8.

Chapter **2**

Exploring AI Business Use Cases

Since the 1980s, artificial intelligence (AI) has been steadily permeating organizations, and each advancement in AI innovation opens up new possibilities for its application in business. Given that technology is the backbone of a multitude of business processes (from accounting to inventory management), every advancement in AI implies that people can automate more processes, or they can enrich existing automated processes in more inventive ways.

Generative AI — a branch of artificial intelligence focused on creating new content (such as text, images, and music) by learning from existing data — stands out as the most significant development in the history of AI development. It gives rise to a plethora of business applications, many of which no one could even imagine until recently. These applications, including drug discovery and video creation, span all operations and functions within organizations. The more sophisticated ones (for example, finding cures for specific disease states) necessitate deep, industry-specific knowledge and access to unique data sets. Indeed, the uniqueness and completeness of the data set used to train an AI tool allows the AI to perform increasingly intricate tasks.

A recent study by McKinsey & Company (a global management consulting firm) highlighted the potential of generative AI to enhance workplace productivity and inject trillions of dollars in value into the global economy. Specifically, the study estimated that generative AI could annually contribute between $2.6 trillion and $4.4 trillion in value across 63 distinct *use cases* (specific, narrow business applications or implementations of the technology within a company). To contextualize these figures, they're roughly equivalent to the entire GDP of the United Kingdom in 2021.

This study doesn't even account for the additional productivity benefits gained by integrating generative AI into existing software for tasks beyond those 63 defined use cases. Notably, the study indicated that three-quarters of the value that generative AI can create would come from customer operations, marketing and sales, software development, and research and development. You can read this McKinsey study yourself online. Just go to www.mckinsey.com, select the Search icon, enter "economic potential of generative ai" in the text box, and click the Search icon again. Select the first search result to access the study.

In this chapter, you can find a pragmatic approach to AI use that examines various functions in a business — from marketing and sales to product development and legal departments — to help you determine which major activities or workflows you can enhance, or even replace, with AI. Because an abundance of generative AI solutions are on the horizon at the time of writing (thanks to the groundbreaking work of OpenAI, Google, Anthropic, and others), this chapter examines the most common use cases by business function, offering insights into the decisions that managers should contemplate when they incorporate more AI into their initiatives.

Automating Customer Service

A logical starting point for using AI in business involves the customer service department, given its extensive history of leveraging technology to automate numerous tasks, all aimed at reducing costs and enhancing business efficiencies. Because customer service typically comes at a significant expense for companies (especially in a post-COVID era, when customer expectations have only increased), it's a natural place to identify opportunities for efficiencies. According to a *Harvard Business Review* article published in August of 2023, AI-driven automations in customer service, such as personalized recommendations and improved support, ultimately lead to increased customer satisfaction and loyalty.

Serving customers by using chatbots

One of the most fundamental use cases for the application of artificial intelligence in customer service falls into the realm of *chatbots*, which are applications designed to simulate human-like conversations based on user input. This technology proliferated across companies in the last decade as a way to handle real-time customer service tasks (such as changing flight bookings) more efficiently and cost effectively than by having a human being available, whether on the phone, at a desk, or through a computer.

Historically, technology limitations resulted in most of the chatbot and virtual assistant use cases being rather rudimentary. Companies and systems integrators (technology consultants) built these chatbots as rule-based decision trees: A live chatbot asked customers a series of questions, and those customers could choose from options in a predefined list of responses. Based on their specific response, the chatbot would ask another question that had another set of predefined responses; or if the customer reached the end of a decision tree without their query being resolved, the chatbot would point them to a web page that may have the answer to their original query.

Generative AI has changed this structure by allowing customers to write their questions in their own words. And in turn, using *natural language processing* (NLP) enables the chatbot to read the question, analyze the query, and then identify the intent and associated entities (articles, web pages, and so on) that it can use to provide a useful response in natural language. These more advanced chatbots use technologies such as OpenAI's ChatGPT plug-ins to analyze and understand the conversation that a human being is having with it. The chatbot then responds by drawing insights from the internal customer service database of the company and putting it in everyday conversational English.

FINE-TUNING CUSTOMER INTERACTIONS WITH GENERATIVE AI CHATBOTS

At the time of writing, a growing number of startups and enterprise-grade companies are introducing AI technology solutions featuring out-of-the-box Generative AI chatbots. You can seamlessly integrate the chatbots with ChatGPT and train them on your company's data through simple integrations. This integration evolves into informed chatbot agents that continually improve with each subsequent customer interaction. The more advanced solutions don't just search company databases to respond to customer inquiries, but also analyze customer activity, payment histories, account notes, call logs, and other behaviors to deliver more pertinent and helpful responses. In some instances, these comprehensive customer views also guide the interactions of customer service representatives with the customers. After all, customers may still prefer to converse with a human representative, even though an AI chatbot may be equally, if not more, knowledgeable.

Resolving customer issues with virtual assistants

Virtual assistants (which are digital helpers that perform tasks and services based on voice or text commands), alongside chatbots (see the preceding section), play a crucial role in customer service. They can significantly enhance operational efficiency for companies by enabling quicker customer service and concurrently reducing the overall expenses related to customer service operations. They integrate the accumulated insights gleaned from customers and optimize interactions while continuously refining their responses and support capabilities. These functions ensure more personalized and effective communication and support.

These technologies serve as supportive tools to more experienced human operators, primarily capturing fundamental customer information and directing customers to the most suitable human operator likely to address their concerns effectively. Virtual assistants automate numerous routine customer service tasks and assist with other support-related activities, such as

>> Dispatching order confirmation e-mails

>> Facilitating product returns

>> Tracking orders

>> Updating delivery statuses

>> Managing renewals and cancellations

>> Updating billing and payment info

Much like chatbots, most businesses have used virtual assistants for some time, albeit with more rudimentary and basic functionalities. Now, with the advent of generative AI and its ability to understand customer service requests, AI-enhanced virtual assistants can navigate customers through more intricate processes in ways previously unattainable. For example, they can manage tasks ranging from altering flight details for airline customers, to aiding a customer in resolving product complaints, to identifying the optimal product or service based on individual needs.

Seeking out trends and solutions with sentiment analysis

Businesses can use AI to discover trends within customer service requests through *sentiment analysis*, a specialized area within natural language processing (NLP; see

Chapter 6) that scrutinizes and categorizes the emotions and opinions expressed by customers in text (whether through e-mails, website chats, or text messages). Especially for large companies that interact with hundreds, thousands, or even millions of customers daily, sifting through myriad customer service inquiries is a routine challenge. These companies need to discern overarching patterns and understand the significance and nature of the volume of customer service requests to better inform future product features or pricing directions, for example.

The AI can swiftly analyze all customer service requests received over a specified period — a day, week, or month — and filter by various criteria such as location, product type, or customer segment. This quick categorization furnishes companies with crucial insights into the nature of customer service requests. These insights can subsequently guide decisions related to

>> **Inventory:** What and how much to keep on hand

>> **Customer service approach:** What type of service to provide and when

>> **Agent performance:** Whether specific agents, either AI or human, need additional training or support

Sentiment analysis also yields invaluable insights into customer sentiments, preferences, and needs, enabling businesses to refine their products and services accordingly. The analysis offers insights by identifying patterns in the data that would be difficult for a human being to discover efficiently.

REMEMBER

Although AI has used sentiment analysis as a part of NLP for some time, recent advancements in NLP and machine learning (see Chapter 5 for more) have facilitated more sophisticated, precise, and insightful analyses that earlier technologies just couldn't do. The nuanced understanding that advanced sentiment analysis provides allows companies to stay attuned to their customers' evolving needs and preferences, and to make strategic adjustments to their products, services, and customer interaction strategies. The enhanced accuracy and depth of these analyses empower companies to

>> Make informed decisions regarding the scope of products and services that they offer.

>> Tailor their product marketing strategies to more closely match customer needs and preferences.

>> Enhance (continually) their offerings and customer interactions based on evolving customer sentiments and expectations. The following table lists five AI customer service offerings that you can explore.

Startup	Website	What It Does
Observe.AI	www.observe.ai	Enables more automated call center operations for your customer service teams
Ultimate	www.ultimate.ai	Enhances your customer service operations with a conversational AI platform
Kore.ai	www.kore.ai	Spans many business functions — including customer service — with its AI platform
Ada	www.ada.cx	Uses AI to automate a range of advanced customer service operations (such as refunds and exchanges)
Capacity	www.capacity.com	Offers the first fully AI-powered Helpdesk, which continuously learns from customer interactions

Enhancing Product and Technology with AI

The business world first got a look at the transformative potential of generative artificial intelligence (AI) in June 2021. The technology giant Microsoft, through its partnership with OpenAI (the AI company behind ChatGPT), integrated OpenAI Codex (a sibling to the GPT-3 and GPT-4 models of NLP, which I talk about in Chapter 8) into its GitHub Copilot offering. GitHub Copilot was an application designed to aid software developers in both creating new code and manipulating existing code more efficiently, serving as a revolutionary tool in the realm of software development. This integration with OpenAI Codex enables developers to receive real-time AI assistance while crafting code, an achievement that marked a pivotal advancement in AI applications.

The innovations in generative AI have a profound impact on every aspect of the product and technology lifecycle by enhancing efficiency and minimizing errors. Generative AI facilitates software development by

>> **Alleviating the workload of developers:** It optimizes the process of generating and modifying code.

>> **Democratizing the code-writing process:** It empowers individuals who have limited coding experience by providing them the tools to help them craft more sophisticated code for a diverse range of applications.

Democratization of the code-writing process extends the scope of who can contribute to coding projects, allowing for a more inclusive and diversified development environment.

The following sections delve into some of the principal use cases across the product and technology functions within an organization.

Streamlining product validation

Many businesses use generative AI to validate or confirm the applicability and usability of new products before they introduce those products to the customer. Much like its enhancements to software that I discuss in the preceding section, generative AI can significantly streamline the validation stages of new solutions and expedite trial phases that traditionally demand more manual and time-intensive approaches, such as the recruitment and coordination of human testers who have highly specific profiles.

In the realm of product validation, generative AI can

>> **Simulate a variety of user interactions and behaviors** to assess how new products perform under different conditions and use cases. This function enables companies to identify potential issues and areas for improvement early in the pre-launch process, which reduces the risk of releasing a flawed product to the market. By simulating user interactions, generative AI eliminates the need for extensive human testing that can require a lot of resources and may not cover all possible use cases and scenarios.

>> **Aid in the assessment of product-market fit** by analyzing market data, customer preferences, and feedback to predict how well the target audience will receive the new product. This analysis ensures that you develop not only technically sound products, but also products that align with market needs and demands, which increases the likelihood of their success.

>> **Automate testing,** including regression testing, whereby products undergo repeated tests to ensure that new modifications don't disrupt existing functionality. AI makes any performance testing more efficient because it can simulate a range of scenarios, analyzing how a product reacts under varied conditions and identifying areas for optimization. These AI testing capabilities enhance the product's overall reliability.

In essence, by employing generative AI in product validation, companies can attain a more comprehensive understanding of product performance, user satisfaction, and market alignment — which, in turn, enables them to refine their products more effectively and efficiently.

Simulating user experience testing

The AI can meticulously analyze every component of a product's user interface, ensuring that each element functions as intended and contributes to a seamless and intuitive user experience. It can identify areas where users may encounter difficulties and suggest improvements, enhancing the overall usability and appeal of the product.

A notable application is *visual testing*, where AI scrutinizes the visual components of a product to ascertain their alignment with design specifications. It examines elements such as layouts, color schemes, and graphical elements to ensure coherence and adherence to design principles. This examination can also identify discrepancies that may detract from the user experience. This testing has the overall goal of ensuring that the visual aesthetics of the product complements its functionality to create a harmonious and engaging user experience.

Writing code

One of the most transformative shifts in technology involves the capability for software developers to leverage AI to automatically generate code based on specific user requirements or descriptions articulated in natural language. This innovation saves businesses a significant amount of time and money, particularly for more mundane coding tasks such as crafting user interfaces, creating basic data models, and producing sample code.

AI has the ability not only to generate fragments of code, but also to propose entire lines or blocks of code in real time while a developer is typing. The AI acts as an intelligent assistant that aids developers in expediting the code-writing process. This advanced feature considerably mitigates the manual effort required from software developers. The AI-proposed code is particularly helpful when dealing with boilerplate code (such as for menus or other user-interface elements), which you need to create in order to provide standard functionalities in applications but that can take a lot of your human developers' time to write.

REMEMBER

Alleviating the mundane aspects of the code-writing process enables developers to delve deeper into the complexities and nuances of their projects. By focusing on the nuanced and unique components of software development, developers can push the boundaries of innovation and functionality, and more easily create high-quality products that are truly groundbreaking and user-centric.

Detecting and resolving software bugs

In addition to aiding developers in code generation (as I discuss in the preceding section), AI can scrutinize existing code and propose solutions for identified bugs or vulnerabilities. The solutions, in turn, can enhance the robustness and security of the software. This capability is akin to how models such as ChatGPT can review text to pinpoint spelling errors, grammatical mistakes, and poor sentence structure.

AI models can thoroughly examine the codebase, comparing individual code components against predefined coding standards and best practices in order to identify deviations and potential improvements. They can also assess the efficiency of the code, suggesting optimizations to improve the performance and resource utilization of the software. For example, an AI can identify instances where it suggests a less time-consuming algorithm or a parallel process that expedites task completion.

Testing software and creating documentation

In its multifaceted software development role, AI is also useful in basic testing and documentation functions. By automating these tedious but essential aspects of software development, AI not only alleviates the workload on developers, but also contributes to the creation of more robust, maintainable, and well-documented software products. For example, you can use AI tools to

>> **Autonomously construct and execute test cases against developed software.** Doing so ensures that the code undergoes rigorous evaluation — or, at a minimum, benefits from an additional layer of scrutiny (even though this scrutiny doesn't come from human eyes!). Specifically, the automated composition of test scripts (or the tasks that user testers execute to check whether the software is working as prescribed) notably diminishes the manual effort required for software testing and (hopefully) enhances the efficiency and reliability of the testing process.

>> **Generate documentation automatically based on the source code, accompanying comments, and any supplementary information provided.** This automation ensures the delivery of precise and consistently updated information. You need detailed, comprehensive, accurate, and up-to-date documentation to maintain code integrity and facilitate future modifications and enhancements.

Such documentation can

- *Provide a level of clarity and understanding* that's essential for fostering collaborative and informed development environments.

- *Enable other developers to comprehend* the construction of the code and to discern the optimal methodologies for modifying the code, as needed.

- *Serve as a road map* that guides developers through the complexities of the codebase and provides insights into the logic and structure of the software.

See the following table for five AI product technology offerings to explore.

Startup	Website	What It Does
Dataiku	www.dataiku.com	Allows users to develop their own AI solutions and applications that uniquely suit their business
Neurala	www.neurala.com	Detects product defects by using AI-powered visual inspections to improve quality control
Prosodica	www.prosodica.com	Measures conversational behaviors and provides insights to improve customer experiences
Uizard	www.uizard.com	Creates professional website designs and mobile apps with minimal coding or design experience
Vision AI from Google	https://cloud.google.com/vision	Allows users to develop high-quality machine learning models without programming knowledge

Accelerating Research and Development

Artificial intelligence (AI) has completely changed research and development (R&D) in business — and, in fact, the entire product development process — by automating, enhancing, or optimizing various aspects of the process. See the sidebar "AI in biotechnology," in this chapter, to discover how generative AI can work in the biotechnology industry to drive drug discovery and development. That's just one example of AI's use to conduct research and unlock product and business innovations that span from physical products and electrical circuits to financial applications and online services. You can find out about some of the specific uses cases in the realm of research and development in the following sections.

AI IN BIOTECHNOLOGY

Artificial intelligence (AI) can propel drug discovery and development by analyzing chemical and biological data to identify compounds that have therapeutic potential. AI models can analyze existing drugs and their interactions to find new applications for previously approved drugs and optimize clinical trials by analyzing patient data to select the most suitable candidates, enhancing the overall efficiency of the clinical development process.

AI can also analyze genomic data to identify disease-associated genetic mutations; examine medical images to detect abnormalities and assist with diagnosis; monitor and analyze production data in real time to ensure product quality; and simulate protein structures and functions, assisting in designing novel proteins that perform specific biological activities. You can find a seemingly endless array of AI applications; and that list becomes even more extensive when you delve into industry-specific technical applications, such as insitro and Exscientia

Generating and exploring ideas

One of the more unexpected yet potent applications of generative AI involves idea generation and exploration. With well-crafted, multi-part prompts, this technology can help businesses conceive innovative concepts and aid researchers in formulating hypotheses by meticulously analyzing existing data and academic literature. Generative AI can generate entirely novel conceptual directions for further research and development by synthesizing seemingly unrelated concepts, thus paving the way for breakthrough innovations.

REMEMBER

When choosing to employ generative AI in your idea generation, you must

>> **Select the appropriate generative AI tool** for the specific job you want it to perform because each tool possesses a unique set of advantages and limitations. The choice of AI tool can significantly impact the quality and relevance of the generated ideas, with some tools better suited to specific domains or types of tasks.

>> **Train your generative AI models by** using in-house proprietary data sets to potentially yield the most sophisticated, albeit specialized, results from this exclusive internal data. Doing so can help ensure that the AI generates highly relevant ideas informed by the unique context and nuances of the business.

TIP

In Chapters 8 and 12, I tell you more about the various AI platforms available and discuss their respective strengths and weaknesses. Visit these chapters to get an understanding of the AI tool options and their potential impacts on idea generation processes. This information helps you make informed decisions regarding the selection of AI tools that give you the optimal utilization of generative AI for groundbreaking idea generation and exploration.

AI VERSUS MBA STUDENTS

In September 2023, three professors at the University of Pennsylvania — Karl Ulrich, Christian Terwiesch, and Lennart Meincke — as well as Karan Girotra at Cornell Tech, involved their MBA students and an AI engine in an experiment to see who could come up with better business ideas. The professors assigned both groups (the 200 MBA students and the AI engine) a task to "[g]enerate an idea for a new product or service that could be offered to college students for under $50." In a single hour, the AI engine produced 200 ideas while the students took 24 hours to produce one compelling idea each. Among the 200 ideas that the AI was asked to generate, for 100 of them, the professors gave the AI engine a few samples of good ideas to steer it in the right direction. To assess the strength of the ideas, the professors subjected both the AI- and student-generated sets to an online purchase intent survey. The results were telling: 47 percent of respondents favored the AI-generated concepts, compared to 40 percent for those ideas proposed by the students. And not surprisingly, the AI ideas that were informed by a few sample ideas performed the best. This study raises an intriguing question: Who among us is truly immune to being outperformed by AI, and how can we best address this challenge? Check out Chapter 12 for strategies and tactics to harness generative AI for ideation.

You can find the research paper on the Social Science Research Network (SSRN) website (www.ssrn.com). On the main page, click the Search icon and enter any (or all) of the authors' last names. The results should include a link to an article titled "Ideas are Dimes a Dozen: Large Language Models for Idea Generation in Innovation." Click that link to access the abstract and a link to the full paper.

Extracting insights from data

Generative AI can quickly and thoroughly sift through vast data sets to discern patterns, correlations, and valuable insights. Insight extraction — which is crucial to every research and development initiative — becomes substantially faster if you allow AI to take charge, giving researchers more time for strategy development, product delineation, and decision-making. AI tools for extracting insights and predicting trends work by

>> **Employing predictive analytics.** The term *predictive analytics* refers to the process of using data to predict future outcomes. AI models can forecast upcoming trends and business results by using historical data and their inherent analyses as the basis for examining the data.

>> **Developing intricate models to analyze complex systems or procedures.**
These models and analyses can furnish insights that fuel future innovations and
empower researchers to examine hypotheses and corroborate theories more
quickly when compared to conventional R&D system engineering process.

Optimizing product designs and production processes

Generative AI serves as a key tool to aid product designers in discovering, assimi-
lating, and experimenting with new materials for new product offerings. A generative AI tool becomes an invaluable asset when a company builds it or customizes
an off-the-shelf version on a foundational model that has been trained on the
research and development processes and possesses extensive knowledge about
diverse material combinations. It can optimize designs not only for manufacturing but also to curtail development and logistic expenses effectively by

>> **Analyzing various material properties, compatibility, and performance
under different conditions:** The generative AI tool can then suggest optimal
material combinations and design modifications to enhance product performance, durability, and cost-efficiency.

>> **Providing insights into the feasibility of integrating new materials and
suggesting adjustments to the design to accommodate them:** These
factors help ensure that the final product meets the desired quality and
performance standards.

>> **Streamlining the production process, minimizing waste, and reducing
the time-to-market:** These aspects strike a balance between creativity and
feasibility by making the entire product development cycle more efficient and
sustainable and enabling designers to push the boundaries of innovation,
while maintaining practicality and viability in the manufacturing phase.

The following table shows five AI research and development offerings to explore.

Startup	Website	What It Does
Arize AI	www.arize.com	Increases model creation velocity (how quickly a model can be devel-oped, trained, and deployed) and improves AI outcomes by using a *machine learning (ML) observability platform* which monitors the performance of the model
Hazy	www.hazy.com	Delivers innovative synthetic data technology in complex enterprise environments

(continued)

(continued)

Startup	Website	What It Does
Lightning AI	www.lightning.ai	Helps build, train, and deploy AI applications quickly by using the PyTorch (http://pytorch.org) open source ML library
Snorkel AI	www.snorkelai.com	Helps companies build, customize, and scale AI applications by using their proprietary data
Weights & Biases	www.wandb.ai	Helps AI developers build better models, and track and iterate on experiments

Giving Marketing an AI Boost

Because this book is titled *Marketing with AI For Dummies*, you're probably not surprised that I cover the marketing use cases for AI extensively in many of the chapters. However, in the following sections, I put the marketing use cases in the context of an overall business.

Creating coherent, consistent content

From crafting blog post headlines, lifecycle e-mails, and various text-based communications, to developing video scripts, campaign taglines, and product imagery, generative AI can transform the content creation processes of marketing departments by creating and optimizing the content itself. *Note:* Although you still need the human touch to craft the right prompts and evaluate the output, generative AI allows for automation of the facets of actual content creation, optimizing the creative process significantly by making it more efficient, less labor intensive and more personalized for each user.

Generative AI extends the content creation capabilities of marketing departments so that those departments can

>> **Support branding efforts.** Generative AI tools can ensure writing consistency among multiple authors and align all content creation endeavors with the brand voice and predetermined writing guidelines. This oversite can ensure a coherent, unified, and consistent brand message across various platforms and content types. Generative AI can also scrutinize the nuances of the brand's communication style, implementing that style meticulously across marketing content.

>> **Facilitate marketing material translations.** Businesses can use generative AI to automatically translate content from one language to another; this convenient feature not only saves significant time, but also broadens the reach of marketing content and reduces costs for the organization. Easy

translation particularly helps businesses that operate in multilingual environments by ensuring the accuracy of translations and enabling consistent communication across audiences that speak different languages.

Personalizing marketing messages

One of the most ubiquitous and influential applications of AI in marketing involves facilitating customer personalization *at scale*, which means creating hundreds if not thousands of versions of a piece of content with each one specifically targeted to different users and based on their specific needs. Marketing teams can leverage AI to craft meticulously personalized messages — messages that align with individual customer interests, preferences, and behaviors — dispatching them when customers are most likely to be receptive (considering the optimal time, day, and format). This personalization not only offers significant automation advantages for a company, but also enhances the customer relationship by making interactions more specific and intimate.

By utilizing the wealth of customer data available, AI can

>> **Analyze individual customer journeys,** purchasing histories, and interaction patterns to generate insights that marketers use to tailor marketing offers and messages more effectively. This level of personalization goes beyond merely addressing the customer by their first name; it encompasses the delivery of content, offers, and experiences that are genuinely relevant and valuable to the individual.

>> **Strengthen brand loyalty and customer satisfaction** by making customers feel valued and understood, and by delivering more relevant and engaging content and offers. The heightened level of personalization ultimately contributes to improved customer retention and business growth.

Managing digital advertising

As I discuss in Chapters 17 and 19, AI can enhance digital advertising efforts for marketers. Platforms provided by major tech companies, such as Google, Bing, Meta, Snap, and TikTok, have integrated AI platforms that can help you figure out which ads to display to specific *customer cohorts* (groups of users who share demographics and do similar activities within a particular time frame), based on the probability that your ad will engage a customer and spur that customer to subsequent action. These algorithms access extensive data to discern the optimal ad-unit format, channel, device, time slot, and creative elements to align with a target audience and aim for peak performance, whether performance means click thru rates, online purchases, or some other marketing metric.

AI specifically helps with targeted marketing by

>> **Diving deeply into consumer behavior patterns, analyzing interactions, and crafting responses that dynamically optimize ad content and placements.** AI tools can intelligently select and adjust various advertising parameters — such as timing, content, and type of ad unit — to resonate more effectively with the intended audience based on that audience's preferences and behaviors. The marketing goal is to drive heightened customer engagement and conversion rates.

>> **Applying real-time analytics and adaptive learning capabilities that enable the continuous refinement of advertising tactics.** AI tools can swiftly assess the impact of ad variants; they can analyze and adjust in real time to ensure that they serve ads most likely to achieve the desired outcomes (whether you want clicks, conversions, or some other metric). This optimization prevents digital advertising strategies from becoming static; instead, they're constantly evolving and improving to maximize the return on advertising spend.

Streamlining search engine optimization (SEO)

In recent years, *search engine optimization* (SEO, which is the process of optimizing the company website content, design, and tagging so that it ranks high in the search engine results) has become crucial for businesses that seek customers online. Many companies consider SEO one of the most efficient and cost-effective marketing channels. Generative AI can automate and optimize the creation of SEO-friendly articles and refine various SEO elements such as page titles, image tags, URLs, keywords, and page descriptions.

Generative AI analyzes search trends and user behaviors to optimize content that achieves higher visibility and ranking on search engine results pages. Using AI in SEO best practices enables a more streamlined and efficient approach to improving online visibility and engagement, with the ultimate goal of contributing to increased organic traffic and business growth. Specifically, when you use AI for SEO, it

>> **Provides insights into optimal, relevant keywords** and automates their strategic placement within SEO elements

>> **Maintains content quality and relevance** — ensuring that the content is user-friendly and informative — and adheres to SEO best practices to enhance web page ranking in search results

Check out the five AI marketing offerings in the following table.

Startup	Website	What It Does
AlphaSense	www.alpha-sense.com	Conducts market intelligence by searching millions of files across more than 10,000 business data sources
Copy.ai	www.copy.ai	AI content generator for producing copy for e-mails, blogs, and social media
Predraft.ai	www.predraft.ai	Researches and writes SEO articles in response to topics and keywords that you input
SoundHound	www.soundhound.com	Uses proprietary voice AI technology to give brands a voice when interacting with customers
Synthesia	www.synthesia.io	Allows businesses to create and personalize video content efficiently with human-like avatars

Optimizing Sales with AI

Generative AI plays an important role in how companies approach sales. The AI can handle mundane activities (such as scheduling appointments and updating sales records) so that sales teams can focus on building customer relationships. This focus, in turn, enables businesses to enhance productivity and drive greater revenue growth. AI also enables an analytical, intelligent approach to sales forecasting that gives companies greater visibility into future revenue for their businesses. At the heart of use cases involving sales and AI, you find three critical drivers, which I cover in the following sections.

Driving profitability

The art of sales fundamentally deals with the number and profitability of transactions that a company completes. AI can enhance profitable growth by extracting insights into customer behaviors, preferences, and needs throughout the sales cycle. AI analyzes consumer data to discern patterns and preferences that serve as a basis for creating personalized and impactful sales strategies and actual sales content such as brochures and web pages to assist in the selling process.

>> **Allow sales teams to identify and strategically target customer segments** that are most likely to purchase their products and services. Teams can then deploy tailored and effective strategies to optimize sales.

>> **Offer real-time recommendations to sales representatives** that foster adaptive and informed interactions with customers. For example, an AI engine

may analyze a client's tone and responses during a sales call and offer suggestions in real time for how the salesperson should steer the conversation, which product features to highlight, or when to discuss pricing. These interactions focus on maximizing *conversion rates* (calculations that measure the effectiveness of a sales strategy). Consequently, the implementation of AI in sales not only optimizes conversions, but also enhances customer relationships and can boost the overall profitability and efficiency of the business.

Nurturing leads

Generative AI can help sales representatives nurture assigned leads more efficiently. The strategic integration of AI in this process makes the lead nurturing stage more effective and streamlined, contributing to overall sales productivity and success. By analyzing past call transcripts, customer profile data, and the features and benefits of products, AI tools can construct personalized discussion scripts that optimize talking points for sales representatives.

These tools can also automate the process of sending follow-up messages tailored to individual leads and can passively maintain engagement with the leads (for example, by sending them thought leadership content on an ongoing basis) until another direct sales message is warranted to move the customer further down the sales funnel.

REMEMBER

By handling the customer analysis and engagement functions, AI relieves the sales representatives of more mundane and time-consuming tasks involving data entry, scheduling, lead scoring, and follow-up. Therefore, they can concentrate on fostering customer relationships. This automation ensures that sales reps can allocate more time to understanding customer needs and providing tailored solutions. This focus enhances the likelihood of successful sales conversions while ensuring that each lead receives adequate attention and nurturing.

Forecasting sales

Artificial intelligence can significantly refine sales forecasting and revenue predictions by factors such as product, SKU, customer type, region, and so on. AI employs machine learning to scrutinize historical sales data, market trends, and other pertinent influencing factors such as weather patterns (you don't sell many umbrellas when it's snowing in Chicago) and consumer sentiment (gleaned from social media conversations). This analysis yields forecasts that surpass the reliability and depth of traditional models. The distinct advantage of contemporary AI models lies in their capability to effectively analyze and interpret real-time data, enabling their forecasting to perpetually adapt to changing market conditions.

TIP

By integrating real-time learning and adaptation, AI helps sales forecasts stay dynamic reflections of the market. These forecasts of current, relevant, and actionable insights enable sales teams to make swifter, more informed decisions. The insights also enhance predictability and help optimize strategic planning and resource allocation for the business.

See five AI sales offerings to explore in the following table.

Startup	Website	What It Does
Conversica	www.conversica.com	Unlocks revenue throughout the lifecycle of sales by using revenue digital assistants
Cresta AI	www.cresta.com	AI sales and customer care solutions to boost productivity and improve satisfaction
Highspot	www.highspot.com	An AI-based sales enablement platform to increase a salesperson's productivity
Orum	www.orum.com	Automates calling, detects voicemails, filters out bad numbers, and provides instant coaching notes to the sales representative
People.ai	www.people.ai	A revenue intelligence platform that selects the most leads, using data to create actionable insights

Adding AI to Legal Activities

In April 2023, the Stanford Center for Legal Informatics announced that GPT-4 had successfully passed the Uniform Bar exam, scoring in the 90th percentile. This score was not only superior to those of previous large language models, but also exceeded the average scores of human examinees. GPT-4 excelled in the multiple-choice section and in both components of the written exam. The fact that an earlier version of the large language model, ChatGPT, had failed the Uniform Bar exam just a few months prior underscores the rapid advancement of this technology.

Undoubtedly, generative AI can profoundly impact the legal function within any organization. The technology demonstrates its versatility by spanning a wide array of applications in the legal domain, including legal research, risk management, workflow optimization, due diligence, and contract drafting. In the following sections, I discuss a few key ways that businesses can use AI in legal departments.

Analyzing documentation for legal research

AI can streamline and simplify the process of legal research by analyzing extensive volumes of case law, legal literature, and statutes to pinpoint the most pertinent precedents, rulings, and regulations related to a specific case. You can accomplish tasks that typically take a lawyer or paralegal hours, or even days, much more swiftly when you can give AI access to the right data sources. The AI tools can subsequently generate summaries, recommend relevant cases for review, and offer insights into the probable success of a particular case in a court of law.

Evaluating and drafting contracts

AI can aid in examining, analyzing, and drafting new contracts. It can also propose alterations to existing contracts — for example, based on compliance with legal standards — by recognizing nonstandard clauses, language discrepancies, and other potential issues. AI can also generate contract templates and automate the creation of new contracts by using predefined criteria and inputs from overseeing lawyers.

REMEMBER

To have AI draft legal contracts, you need to train the AI against a database of existing contracts. Given the variance in contract quality, you run a risk that the AI may propagate subpar legal work, along with the exemplary. Therefore, you still need the oversight of human lawyers in contract drafting, ensuring the quality and accuracy of the legal documents produced.

Performing due diligence

AI can enhance the due diligence process for both internal legal teams and external counsel prior to finalizing a business transaction. It can scrutinize documents, financial records, and related legal agreements to uncover potential risks, liabilities, and compliance issues. Furthermore, businesses can employ AI for *compliance monitoring*, which is the ongoing assessment of a business's adherence to specific legal regulations and standards. In these contexts, AI can formulate reports that summarize the findings and suggest specific actions for the business to take to stay in compliance with state and federal regulations.

Managing intellectual property

AI holds substantial value in intellectual property (IP) management by streamlining the processes of intellectual property creation, protection, and anti-violation enforcement. By automating and aiding in all facets of IP management, AI empowers legal teams to concentrate on more strategic planning, client management (either internal or external stakeholders), and decision-making to optimize the protection and utilization of intellectual property. Specifically, generative AI tools can

>> **Explore patent databases, legal documents, and literature** to identify existing patents, potential infringements, and opportunities for novel intellectual property.

>> **Aid patent attorneys in drafting patent applications,** ensuring thoroughness and adherence to patent office protocols.

>> **Monitor the intellectual property landscape** to notify organizations of possible infringements or violations, which facilitates more immediate and proactive safeguarding of a company's intellectual assets.

Here are five AI legal offerings to explore.

Startup	Website	What It Does
Ascent	www.ascent.io	Identifies the regulations that a company must comply with and keeps the company updated when rules change
Casetext	www.casetext.com	Helps law firms find cases and use machine learning to compose better briefs
Harvey AI	www.harvey.ai	Enables lawyers to describe tasks in simple instructions and receive the AI-generated legal result
Luminance	www.luminance.com	An AI-powered contract management platform that can generate contracts from scratch
Sherpa.ai	www.sherpa.ai	Protects data privacy, improves regulatory compliance, and mitigates against insurance fraud

IN THIS CHAPTER

» Accepting AI as your
marketing partner

» Considering the influence of AI
marketing on business

» Setting foundational elements for
AI marketing

» Developing a strategic approach to
AI marketing

Chapter **3**

Launching into the AI Marketing Era

When you want to enter the world of artificial intelligence (AI) marketing, you may find the question of where and how to begin quite perplexing. Maybe kick-start your journey by delving into AI through library books? Enroll in one of academic institutions' myriad courses specifically designed for executives at your level? Or perhaps seek guidance from friends, colleagues, business partners, and industry thought leaders?

The answer can encompass all of the preceding options while you study and absorb knowledge about AI marketing. But don't overlook the crucial component (which *often* goes unnoticed) that determines how you actively apply what you discover about AI marketing in a thoughtful manner. And instead of diving head-first into a frenzy of experimentation by using tools such as ChatGPT or Midjourney, establish well-defined frameworks to guide your journey.

Don't get me wrong; experimentation is valuable, and if you want to explore various AI tools yourself (I describe various AI tools and their use in Parts 2, 3, and 4 of this book), you can get started right away. But in this chapter, I first explain why diving into AI marketing is a strategic imperative for your marketing efforts. Then, I introduce several frameworks that I've created, which you may consider using when you delve further into the world of artificial intelligence.

Ready or Not: AI Is Your New Marketing Copilot

As I write this chapter, the artificial intelligence (AI) world has had an eventful few weeks. Recently, OpenAI — which seems ready to become a billion-dollar-revenue company — launched its new *enterprise product* (meaning a version of its product that includes the security and privacy features that most companies require before they can use a piece of software), ChatGPT Enterprise. Just a day later, Google Cloud announced a slew of AI products poised to change how people work and collaborate.

REMEMBER

Signs hidden within these announcements of enterprise AI products point to the imminent transformation of marketing. But as of the time I'm writing, no one knows how the marketing function will transform with this seismic shift. While you take your marketing organization deeper into the world of AI (which I explain in the section "Adopting a Strategic Framework for Entering the AI Era," later in this chapter), you must understand and plan for some of the associated impacts.

Putting performance marketers at risk

Today, roughly a third of all digital advertising dollars in the U.S. funnel into Google. Legions of marketers and agency professionals oversee these expenditures by handling keywords, bids, budget optimization, audiences, creatives, and attribution aspects of Google campaigns. The tools at their disposal have steadily moved toward automation over time. Some seasoned marketers contend that Google's automated tools (for example, the Google Performance Max tool) may even outperform both agency and in-house performance marketing teams.

Google's recent announcements (as discussed in the preceding section) indicate that its advertising tools (such as a Keyword and Performance Planner) will become even more automated — not just as individual features or disparate tools, but in seamless orchestration. This development could lead to full automation of the entire marketing campaign process.

Imagine choosing an objective and setting a budget (like you do today in Google), and then completely leaving it to Google to do the rest. Google would

>> Pull first-, second-, and third-party data from various systems (that it has access to), such as internal customer databases and publisher platforms.

>> Create unique customer segments from the data.

>> Identify the right keywords to target the customer segments.

>> Set budget parameters for each account in the campaign.

And for the campaign content and deployment, suppose that a more potent and autonomous Performance Max product (Google's advertising campaign engine) could also automatically

>> Create headlines, ad copy, and creative visuals by using your own website and brand style guide as reference points.

>> Trigger the campaign, assess the results, optimize content and placement based on the performance, and make new choices on its own across all platforms (search, display, YouTube, social media, and connected television).

Note: When you can have everything automated, you don't need as many human beings to do the marketing work. So, in this Google-engineered future, your teams will likely have significantly less to do.

If you extend the line of thought about Google advertising tools to include similar automation capabilities from Meta, TikTok, Amazon, and other advertising platforms, you may begin to question what the future of marketing will entail for marketers and their roles. Each of these platforms already possesses some essential components to automate marketing; it's only a matter of time before they connect the dots to fully automate the campaign-creation process, potentially in collaboration with Google Cloud, ChatGPT Enterprise, or some other player. These platforms together capture the majority of the advertising dollars in America. So if those platforms change dramatically, marketing will also have to change.

Competing with creative directors

In conversation with another senior marketer, I discovered how an advertising agency leveraged generative AI to secure a project. The agency had a looming deadline to present concepts for a large-scale mural intended for a public space. If the agency knew the client well, they would push back on the tight timeline, but because they didn't have a relationship and really wanted the business, they couldn't. Summer vacations had depleted their staffing levels, which made rallying a team for night and weekend work difficult.

Enter a Midjourney generative AI solution that the advertising agency supplied with a series of increasingly focused prompts to quickly generate a mural concept. (You can find out more about prompt engineering in Chapter 13 and Midjourney in Chapter 14.) They presented this AI-generated concept to the client, and that concept won the project. The client never met the team that created the work!

This scenario raises critical questions about whose ability (or capability) the agency should depend on when they need a quick concept solution. The questions include

» Should the agency use prompt engineers, rather than creative staff, for pitches?

» Do members of the creative staff need to become prompt engineers?

» Did the success of winning the project come from the advanced technology of the generative AI, the skillful prompt engineering by the agency's staff, or raw luck?

Now imagine another scenario for the mural project. Suppose that the client used ChatGPT and Midjourney AI to provide prospective agencies with a more detailed specification of what was required upfront. This situation may require a more modest project scope in the first place and make the concept and bidding process even easier. The marketing world faces a challenging reality in which you need fewer people involved in marketing — or, at the least, fewer people creating content and more people prompting the AI tools.

REMEMBER

Generative AI tools can occasionally produce odd results — such as famously messing up the depiction of human hands, as outlined in the article on Britannica.com "Why does AI art screw up hands and fingers?" by Meg Matthias. (To find this article, just enter "ai hands" in the search box at the top of the Britannica website and click Search. It should appear as the first result.) The AI misrepresentation of hands basically comes down to lack of focused data, which programmers are working to overcome at the time of writing. But even though you need human oversight to refine the output, you can't deny that these generative AI tools save marketers and marketing agencies time.

Watching AI Upend the Corporate World

I wish I could say that the idea of artificial intelligence (AI) upending the corporate world is hyperbole, or at least akin to the growth of the World Wide Web. That technology indeed transformed the way we work, play, and live, but the dot-com bust of the early 2000s revealed that the business world collectively misjudged the timing of its impact. As of this writing, many business leaders hope for a similar grace period with generative AI. They recognize AI's transformative potential but hope that the transition will feel more like landing a plane smoothly in an empty field, rather than running directly into a cliff.

However, the business world may find the AI-intrusion timeline unforgiving. In 2023, OpenAI fast-tracked the launch of ChatGPT Enterprise precisely because they observed businesses already redefining their operations through the new technology. Examples of AI's influence include

>> **Adoption of AI for many business tasks:** Citing OpenAI's product launch blog post, organizations began using ChatGPT "to craft clearer communications, accelerate coding tasks, explore complex business questions rapidly, assist with creative work, and much more," as the blog post shared. In June of 2023 alone, ChatGPT garnered 1.8 billion visits, and OpenAI revealed that 80 percent of Fortune 500 companies had already adopted its use.

>> **Investment in AI-related apps and training for employees:** Walmart, the world's largest company (by revenue), made a significant move in 2023, announcing that it would grant 50,000 of its non-store employees access to a generative AI app trained on corporate data. Walmart envisions this technology liberating employees from repetitive, monotonous tasks and aiding them in tasks such as creating new content, summarizing lengthy documents, sorting through benefits, and streamlining new hire orientations. Walmart's direction has vast and varied implications because other businesses often follow Walmart's lead.

Although these examples may not directly relate to marketing, a brief review of your organization's marketing operations probably shows that those operations involve a significant amount of manual work — work that generative AI can potentially revolutionize. If Walmart can adapt so rapidly, other organizations likely also can — and they probably need to.

Taking Foundational Steps Toward AI Marketing

You can follow six foundational steps to kick-start the integration of generative artificial intelligence (generative AI) into your marketing endeavors. Professors at the Wharton School (of the University of Pennsylvania) believe that an astounding 80 to 90 percent of all business documents will soon start as machine-generated drafts. In the constantly changing field of marketing, if you don't use AI for at least half of your preliminary consumer-facing content drafts (just one use for generative AI), you're falling behind.

These six steps can serve as a way to begin the journey to embrace and exploit generative AI in your marketing work. Take a moment to read through these steps and assess your progress on this journey, both for yourself and your teammates. Follow these steps to make meaningful moves into the world of AI marketing —

you're surfing its waves, positioning your brand for growth, and most importantly, taking yourself and your team on an exciting AI journey:

1. **Decipher your brand's voice by using generative AI.**

   Instruct your marketing strategy and brand teams to use conversational AI tools for insights into your brand voice and to generate alternative taglines. Have them input anonymous customer behavioral data into AI analytics tools to identify and segment audiences. Make sure that your teams share the AI prompts that guided these analyses with their peers and you. See Chapter 13 for tips on prompt writing.

2. **Develop AI-driven first drafts of any marketing communication.**

   Urge each marketer to generate a first draft of any content — whether they need a headline, ad copy, image, article, or e-mail — by using an AI tool. Request to see the original draft and the prompts used so that you can understand the subsequent refinements made. Don't outsource this fine-tuning to your agency partners; use it as an in-house exercise because that's the best way for your teams to learn — by doing the work themselves.

3. **Experiment with AI on ad platforms that house your product information.**

   Establish *ghost accounts* (hidden accounts that very few of your customers see) that have experimental budgets on major advertising platforms (such as Google, Meta, Amazon, TikTok, and so on). Direct your growth marketing teams to use every AI-driven automation feature — from copy creation to creative optimization and bidding — that these platforms offer. Deploy the AI-developed features and benchmark the results against your current campaigns.

4. **Create AI-enhanced social media calendars that offer alternative content.**

   Ask your social media team to use AI tools to generate alternative copy for each planned post. Align these posts with your brand voice and adorn them with AI-created captivating headlines and visuals. Then assess whether the AI-created content can provide augmentations or enhancements to the content in your existing calendar.

5. **Address AI bias immediately by consulting your business's legal team and providing anti-bias training to your marketing team.**

   Collaborate with your legal team to draft guidelines for identifying and mitigating bias in AI-generated content. Offer internal training sessions to equip your marketing team with the skills to spot and combat bias. Identify AI tools that can aid this process and share examples of how the data that an AI engine trains on or the phrasing of prompts can bias the results.

6. Evaluate your agency partners' AI capabilities.

Proactively engage with your agency partners to understand their AI road map — what AI enhancements they offer today, their plans for future investments, and their partnerships. Examine how their AI capabilities can enrich your joint projects. Push them to bring their best AI thinking to bear on your marketing challenges.

Addressing the marketing dichotomy

Adopting a new technology in your marketing efforts may seem straightforward, but you need to master more than just how to use the technology. The change also requires cultural adaptation. When you embark on your transformative AI marketing journey, you may encounter a divide within your team describing two kinds of marketers. I call this division the marketing dichotomy:

>> **Marketing intrapreneurs** are both visionary and agile. They're already incorporating AI into their daily tasks. They aim to boost their productivity, enhance the caliber of their work, and ascend the corporate ladder more rapidly. These innovators immerse themselves in AI, harness every AI tool at their disposal, and experiment passionately. Embrace these marketers because they create momentum for the rest of the team to adopt the new technologies.

>> **Marketing traditionalists** are rooted in skepticism and see AI merely as a tech tool. They remain passive (taking a wait-and-see stance) and trapped in the belief that AI doesn't have the potential to transform their roles or the businesses with which they work. Although they may not be overtly undermining your initiatives, their inertia could potentially hinder the enthusiasm and progress of the broader marketing team. Don't let these traditionalists restrain the strides that your team and company can make in the AI world.

Senior marketers and marketing managers may get caught in the crossfire between the intrapreneurs and traditionalists. Some of these marketers may look to external agencies and tech companies for guidance so that they don't have to do their own research (and anticipate lavish dinners and client councils) to discern how to seamlessly integrate AI into their departments.

WARNING

You must overcome a cultural challenge when senior and managing marketers don't deeply engage with the AI technology available. They don't lead the charge and often hold traditionalist perspectives. They may see generative AI simply as a tactical tool and may not recognize its strategic potential to reshape their roles or their businesses. When you encounter marketers in this less-than-all-in camp, be sure to engage with them directly, educate them on the potential of AI, and demonstrate that embracing AI can enhance their careers versus hurt them. Often, pairing up these marketers with the enthusiastic intrapreneurs can lead to the best outcomes for the team and the business.

Assessing progress with the AI checklist

Adopting a proactive and informed approach to AI not only ensures your marketing team's survival, but also places you at the forefront of the marketing revolution where you can leverage AI's transformative potential to its fullest and stay competitive in the evolving technological landscape. I designed the following checklist to help you assess your team's progress in driving AI-centric transformations within your marketing plans. Evaluate your ongoing progress on the following points to ensure that you have your marketing efforts on the path to success:

TIP

» **Exploring all AI technologies:** Begin with yourself by embracing a variety of AI technologies and personally studying and testing a range of AI tools. If you're using only ChatGPT, that's a bad sign because it means you're not being as inquisitive as you probably can be in discovering the specific tools that are optimized for different use cases. I discuss other tools in Part 3 and elsewhere in the book.

The next time you create a slide deck for your CEO, ask three different generative AI tools for feedback on the deck. See which one gives you the best evaluation and talk to your entire team about the exercise and the results.

» **Expanding the AI use cases:** Don't limit generative AI to tactical duties such as text creation or augmentation; explore its potential to drive business strategy, customer segmentation, campaign development, performance marketing, and predictive analytics in new ways.

Start by creating or joining a task force in your marketing department to develop business use cases to unlock AI's full potential, especially in marketing. Doing so can highlight positive economic value for the business. See Chapter 2, which involves use cases for AI, and assess whether your team or your company can benefit from executing some of those use cases.

» **Aligning with the vision of your chief information officer (CIO):** Understand and influence your CIO's AI technology road map of what gets built and when. Create or engage with cross-functional AI task forces (representatives from each function in the company) to have critical discussions around data governance and generative AI.

REMEMBER

If you're a marketing manager, make sure that the organization's overall AI road map factors in marketing priorities. To succeed as a marketer in the AI era means having the best AI tools and technologies at your disposal. You can only have those tools if you partner very closely with the CIO. In fact, having this close association matters now more than ever while the influence of AI in your organization grows.

>> **Balancing external education and influence:** Although your company can benefit from external education from agencies and technology partners, maintain a balance and stay objective — because your company's economic interests may diverge from your external resources' interests.

Get all the help you can, especially from the platforms that are innovating at breakneck speed. But also, do your own homework. Partners and platforms may downplay how transformative AI can be to their own statements of work.

>> **Staying ahead of competitors:** Keep a close watch on competitor behavior and stay abreast of the latest AI advancements to ensure that you don't miss out on opportunities in AI-driven ad targeting, buying, optimization, and personalization.

TIP

For example, if you notice that competitors inexplicably take over shares in Google search auctions, they may be using AI technologies more innovatively than you are. Google *impression share* (the percentage of impressions that your ads receive compared to the total number of impressions that your ads could get) can be telling.

>> **Activating a data strategy:** Recognize the importance of data in machine learning (ML; see Chapter 5) and generative AI (see Chapter 8), in particular. Get involved in developing a robust data strategy (what data you use and which tools do the data analysis) that involves both public and internal data sources as a competitive advantage for differentiating your offerings. Don't leave it to the CIO's team only.

If your organization doesn't have enough valuable proprietary data, help develop a strategy so that you can bring more data in-house over time to feed your own large language models (LLMs; see Chapter 9). And evaluate with your CIO whether to use open or proprietary LLMs.

>> **Prioritizing AI ethics:** Lessons from the social media marketing era underscore the vital importance of embedding AI ethics at the heart of every AI deployment. The data used to train AI models inform those models' biases and necessitate heightened sensitivity to their inputs.

REMEMBER

You must uphold the intellectual property rights of businesses, creators, and artists. And ensure transparency regarding the accumulation and use of data in every AI implementation so that you can guarantee the equitable and responsible use of AI.

>> **Organizing AI inspiration days:** Hundreds (if not thousands) of AI companies help marketing teams like yours learn about AI and how to apply the new technology to business. Take advantage of those services to educate your teams.

Suggest that various companies introduce their latest innovations to your teams and, subsequently, participate in informed and objective decisions regarding partnerships for specific use cases.

TIP

>> **Optimizing your organization's structure:** Adapt the organizational structure of your marketing function to the AI era by retraining and up-skilling (adding concrete abilities) teams; address any talent gaps proactively. AI can revolutionize your marketing; adapt your teams, skills, capabilities, and workflows to stay relevant.

Restructuring may include creating new cross-functional pods, rewriting annual objectives, putting more data analysis tools into the hands of marketers (rather than a separate data analytics team), and bringing more content creation in-house.

Adopting a Strategic Framework for Entering the AI Era

After you embrace the realm of artificial intelligence (AI) marketing and engage the entire marketing team (which I talk about in the section "Taking Foundational Steps Toward AI Marketing," earlier in this chapter), how do you methodically, strategically, and holistically propel an entire business organization forward? The following sections seek to answer this question by presenting a four-part AI Marketing Maturity Model, using the metaphor of a rocket launch.

Going for liftoff

Much like a rocket poised on the launch pad ready to soar, marketers at the beginning stages of entering marketing-with-AI space recognize the significance of AI and its transformative power in the realm of marketing. Although skeptics may exist, the majority of marketing team members understand the need to invest time and resources to grasp AI's influence on marketing.

Marketers who want to explore ways to leverage AI tend to

>> Understand fundamental AI terms and core concepts.

>> Want to attend conferences, take classes, and discuss ways in which they can use AI in their jobs.

>> Explore generative AI tools, such as GPT-4, Midjourney, and DALL-E (see Chapters 13 and 14) in their free time or maybe use those tools to assist with basic day-to-day routine tasks.

>> Rely (still) on traditional marketing tools and processes for the majority of their work efforts because they believe that the AI tools can't yet effectively produce creative content that is on brand, unique, or impactful.

The organizations that these marketers belong to often

>> Display a willingness to explore different AI tools and services by opening up access to those tools from within the enterprise.

>> Make third-party tools available for employee trials and invite enterprise providers to pitch their new AI product features to the organization's teams.

>> Try to identify scenarios in which AI can add value to the business, perhaps by examining the use cases that competitors embrace.

Leaders at these organizations typically

>> Showcase curiosity prompted by inquiries from their C-suite (the realm of the organization's chief officers) personnel and boards of directors. More often than not, evaluation of AI in marketing for a business begins with the board of directors, or even shareholders on earning calls.

>> Prioritize managing the day-to-day operations of the business over AI explorations. Although leaders may become interested in AI, at this (liftoff) stage, leaders still dedicate all their time to keeping the business running.

>> Don't have designated champions in mind for specific teams to spearhead AI education, largely because they haven't wrapped their heads around the importance of AI themselves.

Their data and business road maps may include

>> Establishing basic data security measures and protocols

>> Conducting data accessibility and quality assessments

>> Cataloging the data that they currently have so that they can leverage that data for AI training

They need to determine the following metrics:

>> The number, type, and success rate of their various experiments with AI marketing

>> An accounting of courses that employees have taken and/or certifications they've received

Initiating atmospheric ascent

At the ascent phase of AI incorporation, you (or your marketers) initiate hands-on experimentation in a structured and strategic way. You grapple with deep-seated corporate cultures and business processes, much like a rocket battling gravity and aerodynamic challenges. Achieving breakthroughs and quelling the skeptics can require immense effort. But you can make progress by identifying key use cases, launching experiments, and disseminating insights across both the marketing team and the wider organization.

Marketers in the ascent stage

>> Test AI marketing use cases, beginning with low-hanging fruit (easy tasks), such as copy creation.

>> Move beyond the public AI tools and experiment with AI tools specifically built for enterprises.

>> Engage with internal IT teams and existing tech vendors to integrate AI into the *MarTech stack* (the marketing tools and technologies you use to automate, streamline, and improve marketing efforts).

The organizations to which these marketers belong often

>> Display a new sense of urgency to incorporate the best of AI into the business.

>> Show a willingness to elevate the AI conversations into the C-suite to take place among the organization's chief officers.

>> Formalize cross-functional task forces that have shared responsibilities to assess AI opportunities.

>> Recognize that the AI wave requires talent assessments up and down the hierarchy.

Leaders at these organizations typically

>> Organize cross-functional task forces to audit and elevate functional AI efforts.

>> Integrate experimentation results into one-, two-, and three-year horizon innovation projects so that AI isn't treated as a fad but as an investment that gets integrated into long-term planning.

>> Incorporate AI planning, design, and launch into annual goal setting for the teams. This incorporation can give you a critical way to break through some of the expected apathy toward new technologies.

>> Try to break down silos between departments, inhibitors to success (see the section "Addressing the marketing dichotomy" earlier in the chapter), and organizational apathy.

Their data and business road maps may feature plans to

>> Build generative AI applications on third-party hosted platforms such as Amazon Web Services.

>> Centralize, streamline, and merge separate data silos for a holistic view of customer data.

>> Utilize tools for data visualization to provide predictive insights into marketing.

>> Strengthen the data pipeline by automating data collection, processing, and storage.

These organizations need metrics to

>> Gauge the effectiveness and completion rate of AI-driven initiatives.

>> Assess employee engagement with AI tools.

Reaching escape velocity

In the escape-velocity phase, marketers systematically roll out AI projects across a range of use cases that leverage enterprise-level AI technology and reflect harmony with the company's broader strategy. In the same way that a rocket at this stage no longer needs additional thrust to combat Earth's gravity, an organization at this level of AI maturity can concentrate on successfully carrying out pilot projects and applying those insights to transition an increasing number of use cases to production. By now, the entire organization supports the AI marketing initiatives, fostering a collaborative atmosphere among teams.

Marketers reaching escape velocity do the following:

>> Integrate AI-driven predictive insights into decision making in a consistent, thoughtful, and goal-oriented fashion. (See Chapter 7.)

>> Harness AI tools for planning, buying, and evaluating media performance across all paid, social, and organic marketing channels. (See Chapter 18.)

>> Collaborate with external AI experts and vendors for proprietary and specialized solutions that serve their specific industry, customer, and business needs.

The organizations that these marketers belong to often

>> Display a readiness to integrate AI thinking into the company's three-to-five-year plans.

>> Explore advanced use cases that require domain- and industry-specific customization and personalization that account for legal and regulatory factors.

>> Formalize C-level AI-related visions and goals that get cascaded through the organization. These goals typically get board-level visibility.

>> Incorporate guidelines for ethical AI use, considering biases, transparency, and fairness.

Leaders at these organizations typically

>> Ensure that the organization structure supports the AI initiatives by moving resources, forming SWAT teams to focus on the initiatives, and re-evaluating where the company deploys resources.

>> Hire or train talent in specialized AI roles across marketing, technology, and data science.

>> Pressure-test results of AI efforts, updating all stakeholders on what worked and what didn't.

>> Get their team to shift focus from experimentation to pilot projects that the company can scale across the enterprise if they're successful.

Their data and business road maps may

>> Utilize machine learning (ML, see Chapter 5) to predict customer behavior and forecast sales.

>> Develop propensity models (to predict customer behaviors; see Chapter 7), churn prediction (to pinpoint customers that you may lose; see Chapter 11), and customer lifetime value models (to figure the average revenue customers generate in dealings with the company over the length of their relationship; see Chapter 10).

>> Build or use data lakes that enable the organization to store massive amounts of raw (structured and unstructured) data.

>> Regularly audit data practices for compliance with global regulations and industry-specific concerns.

The metrics that these organizations need may include

>> The return on investments (ROIs) on the various AI initiatives

>> Revenue increases or cost decreases in conjunction with AI initiatives

Dominating deep space

After your organization leaves the confines of Earth's atmosphere, marketers spearhead a comprehensive transformation, with AI-driven marketing fully integrated into operations. The organization uses processes, roles, and responsibilities reshaped for the AI era, transforming how the marketing function achieves its objectives and supports the business. Employees across all levels of the organization acknowledge this pivotal shift in a highly competitive landscape. The roles of many employees have notably evolved to accommodate sophisticated AI copiloting.

Marketers in deep space

>> Have mature AI-driven real-time personalization and customer engagement strategies.

>> Harness dynamic customer journey mapping (that visually represents customers' needs, habits, and so on throughout their interactions with the organization) and one-to-one personalization for all marketing programs (see Chapter 20), from campaigns to always-on marketing activities.

>> Re-evaluate agency and technology vendor relationships through an AI-capability lens and making roster adjustments or, at the very least, statements-of-work changes to make sure that no unnecessary charges occur for work that can be done much more quickly now by AI tools.

>> Provide thought leadership in AI marketing, setting industry and category benchmarks, and showcasing how AI marketing can drive business and marketing performance to new heights.

The organizations to which these marketers belong

>> Natively build and test custom models and have full control over data, customization, optimizations, and so on.

>> Make investments in research and development (R&D) to explore cutting-edge AI tech to further automate marketing, insight generation, predictive

analytics, and greater personalization. (Find out about the tools for these activities in Chapters 7 and 10, for example.)

>> Foster AI partnerships with data providers, tech firms, academia, and ad platforms to augment proprietary generative AI models with their more powerful data.

>> Advocate for ethical and responsible use of AI in marketing — and business more broadly, especially in the use of data to train the large language models (LLMs).

Leaders at these organizations typically

>> Reassess and modify business operating models in light of AI's transformative potential. They seek to use AI to influence or drive every sphere of their business operations.

>> Identify, develop, and invest in new revenue streams enabled by AI across each function. In the context of marketing, these revenue streams include retail media networks and new pricing structures.

>> Engage in public discourse and share knowledge about responsible AI applications, focusing on bias, ethics, and inclusivity.

Their data and business road maps may include

>> Implementing self-service data platforms, plus AI and ML tools for various use in various business functions

>> Launching autonomous systems that self-heal (identify and correct errors) and optimize without manual intervention

>> Applying ML to adapt business data processes based on changing patterns

>> Enabling easy data access across the organization via LLMs while ensuring security

The metrics in this deep-space phase may include

>> The return on investments (ROIs) on the various AI initiatives

>> The success rate of new products, services, and marketing launched with AI copiloting

2

Exploring Fundamental AI Structures and Concepts

Gather, organize, and prepare data for AI models.

Understand machine learning principles and how neural networks work.

Use natural language systems and sentiment analysis to turn customer information into marketing insights.

Discover the importance of predictive analytics, procedures, and filtering systems in AI.

Get to know generative AI, as well as its business applications and potential risks.

Chapter **4**

Collecting, Organizing, and Transforming Data

I n the world of artificial intelligence (AI), data acts as the vital force driving machine learning (ML) algorithms. Data lays the foundation for the construction of AI systems, and you need a sufficient quality and quantity of data to make sure that your AI programs perform successfully. Data is the fuel that trains the AI to discern patterns and interpret the inputs provided.

But simply collecting vast amounts of data isn't the whole story. Imagine having a library that contains millions of books, but you have no index or catalog. You'd find searching for some specific book or information frustrating, right? Metadata and data governance step in to alleviate this frustration for the AI. These elements act like the librarians of the AI world, keeping the data in order and making it easily accessible for your AI tools.

With generative AI, some cataloging becomes significantly easier (or maybe even unnecessary) because the AI can read the data and automatically index it. In fact, generative AI's ability to automatically read unstructured data and classify it appropriately for future uses is an immensely powerful capability for companies. It saves them a lot of time and resources because the former process of reading and tagging documents manually now can be done via the AI tools.

Marketers and business leaders have a big stake in the discussion of data. The success of using AI to propel marketing and business results directly depends on the quality of data that fuels the AI engines. Furthermore, marketers and business leaders need to have constructive, solutions-oriented conversations with the technologists who build the AI engines, so they must understand the concepts and tactics of collecting, organizing, and transforming data.

In this chapter, you can explore the importance of data and its collection, storage, and management. You can also find out about the critical elements of metadata and data governance in the business and marketing landscape, as well as how best to format the data and prepare it so that it is easily accessible by the AI applications.

Defining Data in the Context of AI

When you talk about data in the AI realm, you may just think about numbers, text, and code. But the data discussion encompasses so much more. Data can include that song you heard this morning, the video clip you shared with a friend, or even this book's text that you're reading right now. You have data all around you, and AI feeds on that data to make smart decisions for you.

REMEMBER

You can define *data*, in the context of AI, as raw information that serves as input for machine learning (ML) algorithms and enables those algorithms to make predictions and decisions, or to automate tasks. This data can take various forms, including text, images, videos, audio, structured tables, and more. The quality and quantity of data largely determine the performance and reliability of AI systems.

Considering the quality of data

The *quality* of data refers to its accuracy, completeness, and reliability. AI applications need high-quality data so that they can make precise and trustworthy predictions, which is especially important for developing and deploying successful marketing campaigns. Poor data quality can lead to erroneous results and dangerously biased model outcomes. The advent of *generative AI* (a type of AI that focuses on the production of content) can exacerbate bad output. It may create situations in which poor data quality leads to AI responses that sound authoritative and accurate but that actually aren't.

Data quality issues can arise from various sources, such as human error during data entry, inconsistencies in data formatting, inaccuracies or biases in the data itself, and data corruption during transmission or storage.

For AI input, you can evaluate data quality based on several dimensions:

>> **Accuracy:** *Accuracy* measures how closely the data reflects the real-world information it represents. Accurate data is free from errors and discrepancies. Inaccurate data can lead to incorrect model outcomes. For instance, in a medical AI system, incorrect patient data can have life-threatening consequences for both existing and future patients (if the AI model uses that incorrect data).

>> **Completeness:** *Complete* data contains all the necessary information without any gaps. Missing or incomplete data can hinder AI model training and prediction. For example, if you want to personalize an e-mail marketing campaign but have only partial customer data, the AI may miss key patterns and preferences. This situation, in turn, may lead to the creation and delivery of e-mail that lacks context or (worse still) may be completely inaccurate.

>> **Consistency:** *Consistent* data maintains uniformity in terms of units, formats, and definitions. Inconsistent data can confuse AI algorithms and lead to unreliable outcomes. Over time and with the advent of generative AI, lack of consistency in data has become a smaller issue because the generative AI can fill in some of the gaps itself. But you still need to keep consistency in mind.

>> **Relevance:** *Relevant* data applies to the problem at hand and aligns with the objectives of the AI project. Including irrelevant data can introduce *noise* (meaningless information) that reduces the model's performance and challenges users who want to extract meaningful insights. Like consistency, with generative AI and large language models, relevance has become less of a factor more recently because AI can sort out the relevant data.

>> **Timeliness:** *Timely* data is up-to-date and reflects the current state of the subject matter. Outdated data can lead to outdated model predictions. Timeliness was a key deficiency of ChatGPT when it was released in November 2022. At the time, ChatGPT was limited to a supply of data that was good only up to September 2021. That situation has now changed because ChatGPT has updated its model to include more recent information. In fact, it now also has the capability to search the Internet by using Bing to supplement the existing data that it may have been trained on already.

>> **Validity:** *Valid* data adheres to the rules, standards, and constraints in its field. For instance, in healthcare data, validity would ensure that lab values fall within plausible ranges and diagnoses adhere to medical codes.

>> **Uniqueness:** *Unique* data relates to how distinct the entries are. Duplicate data entries can skew AI model training, leading to biased or inaccurate results. For example, in customer databases, multiple entries for the same individual can lead to erroneous customer insights or marketing strategies.

>> **Granularity:** *Granular* describes the level of detail or depth of the data. You must ensure that the data is detailed enough for analysis but not so detailed that it becomes unmanageable or risks privacy issues.

REMEMBER

To improve data quality, businesses often employ data cleansing and validation processes (see the section "Preparing the Data for Use by AI Algorithms and Models," later in the chapter), which involve detecting and rectifying errors and inconsistencies in the data. Additionally, using structured data entry forms, data validation rules, and data quality tools can help maintain high data quality standards.

Getting an appropriate quantity of data

How much data you have is equally as important as the quality of the data that you use with AI. (You can read about quality in the preceding section.) Machine learning models require a sufficient amount of data to discern patterns and make accurate predictions. This concept is often referred to as the *big data* model. The more data available, the better AI models can generalize from that data.

TIP

More data doesn't always equate to better quality. You must balance quantity and quality. Too much irrelevant data in large data sets can degrade model performance by distracting the AI engine while taking up valuable computational power. In marketing language, this situation may translate into grammatically incorrect responses, inaccurate customer recommendations, or even creative copy that isn't all that creative!

You can describe the quantity of data in terms of volume, velocity, and variety:

>> **Volume:** The sheer size of the data pool. Generally speaking, more data often leads to more accurate and robust models. However, you need to balance volume with data quality — less data of the highest quality provides better results than more data of uncertain quality.

>> **Velocity:** The speed at which a system can process and analyze real-time data to provide recommendations. For example, if an AI engine has real-time social media comments coming in about a particular brand, the velocity is the efficiency with which it can respond to those real-time inputs by collecting the data and generating results based on it. Real-time data streams require AI models that can process data extremely quickly.

>> **Variety:** Data comes in various forms, such as structured, semi-structured, and unstructured data. AI systems and models need flexibility to handle diverse data types. The development of generative AI allowed for the analysis and use in training of unstructured data — a situation that older AI models had difficulty with.

REMEMBER

While AI technologies continue to evolve, the demand for more data grows. However, collecting excessive data without a clear purpose can waste time and resources, and it may even infringe on privacy. Unless you work with a technology platform that's building a large language model (LLM), you may not need as much data to feed your AI engines as you think. Target only the data that you need to collect because you have to pay to acquire, store, and manage large amounts of data — especially when it is used by an LLM to generate new content.

Choosing Data Collection Methods for Marketing with AI

To build effective machine learning (ML) models, you must collect data for artificial intelligence (AI) purposes. Data collection methods vary depending on the type of data required and the specific application (in your case, it's marketing). For successful AI projects, you must recognize and implement suitable data collection strategies.

Even if you're not directly involved in developing AI models, like many marketers, you need to understand the data fueling the AI tools that you use in marketing. In particular, the best type of data collection for marketing purposes may source data from third-party providers such as Acxiom, Nielsen, Equifax, Transunion, and Comscore. In order to trust the outcome from AI models, you must understand what data fuels those AI tools.

Identifying data sources and methods

You can collect data from a variety of sources, including

>> **User-generated:** Individuals generate this type of data through interactions with websites, mobile apps, and social media. User-generated data can provide valuable insights into user behavior and preferences, which are foundational elements that inform product improvement and good marketing campaigns. A good example of this data includes the user reviews posted about your product or service.

>> **IoT devices:** Internet of Things (IoT) devices, such as sensors, wearables, and smart appliances, generate vast amounts of data. These devices can capture a wide range of data, from temperature and humidity to location and user behavior. Industries such as manufacturing, agriculture, and healthcare benefit from this real-time data to help inform decision-making. For example,

Tesla cars serve as IoT devices, capturing massive amounts of traffic data which the autopilot functionality in the vehicles uses to improve performance. For marketing purposes, IoT devices can track customer behavior that, in turn, gives you insights into the best ways to market to them.

» **Enterprise data:** Businesses can tap into their internal data sources, such as customer records, sales transactions, and operational data. This data often needs to be structured appropriately so that it can be used for business intelligence and process optimization. Increasingly, enterprise data — when harnessed by AI engines — can serve to drive business differentiation to distinguish your products and serve your customers better. In the realm of marketing, enterprise data often takes the shape of first-party data, which offers valuable insights about your customer base.

» **Web scraping:** Web scraping involves extracting data from websites and online sources. Many businesses use web scraping to gather data for text, sentiment, and competitive analyses. (See Chapter 6 for information on these types of analyses and their use in marketing.) In addition, businesses use AI to perform more effective web scraping, which makes the data gathered more precise and efficient than ever before. *Note:* Always perform web scraping ethically — only after you seek and receive permission from the website that you're scraping.

» **Publicly available data sets:** You can access numerous publicly available data sets for research and development. These data sets cover a wide range of topics, from purchasing behavior and responsiveness to advertising types to broader economic signals and everything in-between. Although these data sets can help you get a broad picture of potential customers for your marketing efforts, many of these data sets require subscriptions and reside behind paywalls.

You can categorize data collection methods into two main approaches:

» **Passive data collection:** In this method, data is collected without direct user interaction. Examples include monitoring user activities on a website, tracking sensor data from IoT devices, and retrieving historical records (such as past purchases, which you can use for targeted marketing) from databases or websites.

» **Active data collection:** This method involves direct user engagement to obtain data and can include surveys, questionnaires, interviews, and other user feedback mechanisms. You can use active data collection methods to gather specific information that can inform the targeting and design of your marketing efforts. Given that this method requires human involvement and returns much smaller samples, it's becoming a smaller part of the data collection ecosystem.

Minding data privacy and ethics

When you participate in data collection for marketing with AI, you must incorporate consideration for privacy and ethics. Obtaining informed consent from individuals whose data you collect is crucial. And you must ensure that you anonymize the data and protect it from unauthorized access. Your business must adhere to privacy regulations, such as the *General Data Protection Regulation* (GDPR; an EU-based law that governs how organizations can use, process, and store personal data), when collecting and handling personal data. See Chapter 22 for more information about ethics and privacy.

TIP

Regulatory landscapes in the U.S. and globally shift often, and a patchwork of statewide regulations also exist in the U.S. So marketers must stay current on the latest regulations for wherever they do business (as opposed to merely where they're based). For example, a Texas-based business with a website used for selling to customers in California and London must adhere to the rules and laws of their customers' locations.

Moreover, any AI data collection involves serious ethical considerations. Biased data collection can lead to biased AI model outcomes, which can have harmful consequences such as the situation in which the Google Gemini model recommended to users that they eat one stone a day. Preventing discriminatory or unfair data collection practices requires careful thought and oversight.

REMEMBER

I discuss these two aspects of data collection in subsequent chapters (particularly in Chapter 22), but, today, the best way to limit biased data collection involves having appropriate human oversight. As a marketer who uses collected data, don't think that you can absolve yourself of that responsibility.

Putting Your Marketing Data in Its Place

After you collect your data, you need to store it in an accessible, secure, and scalable manner. You can find various storage solutions available for managing data in the context of artificial intelligence (AI), each with its own strengths. In addition to just storing data, managing data in businesses requires factors such as use of *metadata* (specific data that describes and identifies characteristics of other data) and *data governance* (internal standards about how your business collects, stores, processes, and disposes of personal data). These factors ensure that you properly document and organize data, and that you remain compliant with regulatory requirements. Neglecting these aspects can lead to data chaos (where data is organized and accessed badly), compliance issues, and data misuse.

Access to structured, reliable data provides the backbone of AI applications and machine learning (ML). Defined by its well-organized nature, you typically store structured data in databases or spreadsheets that feature clearly defined data types, relationships, and constraints. You must establish structured data systems first if you want to craft a foundation for developing AI models that you can use in marketing — and all aspects of business. Table 4-1 gives an overview of data structures and handling.

TABLE 4-1 **Data Structures and Handling**

Aspect of Data Handling	Specific Processes and Structures	The Impact on Data Available to AI Apps
Data storage	Databases	Relational and NoSQL databases offer both structured and less structured data. AI applications, such as customer segmentation apps, which require rapid access to specific bits of data can use these databases.
	Data lakes	Offer various data types: structured, semi-structured, and unstructured. Also include scalability and tools for data exploration and transformation. Especially suitable for AI apps that rely on big data analytics.
	Data warehouses	Databases optimized for analytics and reporting, and specialized for business intelligence purposes. Offer optimized querying and data retrieval for fast performance.
Metadata	Discovery	Helps users locate relevant data quickly and lessen the time spent searching for the right info.
	Lineage	Tracks the origin and history of data to give a big-picture view of data evolution.
	Quality	Outlines details about data accuracy and reliability.
	Security	Can include security policies and access controls to safeguard data.
Data governance	Policies	Define how companies collect, store, access, and protect data. Align with business (including marketing) goals and regulatory requirements.
	Stewardship	Assign stewards responsible for data quality, security, and compliance; all of which ensure valid data for AI applications.
	Catalogs	Create a centralized repository of metadata that offers quick and easy access to available data assets.
	Compliance management	Ensure that governance practices align with legal and regulatory requirements, such as General Data Protection Regulation (GDPR), Health Insurance Portability and Accountability Act (HIPAA), or industry-specific regulations.

Aspect of Data Handling	Specific Processes and Structures	The Impact on Data Available to AI Apps
	Lifecycle management	Define how companies manage (create, store, and archive) data, from collection to eventual purging.
Data structuring	Data schema	Outline data structure, including tables that have columns and attributes, data types, and interrelationships of data elements and structures. Well-designed schema helps data retain integrity.
	Storage mechanisms	Primarily include relational and NoSQL databases that provide the organization, access, and constraints to ensure data consistency and quality.

Understanding Data via Manual and Automated Systems

You must understand data if you want to foster artificial intelligence (AI) development. The process for understanding data involves both manual and automated systems, and each system type offers unique advantages for gaining insights from the data. Manual data analysis, in particular, helps you identify nuanced and domain-specific insights, which crucially depend on human intuition and expertise. Automated data understanding uses machine learning (ML) techniques and data profiling tools to uncover patterns, anomalies, and other insights in the data.

In the following list, I briefly describe the key elements of the systems that affect the data that your AI marketing model eventually receives:

>> **Manual data analysis** involves the comprehensive examination of data to gain insights through visual and statistical methods. Specific methods include

- *Exploratory Data Analysis (EDA):* A critical phase in data analysis that employs both visual and statistical techniques. Visualizing data by using tools such as scatter plots, histograms, and heatmaps unveils patterns, trends, and correlations in the data. Data scientists can use these connections to identify potential relationships or anomalies.

- *Domain expertise:* Domain experts (humans) can provide context and insights into the data that purely automated processes may not catch. Experts' understanding of the industry or problem domain can guide data exploration effectively.

>> **Automated data analysis** takes advantage of a variety of software tools and techniques, including

- *Clustering:* Techniques that group data points based on similarities. These algorithms automatically identify clusters of similar data points so that the AI engine can more easily identify trends or segment data for further analysis. Clustering can provide insights into customer segmentation, market analysis, and more.

- *Association rule mining:* Detects frequent patterns and relationships within the data. It identifies rules that describe associations between different variables, enabling businesses to understand customer behavior or identify product affinities.

- *Data profiling tools:* Automatically generate summary statistics and detect data quality issues, providing a quick overview of data characteristics. These tools can identify missing values, outliers, and inconsistent data, aiding in data cleaning and preparation.

- *Anomaly detection:* A vital technique for identifying data points that deviate significantly from the norm. In applications such as fraud detection or quality control, automated systems can efficiently identify unusual patterns or outliers that require further investigation.

Preparing the Data for Use by AI Algorithms and Models

After you properly store, govern, and structure your data systems (as I discuss in the section "Putting Your Marketing Data in Its Place," earlier in this chapter), your marketing focus shifts to preparing data for artificial intelligence (AI) applications that you intend to train and use. Data preparation encompasses several crucial steps, including data cleaning, transformation, and splitting. The quality of data directly influences the effectiveness of AI marketing models and adheres to the adage "garbage in, garbage out."

Perfecting data by cleaning

Data collected from various sources often arrives with imperfections, including missing values, outliers, and outright errors. *Data cleaning* is the systematic process of identifying and rectifying imperfections to ensure data quality and consistency. Key aspects of data cleaning include

>> **Addressing missing values:** Techniques such as *imputation* replace missing values to prevent data loss and ensure that machine learning models can effectively use the available data. You can account for missing values by imputing (substituting) them with estimated or calculated values, or by labeling them to indicate their absence. For example, in a data set of customer records, data cleaning may involve filling in missing phone numbers to maintain data completeness.

>> **Dealing with outliers:** *Outliers* are data points that deviate significantly from the norm and can cause skewed models or results. Data cleaning identifies and handles outliers by either notating them as exceptions in the data set or removing them, depending on the context.

>> **Correcting errors:** You can correct errors in data, such as typos or inconsistencies, during data cleaning. This process ensures that data adheres to the predefined schema and quality standards.

Transforming data

Data transformation focuses on presenting data in a format suitable for AI models to use as training data. Transformations may involve various operations, including

>> **Normalization and data scaling:** You often need to *normalize* numerical data, bringing it within a specific range that's appropriate and predefined for the data point. For example, scaling values to fall between 0 and 1 (called *min-max scaling*) for data such as a user's propensity to buy a product again may adjust the input for an AI model's training phase. Another data scaling technique — *Z-score standardization* — normalizes data by transforming it into a distribution with a mean of 0 and a standard deviation of 1. This method works for data that follows a normal distribution so that machine learning (ML) models can work with it.

Normalization ensures that the same data points don't present different value scales, which can contaminate the learning process of AI models.

REMEMBER

>> **Encoding:** You must *encode* categorical data — which includes non-numeric values (such as product or city names) — by converting it into a numerical format for proper processing and learning by AI.

You have to encode data in order for AI models to work efficiently with all data types. Common encoding techniques include *one-hot encoding,* where you represent each category by using a binary vector that consists of 1s and 0s. Encoding techniques such as label encoding (a method that's more space efficient than one-hot encoding) or embedding (which also uses vectors) help ensure that you can effectively integrate categorical data into the model.

Splitting data into subsets

Data splitting is the process of dividing the data set into training, validation, and test sets. You need effective data splitting in AI model development because it enables training, optimization, and evaluation of the model in a controlled and systematic manner.

Each subdivision serves a distinct purpose in AI model development:

>> **Training set:** Teaches the AI model. Through the training set, the model learns from the data to identify patterns and make predictions.

>> **Validation set:** Assists in fine-tuning model *hyperparameters,* which are parameters whose values control the learning process. The validation set helps optimize the AI model's performance before its final testing.

>> **Test set:** Serves to assess the model's *generalization performance* (its capacity to properly adapt to new data that comes from the same data used to create the model). Using a separate data set for the testing phase ensures that the AI model performs well on unseen data and doesn't *overfit* (correspond too closely to the training data and therefore perform poorly on new data).

Trimming down data

The curse of *dimensionality,* which happens when your data has too many variables or features, is a common challenge in AI and machine learning. It occurs because the data volume grows exponentially as the number of features increases. This curse can affect marketing data in AI models by making it more complex and less efficient, leading to the AI engine developing inaccurate insights or providing flawed marketing recommendations.

To tackle this issue, data scientists employ dimensionality reduction and feature extraction techniques to simplify the data set while preserving essential information. In short, these techniques help alleviate the curse by

>> **Reducing the number of features in a data set while retaining the essential information:** Several key aspects in this process include

- *Principal component analysis (PCA):* This widely used method identifies *principal components* by grouping linear combinations of the original features. It then ranks the principal components in order of their importance and projects the data into fewer dimensions based on these components. This process results in a reduced data set that retains as much variation and information as possible.

- *t-Distributed Stochastic Neighbor Embedding (t-SNE):* This technique aids in visualizing data by focusing on preserving local similarities among features. t-SNE creates a simpler representation of the data while trying to maintain the relative distances between data points, making it a valuable tool for understanding data clusters and patterns.

>> **Creating new features based on existing ones:** The process of *feature extraction* reveals latent patterns and relationships in the data (which data scientists may not see) by analyzing the original features. Key points about feature extraction include

- *Convolutional neural networks (CNNs):* A class of deep learning models that automatically extract features in image analysis. By identifying and representing intricate features and patterns (such as edges, textures, and shapes) from raw pixel data, CNNs can perform image processing quite successfully.

- *Latent features:* Features that data scientists may not discern in the original data can provide valuable insights and often lead to improved model performance. For example, in natural language processing, latent semantic analysis can extract underlying semantic information from text documents.

Handling imbalanced and irrelevant data

In cases where data is *imbalanced*, meaning one class that represents a specific feature significantly outnumbers another, you can employ techniques to address this class imbalance and ensure that machine learning (ML) models don't exhibit bias and thereby skew your marketing data. Methods include

>> **Oversampling** by increasing the number of instances of the minority class

>> **Undersampling** by reducing the number of instances of the majority class

>> **Applying specialized algorithms** designed to counteract imbalanced data

In data preparation, you must select relevant features (measurable characteristics or properties) of the data. Irrelevant or redundant features (that don't target the information you are trying to glean) can introduce noise and negatively impact model performance. Data scientists use techniques such as Recursive Feature Elimination (RFE) or feature importance scores to identify key features that contribute significantly to the predictive power of the model. By focusing on relevant features, you can train your AI marketing models more efficiently and effectively.

IN THIS CHAPTER

» Discovering the basics of machine learning and neural networks

» Recognizing the types of learning AI can utilize

» Taking a look at image processing

» Becoming familiar with related tools and terminology

Chapter 5

Making Connections: Machine Learning and Neural Networks

People probably overuse the terms *machine learning* and *neural networks* when they talk about the fundamentals of artificial intelligence (AI). But this situation occurs for a good reason: Together, these technologies form the foundation upon which every other AI innovation is built. Understanding how machine learning and neural networks actually work is important because it gives you a framework for how to think about the potential of AI and what it can and can't do.

In this chapter, I break down machine learning (ML) into simple terms and discuss the process by which machines learn from the data they're exposed to. I also present neural networks as one method of accomplishing machine learning — by using human brain–inspired algorithms to recognize patterns in data.

Understanding machine learning and neural networks is crucial for marketers. These technologies enable personalized marketing, predictive analytics, and automation, which enhance marketing efficiency and customer insights. They help in optimizing content, detecting fraud, and improving customer support. Overall, these technologies empower marketers to make data-driven decisions and deliver personalized experiences in a competitive market.

Examining the Process of Machine Learning

Machine learning (ML) is a branch of artificial intelligence (AI) in which computer scientists train computers to learn from the data that they encounter, instead of relying on explicit programming. To understand how exactly this process works, imagine teaching children to recognize fruits. You show them various fruits and identify those fruits by name. Over time, the children start recognizing fruits without your help. Similarly, with ML, scientists provide data (such as pictures of fruits) and their corresponding labels (names of the fruits) to a computer, and that computer learns to recognize new data (about fruits) on its own. Practically, every image recognition tool today is trained by using machine learning. If you've ever activated FaceID on your iPhone, you've facilitated some machine learning yourself by training the iPhone to recognize your face.

REMEMBER

Machine learning is like teaching computers to learn from experience. By feeding them data, using appropriate algorithms, and fine-tuning models, you can make computers perform tasks without those computers being explicitly programmed for each task. As I mention in Chapter 4, data is the foundation of machine learning. The quality and quantity of data directly influence how well a machine learns. Think of it this way: If you're learning to play a musical instrument, the more you practice (or add data), the better you become. However, if you practice using bad habits (or poor-quality data), you won't become a good player.

Here are some critical factors that determine how well your AI engine incorporates machine learning:

>> **Model and algorithms:** The brain behind the learning is the *machine learning model,* a computer program built to use algorithms that provide instructions on how to handle data. An *algorithm* is like a recipe. Just like you can use various recipes to bake a cake, you can employ different algorithms to process and learn from data. The choice of algorithm often depends on the type of data, the task, and the desired outcome.

>> **Training and testing:** After you develop the algorithms, you train your ML model by using a portion of your data. After training, you test the model by using a different set of data to find out how well the model learned. This training-and-testing process ensures that your model doesn't just memorize the training data (a result that's referred to as *overfitting*) but understands the patterns within it well enough to extrapolate the testing data.

>> **Overfitting and underfitting:** These potential results are common challenges in machine learning. *Overfitting* is like memorizing answers to a specific test without understanding the concepts. If faced with a different test on the

same topic, the student who memorized answers may fail. Similarly, an ML model may perform excellently on training data but poorly on new, unseen data. *Underfitting* is the opposite. The model is too general and fails to capture the patterns in the training data, resulting in poor performance or, in other words, recommendations that are inaccurate or too generalized.

>> **Real-world applications:** Machine learning is everywhere! From recommending songs on music platforms, to predicting weather, to diagnosing diseases, to assisting in financial decisions, to powering voice assistants on smartphones — ML touches various aspects of our daily lives and has for a while. For example, if you use the music service Spotify, you get the benefit of its machine learning algorithms that help the service recommend songs you may like.

Machine learning algorithms enhance marketing programs by providing personalized product recommendations based on customer behavior. They also predict trends and help marketers anticipate customer needs and preferences.

Understanding Neural Networks

To build on the preceding section's discussion of machine learning, you can go deeper by understanding one of the most exciting techniques of machine learning: neural networks. Inspired by the human brain's structure, *neural networks* are sets of algorithms designed to recognize patterns. Machine learning is all about making computers learn from experience, and neural networks are one specific way to achieve that result. Neural networks process sensory data by mimicking the brain's way of labeling or clustering raw input.

Layers of a neural network

Visualize your brain as a bustling city for a moment. The neuron bodies (nodes) are the city's buildings, and the dendrites and axons are the roads connecting them, creating pathways for information. Similarly, in machine learning, a neural network has artificial neurons (also called nodes) connected by "paths" to transmit data.

You can think of the structure of a neural network like this:

>> **Input layer:** The city's main gate, where you feed information (your data) into the city's landscape. Flip back to the fruit-recognition example that I present in the section "Examining the Process of Machine Learning," earlier in the

chapter. In that example, the data input feeds in as labeled data — an image and associated name.

>> **Hidden layers:** The intricate streets and neighborhoods, where data passes through streets and between buildings, and the magic of data processing happens. An essential part of neural networks, the *activation function* is computer logic that decides how much signal to transfer to the next layer. Picture it as a city's traffic lights, controlling the flow of information.

>> **Output layer:** The final destination. Here, based on the data's journey through the hidden layers, the neural network gives its prediction or classification. For example, imagine a network that's been taught to identify a cat. The neural network passes the image data provided through the network, dissects the image, and examines features such as edges and shapes. By the journey's end, it decides on the likelihood of the image being a cat and offers its conclusion as output.

Training a neural network mirrors the supervised learning process in machine learning and has these characteristics:

>> **An iterative learning process:** By using labeled data, the network makes predictions, learns from errors, and refines its approach, a process called *backpropagation*. In neural networks, programmers feed the network with handwritten numbers (which indicate how correctly it made its predictions), allowing the network to adjust its predictions based on the feedback. The goal is to help the network get better with each iteration.

>> **An adjustable system of weights:** Connections between artificial neurons have weights that signify their importance. When data travels through layers and connections, the network refines these weights (giving them more or less importance to the outcome) to improve its predictions.

TIP

Deep neural networks, which have numerous hidden layers that allow the system to recognize intricate patterns, take the potential of machine learning in new directions. Voice assistants such as Siri (for Apple products) or Alexa (for Amazon products) offer great illustrations. These networks process sentences, discern context, and generate accurate responses. In the realm of marketing, deep neural networks provide product recommendations to customers and offer them targeted, contextual advertising by understanding all the customer's interactions with a brand on its website (and beyond).

Challenges with neural networks

Neural networks amplify the principles of machine learning (ML), enabling computers to learn and adapt from data in profound ways. You can train these virtual brains, with their intricate connections and layers, for myriad tasks, from simple image recognition to understanding human language. Integrating the adaptability of ML with the depth of neural networks opens doors to some of the more advanced AI use cases. For example, in marketing, neural networks can better optimize social media advertising that you see in your Instagram feed. This advertising is highly personalized not just to your interests but also to your immediate shopping needs — all thanks to the power of neural networks.

But the power of integrating ML with neural networking has some potential drawbacks:

>> **Overfitting:** Where a model performs well when evaluating training data but not when evaluating new data (as discussed in relation to ML in the section "Examining the Process of Machine Learning," earlier in this chapter). Neural networks can become too specialized and fail to achieve generalized predictions for unfamiliar data.

>> **Computational intensity:** Like with complex ML models, deep neural networks can be extremely resource-hungry and time-consuming. Either of these conditions can make the use of neural networks prohibitively expensive for smaller companies if they're trying to do it all on their own. Fortunately, services such as Google Cloud and Amazon Web Services offer a cheaper opportunity for small companies to take advantage of the best of AI to drive their marketing efforts.

Supervised and Unsupervised Learning

Trying to understand machine learning (ML) and neural networks brings you to the concepts of supervised and unsupervised learning. The section "Understanding Neural Networks," earlier in this chapter, discusses training neural networks by using iterations of labeled data. This type of training is *supervised learning* in action. In *unsupervised learning*, the algorithm in the AI model receives data without explicit instructions on what the data represents or what to do with it. The system tries to learn the patterns and the structure from the data without receiving any labeled responses to guide the learning process.

Following the path of supervised learning

If you employ the bustling city analogy (see the section "Layers of a neural network," earlier in the chapter), supervised learning in this case is like using a GPS. You know your starting point and your destination. In this type of learning, you provide the algorithm with input-output pairs, which are the data points consisting of the inputs and their corresponding correct outputs. This pairing makes the learning supervised because you essentially provide the model with the answers.

You present the network with many examples (the input data), and for each, the network knows the correct output because you provide it with that information. With each training example, the network adjusts its *weights* (the relative importance of the data) to reduce the difference between its prediction and the actual answer.

Research into machine learning shows that — with an increase in labeled data — supervised algorithms, especially neural networks, can achieve impressive accuracy rates. For instance, image recognition models have reached over 95 percent accuracy on specific data sets when trained with millions of labeled images. In fact, examples that fall into the 5 percent or less failure rate typically include images that also trip up humans at first glance — such as the classic example of chihuahuas versus blueberry muffins. (You can find these images online by searching "chihuahuas and blueberry muffins.")

Embracing the freedom of unsupervised learning

Contrast supervised learning (discussed in the preceding section), using GPS to get to your destination, with an adventure in your bustling city without using GPS at all — that's unsupervised learning. When the learning is unsupervised, your AI explores the data without specific destinations in mind. Instead, the AI looks for patterns, structures, or interesting landmarks to provide a basis for identifying and grouping data.

You can use neural networks for unsupervised learning, but they often take on a different structure. One common architecture is the autoencoder. An *autoencoder* is an algorithm designed to encode the input data and then decode it, reconstructing the original data. By doing so, the AI learns the essential features and patterns in the data in real time while it combs through that data.

TIP

One of the strengths of unsupervised learning — especially *clustering techniques* (which group data points based on their similarities) — is that it can help marketers segment their customer base. For instance, a retail company may find that 70 percent of their customers' data cluster around purchasing home and kitchen items, but the other 30 percent are more interested in electronics. This type of data-driven insight can inform targeted marketing strategies.

EXAMPLES OF SUPERVISED AND UNSUPERVISED LEARNING

In the bustling city of machine learning, supervised learning is a guided tour, ensuring that the computer reaches specific destinations. At the same time, unsupervised learning lets the computer freely explore, discovering hidden gems and patterns on its own. You can tailor neural networks, as a foundational infrastructure in this city, for either learning approach, whether it's meticulously training by using labeled data or adventurously seeking out patterns in the uncharted territories of raw data.

Here are examples of each type of learning:

- **Supervised learning:** Imagine that you have a basket of fruits and a label for each fruit. In supervised learning, you show the computer an apple and tell it, "This is an apple." The same goes for other fruits. Over time, and with enough sample images, the computer can recognize a fruit image that it's never seen before and correctly label it as an apple or banana.

- **Unsupervised learning:** Imagine walking through a bustling city and seeing clusters of similar shops — coffee shops in one area, bookstores in another. Unsupervised learning happens when the AI categorizes these shops based on their similarities without being explicitly told the category names. In real-world terms, think of this process as looking at a group of news articles and clustering them into topics (sports, politics, entertainment) without being told what those topics should be.

Together, these learning methodologies expand AI capabilities, giving marketers (and other AI users) tools to harness known truths and uncover hidden insights.

Exploring Reinforcement Learning

In the vast, dynamic cityscape of machine learning (ML), *reinforcement learning* is a type of machine learning where an AI agent learns to make decisions by receiving rewards or penalties for its actions. It's like an adventurous traveler, constantly learning and adapting based on feedback from every twist and turn. By integrating neural networks into reinforcement learning environments, AI models can tackle complex problems, from mastering games to making personalized product recommendations.

To continue with the bustling city analogy for machine learning, think of reinforcement learning as trying to navigate the city by using a combination of intuition, trial and error, and occasional guidance from locals. Every time you make a good decision — such as taking a shortcut that gets you to your destination faster — you get a reward (in the shortcut analogy, a speedy arrival); but if you end up in a traffic jam, your penalty is a late arrival.

REMEMBER

Although neural networks and other machine learning models often rely on structured data (such as the labeled fruit basket in supervised learning, discussed in the section "Following the path of supervised learning," earlier in this chapter), reinforcement learning depends on interacting with an environment and learning from the results of those interactions. You can integrate neural networks into reinforcement learning systems, particularly for complex tasks. Over time, the systems help the AI learner (the neural network) predict which actions will yield the highest rewards based on its past experiences.

Reinforcement learning in e-mail marketing

Here's an example of reinforcement learning from the world of marketing. Imagine an e-commerce company that's looking to enhance its promotional e-mail campaigns. Within its e-mail system, the recipients may serve as the environment and the promotional e-mail marketing system acts as the agent that participates in the reinforcement learning process.

By analyzing customer data, such as purchase history, past *open rates* (the percentage of e-mail messages that recipients actually open), and past *e-mail interactions* (any state or result that occurs related to the e-mail sent), the system experiments with various promotional e-mail designs (revisions in actions). The e-mail marketing system experiences positive feedback when recipients open the e-mails that they receive, and it experiences greater rewards when the clicks result in purchases. The system receives no reward for ignored e-mails (which are like a penalty).

While the e-mail system learns over time, it tailors its e-mail designs to individual customer behaviors, leading to increased click-through rates and sales. This adaptive approach can not only boost the company's revenue, but also elevate customer satisfaction. (Chapter 19 has more information on e-mail marketing.)

Weighing explorations against exploits

A crucial aspect of reinforcement learning is the *exploration-exploitation dilemma.* Should the AI agent try new actions (*exploration*) or stick to what it knows works best (*exploitation*)? Think about deciding whether to try a new restaurant (exploration) or go to a familiar one (exploitation). Going for too much exploration may result in time wasted on subpar meals; going for too little exploration may mean that you miss out on some great cuisine options. In the e-mail system example from the preceding section, the AI system has a choice between redesigning an e-mail completely (perhaps to reach a different type of consumer) or just making minor adjustments to an existing design that already shows favorable results.

REMEMBER

The balance of exploration and exploitation is crucial. Think of online streaming platforms that recommend movies or music. If they suggest only what you've previously liked (exploitation), you have a repetitive experience. But if they always recommend new genres (exploration), you may get recommendations that don't resonate with you at all.

And if you're wondering how impactful reinforcement learning is, take a look at Netflix, which uses reinforcement learning (among other techniques). The company estimates that its recommendation system — which balances exploration and exploitation — saves it over $1 billion a year by reducing customer *churn* (loss; see Chapter 11 for more on combatting customer churn) and enhancing user satisfaction. Needless to say, Netflix also uses reinforcement learning to optimize the e-mails that it sends to its customers.

TIP

Reinforcement learning stands out because it's about continuous adaptation. Unlike supervised learning, where the model may not change at all after training, reinforcement agents constantly refine their strategies, making them versatile in changing environments.

Mastering Sequences and Time Series

In the realm of machine learning (ML), as in all of computer science and digital marketing, sequences and time series play a pivotal role:

>> **Sequence:** in machine learning, ordered sets of data points. Consider the sequence of words in a sentence, such as *Hello* and *world* to create the sentence "Hello, world."

>> **Time series:** A type of sequence that's distinguished by its temporal ordering. Especially crucial when data points correspond to specific moments in time. Think of a machine learning model analyzing heartbeat patterns or predicting stock prices: Each data item is timestamped and forms a continuous data stream.

Seeing how neural networks excel at time series analysis

Neural networks (which I discuss in the section "Understanding Neural Networks," earlier in this chapter) are especially powerful for sequences and time series because of their ability to remember previous inputs. For example:

» **Recurrent neural networks (RNNs)** can process sequences by considering previous data points, making RNNs ideal for time series predictions. This capability is especially important in digital marketing because it allows for accurate forecasting of consumer behavior trends, campaign performance, and demand patterns, enabling more effective and timely marketing strategies.

» **Long short-term memory (LSTM) networks,** a type of RNN, are designed to remember long-term dependencies in sequences. In marketing, LSTM networks are valuable for tracking and understanding historic customer behaviors. The sidebar "Employing LSTM networks," in this chapter, offers an example of using LSTM networks in marketing efforts.

Imagine that you're training a neural network to predict stock prices. Using an RNN, the model analyzes data from previous months:

» **January:** $100/share

» **March:** $110/share

» **May:** $130/share

» **July:** $150/share

The LSTM captures the upward trend and, understanding seasonality from previous years, predicts a slight dip in the coming winter months.

REMEMBER

In machine learning, your AI needs to master sequences and time series through neural networks, especially for marketing and customer loyalty use cases. If your data and analytics teams aren't using these tools to analyze your customer data, you may be missing out on critical marketing optimization opportunities, including extracting customer insights, making accurate sales predictions, and driving innovation for marketing campaigns.

EMPLOYING LSTM NETWORKS

Here's an example of how an online subscription-based service may employ long short-term memory (LSTM; see the section "Seeing how neural networks excel at time series analysis," in this chapter) networks to anticipate customer *churn* (loss). By analyzing time-series data gathered via subscription interactions — for example, daily user activities, customer feedback scores, customer service interactions, and payment histories — the LSTM model predicts the likelihood of a customer canceling their subscription in the upcoming month.

After the model identifies customers who have high churn probabilities, the marketing team can intervene to retain those customers by offering tailored incentives, such as discounts or personalized content recommendations. Through this LSTM-driven marketing approach, the company can effectively reduce customer attrition, enhance loyalty, and promote overall value for the customer.

Embracing time series features, challenges, and tools

Within the context of neural networks, certain features of data-processing methods can help you understand time series. And you can also find tools that enhance the functioning of time series analysis in neural networks. But like with any technology, you may also run into challenges when applying the technology. Table 5-1 offers an overview of features, challenges, and tools related to time series in neural networks.

TABLE 5-1   Specifics of Time Series in Neural Networks

Category	Item	What It Does
Features		
	Embeddings	Represent sequences in compact forms, capturing relationships between different time points.
	Trend recognition	Detects long-term upward or downward movements in a series.
	Seasonality detection	Identifies recurring patterns, such as annual sales spikes.

(continued)

TABLE 5-1 *(continued)*

Category	Item	What It Does
Challenges		
	Overfitting	Training data may fit too closely, causing neural networks to perform poorly when given new data.
	Complexity	Long short-term memory (LSTM) networks and other sequence models can be computationally expensive to operate and intricate to fine-tune.
Tools and Methods		
	Attention mechanisms	Allow the model to focus on certain parts of the sequence more than others, which is useful in tasks such as language translation.
	Transfer learning	Uses pretrained models to improve time series predictions, especially when data is limited.
	Dropout layers	Help prevent overfitting in neural networks by randomly dropping out units during training.

Developing Vision and Image Processing in AI

The marvel of human vision is fascinating to scientists and engineers. Humans' ability to recognize faces, interpret scenes, and differentiate colors is an intricate dance of biological structure and neural analysis. In the world of artificial intelligence (AI), replicating this dance has led to groundbreaking developments in machine vision, where neural networks play the starring role.

The journey of machine vision began in the 1960s, when researchers aimed to teach machines to see and interpret images. The seminal work during this time was rudimentary and focused on basic shapes and patterns. However, while the computational capabilities of the machines grew, so did the ambition of machine vision researchers.

The 2010s witnessed a revolution when convolutional neural networks (CNNs; deep learning models designed to process structured grid data like images) outperformed traditional methods (such as support vector machines and hand-engineered features) in image classification tasks. By 2015, neural network models achieved a staggeringly low 3.57 percent error rate in the ImageNet competition — a yearly challenge for researchers and engineers in visual recognition — surpassing human performance in this competition.

HOW NEURAL NETWORKS PROCESS IMAGES

At its core, a digital image is a collection of pixel values. You start with a certain number of pixels that correspond to the height and width of the image. In color images, each pixel also has three values that correspond to red, green, and blue (RGB) intensities. Along with the number of height and width pixels, a collection of all the pixels' color values forms a three-dimensional array that can be used as input data for analysis by AI models.

Neural networks, especially convolutional neural networks (CNNs), are adept at processing these arrays of image information. A detailed description of this processing is beyond the scope of this book, but in simple terms, CNNs utilize layers of neurons that slide (or *convolve*) over the image data, detecting features such as edges, textures, and patterns. A series of pooling layers interspersed between the convolutional layers help reduce the spatial dimensions (meaning flatten the image array) while retaining important features.

Exploiting the power of convolutional neural networks (CNNs)

CNNs, with their specialized, layered architecture, revolutionized machine vision. Statistically, as of 2020, over 80 percent of image processing tasks in AI research used some form of CNN, highlighting their dominance and efficiency.

CNNs use the following techniques when analyzing images:

>> **Feature learning:** Unlike traditional methods, where features were hand-engineered (that is, manually designed and selected) by experts, CNNs learn these features automatically from image data.

>> **Hierarchical representation:** Lower layers (which are the initial layers of the neural network) may recognize edges, but deeper layers (which are the subsequent layers further into the network) can detect complex structures, such as faces or animals.

>> **Transfer learning:** CNNs trained on one task (for example, recognizing dogs) can adapt to another related task (maybe identifying dog breeds) with minimal additional training.

Prominent examples of machine vision technologies in use involve autonomous vehicles and medical imaging. From Teslas to Ford versions, autonomous vehicles all include cameras that capture imagery for machine vision analysis (interpreting traffic signals and recognizing pedestrians, for example). In medical imaging, neural networks help radiologists detect anomalies such as tumors with extremely high accuracy rates.

In the world of marketing and customer relationship management systems, examples of machine vision abound. For example, a fashion e-commerce platform integrated a CNN to enhance its product recommendation system by

>> **Gathering customer preference data:** When users upload or interact with images of clothing items on social media or the platform itself, the CNN captures the visual patterns and styles of the apparel.

>> **Analyzing clothing preferences:** By recognizing specific features, such as colors, textures, and designs, the CNN builds a picture of what type of clothing the customer likes.

>> **Recommending similar products:** Based on its analysis of product features, the system recommends similar items from the platform's inventory to the user.

TIP

This visually-driven recommendation approach not only streamlines the shopping experience for users but can also boost sales by presenting relevant product options based on visual preferences.

Looking deeper: Advanced vision techniques

Machine vision, in the realm of neural networks, stands as a testament to the incredible power and potential of machine learning. From rudimentary shape recognition in the 1960s to hyper-realistic image generation today, the journey has been transformative.

Going beyond basic CNNs, the evolution of AI's machine vision can help tackle more complex visual tasks with these next-level capabilities:

>> **Generative adversarial networks (GANs):** These dual-network architectures have one network that generates images and the other that evaluates them. GANs can produce hyper-realistic images (of people and places, for example) that are often indistinguishable from real ones.

REMEMBER

If you've ever used AI imagery tools such as Midjourney or DALL-E 3 to create an image for a presentation or a piece of advertising, you've experienced GANs at work.

>> **Segmentation and object detection:** CNNs classify entire images, but networks such as Mask R-CNN can identify multiple objects within an image and precisely outline them. For example, cameras and highway toll booths are trained to recognize car number plates.

>> **Image-to-image translation:** Imagine converting a pencil sketch into colorful artwork. Networks such as Pix2Pix and CycleGAN can achieve this transformation.

Despite the leaps in processing capabilities, challenges with machine vision remain:

>> **Data bias:** Neural networks learn from data. If this data is skewed or biased, the model's predictions can be unfair or inaccurate. For example, early facial recognition systems struggled to recognize individuals who had darker skin tones because of training data bias (these systems received data predominantly relating to lighter-complexioned individuals).

>> **Computational expense:** Advanced networks require significant computational power, making real-time processing or deployment on low-resource devices a challenge.

>> **Interpretability:** Neural networks, often termed *black boxes*, make it hard to discern how they reach a particular decision, which is crucial for sensitive applications such as medical imaging.

Tools for Machine Learning and Neural Networks

The nascent stages of machine learning (ML) in the mid-20th century were dominated by manual computations and limited data sets. However, when the promise of AI began to materialize, the 1990s and 2000s saw the development of early ML tools and libraries. The explosion of deep learning (meaning the use of multilayered neural networks to model complex patterns in data) in the 2010s brought forth a plethora of specialized tools catering to neural networks.

These tools, born from the interplay of academia and industry, make machines smarter and more intuitive. Although you don't need to know these tools well, having knowledge of the ecosystem and how these technology tools connect the dots between machine learning, neural networks, and machine vision can provide you with valuable insights and a deeper appreciation of their capabilities.

Participating with Python

The programming language Python, because of its simplicity and robustness, emerged as the lingua franca of machine learning. Several Python-based *libraries* (code segments that are reusable for specific tasks) have since become cornerstones:

>> **Keras:** As a high-level neural networks application programming interface (API), Keras makes it easy to design and train complex neural models. Initially independent, it's now part of the TensorFlow ecosystem.

>> **PyTorch:** Developed by Facebook's AI Research lab in 2016, PyTorch is lauded for its dynamic computational graph (that allows for on-the-fly changes and debugging), making it particularly attractive for research purposes.

>> **scikit-learn:** Introduced in 2007, this library offers simple and efficient tools for data mining and data analysis. With over 20,000 GitHub repositories using it as of 2021, it's a favorite for classical machine learning tasks.

>> **TensorFlow:** Launched by Google in 2015, TensorFlow has become synonymous with neural network modeling. Its flexibility allows for deployment across various platforms, from servers to smartphones.

TIP

Being familiar with AI programming terminology is helpful. Before you panic, understand that as a marketer, you don't need to master Python or delve into its libraries. But when you partner with data, technology, and analytics teams, you may encounter discussions about Python and its associated libraries. And thanks to advancements in GPT (*generative pre-trained transformer*, a type of machine learning that generates new content in response to a user prompt), as a marketer, you can guide this AI to generate Python code on your behalf. This type of tool enables you to interact with your AI platform seamlessly without needing to be a tech expert.

Diving into deep learning platforms

The rise of deep learning applications (such as image recognition and natural language processing) drove a need for platforms that can handle end-to-end ML workflows. Two deep learning platforms that have risen to prominence are

>> **Google Cloud ML Engine:** Fully managed service that enables developers to build, train, and deploy machine learning models in the *cloud* (meaning the models are developed and executed on remote servers rather than local machines). It seamlessly integrates with TensorFlow (see the preceding section), making the transition from model creation to deployment smooth.

>> **Amazon SageMaker:** Launched in 2017, this platform provides tools to build, train, and deploy machine learning models *at scale* (to match the scope of the data).

By 2024, thousands of companies were using either Google Cloud ML or Sage-Maker for their AI needs.

Chapter **6**

Adding Natural Language Processing and Sentiment Analysis

I n the vast digital universe that's an intricate part of most people's daily lives, words and images are the currency. Every Insta post, product review, or e-mail that you come across represents a goldmine of insights, waiting to be tapped. But with the sheer volume of words circulating every day, how can a business stay on top of customers' (or potential customers') expressed wishes, likes, and dislikes, and extract real value? Enter natural language processing (NLP) — a burgeoning industry that studies our everyday language and extracts insights from it. In the world of marketing, using NLP is akin to having a magnifying glass over your customers' thoughts all the time, every day.

Natural language processing (NLP) is a branch of artificial intelligence (AI) that focuses on the interaction between computers and humans through natural language. In simpler terms, it's the technology behind making machines understand, interpret, and respond to language or the words that humans use when they interact with each other and companies online.

Imagine that you're a retailer who has thousands of product reviews pouring in daily. Manually skimming through them to glean information is not only tedious, but also extremely inefficient. In fact, it's probably impossible for a person (or even a team of people) to do so in a cost-efficient manner. With the help of NLP, you can instantly target specific data and identify trends from those product reviews. If customers are raving about your *soft fabric*, you know where to focus your marketing or your restocking efforts. If they're repeatedly mentioning *slow delivery*, that's a cue to revisit your shipping logistics.

In this chapter, you can find out how natural language processing (NLP) and sentiment analysis can transform digital text into actionable insights when it decodes customer reviews, social media posts, and e-mails to drive smarter decisions and enhance customer experiences. The chapter covers foundational elements of NLP (linguistics and statistics), the integration of machine learning, and the impact of AI transformers and attention mechanisms. It also addresses practical applications and challenges of using these AI technologies to drive businesses' marketing efforts forward.

Demystifying the Backbone of NLP

NLP is more than just a tool; it's the bridge between businesses and their customers in the digital age. By truly understanding the language that customers use, companies can not only listen to customer feedback, but also anticipate, strategize, and deliver greater value to their customers. NLP is so important to businesses because its technology enables them to understand customers through their everyday communications.

In the ever-evolving world of NLP, two foundational elements — linguistics and statistical NLP — form the dual engine that drives the power of most AI solutions that businesses use to comprehend and interact with human language. Linguistics provides a rulebook, and statistics offers adaptability. Together, these elements ensure that NLP tools can understand language as it is today, and also evolve with it.

TIP

You must grasp the essence of these fundamental elements (linguistics and statistics) if you want to understand NLP and its applications for your marketing efforts in the AI era.

Exploring linguistics for NLP

At the heart of every language lies a set of rules, structures, and semantics —the domain of linguistics. When scientists talk about *linguistics* for NLP, they're referring to the application of linguistic principles to help computers understand the intricacies of human language.

Consider the difference in meaning between "Let's eat, Grandma" and "Let's eat Grandma." A tiny punctuation mark (the comma) changes the entire sentiment of the sentence, and the principles of linguistics help NLP systems discern such nuances. By embedding linguistic rules into NLP models, businesses can ensure more accurate and context-aware language processing to fuel their chatbots, transcription services, and other language-focused tools.

The cornerstone of sentiment analysis lies in sophisticated linguistic algorithms. These algorithms are adept at dissecting language, much like a skilled surgeon, by cutting insights out of a tapestry of words. They operate by analyzing text — whether a tweet, a product review, or a customer e-mail — and identifying keywords and phrases that carry emotional weight.

For instance, a customer review stating, "This new skincare line is revolutionary, and my skin has never felt better," would be flagged with positive markers for words such as *revolutionary* and *better*. Harnessing and analyzing these expressions to understand sentiment has helped companies quickly determine what they should be doing next to better serve their customers. This linguistic analysis is a deep dive into language to glean insights.

Seeing the big picture with statistical NLP

Although linguistic rules provide a structured approach to understanding text, language is dynamic and ever-changing. And so, statistical NLP comes into play. Statistical NLP employs mathematical models to analyze language based on patterns and probabilities. Think of it as teaching machines the art of prediction.

For example, if someone types, "I'm feeling under the" into an e-mail message, a statistical NLP model may suggest *weather* as a likely next word, based on the frequency of the phrase's past occurrences. This data-driven approach has revolutionized areas such as machine translation and sentiment analysis (see the section "Unpacking Sentiment Analysis," later in the chapter), allowing businesses to glean insights and make predictions from vast amounts of textual data.

Why linguistics and NLP both matter

Both system components — linguistics for NLP (see the section "Exploring linguistics for NLP," earlier in this chapter) and statistical NLP (discussed in the preceding section) — have their strengths and weaknesses. Linguistics can handle complex language structures and generate grammatically correct sentences.

However, programmers can't create rules for every possible language structure, and rule-based systems are inherently inflexible and difficult to maintain.

Statistical NLP, on the other hand, can handle large amounts of data and recognize patterns that are difficult to capture with rules. On the downside, interpreting statistical models can be difficult, and they may not always produce grammatically correct sentences.

Elevating NLP with Machine Learning

Consider some of the language-based applications that you employ in your customer-outreach efforts — chatbots on your website interacting with customers in real time, smart assistants (such as Alexa) understanding and responding to user commands, or sentiment analysis tools that gauge the mood of social media posts during a product launch.

REMEMBER

These examples aren't just fancy tech tools; they're real-world applications of natural language processing (NLP) that businesses leverage today to serve customers better. NLP has a variety of real-world applications in several fields beyond the ones mentioned in the preceding paragraph, including medical research, search engines, business intelligence, speech recognition, document summarization, machine translation, spam detection, named entity recognition, question answering, autocomplete, predictive typing, and more.

Integrating NLP and machine learning

Because people's interactions with businesses become more digitally driven, the need for machines to understand and respond to human language with precision becomes even more important. Although the roots of NLP are steeped in linguistics and statistics, advances in technology have led to a transformative approach: machine learning (ML) for NLP.

This synergy of AI systems is redefining the boundaries of what programs computer scientists can build in the realm of language technology. It represents a leap from mere language processing to deep language comprehension. For businesses poised for digital innovation, this combination of NLP and machine learning offers a path to creating truly intelligent and intuitive language-based applications that can serve customers in more dynamic, personalized, real-time, and cost-efficient ways.

TIP

For marketing applications, embrace the combo — NLP and machine learning — to fulfill the promise of the well-used phrase in marketing "driving toward the right time, right place, and right message."

Incorporating the two technologies has two levels:

>> **Machine learning in NLP:** As I discuss in other chapters (Chapters 4 and 5, specifically), machine learning involves teaching computers to learn from experience. Instead of manually crafting rules for language processing, ML models are trained on vast data sets, allowing them to identify patterns, nuances, and intricacies of language. Imagine training a model on millions of customer reviews. Over time, the model becomes adept at understanding sentiments, preferences, and even cultural nuances, turning raw text into actionable insights.

>> **Deep learning and NLP:** A subset of machine learning, *deep learning* (meaning advanced learning models that use large data sets and complex algorithms), is even more powerful when paired with NLP. By using neural networks (inspired by the human brain; see Chapter 5), deep learning models dive deep into language structures. Take, for example, the challenge of understanding context in sentences. Although traditional models may struggle with the word *bank* in a phrase such as *I sat on the bank of a river* versus *I went to the bank for money,* deep learning models can discern the difference by analyzing surrounding words, sentence structure, and even prior sentences in the same paragraph.

The fusion of NLP with machine learning offers businesses and marketers a competitive edge like never before. Automated customer support becomes more empathetic and efficient, content recommendations become highly personalized, and real-time language translations become much more accurate. Automated customer support goes beyond just processing language; it can understand and even anticipate customer intent, emotions, and desires.

Adapting to the emotional spectrum

In the dynamic world of customer emotions, one-size-fits-all solutions fail. When it comes to responding to and interpreting customer emotions, machine learning (ML) models shine, offering a more tailored and nuanced approach to sentiment analysis than historical technology solutions that depended heavily on structured data (in which each potential question from a customer had specific responses). Computer scientists train these new models on vast data sets of textual content to help the models learn to recognize and interpret the subtleties and complexities of human emotions.

For example, a marketing team for a sports brand can use ML to discern the subtle differences between *The new running shoes are good* and *The new running shoes are a game-changer!* Despite both being positive, the enthusiasm and intensity are markedly different. By constantly learning and adapting, ML models provide marketers with a dynamic and, most critically, more specific lens to view the emotional landscape of their customers than they would get from basic sentiment analysis alone (see the section "Unpacking Sentiment Analysis," later in this chapter).

TIP

NLP algorithms and models aren't merely tools that capture customer sentiment. They enable businesses to view the world from their customers' eyes and respond to that view by turning raw data into actionable insights. Incorporating NLP and sentiment analysis into your marketing efforts can help drive your business's marketing actions (such as knowing when to push a customer to upgrade based on positive feedback trends), product decisions (based on recurring complaints about a feature, for example), pricing alternatives, and customer support feedback (such as slow response times).

Examining Transformers and Attention Mechanisms

A new buzzword — transformers — has taken the world of natural language processing (NLP) by storm. Along with *attention mechanisms* (which enable models to focus on and prioritize specific parts of the input data that are most relevant for making decisions), *transformers* (advanced neural network architectures that process entire sequences of data simultaneously to capture complex dependencies between distant elements such as paragraphs in a document) are AI technology models that reshape the way machines comprehend human language.

Transformers and attention mechanisms represent the current pinnacle of NLP innovation. By bridging the gap between machine processing and human-like language comprehension, these system elements offer businesses a golden ticket to unparalleled customer engagement and (hopefully) related market dominance.

REMEMBER

For marketers particularly, the advent of transformers and attention mechanisms opened a goldmine with boundless potential. Marketing departments can use these technologies to tailor content that resonates with audiences, extract nuanced insights from customer feedback, or create chatbots that respond with uncanny relevance. In a very practical sense, transformers and attention mechanisms drive the generative AI world, and hence are truly transformative (no pun intended) for marketing.

Here's a quick look at the transformer and attention mechanism technologies:

» **Transformers:** Think of transformers, which were first introduced in 2017, as the latest AI architectural marvel. Unlike traditional models that process words in a sequence, one after the other, transformers can look at entire sentences or paragraphs simultaneously. This scope helps the transformer capture relationships between words, no matter how far apart they are. Imagine the AI examining the sentiment of a customer's feedback that reads,

Despite the frustratingly long wait and having to call back several times to find out when the order will be shipped, I loved the product.

A transformer can effortlessly link *long wait* with *loved* to provide a holistic understanding of the mixed feedback. **Note:** the *T* in the name for the conversational model *ChatGPT* stands for Transformer (and GPT stands for Generative Pre-trained Transformer).

» **Attention mechanisms:** The true power behind the transformer. In the same way that humans pay more attention to certain words when trying to understand a sentence, this mechanism allows the model to focus on specific parts of the input data that are more relevant. For instance, in the sentence, *Jane, who had been to Paris twice, said the Eiffel Tower was breathtaking,* the attention mechanism gives more weight to *Jane* and *Eiffel Tower* when determining the main subject and sentiment of the statement because it recognizes that the primary meaning of the sentence is how beautiful Jane finds the Eiffel Tower and not that she's been to Paris twice.

The Bidirectional Encoder Representations from Transformers (BERT) and GPT language models both use attention mechanisms. BERT studies the text in both directions — both before and after the primary words — to better capture nuance and meaning.

Unpacking Sentiment Analysis

In the age of digital interactions, where every click, review, or comment holds a story, businesses are on a perpetual quest to decipher the sentiments behind these interactions. In this scenario, AI sentiment analysis is the tool that marketers wield to listen to and gauge the heartbeat of their customers. It's like having a window into your customers' minds that reveals not only what they are saying but also how they feel.

And sentiment analysis is more than a tool; it's the bridge between businesses and the emotional landscape of their customers. In a world where emotions often drive buying decisions, it offers marketers a road map to navigate the complex terrains of customer feelings, ensuring every strategy is not only data-driven, but also emotion-aware.

Catching the feeling

Sentiment analysis is an NLP technique that determines whether a piece of text expresses a positive, negative, or neutral sentiment. It's the science and art of extracting emotional tone from words and turning an abstract feeling into measurable data. Picture a review that reads, *The shoes are stylish but terribly uncomfortable.* Sentiment analysis can pinpoint the positive sentiment toward the style and the negative sentiment toward the comfort, providing a multi-dimensional view of the feedback.

The magic of sentiment analysis lies in its versatility. Consider these examples:

>> **For a hotel chain,** it can mean categorizing feedback such as *The ocean view was breathtaking* as positive and *The room service was dreadfully slow* as negative.

>> **For a tech company,** comments such as *The app's interface is incredibly user-friendly* offer a thumbs-up, but *It crashes frequently* rings alarm bells.

>> **In the entertainment industry,** even subtle sentiments, such as *The concert was okay, I guess* (which leans toward neutral or slightly negative) can be detected and categorized.

REMEMBER

For marketers, using sentiment analysis effectively is akin to striking a rich vein of ore; but in this instance, the ore is customer insights. It offers a nuanced understanding of customer opinions — beyond just star ratings or likes. Marketers can analyze campaign feedback, product launches, or even social media trends in real time and use the insights gained to pivot strategies, address customer concerns, or amplify strengths. Sentiment analysis not only collects feedback; it helps you understand the emotions behind the feedback and how to craft resonant responses.

Understanding language nuances

The true challenge in sentiment analysis is grappling with the nuances of context and semantics. Words alone are just the tip of the iceberg; understanding their meaning in context is where the real depth of relevant information lies. Semantic analysis steps in to interpret the meaning behind words by taking into account the subtleties of language such as sarcasm, irony, and metaphor.

In the area of marketing, understanding subtleties means not just knowing that a customer said, "This is the most interesting perfume I've ever smelled," but also deciphering whether that's a compliment or a critique. A report by Digital Marketing Institute highlighted brands that employed advanced semantic analysis and experienced an improvement in targeting customer needs.

Integrating social media analytics

In today's digital age, social media can be the battleground where brands are made or broken. Sentiment analysis marries perfectly with social media analytics, providing real-time insights into public opinion. This integration enables marketers to monitor social media chatter and quickly gauge public sentiment toward a product launch or an ad campaign.

For example, a beverage company may track reactions to a new flavor launch on X (formerly Twitter), discerning in real time whether the sentiment is overwhelmingly positive, mixed, or negative. Data from social media management tool Sprout Social indicates that brands actively using sentiment analysis in social media monitoring are more likely to report increased customer loyalty. Social media analytics involves more than just monitoring; it gives you a finger on the pulse of consumers' current zeitgeist.

Challenges for NLP and Sentiment Analysis

In the digital era, marketers rely heavily on natural language processing (NLP) and sentiment analysis to unlock the treasure trove of customer insights hidden in text data. However, the journey from text to insight is strewn with complexities because these technologies have to deal with the intricacies of human language and emotion.

Understanding the nuances of these challenges isn't just academic; marketers aiming to understand their customers better need to be able to identify and address these challenges. Here are some challenges that AI systems face when dealing with the human element:

>> **Slang and idioms:** Slang and idiomatic expressions are constantly evolving, reflecting cultural shifts and trends. Traditional NLP systems, often built on static dictionaries and rules, struggle to keep up with this linguistic evolution. For instance, a system trained on data from five years ago may be baffled by contemporary Internet slang. This limitation arises from the algorithmic

rigidity of NLP models that lack the ongoing learning mechanisms that would allow them to adapt to new linguistic trends dynamically.

>> **Mixed sentiments:** Mixed sentiments in a single bit of text present a complex scenario for sentiment analysis algorithms. Current technology often relies on keyword-based approaches or simplistic sentiment scoring systems, which can misinterpret or oversimplify nuanced expressions. The challenge lies in the technology's inability to contextually weigh different sentiments within the same text and provide a holistic sentiment score that reflects the overall tone (see the section "Examining Transformers and Attention Mechanisms," earlier in the chapter, for a rundown of how AI systems understand emphasis). More advanced sentiment analysis algorithms that incorporate machine learning can interpret some of these complexities.

>> **Sarcasm and irony:** Sarcasm and irony flip the intended meaning of words, posing a significant challenge to NLP algorithms that primarily analyze text based on surface-level word meanings. Most current systems lack the sophisticated contextual and pragmatic understanding required to detect these subtleties. This limitation is rooted in the technology's inability to incorporate broader world knowledge and emotional intelligence that's essential for interpreting such indirect forms of expression.

>> **Cultural and linguistic diversity:** The global digital marketplace brings a multitude of languages and cultural contexts, each with its unique linguistic structure and connotations. Current NLP technologies often exhibit a bias toward more widely spoken languages, such as English and Spanish, so these technologies can't as accurately process less-common languages. However, advances in machine learning-based NLP have made progress in accommodating a wider range of languages and dialects.

Additionally, these systems often overlook the subtleties of cultural context, which significantly impacts sentiment interpretation. This challenge stems from the fact that AI technology can't account for the vast and varied cultural nuances that influence language use.

Engaging Best Practices for Using NLP and Sentiment Analysis

In the realm of modern business, the convergence of natural language processing (NLP) and sentiment analysis has opened new avenues for understanding and engaging with customers. To harness the full potential of these technologies, businesses must adhere to a set of best practices that address both the technical and ethical aspects of these AI tools:

>> **Prioritize accurate and diverse data collection.** Effective NLP and sentiment analysis start with the collection of high-quality, diverse data. Businesses must aim to gather data from a variety of sources, such as social media, customer reviews, surveys, and direct customer interactions. For example, the clothing company H&M diversified its data collection and therefore achieved a more rounded understanding of customer sentiment, leading to a significant increase in customer satisfaction.

WARNING

Don't rely solely on a narrow range of data sources; otherwise, you end up with biased and incomplete insights.

>> **Select appropriate NLP and sentiment analysis tools.** Tailor your tool selection to specific business needs, considering factors such as language support, integration capabilities, and the sophistication of analysis required. Companies that use tools that align with their unique requirements can expect a marked increase in the accuracy of insights.

REMEMBER

Don't decide which tools to use based purely on cost or popularity because these criteria may not correlate with your business's specific needs.

>> **Contextualize analysis and understand limitations.** Both NLP and sentiment analysis must be context-aware to be effective. For example, Netflix's approach considers the specific context of user comments, leading to more accurate content recommendations. Current NLP technologies have their limitations, especially in dealing with ambiguity, sarcasm, and cultural nuances (see the preceding section). Misinterpreting these elements can lead to inaccurate analyses and potentially harmful business decisions.

>> **Ensure continuous learning and adaptation.** The field of NLP is continuously evolving. Make sure that your NLP and sentiment analysis models are updated regularly to understand new linguistic patterns, emerging slang, and evolving language usage so that you can maintain the relevance and accuracy of analyses. Amazon's approach to continuously updating its algorithms stands as a testament to the effectiveness of this practice.

>> **Integrate quantitative and qualitative insights.** Although NLP and sentiment analysis offer quantitative data, you can supplement this data with qualitative research to provide a deeper understanding of customer sentiments and preferences. Starbucks' strategy of combining algorithmic analysis with direct customer feedback is a prime example of this approach. Relying solely on quantitative data may overlook the nuanced insights that human beings can glean from qualitative analysis based on data gathered by asking people to share their opinions more conversationally.

>> **Adhere to ethical standards and privacy compliance.** Use NLP and sentiment analysis ethically. Businesses must respect privacy laws and maintain transparency in their data processing practices. You have to comply with regulations such as the General Data Protection Regulation (GDPR) not only for legal reasons, but also so that you can maintain customer trust. (See Chapter 22 for more on ethics and privacy.)

>> **Leverage multilingual capabilities for global reach.** If your business operates globally, you need to leverage NLP tools that can handle multiple languages and dialects. This capability ensures that your tools' insights aren't limited to a single language group, providing a more inclusive understanding of the global customer base. Failing to account for linguistic diversity can result in skewed insights and missed opportunities in international markets. (Check out Chapter 17 for information about using AI to translate and localize marketing content.)

>> **Collaborate with NLP experts and linguists.** This collaboration can greatly enhance the effectiveness of sentiment and linguistic analyses. These professionals can provide valuable insights into the subtleties of language and help fine-tune algorithms for more accurate results. Don't underestimate the complexity of language processing — seek expert guidance when you need it, such as when developing sophisticated language models or addressing specific language nuances in customer feedback.

By implementing the best practices in the preceding list, your business can effectively navigate the complexities of NLP and sentiment analysis, leading to more insightful and impactful marketing strategies. These practices underscore the importance of a holistic, ethically sound, and continuously evolving approach to understanding and engaging with customers in today's digital landscape.

Chapter 7

Collaborating via Predictions, Procedures, Systems, and Filtering

I n the evolving field of artificial intelligence (AI), the concepts of predictions, procedures, systems, and filtering stand out as fundamental pillars underpinning AI's potential for data manipulation. These components not only drive core functionality of AI systems, but also shape the way humans interact with and benefit from those systems. *Predictions*, at the heart of AI, leverage historical data to forecast future outcomes. This function is particularly transformative in fields such as healthcare, where AI-driven predictions help to diagnose diseases with a precision rate often surpassing that of human experts.

Procedures in AI refer to the algorithms and protocols that govern how AI systems learn and adapt. Programmers must meticulously design these procedures to ensure both efficiency and accuracy. For example, properly designed AI algorithms can potentially process and analyze data exponentially faster than humans can. However, AI systems that have badly designed procedures can, in turn, cause immense problems. And the systems in AI encompass the infrastructure and architecture that support these intelligent capabilities.

Lastly, *filtering* helps AI systems sift through vast amounts of information, extracting only what's relevant and useful for the task at hand. AI driven filtering has revolutionized fields such as content recommendations, in which filtering algorithms create personalized experiences for users. Advancements in AI filtering contribute to a significant increase in user engagement across various platforms.

In this chapter, find out how predictions, procedures, systems, and filtering together form the backbone of modern AI.

Understanding Predictive Analytics

In the AI world, *predictive analytics* (a crucial branch of advanced analytics) serves to make predictions about unknown future events by employing data, statistical algorithms, and machine learning techniques. Predictive analytics

>> Is grounded in the field of data mining and examines large databases to generate new information.

>> Relies heavily on *machine learning,* a subset of AI technology that allows systems to learn and improve from experience autonomously (see Chapter 5 for more on machine learning).

You can see the effectiveness of predictive analytics in AI by considering its impressive successes in the business world. In specific sectors, such as fraud detection, these systems achieve accuracy rates upwards of 95 percent.

TECHNICAL STUFF

The market for predictive analytics applications is experiencing rapid growth at the time of writing, with projections suggesting an increase in revenue from $7.2 billion in 2020 to $22.1 billion by 2026 (statistics available from Gartner articles at www.gartner.com/). This increase indicates a compound annual growth rate (CAGR) of 21.2 percent. Over 52 percent of enterprises are leveraging advanced and predictive analytics for greater insights and contextual intelligence into operations according to a MicroStrategy survey (https://community.microstrategy.com/) updated in January of 2024.

Using predictive analytics in various industries

Various industries leverage predictive analytics to revolutionize their operations, and AI continues to be a major driving force in the evolution and application of predictive analytics across various sectors. Consider these examples:

>> **In healthcare:** AI models, such as IBM Watson, demonstrate a blend of structured and unstructured data analysis to analyze patient data patterns to predict the occurrence of diseases such as cancer. Other applications enhance patient outcomes and reduce treatment costs.

For instance, Google's DeepMind Health uses AI to predict patient deterioration, specifically acute kidney injury (AKI), up to 48 hours before it occurs. This capability to foresee critical health events improves patient outcomes by an impressive 30 percent while cutting treatment costs by half. (Check out related information at https://deepmind.google/discover/blog/using-ai-to-give-doctors-a-48-hour-head-start-on-life-threatening-illness/.)

>> **In the finance sector:** Companies use predictive analytics for credit scoring and risk management. They can evaluate borrowers' likelihood of defaulting and also predict market trends to aid in investment. AI-fueled predictive analytics play a crucial role in fraud detection; with more than 70 percent of banks using AI solutions to help fight fraud.

Prime examples include PayPal and Visa, which employ sophisticated AI algorithms to scrutinize millions of transactions daily. These AI systems accurately identify fraudulent activities and ensure secure transactions for users globally. (See information on PayPal security at www.paypal.com/us/security/learn-about-paypal-secure-technology.)

>> **In the retail industry:** Predictive models aid companies' understanding of customer behavior and optimize inventory management, which enables effective stock level management and personalized marketing campaigns.

Amazon, a leader in the retail space, uses predictive models to forecast customer purchases, a strategy that has led to a 20 percent surge in sales and a 5 percent reduction in inventory costs over time. They use an anticipatory shipping method to ship products even before a customer places the final order. This proactivity exemplifies the power of predictive analytics in retail.

>> **In manufacturing:** AI supports predictive maintenance and supply chain optimization, which results in reduced equipment downtime (by up to 50 percent), prolonged machine life (by 20 to 40 percent), and enhanced supply chain efficiency.

Siemens' use of predictive analytics in their gas turbine operations stands out. By predicting failures before they happen, Siemens schedules maintenance more effectively, enhancing both reliability and efficiency of their equipment.

>> **In transportation:** Predictive analytics helps reduce travel time for travelers by rerouting their routes based on the amount of traffic on the road.

Uber's application of AI for route optimization provides a notable example. By predicting the fastest routes, Uber decreases wait times for customers, enhances the ride-hailing experience, and reduces actual travel time by up to 25 percent.

- » **In cybersecurity:** The implementation of predictive analytics detects up to 95 percent of potential hacking threats and drastically reduces response times for security issues.

  Companies such as Darktrace use AI-driven analytics to proactively identify and mitigate threats, staying ahead of potential cyberattacks and safeguarding digital assets.

- » **In energy industries:** This sector benefits from using AI predictive analytics in demand forecasting that increases accuracy up to 20 percent.

  GE's Predix platform uses AI to help optimize energy production and distribution. It ensures efficient alignment with fluctuating demand patterns and leads to more sustainable and cost-effective energy management.

- » **In marketing efforts:** Marketing campaigns become more effective with the use of predictive analytics and witness a 10 to 20 percent increase in customer response rates.

  Netflix's recommendation algorithm, based on individual viewing habits, provides a stellar example. This personalized approach not only enhances user engagement, but also plays a key role in maintaining Netflix's position as a top content provider.

In each of the business domains in the preceding list, predictive analytics not only streamlines operations, but also introduces significant improvements in efficiency, cost savings, and customer satisfaction. While AI continues to evolve, the influence and application of predictive analytics can expand further, bringing about more valuable and business–critical solutions across many industries.

WARNING

Predictive analytics, which depends on AI, has its own challenges. The accuracy of predictions depends greatly on the quality of the data used — a situation that highlights the need for robust data collection and processing methods. Ethical concerns, such as privacy, consent, and bias, also play a critical role in the deployment of predictive analytics. Also, the complexity of AI models can present challenges in terms of understanding and managing these systems effectively.

Building predictive models

Businesses use predictive models to forecast future events. Fundamentally, to build a predictive model, you have to blend science and art: You must

- » Include a problem definition that has very little ambiguity.
- » Conduct meticulous data handling so that the AI models stay accurate
- » Select and train your algorithm based only clean data

>> Rigorously test your model for accuracy, performance, and bias

>> Perform ongoing monitoring to assess whether your model continues to provide accurate, and appropriate responses.

The process may seem complex, but you just need to follow a series of logical steps. These steps, when executed effectively, can help technologists create powerful tools that drive decision-making and strategy in companies across various industries.

Industries follow these steps to build and test valid predictive models:

1. **Define the problem by specifying what you need to predict.**

   Detail what you need to forecast, whether it's the likelihood of a customer making a purchase, the risk of a machine failure, or the future trend of a stock market index. For example, a retail company may want to predict which products will be in high demand during the holiday season.

2. **Collect the right kind and right amount of data.**

   Predictive models are only as good as the data you train them on. In the retail-product example, the company may choose to gather data on past sales, customer demographics, and seasonal trends.

REMEMBER

   Quality data collection can improve the accuracy of predictive models by up to 60 percent. This step often involves cleaning and preprocessing the data (see Chapter 4 for more information about handling data) to make it suitable for analysis.

3. **Select the AI algorithm that you want to use as the predictive model.**

   You have various algorithms to choose from, including decision trees, neural networks, or regression models. Each algorithm can best solve specific types of problems. For instance, neural networks work especially well for complex problems that have large data sets, such as image recognition.

4. **Train the chosen algorithm on a portion of the data.**

   During this training, the algorithm learns to recognize patterns and relationships. In a retail example, the algorithm may learn how different customer demographics correlate with the demand for certain products.

5. **Test and validate the model's accuracy by using a separate set of data that you haven't provided to the algorithm before.**

   This step is vital for assessing the model's real-world applicability. Models commonly achieve over 90 percent accuracy in this phase, but you need to look out for *overfitting*, a situation in which a model performs well on training data but poorly on new, unfamiliar data. (I cover the details of overfitting in Chapter 5.)

6. **Deploy the predictive model and monitor its results.**

   Put the model into use, making predictions about new data. In the retail scenario, the model may now predict future product demand.

7. **Continue to monitor the algorithm to ensure that the model remains accurate over time.**

   The work doesn't stop with deployment because patterns and trends can change.

Best practices for predictive analytics

Creating effective predictive analytics requires adherence to a set of best practices. Each of these practices plays a vital role in the success of a predictive model. By following them, organizations can maximize the accuracy and effectiveness of their predictive analytics efforts, leading to better decision-making and enhanced outcomes in their respective fields.

Table 7-1 contains ten crucial best practices, each one accompanied by appropriate examples to illustrate their application.

TABLE 7-1   **Creating Successful Predictive Models**

Best Practice	What It Means	Real-World Example
Start with a clear objective.	Define what you want to achieve with your model.	A bank can use predictive modeling to identify which customers are likely to default on loans.
Ensure data quality.	Garbage in, garbage out: Ensure good data going in.	A healthcare provider uses clean, well-labeled patient data to accurately predict health outcomes.
Use relevant features.	Select data features that are most relevant to the problem.	A retailer uses relevant features such as the number of previous purchases to predict customer buying patterns.
Handle missing data carefully.	Develop strategies for dealing with gaps in data.	An airline may use average values to fill in missing data points in flight arrival times for better delay predictions.
Split data into training and testing sets.	Avoid using the same data for both training and testing predictive models to prevent overfitting.	A streaming service such as Spotify likely uses separate data sets to train and validate its music recommendation algorithm.
Choose the right algorithm.	Match the algorithm to the problem and data type.	Using a convolutional neural network (ConvNet) rather than a linear regression model can more effectively address a complex problem such as image recognition because the ConvNet learns directly from the data.

Best Practice	What It Means	Real-World Example
Avoid overfitting.	Use techniques such as regularization or cross-validation that calibrate the model and vary the data used.	An e-commerce company may use cross-validation to ensure that their product recommendation model *generalizes* well to new customers, or in other words, provides valuable recommendations for new customers that haven't interacted with the company before.
Adopt an iterative approach.	Continuously refine the model based on feedback.	A computer programmer may need to regularly update a traffic management system to adapt to changing traffic patterns based on time of day, day of week, and season.
Include interpretability.	Ensure that users can understand and explain the model's decisions.	A financial institution must be able to explain how its AI model assesses creditworthiness data to comply with regulatory requirements.

Putting AI Procedures into Practice

Procedures encompass the specific algorithms and protocols that shape how AI systems process information, learn, and make decisions. This facet of AI represents both a theoretical framework and a practical necessity because it underpins the mechanisms that enable AI systems to function effectively.

At its core, *procedure theory and practice* involve the systematic development and implementation of AI systems. This multifaceted process spans data collection, data preprocessing, model selection, model training, and model evaluation. The process aims to create AI systems that are accurate, reliable, and effective, and the development of these systems requires a multidisciplinary approach. The approach combines elements of mathematics, computer science, linguistics, and psychology.

REMEMBER

By meticulously designing and implementing sophisticated algorithms via established procedures, AI can automate tasks, refine decision-making, and resolve complex problems. The results can significantly impact technology, industry, and daily life. Consider these elements of applying procedure theory and practice to AI systems development:

>> **Coding and integrating algorithms into software systems:** Grounded in algorithmic design and computational theory, procedures in AI manifest through *algorithms* — sets of rules or instructions designed for specific tasks such as pattern recognition or predictive analysis. For instance, in healthcare, AI algorithms analyze medical images to aid in early disease detection. Research indicates that rigorous procedures and practices that optimize algorithms can improve the efficiency of an AI medical analysis system by over 50 percent.

>> **Automating decision-making processes:** AI systems employ procedural logic to automate complex decision-making processes through technologies such as robotic process automation (RPA). RPA tools, powered by AI, automate repetitive tasks in business processes, adhering to predefined procedures to interact with digital systems, thus enhancing efficiency and reducing human error.

>> **Streamlining decision-making processes:** *Heuristics,* meaning rules of thumb strategies, form a significant part of procedure theory in areas that involve streamlining how decision-making occurs. Heuristics greatly enhance AI's role in natural language processing (NLP; see Chapter 6 for more on NLP), assisting in tasks such as language parsing and sentiment analysis. For these functions, AI procedures enable machines to understand and generate human language, a feat that involves navigating the complexities of syntax, semantics, and context.

>> **Including learning algorithms to support AI self-modification:** Adaptation and learning are central to procedure theory. AI systems often include learning algorithms that enable them to modify their procedures based on new data or experiences. You can see this adaptability at work in autonomous vehicles, which combine sensors and AI algorithms to navigate and adjust to changing road conditions in real time.

WARNING

As a marketer who uses AI in practice, you must recognize the pitfalls of inadequately implemented AI procedures. These drawbacks can involve issues with data quality, problem complexity, and potential biases in algorithmic decision-making. Although AI procedures may seem like a technical and dry aspect of AI to a marketer, you need to understand the significance of procedures that impact what the AI recommends for the marketing campaigns. They often act as the deciding factor in whether you can depend on an AI system.

The AI System Development Lifecycle

Programmers use the AI system development lifecycle (SDLC) to design, develop, and deploy artificial intelligence systems. This lifecycle is akin to traditional software development, but with specific nuances and complexities inherent to AI. Although marketers may not drive (or even directly affect) the development lifecycle, your role as a marketer may make you a customer of the AI system. And so, if you understand the steps that a technology team goes through when developing an AI application for marketing, you can provide input for their development process — at the right times and in the right way — to make sure that the resulting application serves to support marketing activities. *Note:* The

AI SDLC incorporates the creation of procedures (see the preceding section) while developing the new AI system.

A technology team follows steps like these when developing the AI applications that you use for marketing:

1. **Define the problem to solve and the scope of the system.**

   This initial phase involves clearly defining the problem that the AI system aims to solve, which includes understanding the business objectives, the data available, and the desired outcomes.

   A study by McKinsey in 2020 (www.mckinsey.com/featured-insights/artificial-intelligence/ai-adoption-advances-but-foundational-barriers-remain) revealed that about 35 percent of AI projects fail due to a lack of clear problem definition and alignment with business goals. For instance, when IBM Watson Health aimed to revolutionize cancer treatment, the project faced challenges partly because of the initial broad scope and complexity of the problem.

2. **Gather and prepare the required data.**

   Data provides the cornerstone of any AI project; systems rely heavily on relevant, valid, and properly structured data. This stage involves gathering relevant data (which can be a massive undertaking) and then cleaning, formatting, and partitioning it appropriately.

   According to Gartner, companies may spend millions of dollars on data collection and cleaning. For example, Google's development of its AI-powered assistant required extensive data from voice samples across dialects and languages to ensure accuracy and inclusiveness.

3. **Choose and tailor the right AI model that's suited to the defined problem.**

   The model may involve machine learning, deep learning, or other AI methodologies. The choice depends on the nature of the problem, the data available, and the desired outcome.

   For example, OpenAI created GPT4, one of the most advanced language processing models, by using meticulous model selection and development, aligning with specific goals of language understanding and generation. GPT4 is recognized as one of the best generative AI models in the world, but Anthropic's Claude is recognized as being better for long-form writing.

4. **Train and test the chosen AI model by using the prepared data.**

   This step involves first adjusting the model parameters so that that model can make accurate predictions or decisions; this training phase requires a lot of resources, in the form of computing power, electricity, and monetary investment (maybe upwards of hundreds of thousands of dollars). After this training piece, development teams rigorously test the model.

Problems with Tesla's Autopilot system (in their self-driving cars) exemplifies the need for rigorous training and testing by using vast amounts of driving data to ensure reliability and safety.

5. **Deploy AI systems to real-world situations and monitor the results.**

Development teams must deploy systems carefully into a real-world environment. And after deployment, they must conduct continuous monitoring to ensure that the system operates as intended and to gather data for further improvements.

Amazon's AI recruitment tool, which was scrapped due to bias against women, underscores the importance of continuous monitoring and evaluation post-deployment. On a positive note, Spotify's deployment of its music recommendation engine shows how ongoing monitoring can lead to successful adaptation and improvement over time.

6. **Employ regular system maintenance and updates.**

Don't think of AI systems as set-and-forget solutions. Part of the system monitoring (see Step 5) provides the information that you need to adjust the systems by conducting regular updates and maintenance that keeps those systems relevant and effective.

Microsoft's AI-driven chatbot, Tay, had to be quickly adjusted after its release due to unexpected interactions (for example, when it began tweeting highly offensive and racist comments) with users.

REMEMBER

Companies that adhere to a structured AI SDLC have a better chance of developing AI systems that don't fail and, instead, stand the test of time. The journey through the AI SDLC does come with some challenges, though. Deloitte's survey (www2. deloitte.com/ph/en/pages/technology-media-and-telecommunications/ articles/now-decides-next.html) on AI adoption highlighted concerns such as misuse of client or customer data (identified by 34 percent of respondents) and the lack of explainability/transparency (31 percent of respondents).

Understanding Filtering in AI

Think of filtering in AI like expertly navigating through a vast ocean — but this ocean has information that holds invaluable pearls of wisdom. In AI, *filtering* involves deploying algorithms to wade through immense volumes of data and then zeroing in on and extracting just the bits that are most pertinent for a particular task or decision-making process.

When AI filters data, it's like you have a highly intelligent assistant in a massive, seemingly infinite library of data. This assistant not only understands what you're looking for, but also knows exactly where to find it. For example, when you're using Netflix, the service has AI-powered filtering at play. This filtering provides suggestions that lead to users choosing an impressive 80 percent of the content watched on the platform, according to company reports (per CEO Reed Hastings, https://stratoflow.com/how-netflix-recommendation-algorithm-work/). The AI analyzes your viewing history and preferences, then filters through countless movies and shows to recommend ones that align with your tastes.

Knowing where you encounter filtering

Here are some other examples of AI filtering the online content that you see:

>> **Online shopping:** Platforms such as Amazon employ filtering to enhance your experience by offering you targeted suggestions. They scrutinize your browsing habits, past purchases, and search queries with the goal of presenting products that you're more likely to consider purchasing. This feature plays a big role in sales; Amazon's recommendation engine, a prime example of AI filtering, is significantly boosting its revenue.

>> **Social media platforms such as Facebook and Instagram:** You see a curated news feed that relies heavily on AI filtering. The AI assesses your interactions — likes, shares, and comments — and then filters the massive stream of available posts to show you content that it predicts will keep you engaged and interested.

>> **Your e-mail service:** Services such as Gmail use sophisticated AI algorithms to sift through the barrage of e-mails, effectively filtering out spam and keeping your inbox organized and relevant, which isn't a small job, considering the endless stream of e-mails many people receive daily.

International Data Corporation (IDC, a premier global market intelligence firm) predicts that the worldwide data volume will soar to 175 zettabytes (every zettabyte is one billion terabytes) by 2025 (www.datauniverseevent.com/en-us/blog/general/AI-and-the-Global-Datasphere-How-Much-Information-Will-Humanity-Have-By-2025.html). In this world, the role of AI in filtering information can help you sort through endless options and present you with exactly what you need, often before you even realize you need it.

Filtering in AI is the unsung hero of our digital experiences, silently and efficiently working in the background to make our interactions with technology more personalized and manageable. As AI evolves, its prowess in filtering will only become more refined, further enhancing everyone's digital lives in ways that you may not even imagine.

AI filtering in recommendation systems

You can find a rich and varied world of AI-based recommendation systems, employing different techniques to deliver personalized content. Each type of system — whether collaborative filtering, content-based filtering, or hybrid — uses unique methodologies to understand and cater to individual user preferences. Here's a quick look at each type of filtering system:

» **Collaborative filtering:** Can make recommendations based on collective user behavior. This approach hinges on the idea that if two users have similar tastes, if one user likes something, the other will likely appreciate it, too. This technique can really provide users with strong recommendations in environments that have a lot of user interaction data.

For instance, Spotify's Discover Weekly playlist shows collaborative filtering in action. By examining listening patterns across its vast user base, Spotify can identify users who have similar music preferences and suggest songs that those similar users enjoyed. This intuitive and dynamic method of recommendations continually evolves while it absorbs new user data.

» **Content-based filtering:** Takes a more individualized approach than collaborative filtering, making recommendations by comparing the available pieces of content to a user's profile, which is shaped by their past interactions. This method is akin to having a personal curator who knows your preferences down to the smallest detail.

Netflix employs this strategy effectively by analyzing your watched movies and shows, focusing on characteristics, such as genre, cast, and plot, to recommend similar content. This approach ensures that the recommendations are closely aligned with your specific interests, making for a highly personalized viewing experience.

» **Hybrid systems:** Hybrid recommendation systems combine the best of both collaborative and content-based filtering, offering a more robust solution. These systems are particularly adept at addressing common challenges such as the *cold-start problem*, where new users or items have little interaction history.

Amazon's recommendation engine gives you a prime example of a hybrid system at work. It uses your past purchase history (collaborative data), along with the details of the items you browsed or bought (content data), to generate suggestions. This fusion approach allows Amazon to make highly relevant recommendations, contributing significantly to customer satisfaction and sales.

Moving beyond collaborative and content-based filtering, companies may use one of these methods:

>> **Contextual recommendations:** Add another layer of sophistication by considering additional contextual factors, such as time of day, location, or the device that the consumer is using. This method can enhance relevance by understanding not just what you like, but also when and where you prefer it.

For example, a news app that employs contextual recommendations may offer different types of articles in the morning, compared to the evening, adapting to the user's changing reading habits and preferences throughout the day.

>> **Knowledge-based recommendations:** Lastly, knowledge-based recommendations can provide acceptable recommendations when you don't have a lot of explicit preference data. These systems rely on specific domain knowledge about how certain item features meet user needs and preferences.

An online interior design service, for instance, may use this approach to suggest furniture and decorations based on a user's stated style preferences and the dimensions of their living space.

Chapter 8

Getting Comfortable with Generative AI

Generative AI was introduced to the world on November 30th, 2022, when the organization OpenAI made ChatGPT accessible to the general public. ChatGPT became the fastest growing application in history: It quickly reached 100 million active monthly users by the end of January 2023. Fast forward to the end of 2023, and OpenAI briefly stopped new users from signing up for the premium (paid) version of the AI engine because it didn't have enough servers and computing power to meet consumer demand.

Generative AI refers to a subset of artificial intelligence (AI) that focuses on creating new content, ranging from text and images to music and code. At the core of generative AI are machine learning models, particularly those that are based on deep learning techniques and trained on extremely large data sets. These models then generate outputs that use cues from their training data to predict the most appropriate next word, phrase, or pixel, based on their learnings. As Google explains in its overview of generative AI (which you can find at https://ai.google/discover/generativeai/), the phrase *peanut butter and (fill in the blank)* is more likely to end with *jelly* than with, for example, *shoelace*. And so, the generative AI engine is trained to guess that *jelly* is the likely next word in the phrase.

In this chapter, I introduce you to generative AI in various forms, discuss its importance (specifically in the business and marketing worlds), and give you an idea about its structure and applications.

Changing the Game with Generative AI

Generative AI democratizes creativity in ways that no other technology has before. The effect is twofold: By providing tools that can generate high-quality content, it lowers the barrier for entry into creative fields and provides content creators with the means to do more in less time. That is, content creation becomes easier and quicker. In turn, small businesses and independent creators can now produce professional-grade content without the need for large budgets or specialized skills.

Thanks to generative AI (and more specifically the launch of ChatGPT), I confidently say that AI has finally captured human imaginations. Consumers can experience AI outputs firsthand through the simple chatbot interfaces of ChatGPT — even on smartphone apps such as ChatOn and Alissu.

And other competitor platforms offer not just AI apps for text, but also apps for imagery and video. Some of the other generative AI platforms include

- » DALL-E 3 (https://openai.com/index/dall-e-3/)
- » Gemini (http://gemini.google.com)
- » Midjourney (www.midjourney.com)
- » Stability AI (www.stability.ai)

You may underestimate the importance of generative AI and consider it as simply an automation technology tool like others that have come before (for example, when the automobile was introduced and replaced the carriage). But that view of generative AI ignores its potential to transform businesses by significantly reducing their cost structures and expanding productivity.

Here are some examples of the potentials of generative AI:

- » **In the entertainment industry,** AI-generated content is expected to reduce production costs by up to 20 to 30 percent, as reported by a PwC analysis. (PwC, also known as PricewaterhouseCoopers, is one of the largest business and accounting consultancies in the world.) At the same time, generative AI is causing immense concern among actors and screenwriters as they worry that their work may be used as data to train the AI models that then, in turn, will produce video and written words — a situation that can leave them with fewer job opportunities.

>> **In software development,** Microsoft's GitHub Copilot (www.github.com/features/copilot) — powered by OpenAI's Codex — assists programmers by suggesting whole lines or blocks of code, effectively boosting productivity. A study by OpenAI found that this boost can increase coding speed by up to 50 percent and reduce the cost of development.

>> **In the fields of architecture and design,** AI tools such as Autodesk's Project Dreamcatcher (www.research.autodesk.com/projects/project-dreamcatcher) allow for the generation of numerous design alternatives that are optimized for specific goals and constraints. This capability streamlines the design process and gives humans time to focus on more creative parts of the design.

Knowing core generative AI concepts and techniques

When you understand the core concepts and techniques of generative AI, you can begin to grasp its capabilities and potential applications. This familiarity is vital for anyone looking to delve deeper into the world of generative AI, whether for academic, professional, or personal interests. Each element in the technical architecture not only defines the technical aspects of generative AI, but also opens doors to various applications and the ethical considerations that come with them.

Table 8-1 gives you a quick look at the fundamental concepts and techniques of generative AI systems.

TABLE 8-1   **Generative AI Concepts and Structures**

Concept or Structure	What It Is	What It Does	Why It's Important
Generative adversarial networks (GANs)	A system that has two parts: The *generator* creates data (images or text), and the *discriminator* evaluates the created data against real data. (See Chapter 5.)	Iterative training on huge data sets enables GANs to produce highly realistic synthetic data often indistinguishable from human-created content.	Widely used in image generation, video game design, and even in creating realistic-sounding speech (such as for non-human customer service).

(continued)

TABLE 8-1 *(continued)*

Concept or Structure	What It Is	What It Does	Why It's Important
Variational autoencoders (VAEs)	A generative model primarily used for image generation.	Encode data into a latent space (see the entry "Latent space," in this table) and then decode it to generate new data points.	Used in style transfer applications and to generate synthetic data that maintain statistical characteristics of the original data set.
Transformer models	Originally designed for natural language processing (NLP) tasks, transformer models have shown remarkable ability in generative tasks. (See Chapter 6.)	Generate human-like text (in models such as GPT-4), which makes them useful in applications such as content creation, conversation AI, and even coding.	Their architecture allows them to handle sequential data effectively, making them suitable for tasks that require understanding of context or sequence, such as language translation or text summarization.
Reinforcement learning	Primarily known for its applications in robotics and gaming, but can improve decision-making algorithms in generative AI. (See Chapter 5.)	Involves training models to make sequences of decisions by rewarding them for achieving specific goals.	This technique is crucial in scenarios where AI must generate outputs based on complex and dynamic environments.
Neural style transfer	Involves applying the style of one image to the content of another, using deep neural networks.	Enables a popular technique in art and design, allowing for the creation of unique artistic images by blending different styles and contents.	This technique demonstrates the intersection of AI and creativity, showcasing AI's capability in augmenting artistic expression.
Latent space	In generative models, latent space represents a compressed knowledge representation of the data.	Generates new data instances that have varying features by exploring and manipulating this latent space.	Understanding latent space is crucial for controlling and improving the quality of generated outputs.
Synthetic data generation	Generative AI can create synthetic data sets that mimic the statistical properties of real-world data.	Proves particularly useful in scenarios where data is scarce, sensitive, or expensive to collect, such as a healthcare application.	Can be used in healthcare, finance, and autonomous driving, where real data may have privacy or safety concerns.
Deepfakes	Synthetic media where a person's likeness is replaced with someone else's by using AI.	Showcases the advanced capabilities of generative AI, while also raising significant ethical concerns regarding misinformation and consent.	Developers must understand the ethical implications of generative AI for responsible development and application.

AUTOMATING THE CREATIVE PROCESS

The transformative nature of generative AI lies in its ability to automate and enhance creative processes that used to be solely the domain of human beings. In the field of digital art, AI algorithms can produce original artworks that rival those created by humans. For example, an AI-generated portrait called "Edmond de Belamy" sold for $432,500 at Christie's auction house, signaling the commercial viability and artistic value of AI-generated art.

In music, AI can compose pieces in the style of classical composers, create entirely new genres, or co-create new music with human beings. These applications aren't just theoretical; projects such as OpenAI's Jukebox have demonstrated the capacity to generate music in various styles, from rock to classical. Needless to say, generative AI's impact is evident in content generation for marketing, where AI tools can produce unique and engaging written content, significantly reducing the time and effort involved in content creation.

Reviewing the training process for generative AI models

The training process of generative AI models (also commonly referred to as large language models, or LLMs) is a sophisticated procedure that enables these models to generate new data that closely resembles the training data set. The training process is *iterative* (involving repetition) and complex. It requires careful monitoring and adjustments to ensure that the model learns effectively and produces high-quality results. The success of this process hinges not only on the technical aspects of the models, but also on the model's ability to understand the data and the specific nuances of the task at hand.

If you had the opportunity to participate in the generative AI training process, you'd follow these key steps:

1. Collect and preprocess the dataset.

The data set must be substantial and diverse. For example, if you intend for the model to generate images of human faces, you need a large data set of human face images to work from. After data collection, you must clean and preprocess the data by using techniques such as normalization, scaling, and (possibly) augmentation to improve model performance. (See Chapter 4 for information on data techniques.)

2. **Depending on the type of data and the desired output, select a specific generative model.**

   Choose a model architecture — such as GANs — to match your data based on the model's defined hyperparameters (for example, learning rate, number of layers, and so on). This choice significantly influences the model's learning ability and output quality. For example, these choices influence whether a model is better at generating text for long form writing versus generating answers to math problems.

3. **Train the chosen model by feeding it with the collected, preprocessed data set.**

   The model begins to learn the data's underlying patterns. In the case of GANs, this learning involves training two network components — the generator and discriminator — simultaneously in a competitive manner. The generator creates data, and the discriminator evaluates it. (See the preceding section for a description of GANs.)

4. **Evaluate model performance throughout the training process.**

   Regularly monitor the model's performance to ensure that it's learning correctly and making progress by testing against a set of validation data that the model hasn't already seen. If the model isn't performing as expected, you can adjust the model architecture or training process. The adjustments may involve tweaking hyperparameters or changing the model structure.

5. **Apply strategies to overcome training challenges that you detect.**

   Sometimes, the model learns the training data too well and fails to generalize to new data and produce a good range of output (a situation called *overfitting*). Particularly in GANs, *mode collapse* occurs when the generator produces limited types of outputs that the discriminator easily identifies as fake. You can employ various strategies, such as using different architectures, augmenting data, or modifying the training method to prevent mode collapse.

6. **Fine-tune models to improve performance or accomplish specific tasks.**

   After the initial training, you may need to fine-tune your model by supplying a smaller, more specific data set for particular tasks such as data that includes common responses to customer queries (if your goal is to use the model as chatbot to help customers). You may also use a pretrained model as a starting point and adapt it for a specific task, which is particularly useful when you have limited available data for the new task.

7. **Test and deploy the trained model.**

   After you experience an effective training cycle, you can test the model by supplying new data to ensure that it generalizes well (produces a good variety) and can generate high-quality outputs in real-world scenarios. You can then deploy the trained model for practical use by integrating it into software applications, online services, or other technological tools.

Getting to Know GPT Models

Generative Pre-trained Transformer (GPT) models emerged as a significant breakthrough in the field of natural language processing (NLP, which I cover at length in Chapter 6) and generative AI. Getting to know GPT models involves understanding their structure, how they're trained, and their applications. But a true understanding of GPT models involves not just appreciating their technical sophistication, but also recognizing their potential impact, the challenges in their development and deployment, and their transformative role in various industries.

GPT models are based on the transformer architecture (see the section "Knowing core generative AI concepts and techniques," earlier in the chapter), which is renowned for its ability to handle sequential data, particularly text. GPTs are composed of layers of transformer blocks that process text in parallel, which allows for efficient training and generation.

Training the models is intensive

Training involves large and diverse data sets that cover a broad spectrum of language usage. These models are pre-trained on a vast amount of text and then fine-tuned for specific tasks. (See the steps of the training process in the section "Reviewing the training process for generative AI models," earlier in the chapter.) The training process is computationally intensive, often requiring advanced computing hardware and a substantial allotment of time.

The pre-training helps models learn a general understanding of language, and fine-tuning tailors the model to specific applications. GPT models continue to learn and adapt during the fine-tuning process, which tailors them to specific tasks or industries. Because of the computationally intensive nature of the training, only a few companies in the world have the resources to invest in developing large language models (LLMs) similar to what OpenAI has developed with GPT-4.

WARNING

GPT models can inadvertently learn and replicate biases present in their training data, which raises ethical concerns. Their ability to generate realistic text also poses risks of misuse in creating fake news or other misinformation. Also, the extensive computational resources required for training and running these models have environmental impacts.

Exploring the models' operation

GPT models generate text in an *autoregressive* manner, which means that they predict the next word in a sequence based on the previous words. They can understand and generate text based on context, making them suitable for tasks such as helping AI mimic conversation, summarize text, and create written content. The scalability of GPT models is evident through their increasing size and capabilities that developed from GPT-1 to GPT-4.

From writing articles to creating poetry, GPT models can generate coherent and contextually relevant text. Their understanding of context and language nuances makes them suitable for translation tasks. For example, they can

>> **Power sophisticated chatbots** and virtual assistants capable of natural and context-aware conversations. Businesses use these assistants in their marketing and customer support efforts to offer buying suggestions and answer product questions.

>> **Assist in software development** by generating code snippets.

>> **Support educational applications** for tasks such as tutoring and creating educational content.

REMEMBER

The trend of increasing the size and complexity of GPT models is likely to continue, leading to even more powerful and capable systems. Academic researchers and AI companies alike are working to make these models more efficient and less resource-intensive. Ongoing research focuses on mitigating biases and ensuring the ethical use of GPT models. Time will tell whether the research can progress enough to limit the inherent biases in the results; these biases are commonplace in the data that is used to train the models in the first place.

Creating New Text, Images, and Video

In this section, I unpack how employees use generative AI to generate text, images, and videos. Current marketing efforts use a lot of *synthetic data* (data created by technology). For example, as I discuss in Chapter 9, businesses use generative AI to create synthetic panels — artificial focus groups that help market researchers learn more about their customers. If you use this technology (or plan to) for marketing, understanding how generative AI does its magic can help you develop a strong awareness of the related opportunities and pitfalls.

Generating text

Generating text by using generative AI involves creating coherent and contextually relevant text, akin to human writing. This process is primarily driven by models such as GPT (see the section "Getting to Know GPT Models," earlier in the chapter), which are trained on extensive text collections specifically used for language research. During training, these models learn language patterns, structures, and nuances. They function as *autoregressive models*, generating text by predicting the next word or character based on the preceding context. This sequential prediction is iteratively repeated, enabling the generation of sentences and entire paragraphs.

REMEMBER

A key to GPT models' effectiveness is their ability to understand and maintain context over long stretches of text, which allows them to produce narratives that are not only grammatically correct, but also contextually coherent and meaningful. Over the last few years, the context window — the amount of context that a generative AI model can hold — has increased significantly and makes these tools much more powerful. For example, you can now input an entire book into GPT-4, and have it use the book as context when answering specific questions for you.

The advanced capabilities of these models are beginning to revolutionize fields such as content creation, chatbots, and even creative writing, showcasing the sophisticated level of understanding that AI has achieved in natural language processing (NLP). In a fascinating example, one of the founders of LinkedIn, Reid Hoffman, co-authored a book *Impromptu: Amplifying Our Humanity Through AI* with GPT-4 (published by Dallepedia LLC) to show how much the technology can do.

Creating images

When it comes to image creation, GANs play a transformative role. As noted in the section "Knowing core generative AI concepts and techniques," earlier in the chapter, a GAN consists of two parts: a generator that creates and a discriminator that evaluates what's produced.

The generator learns to produce increasingly realistic images based on the training data set, striving to make them indistinguishable from human-created or captured images. Simultaneously, the discriminator improves its ability to differentiate between real and AI-generated images. This competitive process enhances the quality and realism of the generated images.

Apart from GANs, image generating models use techniques such as *neural style transfer*, where the style of one image (such as a painting's texture, for example) is applied to the content of another (such as a photograph), creating unique, stylized outputs.

Producing video

Video generation through generative AI is a complex process that extends beyond single image creation and requires the maintenance of *temporal coherence*, which means that successive frames generated by the AI must be consistent with each other to ensure fluid motion and continuity.

The AI models used for video generation are trained on extensive video data sets, allowing them to understand the dynamics of movement and change over time. The process often combines image creation techniques (for individual frame quality and realism, which I talk about in the preceding section) with sequence prediction methods (similar to those used in text generation, discussed in the section "Generating text," earlier in this chapter) to create a sequence of images that form a coherent video.

This ability to generate realistic and contextually consistent videos has vast applications in areas such as film production, game development, and virtual simulations, pushing the boundaries of how AI can replicate and augment complex dynamic visual experiences. We already have films — for example *The Frost*, *Check Point*, and *Glitch* — that all use generative AI, with oversight from humans, to create the entire film or just parts of it.

Introducing Major Consumer-Facing Generative AI Models

You can find dozens of generative AI models — ranging from content creation to programming, along with a myriad of other use cases. Discussing each one would create enough content to fill a few books on their own! In Table 8-2, I present the major generative AI models that invariably serve as the foundation for the other AI tools.

TABLE 8-2   **Major Generative AI Models**

Model	Features	Pros	Cons	Cost
GPT-4 from OpenAI	Features 100 trillion parameters and excellent factual performance, steerability, image input capabilities, and multilingual support	Touted for its inventiveness, accuracy, safety, and stability; a consistent time-saver and cost-effective	Potential biases and the possibility of incorrect answers	Free, with additional charges for prompt and completion tasks, as well as a paid membership option
AlphaCode	Training in programming languages, including Python, C++, and Java; 41.4 billion parameters, with a complete transformer-based language model	Smart filtering mechanisms following large-scale code generation; advanced language processing; provides access to about 13,000 example tasks	Less accessible for smaller projects and can seem unnecessarily complex with a steep learning curve	Free

Model	Features	Pros	Cons	Cost
GitHub Copilot	Designed for code completion; includes code suggestions and supports multiple programming languages; learns from open-source code and seamlessly integrates with various integrated development environments (IDEs)	Rapid prototyping and exploration; context-aware suggestions; improves developers' productivity and efficiency	The quality and security of the code generated may vary; potential risk of a negative impact on developers' skills	Monthly subscription at $10/month; annual subscription at $100/year
Google Gemini	Advanced language-understanding capabilities and up-to-date information; integrated into Google Search; assists with tasks related to software development and programming	Incorporates a rating system to enhance the performance feedback loop; Google's commitment to ethical and transparent AI development	Integration with other systems may limit choice for users as they're forced to use only products that integrate with Gemini	Free, with an enhanced version for $19.95 a month
Claude	Helpful, fair, and safe AI assistant; can process vast amounts of text and can conduct natural conversations; versatile in languages (both human and programming)	High level of user engagement and feedback; provides detailed and easily understood answers	Limited availability outside select regions; restricts its accessibility for a global user base	Claude Instant: $1.63/million tokens for prompts and $5.51/million tokens for completions; more robust Claude-v1: $11.02/million tokens for prompts and $32.68/million tokens for completions
Perplexity	Combines generative AI with web search to produce ready-made answers; cites its sources for the information it returns	Uses real-time information retrieval and has a user-friendly interface; good at coding and solving hard math problems	Can sometimes generate overly complex or ambiguous responses	Free version with ads; pro version $20/month or $200/year

Addressing the Challenges of Using Generative AI Models

Although using generative AI models can provide you with revolutionary efficiencies by doing so much work itself for you, it comes with a set of challenges and risks. These negatives range from technical limitations to ethical concerns, impacting various sectors that use these models. Addressing these challenges involves a multifaceted approach, including improving data set diversity, implementing robust ethical guidelines, enhancing transparency and interpretability of models, and developing strong legal frameworks to govern the use of generative AI.

TIP

As AI technology evolves, the development and deployment of generative AI models must be accompanied by thoughtful consideration of the related challenges and risks.

Seeing the technical challenges and limitations

>> **Data quality and bias:** Generative models are only as good as the data that you train them on. A notable example is the case of Tay, Microsoft's AI chatbot, which had to be taken offline within 24 hours of launch because it generated offensive and biased tweets. This incident highlighted the risk of models adopting biases present in their training data.

Similarly, in image generation, biases in data sets can lead to the reinforcement of stereotypes. For instance, a generative model trained predominantly on images of male doctors and female nurses may perpetuate this gender stereotype.

>> **Computational cost and environmental impact:** Training large-scale generative models such as GPT-4 requires significant computational resources, leading to high energy consumption. The carbon footprint associated with training such models has raised environmental concerns.

>> **Model interpretability:** Humans often have trouble understanding how generative models make certain decisions or generate specific outputs. In fact, it is a huge concern in scientific circles — if we can't understand exactly how the models product output, how can we trust them? This lack of interpretability can cause problems, especially in critical applications such as healthcare or law. For example, in drug discovery, not knowing how a model proposes a certain molecular structure can hinder its practical adoption.

>> **Output control:** In cases where specific outcomes are undesirable or harmful, programmers and users of these AI tools do not have ways to ensure that the model avoids these outcomes consistently.

Exposing ethical and societal consequences

The benefits of generative AI are immense, but difficulties in understanding and controlling the technology that leads to the outputs create risks. (See the preceding section for this discussion.) These risks are further amplified when human beings intentionally or unintentionally cause harm to society with the use of generative AI technology.

Here are some examples:

>> **Deepfakes and misinformation:** Generative AI has led to the proliferation of *deepfakes* — highly realistic and convincing fake videos or audio recordings. This technology poses significant risks for misinformation and manipulation; for example, deepfake videos have created false representations of public figures, which potentially influenced public opinion or caused reputational damage.

>> **Privacy concerns:** The use of real data to train generative models raises privacy issues. For instance, Clearview AI faced backlash and legal challenges for training its facial recognition system with billions of images scraped from the Internet without consent of the image subjects. This practice raised concerns about the infringement of individual privacy rights.

>> **Intellectual property and creative rights:** AI-generated art, music, and literature pose questions about intellectual property rights. The case of "Edmond de Belamy," an AI-generated painting sold for a significant sum at auction, sparked debate over who holds the copyright — the creators of the algorithm or the AI itself. In the music industry, AI-generated music that closely resembles the style of existing artists raises concerns about originality and copyright infringement.

>> **Unpredictable outputs:** Generative models may produce outputs that have unintended or unforeseen consequences. For instance, an AI model designed to generate creative story plots can potentially produce narratives that are offensive or culturally insensitive.

>> **Security risks:** There are also concerns about the potential malicious use of generative AI, such as creating realistic phishing e-mails or forging legal documents, which can pose significant security threats.

3

Using AI to Know Customers Better

Explore how AI enhances understanding and predicting customer behaviors.

Figure out which AI applications can help you with lead scoring, customer lifetime value, and dynamic pricing.

Discover best practices and common pitfalls in integrating AI into business operations.

Do effective customer churn modeling and measurement by using AI techniques and tools.

Chapter **9**

Segmentation and Persona Development

I n today's competitive business environment, understanding and responding to consumers' needs and behaviors is critical to drive more impactful and memorable marketing. Brands differentiate their offerings by knowing their customers well and responding to their distinct needs in a manner that's as personalized as possible. Staying customer-centric matters even more when performance marketing tactics become more automated and product-specific. *Segmentation*, a cornerstone of marketing today, enables businesses to categorize their customers based on purchasing behaviors, demographics, life-stage preferences, interactions, opinions, and so on.

Behavioral segmentation, in particular, is a multifaceted approach to helping you understand and engage with your customers. This segmentation strategy goes beyond the factors of demographics and *psychographics* (classification of people by their attitudes and other psychological criteria). Instead, behavioral segmentation relies on observing and analyzing real consumer behaviors (purchasing habits and product usage, for example) to unveil deeper insights into their motivations and decision-making processes. For marketers, analyzing consumer behavior online has gotten easier over time, which makes behavioral segmentation an increasingly powerful and more accurate way to segment and market to consumers.

In this chapter, you can explore the fundamentals of behavioral segmentation, specifically, along with related data requirements. You can also find out about AI-driven segmentation factors, as well as how to integrate AI-generated personas and research-based methods into your company's marketing approach.

Exploring Behavioral Segmentation Elements

Segmentation methodology dissects how consumers interact with products, services, or (more broadly) brands. Unlike demographic factors, such as age, gender, or location — which remain relatively static — customer interactions that marketers observe to create behavioral segmentation provide a dynamic look at consumer behavior. The analysis hinges on actions — such as purchasing patterns, product usage, and decision-making dynamics. These factors offer a more profound insight into what drives consumer choices.

Behavioral segmentation is typically divided into the following elements:

>> **Purchasing behavior:** Consumers' raw purchasing patterns, which encompass the

- Frequency and volume of purchases
- Types of products or services bought
- Timing of purchases
- Brand choices

Understanding whether a customer is a frequent buyer, a big spender, or exhibits preferences for specific product categories allows you to create more targeted marketing and better customer *lifecycle marketing programs* (programs that keep a customer engaged throughout their relationship with the company, typically via e-mail nurturing with informational and entertaining content). Companies such as Amazon and Walmart excel in leveraging purchase behavior by using past purchases, browsing history, and similar customer behaviors to offer personalized product recommendations and e-mail–driven incentives to strengthen the shopping experience and encourage future sales.

>> **Usage behavior:** How consumers use products or services, including

- Analyzing the frequency, manner, and context in which products are used

- Evaluating the overall consumer sentiment and direct experience with using the actual products

Consider subscription-based services such as Netflix or Spotify, which tailor their offerings based on users' ongoing consumption patterns. By examining consumers' usage behavior — such as preferred genres or viewing habits — these platforms curate personalized recommendations designed to foster greater customer engagement and loyalty.

>> **Decision-making process:** Reveals insights into the factors influencing consumers' purchase decisions, such as

- *The speed at which consumers make buying choices:* Some consumers may be impulsive buyers who decide to purchase quickly.

- *The level of effort involvement in the customer's buying journey:* Other consumers perform research — meticulously and extensively — before making a purchase decision. This kind of research represents a much greater level of involvement in the decision-making process.

Recognizing these distinctions in decision-making habits enables you to tailor your marketing strategies, providing relevant information and messaging aligned with consumers' decision-making preferences at specific points in the process.

TIP

Behavioral segmentation's real power lies in its capability to help you personalize marketing tactics, refine product offerings, and elevate the overall consumer experience based on how consumers actually behave. By deciphering behavioral signals, your business can craft targeted campaigns that resonate with specific consumer groups. This approach fosters stronger connections, boosts customer satisfaction, and cultivates lasting brand loyalty.

Sourcing the Right Customer Data

In behavioral segmentation, the crux lies in accessing and interpreting an array of data sources that serve to unpack the intricacies of consumer behavior. These data sources serve as the bedrock that you can use to develop your marketing plan for effective customer engagement and management via customer relationship management (CRM) programs such as e-mail campaigns. The capabilities of AI and, specifically, behavioral segmentation models offer deeper insights into this customer data.

So if you're planning to apply this AI technology to your marketing efforts, you must first know what types of data you need and where to get them. Check out Table 9-1 for a breakdown of this information.

TABLE 9-1   **Behavioral Segmentation Data**

Data Type	Data Points	Sources	Why You Need It
Transactions	A history of customer purchases, including frequency of consumer transactions, preferred products or services, chosen brands, and financial value	Point of sale systems (where you pay at the cashier in a store), online shopping carts, and credit card companies	To gain insights for tailored marketing campaigns and personalized product recommendations. Also to discover (from companies such as Visa) where customers are spending outside of your business
Web and mobile analytics	Online behaviors, such as click-through rates, browsing patterns, and time spent on specific web pages	Web analytics solutions such as Google Analytics	To help optimize online customer experiences, refine user interfaces, personalize content, enhance navigation, and tailor online environments to specific user needs
Social media	Metrics such as engagement levels, sharing behaviors, comments, and tone (*Likes*, for example)	Social media platforms such as Facebook, X (formerly Twitter), TikTok, and Instagram	To gain insights into consumer preferences and sentiment that guide behavioral segmentation strategies and persona development
Customer feedback	Outlines customer experiences, preferences, pain points, and sentiments	Surveys, reviews, customer service transcripts, and other related channels	To (re)shape marketing and sales strategies that address consumer needs effectively and to guide business efforts toward a customer-centric approach

According to a Microsoft study on customer service (from `https://info.microsoft.com/rs/157-GQE-382/images/EN-CNTNT-Report-DynService-2017-global-state-customer-service.pdf`), 77 percent of consumers exhibit a stronger inclination toward brands that demonstrate a comprehensive grasp of that consumer's preferences and requirements based on the interactions that customer has with the brand.

The data you collect underscores the critical role of behavioral segmentation, not just in reaching audiences, but also in fostering genuine relationships and cultivating consumer loyalty: It steers your business toward strategies that prioritize personalized interactions and tailored experiences. See the section "Leveraging AI Personas for All Business Efforts," later in this chapter, for examples of putting the right data to work in your marketing efforts.

Seeing How AI Performs Segmentation

The integration of artificial intelligence (AI) and machine learning in behavioral segmentation models revolutionizes the way businesses comprehend and engage with their customers. The combined technology excels at processing colossal volumes of data, uncovering intricate patterns, and constructing segmentation models that can amplify your understanding of consumer behavior. AI plays two specific roles in the world of behavioral segmentation:

>> **Processing data at scale:** AI and machine learning algorithms can handle vast data sets with unparalleled efficiency. Their computational capabilities can analyze immense volumes of data to reveal intricate behavioral patterns that human beings may not see. AI decodes these complex patterns, and companies gain nuanced insights into consumer behaviors, preferences, and decision-making processes.

REMEMBER

AI's ability to process data on a large scale enables businesses to uncover hidden correlations and trends that offer a comprehensive understanding of their customer base and guide informed marketing decisions. Not every company takes advantage of AI's capabilities, but those that do gain a competitive advantage in all areas of marketing — for example, in the ways they build awareness, drive sales, practice lifecycle marketing, and foster customer loyalty.

>> **Automating segmentation:** Advanced AI algorithms automate segmentation by using scenarios in which the AI autonomously groups consumers based on their behavioral attributes, repeatedly and in real time. These algorithms — equipped with machine learning capabilities — streamline the creation of specific and dynamic segmentation models.

By automating the customer segmentation process, you can quickly generate marketing campaigns for customer lifecycle marketing, targeted marketing, and personalized experiences. The agility and accuracy offered by automated segmentation models also enables you to swiftly adapt your approaches in response to evolving consumer behaviors.

Your business can use AI-driven behavioral data and segmentation derived from it to deliver hyper-personalized experiences to its customers. You can not only optimize your marketing strategies, but also foster deeper connections with your target audiences to improve customer loyalty and those customers' desire to tell others about the brand. Using AI for behavioral segmentation enables you to stay agile in a rapidly evolving market landscape.

Consider these two examples of how companies use behavioral data:

>> **Netflix curates personalized recommendations for each user.** Netflix leverages AI algorithms to segment users based on their viewing habits in real

time by analyzing viewing patterns, preferences, and interactions. This personalized approach is designed to enhance user experience by offering curated recommendations, extend the amount of time a person is engaged with the product, and significantly impact user satisfaction and retention.

Netflix released a report in 2023 (https://about.netflix.com/en/news/what-we-watched-a-netflix-engagement-report) showing how many hours users had watched more than 18,000 of their viewable titles — 100 billion hours viewed. The report draws attention to the consumer behaviors associated with the types of titles that those consumers viewed. *Note:* What Netflix didn't share (and wouldn't publicly) is how they use that data to then drive their own marketing efforts.

>> **Spotify provides each user with insights on the music they — and other customers — listened to for a year's span.** Spotify uses machine learning algorithms to categorize users based on their music preferences. By examining listening behaviors, preferred genres, and even skipping patterns, Spotify tailors playlists and recommendations to offer a personalized musical journey for each user. Because Spotify tracks listener data incredibly closely, the platform uses the Spotify Wrapped marketing program, which offers customers information on individual, as well as aggregate, listening habits for its 574 million listeners, such as

- Top 5 Artists and Top 5 Genres

- Specific highlights for artists or works, including Taylor Swift as the number one artist of 2023 (not very surprising), the spike in Rihanna's music after her Super Bowl performance in 2023, and the popularity of the *Succession* theme song when its fourth season premiered

REMEMBER

Spotify Wrapped is an example of using behavioral data as a marketing program (people share their Spotify Wrapped summaries across social media), and it also draws attention to how much behavioral data the platform has and what it can do with that data.

Refining, Validating, and Enhancing Segmentation Models

Marketers use behavioral segmentation models in pursuit of accurate and relevant data analysis. In this pursuit, *refinement* stands as a pivotal process; it helps to ensure that segmentation models evolve and remain aligned with ever-changing consumer behaviors. The iterative approach to model evolution involves incorporating new data, fine-tuning algorithms, and validating the segments against real-world behaviors.

Two aspects of AI model refinement

The essence of continuous refinement lies in the ongoing infusion of relevant, updated data into existing segmentation models. But beyond the data, programmers make adjustments to model algorithms to enhance the sophistication and efficacy of the models.

Consider these points regarding the two refinement strategies:

>> **Incorporating new data:** The ongoing influx of data serves as the segmentation models' lifeblood, which fuels their adaptability and evolution, and keeps them in sync with the ever-shifting landscape of consumer behaviors. By integrating fresh insights (the data), these models remain dynamic, responsive, relevant, and accurate.

>> **Algorithmic adjustments:** The agility of segmentation models relies heavily on the adaptability and fine-tuning of underlying algorithms. Whether it's accommodating new data trends, optimizing performance, or refining the algorithms' learning mechanisms, these continual adjustments help ensure that the AI models remain agile enough to swiftly assimilate and process new information, and also maintain the precision required for insightful segmentation. And so, the models evolve in line with the dynamic consumer landscape and empower businesses to make informed, data-driven decisions.

Procter & Gamble continuously refines their segmentation models by using AI-driven techniques. The company refers to its strategy as "Smart audience work," which it uses to move away from mass marketing to *mass one-to-one brand building* (where you speak to each customer in a very personalized way). Driven by the data (their 1 billion consumer IDs), Proctor & Gamble built specific audience segments and refocused its marketing efforts from a few dozen segments to more than 350 precise, smart audiences (or behavioral segments).

Validation techniques

Some of the validation techniques used to strengthen the behavioral models are

>> **Cross-validation,** which involves testing segmentation models on different data sets to ascertain consistency and reliability. By subjecting the models to diverse data sets, you can validate that your models support robust and generalized segmentation strategies.

>> **Predictive analysis,** which can forecast customer behavior based on specific segments. By predicting consumer behavior using the segmentation models, you can assess the accuracy of your predictions against actual behaviors, thus validating the effectiveness of the segmentation approach.

Aligning Persona Development

The fusion of behavioral segmentation (which you can read about in the section "Exploring Behavioral Segmentation Elements," earlier in this chapter) and *persona development* (developing representative customer profiles) can make your company's marketing efforts more sophisticated. After you identify behavioral segments, you can then develop personas by studying the customer research, analyzing the segmentation, and reflecting on experiences with customers. These elements provide vivid representations (including customer descriptions, interaction scenarios, and backgrounds) that breathe life and depth into the segmented data. This synthesis humanizes raw data and provides you with the context and empathy that's crucial for crafting targeted marketing (and other business) strategies.

The components of AI-generated personas include

>> **Demographics:** AI-driven personas encapsulate demographic traits such as age, gender, income, and other pertinent identifiers. These factors offer a foundational understanding, but you need to include behavioral insights to form a comprehensive representation.

>> **Behavioral traits:** Beyond demographics, personas derived from segmentation incorporate intricate behavioral nuances. As I discuss in section "Exploring Behavioral Segmentation Elements," earlier in this chapter, these traits — buying habits, shopping preferences, motivations, and decision-making patterns — enrich personas with detailed behavioral profiles.

WARNING

Aligning the attributes of personas with real-world individuals poses a challenge. Marketers must balance specificity and accuracy while ensuring that personas reflect actual consumers if they want to create meaningful personas.

Verifying the authentic core of AI-created personas

AI-generated personas can help you recognize consumer behavior because AI can create the personas — and specify their attributes — much more quickly than a marketing team normally would. But ensuring the personas' accuracy and ethical integrity requires human oversight. Having humans validate the authentic core of these personas not only strengthens the accuracy of the representation, but also upholds ethical considerations (such as making sure that the AI-generated personas aren't biased in any way), which are crucial in today's world.

Human oversight of personas involves these functions:

>> **Expert validation:** Human expertise is indispensable in the validation process for AI-generated personas. The experts wield a discerning eye and specialized knowledge to meticulously examine AI-derived personas against real customer data.

Human oversight allows for a thorough and nuanced evaluation, and their scrutiny guarantees that the personas accurately mirror the essence — the diverse traits and behaviors — of the audience that they represent. Making the personas reflect the customer base as accurately as possible helps marketers gain a deeper understanding of customer needs and preferences.

>> **Continuous feedback loops:** Establishing continuous feedback loops forms a dynamic framework for ongoing validation and evolution of AI personas. Feedback mechanisms serve as conduits for capturing and integrating insights gleaned from evolving consumer behaviors, preferences, and tendencies. By actively incorporating real-time feedback and data, personas evolve organically based on the latest data. It's an iterative process that safeguards personas' relevancy and accuracy over time.

REMEMBER

This adaptive approach enables you to keep up with the market and respond swiftly to changes in consumer behavior by ensuring that personas reflect an up-to-date and authentic representation of the target audience. Ultimately, these feedback loops perpetually refine and enhance the personas' ability to guide strategic marketing decisions.

Ethical considerations in persona development

The synergy between AI technology and human expertise in persona validation strikes a delicate balance. The AI-driven personas offer unparalleled insights, but human oversight ensures accuracy, ethical integrity, and alignment with real-world consumer behaviors. By keeping ethical considerations at front of mind during persona creation, you can leverage data effectively, demonstrate accountability and responsibility, and foster trust and credibility in your consumer-centric strategies.

These operational elements help you maintain an ethical balance when developing personas for marketing efforts:

>> **Transparency and customer consent:** Ethical persona development operates on the foundational principles of transparency and respect for customer data. Upholding these principles necessitates a transparent

approach to data usage, which ensures that customers are well-informed about their data's involvement in persona creation.

TIP

Obtaining explicit consent from customers to use their data upholds ethical standards and data privacy, and it also fosters a customer relationship built on trust and respect. Businesses often send customers e-mails specifically requesting their consent to use data, or they may require customers to accept a privacy policy when they visit the business website. This transparency not only aligns with regulatory requirements, but also reflects an ethical commitment to safeguarding customer privacy and using their data responsibly. Chapter 22 has more information about ethics and privacy for marketing practices.

» **Avoiding stereotyping and bias:** Ethical considerations demand that businesses avoid stereotypes and biases in persona creation. Human oversight stands as a crucial checkpoint in this process. A human monitor can detect and rectify inadvertent biases that may seep into persona development. Your business must meticulously examine and correct any unintended biases and ensure that the personas that you use for marketing strategies authentically and accurately represent the rich diversity and complexity of real consumers.

Leveraging AI Personas for All Business Efforts

AI-generated personas stand as invaluable assets that inform diverse business domains and marketing and product development strategies. Derived from behavioral segmentation, personas provide comprehensive insights into customer profiles that can help you optimize your approach to marketing efforts and curate tailored customer experiences. Your business can create these personas quickly and disseminate them across all enterprise offerings — if you collect the right data and vet it by using human beings (see the section "Verifying the authentic core of AI-created personas" earlier in this chapter).

Similarly, AI personas play a critical role in product development and innovation. AI personas channel valuable insights into the intricate landscape of consumer needs, preferences, and pain points; you can use these insights to craft offerings of solutions and resonant experiences that precisely address the desires and challenges of your target audience.

Driving the customer experience

AI personas help you create personalized experiences for customers and tailored interactions across diverse customer touchpoints. From customer support to customer interfaces, these personas guide the customization of experiences according to the nuanced preferences delineated by each persona.

Personas pave the way for customized service delivery, customer support mechanisms, and engagement strategies (such as targeted social media outreach) that resonate authentically with the customers behind the personas. By tailoring interactions and experiences to align with the preferences and behaviors of personas, you can create a more personalized and engaging customer journey. This personalization can not only enhance satisfaction but also nurture lasting relationships.

Airbnb uses personas derived from behavioral segmentation, refining their customer journey based on personas that they developed. By using these personas, Airbnb achieved a substantial increase in user engagement. This success story underscores the transformative power of employing personas derived from behavioral segmentation in enhancing business outcomes.

REMEMBER

The more real time you make the personas (with the appropriate capturing of behavioral data and resultant segmentation), the more your business can serve up current nuanced preferences. This tailoring of interactions can elevate customers' satisfaction (and their sense of being understood and valued) by providing precisely what they seek. You get a heightened level of engagement and loyalty because customers feel more connected and catered to throughout their journey.

Understanding the behavioral intricacies within personas allows you as a business to transcend mere response and delve into proactive anticipation of customer needs. With this proactive approach, you can address customers' needs before they even articulate those needs. You not only can meet customer expectations but also exceed them by forging a path that aligns precisely with the customer's desires.

Directing marketing with personas

As I discuss in the section "Aligning Persona Development," earlier in this chapter, AI personas enable precise targeting by aligning messaging and content with the nuanced preferences and behaviors of specific audience segments. This customization can make your campaigns resonate with your targeted audiences, engage them with your brand, and convert shoppers into customers, helping you foster deeper customer connections and increase sales. AI personas can also amplify the efficiency and impact of marketing campaigns. This tailored approach can hopefully maximize campaign effectiveness, optimize resource allocation, and enhance return on investment (ROI).

TIP

By precisely catering to the needs and preferences of distinct personas developed from valid marketing and sales data, businesses can build a more impactful and cost-effective outreach strategy that, ideally, results in heightened marketing campaign success.

Behavioral segmentation and AI-driven persona development redefine modern marketing by enabling you, the marketer, to create targeted marketing campaigns. You can finely calibrate your messaging, content, and advertising across a variety of channels and tactics. This precision targeting ensures that your marketing efforts resonate directly with specific personas and hopefully enables a deeper connection and resonance with the customers represented by the personas.

Aligning product offerings with personas

Personas can serve as guiding stars during the product development cycle, starting with the critical ideation phase (see Chapter 12), illuminating the path that marketers and product designers can follow to develop products and services that strike a chord with a specific persona. Using personas in product development nurtures a consumer-centric ethos and helps ensure that every feature and aspect of the product aligns with the personas' expectations.

You can use the insights derived from AI-powered personas when shaping product ideation and development by identifying the needs, preferences, and behaviors of specific consumer groups. You can then leverage these insights to craft offerings that precisely cater to the requirements of distinct personas and, therefore, to the audience represented by the personas. This alignment can enhance the likelihood of product adoption and related customer satisfaction.

The integration of AI personas into the fabric of product development can foster a culture of continuous evolution and enhancement in which iterative product improvements evolve at the same pace as shifting consumer behaviors. Constant alignment with the changing expectations and needs of personas acts as a real-time guide for product evolution. As a result, you end up with a suite of offerings finely tuned to resonate deeply with the audience, leading to greater relevance, satisfaction, and loyalty.

WARNING

In an ideal world, marketing and product development departments share the same personas and use them to drive both of their corresponding efforts. In reality, this isn't always the case, which can cause disconnects between how a company markets its offerings and what product features those offerings contain.

Employing Synthetic Customer Panels

For any marketer, overseeing a customer research program comes with inherent challenges. You have to set a solid learning agenda for the marketing team (what you want to learn about your customers over the course of a quarter or year), get the *C-suite* (the top executives) on board, safeguard the budget, recruit customer panels, derive behavioral insights from the research, and ensure that these insights influence actual marketing and product decisions. But with the advent of Generative Pre-trained Transformers (GPT) — for example GPT-4 and other generative AI models — you may find some of these tasks significantly more manageable.

Some agencies, such as Pereira O'Dell and Dentsu, are leading the way with persona creation experiments. Consider the practical scenario presented in the following sections, complemented by research out of Harvard Business School in the paper "Using GPT for Market Research," by Harvard Business School professor Ayelet Israeli and Microsoft economists James Brand and Donald Ngwe (2023). This paper outlines both the risks and the possibilities that this scenario presents. To access the paper, go to www.hbs.edu, select Insights ⇨ Faculty Publications, and then enter in the search text box "Using GPT for Marketing Research."

Creating synthetic panels

Marketing agencies are increasingly using social media comments to create synthetic customer panels. Their method involves exporting all comments from a brand's TikTok account and feeding those comments into ChatGPT. The agency may then instruct ChatGPT to form a panel of four different personas, defined by them, using insights from the uploaded data. ChatGPT then acts as the moderator, posing questions about the brand and its products to the panelists. After observing the interactions for a while, the agencies open the floor to questions from their teams, injecting some of their own queries and paying close attention to the responses. This process is not only cost-effective and easy to implement, but it also yields significant insights.

Now, imagine elevating this panel creation approach by

>> Uploading actual customer demographic and psychographic data from internal databases or external sources, such the U.S. Census data tables, instead of relying on social media comments

>> Integrating all conversations with sales and customer service representatives over the past year

Think about the potential depth and diversity of the panel created with this specific customer data, the unique artificial personas created, and the richness of the questions and responses as a result. As a bonus, this method can dramatically reduce the cost of customer research programs while delivering comparable (or even better) insights than the ones that you can obtain by using human–centric research methods, such as customer panels and surveys.

Embracing the opportunities

Synthetic panels have their own sets of opportunities and risks, and synthetic panels may not provide as much insight as human ones if not managed correctly. The Harvard University professor and two Microsoft economists who wrote the paper referenced in the section "Employing Synthetic Customer Panels," earlier in this chapter, wanted to study how large language models (LLMs) performed for researchers and practitioners who wanted the LLMs to provide them with an understanding of consumer preferences.

The following are summaries of what the researchers figured out in this study:

>> **GPT for research works.** Their analysis suggests that GPT — and LLMs, more broadly — can effectively help you uncover customer preferences. When prompted, GPT exhibited a number of behaviors consistent with economic theory, including declining price sensitivity with higher income (which appears in traditional research time and again), as if the GPT was a randomly selected customer.

Unlike human beings, the GPT typically has fewer issues with stated preferences versus revealed preferences because it doesn't try to appease researchers in any way — it simply tells the truth. On the other hand, humans responding to research questions may tend to provide answers that they think the researcher wants versus what they may actually think.

>> **GPT generates more insightful results than you can get from humans.** These results were also specific and detailed while being realistic and consistent with results obtained from existing, human-based research. Furthermore, the results didn't suffer from the shortcomings — such as human bias — that research which depends on human subjects typically does. In fact, the results suggested that GPT could also help develop new products and, at the very least, complement the results from human-centric research, reducing the number of human participants required for a study.

>> **GPT serves as a realistic simulator of customer choice.** The authors of the paper believe that GPT can serve as a realistic simulator of customer choice without the need for large human panels, beyond choosing the types of prompting. The study used GPT effectively for *conjoint-type analysis*

(a statistical technique) to understand which attributes of a product were most valuable. The authors believe that by providing various forms of *knowledge* (meaning background information like previous research studies conducted, to use their language), and building in personas, GPT can be more context-specific.

>> **GPT and other LLMs are only getting more accurate.** The authors of the paper believe that LLMs can increasingly assist customer research over time. Increases in LLM accuracy and access to more real-time data can lead to the LLMs absorbing and inferring even deeper and more insightful aspects of consumer behavior. This sophistication may lead to an eventual reevaluation of the idea that customer research fundamentally (and ideally) requires businesses to recruit, interview, and or survey human beings.

Managing the risks

All is not rosy with synthetic panels. The researchers of the Harvard paper "Using GPT for Market Research" (2023) came up with some clear risks to keep in mind when you explore the idea of using synthetic panels to complement your traditional research efforts.

Here are some of the risks outlined in the paper:

>> **Preferences may be dated.** Because GPT is pre-trained without specific data typically provided by customer research and without access to the real-time Internet (a limitation that's changing at the time I write this), some of the preferences revealed may be static or dated.

REMEMBER

Pay careful attention to what data you're depending on to train the LLM for your market research. Keep in mind that there may be some extreme consumers who don't post online or may not even have Internet access. GPT can't reflect their thinking unless you provide it with extra data that captures these consumers' points of view.

>> **Wording matters with GPT.** The research highlighted that GPTs have sensitivities to how you word prompts. (**Note:** You can test out these sensitivities yourself by asking GPT specific questions about consumer behavior but using different words to describe your target customer each time.) Although the study didn't see significant differences in results based on the different ways that you can word questions, keep choice of words in mind as a potential risk. Arguably, this risk applies just as much to traditional, human-centric research, where the survey design can greatly influence the survey takers.

>> **LLMs can hallucinate (which is both good and bad).** In this context, *hallucination* means confidently returning incorrect information, which can mislead the researcher, leading to false conclusions about the customers. However, LLMs may hallucinate their way into unpacking insights or potential product features that no human being may ever have thought of, such as predicting how consumers may interact with new technology that has yet to be launched.

>> **LLMs lack ethical judgment.** LLMs, such as GPT-4, lack the ethical judgement and reasoning capabilities that human beings need to navigate more thorny ethical issues around customer behavior. In addition to that, GPTs run the risk of providing biased responses, depending on the data used to train or enhance them. Human judgment and oversight will continue to play an important role in the use of synthetic panels for some time.

>> **Contextual understanding may get lost.** LLMs may miss contextual understanding. As I mention in Chapter 1, humans are still far from a developed *artificial general intelligence* (AGI; a state in which AI possesses reasoning, learning, and common sense akin to human cognition), and LLMs may miss broader insights and more nuanced context simply by virtue of still being young in their own development.

REMEMBER

AI is sophisticated enough to serve as a meaningful complement to human-oriented research; and in cases where the process has appropriate oversight and the right data inputs, it may even adequately supplant existing research methods. That thought alone is mind-blowing for a marketer. Will human-centered customer research, which is typically a lot more time consuming and costly, evolve or simply go extinct at some point in the future? Only time will tell.

Chapter 10

Lead Scoring, LTV, and Dynamic Pricing

Lead scoring, lifetime value (LTV) metrics, and dynamic pricing emerge as foundational pillars of a marketing program that drives sales performance. Although they're independent concepts, they work together to orchestrate a series of real-time pricing decisions that inform how much a business should spend to acquire a lead based on projections for its lifetime value.

Lead scoring (assigning a value to a *lead*, a potential customer), *lifetime value metrics* (estimates of the revenue potential over the life of a customer relationship), and *dynamic pricing* (varying the product price to match market conditions) relied, at one time, on human expertise, judgment, and basic financial calculations. With advancements in artificial intelligence (AI), these concepts take on a powerful role that's automated and based on collected data.

As a marketer, you must understand these three concepts so that you can foster profitable, continuous growth in your business — especially if your company depends on digital channels to acquire and retain customers. In fact, every company in the world that depends on e-commerce acquisition — especially online marketplaces such as Amazon, Uber, Expedia, and Etsy — harness these concepts to drive their business performance.

In this chapter, I begin by describing each of the three concepts and explaining how businesses use them. Then I discuss how AI influence changes the application of the concepts, and I also introduce some of the newer companies at the forefront of the related transformations.

Working Together: Three Core Concepts

In the world of marketing, lead scoring, lifetime value (LTV) assignments, and dynamic pricing work hand in hand to drive profitable growth. These concepts make up the nuts-and-bolts processes of customer engagement over time.

Here are the major roles of these three related concepts:

» **Lead scoring acts as the gateway,** sifting through potential *leads* (meaning target customers that you can market to) to evaluate the most promising prospects against the investments needed to acquire them.

» **LTV calculations determine long-term potential.** As part of the lead acquisition decision, these calculations estimate not only the immediate value, but also the longer-term potential of a customer's revenue contribution based on repeat transactions over an extended period. That way, the money spent to acquire the lead reflects the financial return provided by the immediate purchase and the propensity for purchase over a longer period.

» **Dynamic pricing adds agility** into business tactics by adapting the product pricing (probably lowering it) for the consumer based on the expected LTV.

Identifying potential leads

Lead scoring assigns distinct values or scores to individual leads by meticulously evaluating multifaceted customer criteria that include demographics, behavioral patterns, lead source, and levels of engagement with the brand. This process enables your business to divide your leads into groups more effectively. By identifying the highest potential for *conversion* (a customer buying right now) among these leads (and their lifetime value; see the following section), you can channel your efforts and resources to focus on the leads most likely to yield greater benefits over the long term.

For instance, envision an e-commerce platform that uses lead scoring algorithms to identify visitors who demonstrate a heightened propensity to purchase. These algorithms identify these potential customers through their browsing history, engagement patterns (such as how often they click on specific links on your website), and previous interactions with the brand so that you can know where to focus your marketing efforts.

TIP

For your business's marketing and sales efforts, deploying lead scoring algorithms can help you prioritize and tailor customer engagement strategies. The goal, ultimately, is to foster enhanced conversion rates and optimize the resources that focus on the most valuable leads.

Maximizing customer potential

Lifetime value (LTV) calculations transcend the realm of immediate transactions and project the potential long-term value each customer brings to a business. This analysis considers past purchasing behaviors and retention rates. It also anticipates potential future interactions to estimate the profitability each customer may contribute over the lifecycle of their involvement with the business.

LTV calculations can help you decide how to tailor marketing efforts, design loyalty programs, and craft service provisions to maximize the overall value derived from each customer interaction. By understanding the long-term potential of customers, you can allocate resources and design engagement strategies based on that potential.

In a practical scenario, a brand may identify that consumers who have certain demographic and behavioral characteristics (for example, those of certain ages and having specific website usage patterns) invariably take fewer steps to complete a purchase, and then, over an 18-month period, make more purchases than the average consumer. Calculating the profitability of all the purchases together — and subtracting the original acquisition cost — gives the brand the lifetime value of that customer.

Adapting to market conditions on the fly

Dynamic pricing epitomizes the flexibility and adaptability demanded in today's fiercely competitive business environment. This strategy involves the swift and real-time adjustment of prices based on multiple factors, including demand fluctuations, competitor pricing analyses, lifetime value calculations, and an evolving understanding of customer behavior based on criteria such as seasonality.

REMEMBER

By dynamically adjusting prices and offerings, you can help your business optimize short- and long-term revenue generation. This personalized pricing approach can help your business stay aligned with evolving market trends and your consumers' preferences.

For instance, ride-sharing companies dynamically alter prices during peak hours or high-demand periods — effectively balancing supply and demand — with the goal of optimizing revenue streams without hurting customer satisfaction *too* much. Those same ride-sharing companies may also set varied pricing based on an individual's loyalty to their brand and the acquisition costs in that particular local market at a given time.

Scoring Leads with the Help of AI

Incorporating machine learning (ML) algorithms, predictive analytics, and related artificial intelligence (AI) tools into marketing efforts heralds a paradigm shift that revolutionizes how your business can approach *lead scoring* (which is assigning a value to each lead based on their likelihood to convert and overall value to the business). You can harness this transformation in your marketing plans to increase the accuracy of lead scoring (targeting the right high-value leads), which can then yield substantial improvements in conversion rates (making more sales) and enhance customer engagement (meaning that you keep your customers involved with your brand and business).

Instilling precision with AI solutions

AI technologies lend adaptability, precise forecasting, and real-time prioritization to lead scoring methodologies. In this section, I examine the changes brought on by AI to a formerly rigid approach to lead scoring.

Leveraging machine learning algorithms

At the heart of AI's integration into lead scoring lies the sophisticated machine learning algorithms that it uses. These algorithms and related AI models — when trained on vast customer data sets — perpetually evolve and adapt. By using this feature, your business can forecast customer behaviors and preferences with precision, which in turn, enables you to make better decisions when you assign a value to a lead.

REMEMBER

Rather than using just a few customer attributes as a basis for lead scoring, machine learning algorithms can analyze hundreds of attributes in real time. Their speed and quantity of attributes analyzed can lead to much more precise prioritizations for targeting and acquiring your marketing leads.

Achieving precision through predictive analytics

An indispensable facet of AI-powered lead scoring is predictive analytics, which empowers your business to foresee customer actions and preferences. By extracting insights from historical data, predictive analytics fine-tunes lead scoring models and ensures more accurate identification and prioritization of high-value leads. Predictive analytics also can allow for more accurate lead scoring based on real-time customer decision making that occurs while a customer is on a specific *customer journey*, or path to purchase the product.

REMEMBER
Functioning as *precision enhancers*, AI-powered tools leverage the characteristic capability of AI to detect subtle patterns and correlations within data, which supports the refinement of lead-scoring models. The result is enhanced granularity and precision for identifying high-value leads that have a greater potential for conversion.

TIP
Combining historical and real-time perspectives through predictive analytics helps your business foresee how customers may behave in the future based on historical data, every previous customer interaction with the business, and general market factors. For example, you can adjust lead scoring by using predictive analytics to forecast Christmas season product sales for specific customer segments based on customer data, as well as competitive market and macro-economic factors, all at once.

Enhancing customer interfaces (and experiences) with AI

AI-driven interfaces allow you to use lead-scoring methodologies that pinpoint customers with accuracy and achieve greater conversion rates. These tools — which range from AI-powered chatbots to personalized shopping experiences — streamline lead evaluation and deepen your business's understanding of customer interactions. Although these tools may appear to serve only at the customer-interface level, they capture more specific and more detailed data on the user.

By looking at behavioral patterns and contextual data, AI lead-scoring tools segregate and categorize leads relating to customers who are most inclined to convert. This differentiation can enable your business to channel resources and tailor engagement strategies toward these promising prospects to maximize conversion potential.

Validating AI-powered lead scoring via empirical evidence

Supported by human oversight and rigorous statistical analyses, new tools underscore AI's ability to optimize critical lead-scoring processes. Real-world empirical data can help you validate the improvements in lead accuracy and conversion rates achieved through AI-powered lead-scoring systems.

TIP

Before you deploy AI-generated recommendations widely in your lead-scoring program, validate those recommendations by using common-sense tests (such as manually checking whether the AI is providing the right recommendation for the right leads) against small customer samples. Otherwise, you run the risk that the lead scoring may not be as accurate as you want it to be. You must carefully test and validate any AI integration into a business practice.

With AI tools, you can update lead scoring in real time, providing immediate feedback on how leads are interacting with marketing efforts. With this capability, marketers can validate their approach and also quickly adjust strategies and tactics in response to lead behaviors. For example, if a specific customer lead suddenly increases engagement with a particular product or service, the AI system can immediately update the lead score for that lead which can trigger different marketing actions, such as targeted e-mails or personalized offers.

Enhancing data analysis with AI tools

The integration of AI into lead-scoring tools creates a leap in analytical capabilities. More specifically, tools that include ML algorithms and predictive analytics enable companies to effectively incorporate extensive data sets with greater agility. Including more data adds depth to the foundation used for AI lead-scoring recommendations.

Here are examples of how the strong data-analysis capabilities of AI can bring improvements to your lead-scoring efforts:

>> **Integration of diverse data sources:** AI systems can integrate and process data from a wide range of sources, including social media, e-mail interactions, customer relationship management (CRM) systems, and website analytics. This comprehensive view of your consumer base ensures that lead scoring is based on a holistic understanding of the customer's interactions with the brand across various channels. It allows for a more accurate and comprehensive scoring system than traditional methods (such as evaluating the lead simply based on which marketing channel it came through), which may miss out on these diverse data points because the channel alone doesn't always dictate the likelihood of the lead converting to a customer.

» **Enhanced efficiency and reduced bias:** AI-driven lead scoring automates a process that was traditionally time-consuming and prone to human error and bias. By relying on data-driven algorithms, AI reduces the likelihood of subjective biases (such as evaluating a lead based the gender or the ethnicity of the person) that can affect lead scoring by ignoring high potential leads by over-generalizing about the user.

Instead, AI tools that include ML algorithms continuously improve their own performance over time via reinforcement learning techniques (see Chapter 5 for more on these techniques). And as an advantage for your business, AI's involvement also frees up marketers to focus on strategy and creative aspects of marketing, rather than the mechanical process of scoring leads.

» **Personalization at scale:** AI tools enable marketers to score leads based not only on broad categories but also on nuanced, individual behaviors and preferences. Incorporating this granular approach to analyzing customer data allows for a high degree of personalization in your related marketing efforts. For instance, AI can

- *Track an individual lead's engagement* with specific types of content, time spent on various website sections, and reaction to different marketing campaigns. This level of detail can help your business create personalized marketing strategies and interactions tailored to individual leads by including the promotion of more relevant and specific products only, for example. Personalization like this can significantly improve conversion rates because the customers are sure to see the products that you know they like.

- *Focus on high-value leads* by taking advantage of the depth and precision of data provided by AI-powered lead-scoring tools. You can use the data gleaned from your AI's data analysis to focus on high-value leads and tailor their *engagements* (messaging, product selection offered, and so on) to foster a heightened level of customer satisfaction.

» **Streamlined analytical processes:** AI-driven lead scoring tools can help your business streamline effective analytical processes. Before AI, intricate and time-consuming procedures (such as manually reviewing each lead to determine its score) hindered marketers from swiftly identifying potential prospects. Now, AI's proficiency in managing vast amounts of data expedites this identification process. AI tools can swiftly analyze diverse consumer behaviors and extract valuable insights that were formerly buried within layers of complex data.

Finding companies that offer AI-infused lead-scoring capabilities

Existing companies that offer lead-scoring capabilities are fast integrating AI technologies into their offerings. At the same time, you can also find new AI startups that approach lead scoring very differently than the existing established companies by building their systems to incorporate AI-based solutions at the heart of their offering.

Table 10-1 highlights a selection of companies that show promise for expediting lead scoring by using AI.

TABLE 10-1 **Companies Offering AI in Lead-Scoring Solutions**

Company Name	Website	Solution Specifics
Adobe Marketo	http://business.adobe.com/products/marketo	A part of Adobe since 2018, Marketo offers a marketing automation solution that includes AI-driven lead scoring to identifying the most promising leads based on their interaction with marketing content and online behavior.
Apollo.io	www.apollo.io	A sales platform offering lead scoring, analytics, and a vast database for prospecting and customer relationship management (CRM) integration, offering rich data on millions of companies and decision-makers to help businesses identify and connect with potential customers.
Forwrd	www.forwrd.ai	A business-to-business AI platform specializing in predictive analytics to help companies increase their revenue. It enables businesses to build no-code predictive scoring apps (letting a business user create the app without the need for a developer) for identifying sales-ready prospects and at-risk customers (those that are at risk of lapsing), enhancing lead prioritization and customer engagement strategies.
HubSpot	www.hubspot.com	A comprehensive CRM platform that includes advanced lead-scoring features. Its AI-driven system allows businesses to score leads based on those leads' behavior and engagement, making it easier to prioritize prospects.
Infer	www.getinfer.io	Provides a predictive lead scoring platform that uses AI to help businesses identify and target their best prospects, and it integrates with existing CRM and marketing automation tools.
LeadSquared	www.leadsquared.com	Offers a sales execution CRM that has a strong focus on lead scoring, using AI to track and score leads based on those leads' interactions with the business.

Company Name	Website	Solution Specifics
Oracle Eloqua	www.oracle.com/cx/marketing/automation	Part of Oracle's marketing cloud, Eloqua provides AI-based lead scoring, enabling businesses to score and nurture leads more effectively based on detailed customer insights.
Salesforce Einstein	www.salesforce.com/products/einstein	Part of the Salesforce platform, Einstein AI uses machine learning to analyze historical sales data and predict which leads are most likely to convert.
Zoho CRM	www.zoho.com/crm	Includes an AI assistant, Zia, that provides predictive lead scoring. Zia analyzes customer interaction data to predict the likelihood of a lead converting.

Calculating Lifetime Value to Affect Lead Scoring

In the following sections, I discuss the relationship between lifetime value (LTV) calculations that are fueled by artificial intelligence (AI) and lead-scoring methodologies to demonstrate their joint impact on businesses' decision-making abilities. By dissecting the predictive models and algorithms foundational to LTV calculations, you can choose how to extract more granular insights about your existing and potential customers. And armed with this level of understanding, you can make more robust data-led marketing decisions.

Allowing for predictive customer analysis

Businesses formerly calculated *historic lifetime value* as the cumulative purchases of a product in a specific time period by analyzing the average order size, the average number of transactions, and the average duration over which customers placed orders. For example, if a customer buys a Christmas tree for $50 each year for 10 years, their historic LTV is $500 over 10 years.

But by using AI-enhanced tools, a business can take the LTV calculation much further by making assumptions (based on historic purchasing behavior) or by figuring *predictive customer lifetime value* based on a customer's propensity to buy in the future. Predictive customer lifetime value can take current and future customer acquisition costs, purchase frequency, expected business overheads, and other macro factors all into account.

REMEMBER

AI's role in analyzing historical data for LTV calculations goes beyond history to transform large, complex data sets into predictions of customer behavior — actionable insights — that enable your business to make more informed decisions about your prospective customers.

Here's a more specific and factual breakdown of how this predictive LTV concept works, along with real-world examples:

>> **Analyzing historical customer data:** AI solutions can help your company deeply analyze past customer data, which was previously a challenging task. For example, a retail company can use AI to examine years of sales data, customer feedback, and online engagement. This analysis helps the company understand which products are most popular, which marketing strategies are most effective, and which customer segments are most valuable over time.

>> **Extracting detailed insights from past interactions:** AI technologies use advanced algorithms and machine learning (ML) models to sift through extensive historical data. These tools can identify patterns that human analysts may miss. For instance, a streaming service such as Netflix uses AI to analyze viewing histories and ratings provided by millions of users. This analysis helps Netflix understand viewer preferences in granular detail and helps inform decisions about the types of profitable shows or movies to invest in.

>> **Understanding customer lifetime value more accurately:** AI's ability to do deep analysis can help your business understand the true value of various customer segments. For instance, an airline may use AI to analyze flight booking data and identify which customers are frequent flyers, leading to more targeted loyalty programs and personalized marketing strategies for these high-value customers.

>> **Informing future business strategies:** Insights gained from AI-driven analysis of historical data guide future business decisions. For example, an e-commerce company may use AI to identify that customers who buy certain products are more likely to make repeat purchases. This insight can lead to targeted marketing campaigns and product recommendations designed to increase customer retention and lifetime value.

>> **Shaping proactive business strategies:** AI not only helps in understanding past customer behaviors but also in predicting future trends. For example, a car manufacturer may use AI to analyze past sales data and predict which features are likely to be popular in the future, guiding the development of new models. (Humans can find analyzing such vast amounts of data manually too difficult, and they may be unable to predict new model features that matter.) Also, car manufacturers may use predictive modeling techniques from AI to understand which customers are likely to *churn* (go elsewhere to purchase) when they're due for a new car, so the manufacturer knows to offer those customers unique incentives to stay with the brand.

Finding companies that offer AI-infused LTV calculations

You can find a range of companies that provide AI-based solutions in the space of LTV calculations. Table 10-2 features some of the more notable players that are worth exploring.

TABLE 10-2 **Companies with AI-Based LTV Solutions**

Company Name	Website	Solution Specifics
Adobe Analytics	http://business.adobe.com/products/analytics	AI-powered analytics tools that can facilitate deep insights into customer behavior, enhance LTV calculations, and help your business tailor your marketing strategies effectively.
Bloomreach	www.bloomreach.com	Specializes in digital experience and personalization; uses AI to analyze extensive customer interactions, providing detailed LTV calculations for improved marketing and customer experience strategies.
Google Cloud AI	http://cloud.google.com/products/ai	Advanced AI tools for analyzing extensive customer data sets, aiding businesses in accurately calculating LTV and making informed marketing decisions.
IBM Watson	www.ibm.com/watson	Offers sophisticated AI models that analyze customer behavior, providing insights for LTV calculations and enabling your business to create personalized customer engagement strategies.
Pecan	www.pecan.ai	An AI startup that simplifies predictive analytics, allowing your business to easily calculate LTV and other key metrics, enhancing decision-making processes without requiring deep technical expertise.
Salesforce	www.salesforce.com	Incorporates AI-driven analytics in its customer relationship management (CRM) platform, enabling your business to estimate LTV and gain predictive insights about customer behavior for more effective sales strategies.
SAP	www.sap.com/products/artificial-intelligence.html	SAP's AI integration in CRM and analytics tools provides deep insights into customer LTV, helping your business make data-driven decisions for targeted customer engagement.
Voyantis	www.voyantis.ai	An AI startup that specializes in growth prediction and LTV calculations, offering tools that optimize your money spent on marketing and enhance revenue growth strategies through predictive analytics.

(continued)

TABLE 10-2 (continued)

Company Name	Website	Solution Specifics
Zeta Global	www.zetaglobal.com	A marketing technology company that leverages AI for real-time data processing, enabling accurate LTV calculations and aiding in efficient customer acquisition and retention strategies.
Zoho Analytics	www.zoho.com/analytics	Utilizes AI for data analysis, helping businesses effectively calculate LTV, thereby facilitating more targeted and efficient marketing and sales efforts.

Turning Lead Scoring and LTV Insights into Dynamic Pricing

You can combine the elements of lead scoring (which I talk about in the section "Scoring Leads with the Help of AI," earlier in this chapter) and lifetime value (see the section "Calculating Lifetime Value to Affect Lead Scoring," earlier in this chapter) into *dynamic pricing* (a process that adjusts prices in real time based on market demand, competition, and other external factors). When you do, you hone your marketing practices to enhance customer engagement, maximize revenue potential, and maintain a competitive edge in your particular market.

Here are some ways that your business can maximize these opportunities:

>> **Making dynamic pricing adjustments:** AI algorithms analyze customer data, market trends, and competitor prices to adjust product or service costs dynamically. For example, a fashion retailer can use AI to modify prices based on seasonal trends, inventory levels, and individual customer purchase history. These price adjustments ensure that the retailer keeps pricing competitive and profit margins optimized.

>> **Leveraging lead scoring in pricing strategy:** *Lead scoring* involves evaluating potential customers based on their likelihood to convert or make a purchase. A software company may use lead scoring when creating dynamic pricing by offering personalized subscription plans. High-scoring leads — identified as likely to purchase premium services — can receive offers for high-tier plans, while others are targeted with basic or intermediate options.

>> **Incorporating customer lifetime value (LTV):** LTV helps you understand the long-term value of customers, and your business can effectively use it to guide pricing strategies for different market segments. A luxury car dealership may use LTV scoring methodologies to identify high-value customers who like to drive new cars and are more likely to buy a new model every four years over

a 20-year period. For these customers, the dealership can offer exclusive deals or incentives tied to future purchases, recognizing their higher potential for a long-term relationship.

>> **Harnessing behavioral data:** Streaming platforms such as Netflix or Hulu can use AI to adjust subscription fees based on viewing habits, the popularity of specific content, and competitor's pricing strategies. Hotels and resorts may implement dynamic pricing to adjust room rates so that they can optimize occupancy and revenue based on demand for specific room types, guest LTV, and seasonality.

Table 10-3 shows eight significant AI startups and companies that specialize in dynamic pricing solutions.

TABLE 10-3   **Companies with AI in Dynamic Pricing Solutions**

Company Name	Website	Solution Specifics
Competera	www.competera.net	Helps retailers set competitive prices through market data analysis
Dynamic Pricing AI	www.dynamicpricing.ai	Enables businesses to optimize prices in real time based on market demand, competition, and other relevant factors
Earnix	www.earnix.com	Pricing and product personalization solutions for the banking and insurance industries, focusing on risk assessment and demand analysis
Feedvisor	www.feedvisor.com	Algorithmic repricing and revenue optimization platform designed for online retailers, focusing on maximizing profitability
Imprice	www.imprice.ai	Helps e-commerce businesses set optimal prices, maximize profits, and stay competitive in the market
Omnia Retail	www.omniaretail.com	Dynamic pricing and marketing automation, tailored for retailers to optimize pricing strategies efficiently
Pricefx	www.pricefx.com	Comprehensive cloud-based pricing software that has AI capabilities, helping businesses to implement effective dynamic pricing strategies
PROS	www.pros.com	AI-based solutions for pricing and revenue management, enabling real-time pricing decisions across various sectors
Revionics	www.revionics.com	AI-driven price optimization and promotion solutions for retailers, enhancing pricing strategies and competitiveness
Zilliant	www.zilliant.com	AI-based dynamic pricing and sales growth solutions, helping companies make data-driven pricing decisions to maximize profitability

Chapter 11

Churn Modeling and Measurement with AI

*C*hurn modeling (a technique for predicting customer behavior) helps your business make better decisions about its marketing strategies for customer retention. This chapter delves into the nuanced aspects of churn modeling, beginning with an overview and then exploring artificial intelligence (AI) techniques that make churn modeling all the more effective in the AI era. Identifying *churn* (losing customers) before it happens can help your business take proactive actions to retain customers. And so, in this chapter, I tell you about using AI-based churn modeling to define and inform customer retention strategies.

Effective churn management heavily depends on the sophistication of your *measurement operations* (which are how you collect, process, and analyze customer data). You can use AI-driven data collection and monitoring techniques to provide a deeper, more accurate insight into customer behaviors and sentiment. And AI-based tools for visualization and reporting can help you, as a marketer, understand complex data sets and make informed decisions about the health of your customer base and the likelihood of a specific customer to churn.

Finally, I can't overstate the transformative potential of AI tools in churn modeling and measurement operations. In this chapter, I introduce a sampling of the more effective AI tools that you can use to enhance both predictive accuracy and operational efficiency in the practice of churn modeling.

Getting the Scoop on Churn Modeling

The traditional formula for *churn rate* (how many customers you lose over time) was a simple calculation figured for a specific time-frame (such as monthly, quarterly, or yearly):

$$\text{Churn rate} = \frac{\text{Beginning customers} - \text{Ending customers}}{\text{Beginning customers}} \times 100$$

However, businesses found that calculating the current churn rate didn't provide enough actionable value to decision making, so they tried to project their future churn rates to help them more effectively manage their cost structures.

Enter *churn modeling*, which is a predictive technique that brings in analytical processes to predict the likelihood of customers discontinuing their use of a service and when they may do so. Churn modeling processes use historical customer data to detect patterns of behavior and indicators that precede customers' cancellation of a product or service. Today, the art of churn modeling includes both traditional statistical methods and newer, AI-driven approaches.

By analyzing various customer attributes — such as demographics, usage behavior, service interactions, and satisfaction levels — businesses can construct a predictive model that estimates the probability of churn for each customer. Businesses use techniques such as the Net Promoter Score (NPS) — which gathers information directly from the customers via first-hand feedback (such as surveys) — to measure customer loyalty and satisfaction as input for their predictive modeling.

Building your churn model

Developing a churn model begins with data collection and preparation, which is a critical step in ensuring the accuracy of the predictions that you get from your AI tools. You must

>> Clean, normalize, and transform data to make it suitable for modeling (see Chapter 4).

>> Extract the data features that are relevant to predicting churn, such as how frequently customers interact with the business, changes in patterns of interaction, billing information, and customer support interactions.

Best marketing practice: Use generative AI to automatically generate and select predictive features that are most indicative of churn. This involvement can include generating new variables from existing data points through advanced data techniques, such as feature transformation and discovery, used by machine learning (ML) models. See Chapter 5 for more on machine learning.

Then follow data preparation by selecting a modeling approach, which can vary from logistic regression and decision trees to more complex ensemble methods or neural networks. (See Chapter 7 for more information about building predictive models.) Your selection of a modeling approach and appropriate tools depends on the business context (meaning the type of business and industry you are in) and the data available.

Validating, calibrating, and integrating your churn model

After you build the churn model (discussed in the preceding section), you need to validate and calibrate it to ensure that it performs well on *unseen data*, meaning new data that isn't involved in the initial model development. You can typically assess the performance of a churn model — test its predictive power — by using metrics such as *accuracy* (the proportion of correct predictions), *recall* (the ability to identify all actual churn cases), and *precision* (the accuracy of identifying churn cases), and employing techniques such as *cross-validation* (dividing data into subsets to train and test multiple times) or using a *hold-out data set* (reserving a portion of data for final model evaluation).

REMEMBER

Testing your model by applying accuracy, recall, and precision metrics helps determine how well the model can distinguish between customers who will churn and customers who will stay. If the model can't successfully make this distinction, using it is pointless.

Best marketing practice: Employ generative AI to simulate real-world scenarios and stress-test models in virtual environments. These simulations allow for continuous validation and refinement of models without waiting for long-term business cycles to complete.

To make the results of churn modeling more actionable, you must integrate the results into your customer relationship management (CRM) systems (see Chapter 19 for more about CRMs). This integration enables you to proactively manage customers that you identify as at-risk through targeted retention strategies tailored to the specific reasons behind their predicted churn. Strategies may include personalized offers, timely resolutions of service issues, or changes in customer engagement tactics. (See the section "Combating churn with customer retention strategies," later in the chapter, for more on these techniques.)

TIP

Incorporating churn predictions into CRM systems and other regular business operations requires the following efforts:

>> **Ongoing refinement and recalibration** of the churn model to adapt to new customer behaviors and market conditions

>> **Continuous learning** from new customer data and feedback loops to enhance the model's sensitivity to shifts in customer dynamics

Best marketing practice: Implement automated re-training of churn models using the latest data, facilitated by generative AI. This training setup ensures that the models stay updated with the latest customer trends and behaviors without manual intervention.

Improving churn insights with generative AI

The advent of AI, particularly generative AI, has significantly transformed churn modeling by enabling more nuanced insights and predictive capabilities. Generative AI, through its ability to analyze and generate data that mirrors real customer interactions and behaviors, provides a deeper understanding of customer churn. This capability marks a shift from traditional statistical models to more dynamic, self-improving AI systems that tend to adapt and become more precise over time by learning from their own mistakes.

Generative AI enhances churn modeling by simulating customer behaviors and responses to various stimuli or changes in service. For instance, by using techniques such as *generative adversarial networks* (GANs; machine learning models that create new data that resembles training data), businesses can create synthetic yet realistic customer profiles and interaction data. These profiles help in testing and refining churn prediction models under varied conditions without the need to wait for real events to occur. This ability to generate synthetic data is valuable for filling in the gaps when the real data is sparse, or when privacy concerns limit the use of actual customer data.

Best marketing practice: Use generative AI to create synthetic data that mimics real customer behaviors and interactions. This practice allows for more robust testing and training of churn models without compromising personal privacy or relying solely on available historical data.

AI expands the scope of the data available to businesses for use in churn modeling and related marketing decisions in other ways. You can

- **»** **Develop more sophisticated customer journey mapping.** *Customer journey mapping* captures the path a customer follows when interacting with a company. By predicting potential future interactions based on past behavior patterns, AI models can forecast churn at different stages of the customer lifecycle. This predictive capability allows businesses to implement preemptive actions tailored to the specific needs and preferences of individual customers at various points in their journey. And predictive insights can enhance your personalized marketing strategies and help improve overall customer satisfaction.

- **»** **Integrate multi-modal data sources into a cohesive analytical framework for your AI-driven churn modeling.** These data sources can include text, voice, and digital interactions. This integration allows for a holistic view of the customer experience and captures nuances that you may miss when analyzing separate data silos. For example, natural language processing (NLP) techniques can analyze customer sentiment from customer service support tickets or social media posts, providing early warning signs of dissatisfaction that can lead to churn.

REMEMBER

In practice, implementing AI in churn modeling requires you to maintain a robust infrastructure and a strategic approach to data management. And you must make data quality, customer privacy, and ethical considerations a priority so that you maintain customer trust and regulatory compliance in your AI-driven efforts. Also, have humans interpret the outputs of AI models and validate the insights generated. Then add these insights as actionable strategies by (ideally) integrating them into your business's CRM systems.

Best marketing practice: Maintain a high standard of ethics in the use of generative AI and ensure transparency about how you use customer data and make related decisions. Clearly communicate these practices to customers so that you can build trust and reinforce the value of personalized services.

T-MOBILE'S AI-POWERED CHURN PREDICTION

In the highly competitive telecommunications industry, T-Mobile (www.t-mobile.com) leverages AI to predict and manage customer churn with precision. The company integrates data from a variety of sources, including call records, data usage patterns, billing history, network quality, customer service interactions, and even social media activity. With this comprehensive data set, T-Mobile can build robust churn prediction models. It uses machine learning algorithms to analyze customer behavior, predict the likelihood of churn, and identify at-risk customers with high accuracy.

(continued)

(continued)

Here are some of the methods T-Mobile uses with the help of AI in its customer retention strategy:

- **Risk categories:** By categorizing users into different risk categories, T-Mobile tailors its retention efforts to address the specific needs and concerns of each group. High-risk customers may receive special offers, loyalty rewards, or personalized customer service interventions to enhance their satisfaction.

- **Real-time interventions:** The AI system detects early warning signs of churn in real time, allowing the company to promptly address issues through proactive customer service outreach, targeted promotions, or network improvements.

- **Continuous feedback and model adaptation:** Ensure that T-Mobile's AI system remains effective and up to date with evolving customer behaviors and market conditions.

This comprehensive AI-driven approach has resulted in higher customer satisfaction, reduced churn rates, and a more loyal customer base for T-Mobile, according to T-Mobile and its technology partners.

Combating churn with customer retention strategies

Customer retention strategies are essential for businesses aiming to reduce *churn* (customer loss) and enhance *customer lifetime value* (the total profit that comes from a customer over the life of their involvement with a business). You must proactively implement effective retention tactics by using both data-driven insights (such as predictive analytics to forecast customer behavior and identify churn risks) and personalized customer engagement (direct messaging via e-mail or text, for example).

REMEMBER

Many companies believe that by focusing on customer retention, their businesses will grow at a faster pace because retaining an existing customer is typically cheaper than acquiring a new one. And those happy customers can help encourage others to become customers, as well.

Best marketing practice: Implement AI-driven analytics to monitor the effectiveness of churn-reduction strategies in real time and allow for immediate adjustments and optimizations.

Personalizing customer interactions

Marketers use data analytics (powered by AI) to segment customers based on their behavior, preferences, and past interactions. Then, they create personalized communication and marketing strategies for the various segments.

For instance, they may tailor e-mail marketing campaigns with offers and content designed to appeal to individuals' preferences or past purchasing behavior — especially to those customers whose analytics indicate that they're likely to churn. Marketers also use personalized product recommendations on websites or in apps to enhance user engagement and increase the likelihood of repeat purchases.

Best marketing practice: Take advantage of insights derived from generative AI and data analytics to design highly personalized customer retention strategies. Use predictive insights to anticipate customer needs and address them proactively with the goal of enhancing customer satisfaction and loyalty.

Enhancing customer support

Encourage your business to provide multiple channels for customer support, such as phone, e-mail, live chat, and social media to ensure that help is readily accessible for your customers. Invest in training support staff to handle inquiries efficiently and empathetically. Then regularly assess the quality of support provided and seek customer feedback to continually improve your service.

REMEMBER

Implementing AI-driven chatbots as part of your customer support strategies can provide immediate responses to common queries and free up human resources for more complex issues.

Implementing loyalty programs

Develop loyalty programs that reward repeat customers with discounts, special offers, or exclusive access to new products. You can design these programs not only to reward purchases but also to encourage engagement with the brand through various channels, such as social media interactions and participation in surveys or reviews. And consider adding *gamification elements* (typical elements of game playing) — such as earning points for social media interactions or for completing profiles — to your customer retention efforts. These types of activities can increase customer involvement and commitment.

TIP

Use AI to personalize your loyalty program rewards by analyzing customer data to tailor offers to individual preferences and behaviors. Automate the tracking and rewarding of gamification elements, such as social media interactions and survey participation, to boost customer engagement and commitment.

Conducting regular feedback and follow-up initiatives

Design your marketing outreach to engage with customers regularly so that you can gather feedback about their experiences with your products, website, and so on, and their expectations for such interactions. You can use surveys, polls, and direct communication (e-mail or text, for example) to solicit feedback regarding customer satisfaction and areas for improvement.

REMEMBER

Follow up on the customer feedback that you receive — especially negative criticisms — and let customers know what changes you're making because of their suggestions. Adding this transparency to your follow-up initiatives can build trust and show customers that you value their opinions.

Best marketing practice: Integrate feedback mechanisms directly into the customer journey, for example, after a purchase or interaction with customer service. Then use generative AI to analyze and act on this feedback in real time, perhaps by offering personalized discounts or special access to limited quantity products. This immediate analysis and response can help to quickly identify dissatisfaction or potential churn triggers.

Using exit surveys and win-back campaigns

When customers decide to leave — by canceling a subscription or abandoning a shopping cart, for example — conduct an exit survey to understand their reasons for leaving and identify any common trends that you can address. Use the power of AI to analyze this feedback, identify patterns, and implement targeted strategies related to the feedback issues to improve customer retention.

TIP

Implement win-back campaigns that offer special incentives or address the specific concerns that led to a customer's departure decision. For example, if customers leave for a competitor that offers a better price, consider making a targeted offer that provides a price match or a discount on the customer's next purchase.

CASE STUDY: CHEWY USES AI TO FIGHT CUSTOMER CHURN

Chewy (www.chewy.com), an online retailer specializing in pet products, is recognized for its exceptional customer service, a reputation built through consistent, personalized care for its customers. One of their standout practices is a proactive approach to customer satisfaction. For instance, Chewy often surprises customers with handwritten notes and unexpected gifts, such as sending flowers or a condolence card when they learn of a pet's passing. This empathetic touch not only demonstrates their commitment to customer care, but also fosters deep emotional connections with their clientele. Their customer service team is available 24/7, which helps ensure that they can promptly address any issue, from order inquiries to product advice. This availability showcases Chewy's dedication to accessibility and support.

Moreover, Chewy excels in handling returns and refunds, making the process seamless and stress-free for customers. If a customer reports an issue with a product, Chewy often issues a refund or replacement without requiring the item to be returned, prioritizing convenience and trust. In addition, Chewy goes above and beyond by sometimes donating returned items to local animal shelters, turning a customer service challenge into a positive community impact. This combination of thoughtful gestures, round-the-clock support, and hassle-free problem resolution exemplifies Chewy's phenomenal customer service, setting a high standard in the e-commerce industry. And not surprisingly, it leads to more loyal customers who churn much less frequently.

Ramping Up Your Measurement Operations

The goal of *measurement operations* in business is to assess the effectiveness of measurement approaches, optimize measurement processes, and use the resulting insights to drive business growth. An effective measurement system provides actionable insights that can guide decision-making and strategic planning. In the context of marketing, your business can establish measurement operations that continuously track performance metrics, analyze customer data, and adjust strategies to enhance overall effectiveness.

Follow these steps in implementing these strategies to set up measurement operations that support marketing within your business:

1. **Define clear objectives and key performance indicators (KPIs) that underpin measurement operations.**

   Outline goals that show what success looks like for your organization — specifically, your marketing function —and identify the KPIs that

   - *Measure progress toward your specific goals.* KPIs must be aligned with your business objectives and be easily measurable, relevant, and insightful into business performance.

   - *Include common business success metrics.* For example, you can choose to gather financial metrics, customer satisfaction scores, customer acquisition metrics, *brand health numbers* (such as how many customers are likely to buy in the near future), and operational efficiency.

2. **Establish robust data collection systems that gather accurate and relevant operational data for analysis.**

   Implementing these systems involves

   - *Setting up automated data collection tools* such as customer relationship management (CRM) systems, web analytics, and customer feedback platforms.

   - *Ensuring that the data collected is high-quality,* which means that the data must be complete, accurate, timely, and consistent. See Chapter 4 for information about quality and quantity of data.

   - *Performing regular audits of the data collection processes* to maintain the integrity of the data.

   - *Making certain that data collection systems all talk to one another* and use a common *taxonomy,* that is, a common way to describe the same type of data across multiple systems.

3. **Source and deploy advanced analytics and AI technologies to analyze the collected data.**

   Machine learning models can identify patterns and trends that don't seem obvious through traditional analysis methods. For example:

   - Predictive analytics can forecast future trends based on historical data to help businesses make proactive decisions.

   - AI-driven analytics can highlight anomalies in data that may indicate issues needing immediate attention.

REMEMBER

In the context of churn modeling, AI-driven predictive analytics can analyze much larger data sets with greater accuracy than a human can when using any previous analysis method. This advanced capability allows businesses to identify patterns and predict customer behavior more effectively, leading to improved retention strategies.

4. **Deploy a reporting dashboard that provides real-time insights into KPIs.**

TIP

Make your reporting dashboards interactive, friendly, and accessible to stakeholders at all levels within the organization. Ideally, make the dashboards customizable and available for a wide range of users within the business to view data from different perspectives and drill down into metrics for deeper analysis and insights needed for making decisions — about marketing practices, for example.

5. **Set up a process for regularly reviewing and adapting the overall measurement operations.**

Avoid static measurement operations by regular reviews and adaptations to

- *Periodically reassess* the set KPIs, the data collection methods, and the analytical tools used against the original goals and the business's changing needs.

- *Refine processes* by adjusting data collection methods, updating KPIs, or integrating new analytics technologies to enhance data analysis capabilities.

Best marketing practice: Implement a range of AI-driven analytical models in your measurement operations, including models capable of continuous learning, such as neural networks and reinforcement learning models. (See Chapters 5 and 6 for more about AI models.) These models can adapt to changes in customer behavior or market conditions more fluidly than traditional models.

Letting AI drive data collection and monitoring

Integrating AI-driven data collection and monitoring can transform measurement operations into dynamic systems that track performance and enhance decision-making by providing intelligent, data-driven insights. The management of measurement operations may sit within the marketing function but is just as likely to reside within the technology teams. If it is the latter, then marketing leaders must help the technology teams access the right data inputs (often from third-party providers) and integrate them appropriately.

AI-driven data collection and monitoring can enhance measurement operations by

>> **Strengthening the precision and speed** with which you gather and analyze data

>> **Improving scalability** by increasing the amount of data that you can handle in your measurement processes

>> **Infusing your operations with continuous monitoring and the benefits of deep learning** to not only improve the quality of the data collected, but also provide deeper insights into the data

Follow these broad steps to integrate AI-driven techniques into data collection and monitoring within a marketing organization:

1. **Deploy AI technologies to automate the collection of data across various _touchpoints_ (areas of interaction) in the _customer journey_ (a person's series of interactions with your business).**

    You can use web scraping tools, such as Internet of Things (IoT) sensors and application programming interfaces (APIs), to gather raw, real-time data from websites, physical devices, and third-party services (all used by customers) that you include in your marketing programs. Then use AI tools to turn this unstructured data into structured data that reveals customer behavior, preferences, and engagement levels. Automating the data collection process ensures a consistent flow of data and reduces the likelihood of human error.

2. **Apply machine learning (ML) algorithms to cleanse and preprocess the data so that you can enhance data quality.**

    AI algorithms can detect anomalies, remove duplicates, and correct inconsistencies in the data set. (See Chapter 5 for more about machine learning.) For example, you can use natural language processing (NLP; see Chapter 6) to interpret and standardize textual data — such as customer feedback or social media posts — from various sources.

3. **Use AI technology to monitor data streams in real time and trigger alerts when the AI detects anomalies or significant events that may require immediate action.**

    Critical trends include a sudden drop in user engagement for the products that you market, a change in the bidding requirements for the search advertising that you buy (see Chapter 15 for more on search advertising), or a spike in transaction failures.

4. **Incorporate predictive analytics into your measurement operations to forecast future trends based on historical data.**

    AI models can analyze patterns in large data sets to predict outcomes (see Chapter 7), such as potential churn rates, sales spikes, or inventory shortages. These insights enable your business to make proactive, strategic decisions, such as adjusting marketing campaigns, optimizing inventory levels, or enhancing customer service initiatives before issues arise.

5. **Set up your AI-powered measurement systems for continuous learning, as well as automatic adaptation and improvement, based on new data and outcomes.**

    You can accomplish continuous learning and improvement in your systems by regularly updating the AI models that you use with fresh data and recalibrating those models as needed to reflect changing market conditions or business strategies.

Optimizing measurement operations with AI techniques

If you want to strengthen your business's measurement operations, deploying AI techniques offers a new way to understand and optimize various aspects of marketing performance. You can integrate several AI techniques effectively into measurement operations to yield actionable insights and facilitate more informed decision-making processes. These techniques include

>> **Cluster analysis for customer segmentation:** AI-powered cluster analysis helps to segment customers more accurately based on their behaviors, preferences, and demographic profiles. (See Chapter 9 for information on customer segmentation.) This technique employs algorithms that analyze and group large data sets into clusters that share similar characteristics — without relying on predefined categories. This clustered segmentation not only allows for more personalized marketing and customer service, but also enhances the precision of measurement operations because the measurements align with distinct customer groups' needs and responses.

   Best marketing practice: Apply generative AI models to dynamically segment customers based on evolving patterns and behaviors. This approach allows for real-time segmentation updates when customer behaviors change, which gives you more accurate and timely insights for personalized interventions that can reduce churn rates.

>> **Time series forecasting for trend analysis:** Implement AI-driven time series analysis to forecast future trends based on historical data. You may find this forecasting particularly useful for predicting sales volumes, customer demand, or market movements over time. AI models that incorporate time series forecasting — such as autoregressive integrated moving average (ARIMA) or long short-term memory (LSTM) networks (see Chapter 5 for more) — analyze the data for patterns, seasonal variances, and cyclical changes, providing forecasts that can help your business plan more effectively and allocate resources more efficiently.

>> **Sentiment analysis for consumer feedback:** Apply natural language processing (NLP) techniques (see Chapter 6) to analyze customer feedback, reviews, and social media mentions so that you can gauge customer senti-ment and understand public perception. Sentiment analysis helps businesses measure the impact of marketing campaigns, product launches, or customer service changes in real time.

>> **Anomaly detection for operational efficiency:** Use AI to monitor opera-tional data and identify anomalies that can indicate inefficiencies or errors in business processes. Techniques such as *outlier detection* (which is identifying data points that deviate significantly from the norm) or neural networks can

automatically flag unusual data points, such as unexpected drops in productivity, unusual financial transactions, or faults in manufacturing processes. Detecting these anomalies early allows you to take corrective actions swiftly, thereby reducing potential losses and maintaining operational integrity.

» **Optimization algorithms for resource allocation:** Deploy optimization algorithms to ensure resources are allocated most efficiently across various business operations. AI can analyze multiple variables and constraints to suggest optimal combinations of resource deployment that maximize output or minimize costs. Whether AI-driven optimization offers insight on adjusting staffing levels, optimizing supply chain logistics, or managing energy consumption, it can give you a strategic advantage by ensuring that your business uses resources effectively to achieve the most valuable outcomes for the business.

AMAZON PRIME'S AI-DRIVEN CHURN MODELING

Amazon Prime (www.amazon.com/amazonprime) employs advanced AI techniques to effectively manage and predict customer churn. The foundation of their strategy lies in extensive data collection from multiple sources, including purchase history, streaming habits, search queries, and interaction with various Prime services. This rich data set is fed into sophisticated machine learning algorithms that analyze customer behavior so that they can predict *churn* (when a business loses customers). These algorithms look at a range of factors, such as the frequency of purchases, streaming activity, engagement with Prime benefits, and even customer service interactions. Amazon can analyze this comprehensive data to identify early signs of potential churn and understand the underlying reasons behind it.

To combat churn, Amazon Prime uses AI to personalize the customer experience. For example, if a user shows a decline in streaming activity, AI-driven recommendations suggest new shows or movies based on their viewing history, and personalized e-mails and notifications remind users of the various benefits of Prime membership, such as exclusive deals and free shipping. Proactive interventions are also a key part of their strategy. When potential churn is detected, Amazon may offer targeted promotions or discounts to re-engage the customer.

Continuous improvement is a hallmark of Amazon's AI system, and the models are regularly refined with new data and feedback, ensuring that they remain accurate and relevant. This approach enables Amazon Prime to proactively address potential churn, enhance customer satisfaction, and maintain high retention rates.

Incorporating visualization and reporting solutions

Visualization and reporting solutions that provide marketers with a detailed view of measurement results are essential components of effective measurement operations. They transform the raw insights from your operations into comprehensible and actionable insights that are easily digestible and support better decision making.

Here's how you can deploy advanced visualization and reporting tools that enhance your business's data-driven insights around churn modeling:

» **Implement interactive dashboards and real-time data visualization mechanisms** that provide a centralized view of key performance indicators (KPIs) and metrics for churn modeling across different departments and operations. This real-time capability ensures that decision-makers always have access to the most current data, facilitating immediate responses to emerging issues or opportunities.

Tools such as Tableau (www.tableau.com), Microsoft's Power BI (www.microsoft.com/power-platform/products/power-bi), or Qlik Sense (www.qlik.com/products/qlik-sense) allow you to create dynamic data visualizations that update in real time and enable users to see the impact of their interactions instantly. Make the dashboard for the tool you choose user-friendly and customizable, enabling users to drill down into specific data points or zoom out for a broader perspective.

» **Develop automated reporting systems** that regularly generate comprehensive reports tailored to the specifics of various customer segments at different stages of churn. Automation in reporting both saves time and ensures consistency and accuracy in the data presented.

REMEMBER

Advanced reporting tools can integrate data from multiple sources and provide a holistic view of the business landscape. You can schedule reports to deliver insights directly to stakeholders' inboxes, which ensures that all relevant parties in your marketing department (and other business functions) stay informed about the latest trends, achievements, and areas of operations that need attention.

» **Employ tools that use predictive analytics and scenario visualization** to forecast future trends and visualize different scenarios based on varying parameters. This forward-looking visualization enables your business to prepare for potential future states, when churn may increase or decrease significantly, and make proactive decisions. Visualization tools can help illustrate *what-if scenarios*, which show how different strategies may affect outcomes such as customer retention rates, revenue projections, or market expansion.

Checking Out Tools for Churn Modeling and Measurement Operations

Table 11-1 talks about some tools to consider using for churn modeling and measurement operations in businesses large and small. These tools provide robust support for companies looking to implement advanced AI-driven data strategies.

TABLE 11-1 AI Tools for Churn Modeling and Measurement

Tool	Website	What It Is	What It Does
TensorFlow	www.tensorflow.org	An open-source, model-training platform tailored for complex data sets.	Develops custom churn prediction models by using deep learning techniques
PyTorch	http://pytorch.org	An open source machine learning library that supports dynamic computational graphs	Provides iterative model adjustments in churn prediction scenarios
H2O.ai	www.h2o.ai	An automated machine learning platform useful for non-experts	Develops powerful models quickly, such as for churn analysis
Apache Spark MLlib	http://spark.apache.org/mllib	A scalable machine learning library that handles data clusters and large data sets	Use for churn prediction in environments that have massive data volumes
Altair RapidMiner	www.altair.com/altair-rapidminer	A data-science platform that offers an integrated data manipulation environment	Suitable for designing detailed churn models
Alteryx	www.alteryx.com	A model that excels in data blending and advanced analytics	Integrates with data sources to predict churn and customer behavior
Tableau	www.tableau.com	A presentation tool known for its advanced visualization capabilities	Use with churn models for insights through dashboards
Microsoft Azure Machine Learning	http://azure.microsoft.com/products/machine-learning	Cloud-based advanced analytics tools that can help build and deploy machine learning models	Automates churn modeling from data collection to insights, with scalability
IBM Watson Studio	www.ibm.com/products/watson-studio	A suite of tools to collaboratively and easily build, train, and deploy models	Predicts churn and supports learning frameworks and libraries

4

Transforming Brand Content and Campaign Development

Explore AI's role in creative processes and planning.

Work with use cases in conversational interfaces and get better at prompt design.

Use AI for developing new creative assets and enhancing existing assets.

Improve your search engine optimization (SEO) efforts by using AI.

Conduct A/B testing with the help of AI tools.

Put AI to work for localization and translation of your marketing messages.

Chapter 12

Using AI for Ideation and Planning

U sing artificial intelligence (AI) to help with creativity and *ideation* (coming up with new ideas), in particular, is not a new thought. In 2018, the AI-generated artwork "The Portrait of Edmond de Belamy" sold for $432,500 at Christie's auction house. This price was almost 45 times its pre-auction high estimate. This piece was created by a generative adversarial network (GAN), which trained on a data set of 15,000 portraits spanning six centuries. (See Chapter 8 for a discussion of GANs.)

When you put the thought of creativity into the context of your business, ideation serves as a foundational exercise for the development of successful marketing strategies, content, and campaigns. Ideation isn't just about tossing around ideas; it also involves the art of exploring your customer base, the quest to uncover possibilities for enhancing market success, and the identification of potential paths forward. And ideation doesn't happen in a vacuum. Customer research, business objectives, competitor dynamics, product plans, and previous marketing results all serve as the ingredients for the ideation process.

On the flip side, your marketing planning takes the diverse ideas developed through the ideation process and meticulously orchestrates them into actionable steps and strategies that sketch out a road map for achieving desired outcomes.

These outcomes can take the form of an annual marketing plan, a campaign brief, a creative concept, or even a media plan.

The emergence of generative AI ushers in a new era of possibilities and efficiencies in how businesses can ideate, conceptualize, strategize, and develop marketing (and even new product) innovations. In this chapter, I discuss how you can use AI and, specifically, generative AI to fuel the ideation processes.

Engaging AI to Ideate on Behalf of Human Beings

Until recently, the notion that AI can match human ideation seemed fantastical. Conventional wisdom dictates that AI tools aren't sophisticated enough to generate ideas, develop names for products, identify solutions for unmet needs, or unpack creative insights.

To test this hypothesis, two University of Pennsylvania Wharton School of Business professors ran a controlled experiment to understand how an AI performed on an unstructured assignment relative to the professors' MBA students. This study was highlighted in a *Wall Street Journal* article "M.B.A. Students vs. AI: Who Comes Up With More Innovative Ideas?" from September 9, 2023. See the article at www.wsj.com/tech/ai/mba-students-vs-chatgpt-innovation-679edf3b and the sidebar "ChatGPT versus Wharton MBA students," in this chapter, for details of this study.

This pivotal study from the fall of 2023 has altered the perception of AI's deficiencies. The study specifically highlights the capabilities of generative AI — with ChatGPT 4.0 as the prime example — and demonstrates that AI can ideate with a sophistication akin to that of humans.

REMEMBER

Please be aware that this level of ideation typically requires that human beings engineer precise prompting for the AI and provide domain-specific context to the large language model (LLM) involved (unless the model already possesses the relevant information). Nonetheless, the results of specific ideation studies have shown AI-generated ideas to be viable and on par with (if not better than) human-generated ones.

CHATGPT VERSUS WHARTON MBA STUDENTS

Professors Christian Tardiest and Karl Ulrich gave 200 randomly selected MBA students from the University of Pennsylvania Wharton School of Business the task of generating an idea for a new product or service appealing to college students that a company could make available to those students for $50 or less. The professors gave the same assignment to ChatGPT-4, asking it to develop 100 ideas. To further the hypothesis, the professors asked ChatGPT-4 to develop an additional 100 ideas after some coaching, which involved providing ChatGPT-4 with a sample of successful ideas from past courses. After that exercise, they now had 400 ideas — 200 from MBA students and 200 from ChatGPT-4.

To assess the strength of the idea generation, the professors looked at the efficiency with which the ideas were generated per unit of time, the average quality of the ideas, and the number of truly exceptional ideas. Not surprisingly, ChatGPT-4 produced ideas very quickly — spitting out 200 ideas in about an hour (with some human supervision). The human-generated ideas took longer to develop. The study employed an online purchase-intent survey directed toward the targeted customer base to assess the quality of the ideas by asking the following question:

> "How likely would you be to purchase based on this concept if it were available to you?"

The possible responses ranged from *Definitely Wouldn't Purchase* to *Definitely Would Purchase.*

The professors got some very interesting results in the following average purchase probabilities:

- **Human-generated idea:** 40 percent
- **Uncoached ChatGPT-4 idea:** 47 percent
- **Coached ChatGPT-4 idea:** 49 percent

These results show that not only was ChatGPT-4 much faster in generating ideas but also that the overall quality of the ideas was stronger.

But the study offered more results than just the purchase probability information. To determine whether students or AI produced exceptional ideas (after all, a business typically needs only one exceptional idea, rather than dozens of above-average ones),

(continued)

(continued)

the study reviewed the top 10 percent of the ideas in each pool. Of these 40 ideas, a whopping 35 were created by ChatGPT-4, with 20 from the pre-trained ChatGPT-4 set and 15 from the untrained version of ChatGPT-4. ChatGPT-4 clearly came out on top in these results, as well, demonstrating that generative AI not only can perform basic copywriting tasks, but also provide higher-order critical thinking and ideation.

The Wharton study, which included both MBA students and an AI tool, generated 400 product ideas (200 from students and 200 from ChatGPT-4). After market testing for quality of all ideas, the average probability of purchase for human-generated ideas was 40 percent, whereas the average probability of purchase for the AI-generated ideas was 47 to 49 percent. The study also accounted for speed of idea generation to note efficiency. (Unsurprisingly, ChatGPT-4 generated its ideas much faster than the students generated theirs.) Further review of the top 10 percent of ideas (40 ideas) revealed that AI generated 35 of those ideas.

This groundbreaking study highlighted the quality, quantity, and efficiency of AI-generated ideas, and provided these important takeaways:

>> **Generative AI can be an effective idea-generation tool.** Arguably, no piece of technology in the history of humankind has been able to achieve the kind of results demonstrated in the Wharton study. Using AI to generate ideas marks a distinct departure from the past uses of technology, which typically centered around knowledge management, automation, and calculations.

>> **The role of human beings may shift in a world where AI generates ideas.** Rather than only human beings serving as idea generators, our roles may now shift to becoming the prompters and evaluators of good ideas. The mechanism used for selecting ideas becomes even more important, and a mix of AI and humans (who have good taste) can best determine what ideas are most applicable in a specific business context.

>> **The more human beings guide the AI, the better the AI gets as an idea generator.** Think of the AI like a copilot who can generate ideas with strong human inputs, rather than like an idea generator that competes with human beings to come up with the best ideas.

>> **You need human-machine collaboration to deliver better products and services in the future.** The authors of the Wharton study pointed out this fact in their study described in this section. Human-AI collaboration at every stage of the idea-generation process can allow for stronger ideas than humans developing them alone.

If you still feel skeptical about the use of generative AI in ideation and consider the described Wharton study a theoretical exercise, take a look at these real-world examples:

>> **Mattel harnessed AI to drive product development ideas for its Hot Wheels brand.** The company used generative AI to create four times as many product concept images as it normally would in the same amount of time. As a study from McKinsey & Company (a management consulting company) titled, "How generative AI can boost consumer marketing" pointed out, this large number of concept images inspired new features and designs for products. You can find the study at www.mckinsey.com/capabilities/growth-marketing-and-sales/our-insights/how-generative-ai-can-boost-consumer-marketing.

>> **Coca-Cola released a limited-edition soda flavor called Y3000, which was co-created with AI.** Coca-Cola used generative AI to analyze consumer flavor preferences so that it could design what turned out to be a raspberry slushy-like beverage that contained different artificial sweeteners. The company also used AI to create futuristic artwork for the packaging. (The specific tool used to create the artwork was Stable Diffusion, from Stability AI [www.stability.ai].)

>> **Airbus applied AI-powered generative design and optimization to the A320neo aircraft.** By using generative design technology, Airbus optimized the A320neo's wingtip design, cutting the aircraft's fuel consumption by 3.5 percent, thereby setting a prime example of AI application in product design.

>> **Adidas harnessed AI to design its Futurecraft 4D shoe.** The AI-influenced product design enhanced the shoe's sole comfort by including an internal lattice-like structure born out of the AI guidance. This design offers support and cushioning while maintaining durability and lightness.

Deciding whether AI Hallucinations Are a Feature or a Bug

Inherent in large language models (LLMs; advanced AI systems trained on vast amounts of text data to generate human-like text) are *hallucinations*, the scenarios in which the LLMs generate incorrect, fabricated, or misleading information. This unique and relatively uncommon phenomenon causes the model to confidently present its results as accurate, even though the results may have no basis in reality.

Hallucinations may develop for a number of reasons, including

>> **The vast data sets used to train LLMs** have gaps or inaccuracies, leading to incorrect generalizations.

>> **The LLMs lack personal experience** and may be exposed to data that has limited time frames. In these cases, LLMs don't get the benefit of learning from what happened outside their data set or processing parameters.

>> **Inherent model limitations** related to statistical correlations or complex and ambiguous human-created prompts that can misdirect results.

On the surface, you can view hallucinations as a bug — a negative result to watch out for. I encourage you (and all users of generative AI solutions) to apply common sense tests and verify outputs so that you can determine whether the AI is being factual. But when it comes to ideation, hallucinations have another side. You may view the capacity of the LLM to fabricate information as creative output that opens other possibilities for more novel outcomes.

REMEMBER

By integrating generative AI into the creative process in marketing, you can unlock new types of ideas, while also helping your human teammates confront their own biases. And when you layer in the opportunities driven by AI hallucinations, the potential benefits increase exponentially. So, hallucinations can actually help you with creative marketing.

Bringing in unexpected ideas and concepts

AI hallucinations can lead to unexpected, novel, and completely new ideas that break conventional thinking patterns (you know, break out of that box). These ideas likely happen because the AI engine isn't an entity grounded in real-world experience but, instead, is a text-driven statistical model.

Suppose that your marketing team uses an AI tool such as ChatGPT to brainstorm ideas for a new advertising campaign for a sports drink. Your team members input various prompts related to sports, energy, and refreshment. The AI, experiencing a hallucination, generates a concept about a futuristic sport that doesn't exist.

Instead of discarding this output as irrelevant, the team finds inspiration in the AI's mistake. The team members work together to develop a campaign around this imaginary sport, creating a series of drink ads that depict athletes training for this futuristic game. This kind of idea can capture the audience's imagination, setting the brand apart and highlighting the drink's association with innovation, energy, and forward thinking.

Branching out with non-traditional storytelling

You can harness AI-induced mistakes to create a new dimension for the brand's narrative by creating new stories that resonate with audiences in unexpected ways. This storytelling is particularly valuable in social media marketing because it captures attention, sparks engagement, and fosters a sense of authenticity and spontaneity.

Imagine that a travel agency uses AI to generate marketing content for promoting vacation packages. The AI, experiencing a hallucination, generates a description of a fictional, exotic destination that has unique cultural attributes and natural wonders that don't actually exist. Instead of dismissing this generation as an error, the marketing team sees an opportunity for an imaginative campaign. They develop a thematic campaign titled *Imagined Destinations*, which invites people to explore these AI-created places through a series of interactive online experiences, including virtual tours, digital art, and creative storytelling that showcase these fantastical destinations.

To increase engagement, the campaign includes an interactive element through which customers can submit their own ideas for imagined destinations, which the AI then expands upon. This user-generated content not only fosters community engagement, but also provides insights into what types of vacations and destinations appeal to their clientele.

The campaign garners widespread attention for its creativity and use of technology, enhancing the travel agency's reputation for innovation. It also serves as a fun, engaging way for potential customers to dream about travel, keeping the agency top-of-mind when those could-be clients get ready to book real trips.

Facilitating testing and experimentation

You can put AI hallucination ideas into market research and test them in a similar fashion to the new ideas developed by the Wharton School study mentioned in the section "Engaging AI to Ideate on Behalf of Human Beings," earlier in this chapter. Even if these ideas don't lead to successful products, the exercise can show you what not to do or may encourage new ways of thinking for the marketing teams involved.

Suppose that a food company uses an AI model to explore new flavor ideas for a line of snacks. During a brainstorming session, the AI, because of a hallucination, suggests a bizarre and seemingly unpalatable flavor combination — something that no human being would consider.

Intrigued by the unusual suggestion, the product development team decides to experiment with this idea. They refine the concept and create a small batch of a snack that has this unique flavor. The snack turns out to be surprisingly appealing in taste tests. The flavor, positioned as a limited edition, generates buzz because of its novelty and the story of its AI-inspired origin. The snack gains attention, particularly among adventurous consumers and food enthusiasts, driving sales and enhancing the brand's image as innovative and daring.

Staying the course with generative AI

Over time, I believe that LLMs can deliver more accurate results with fewer hallucinations. Sam Altman, the CEO of OpenAI, said as much when discussing the future of ChatGPT. He fully expects generative AI to become more predictable, accurate, and — in his own words — "boring" over time. Altman's projections may be right, but the very nature of how generative AI works can allow for forced hallucinations or pushing the boundaries of conventional thinking via specifically chosen input data and carefully crafted prompts.

TIP

You may, in general, view AI hallucinations as errors that you need to correct, but you can leverage them as a source of creative inspiration that can lead to unique and innovative marketing outcomes. When you explore specific ways to drive ideation and planning by using generative AI, keep in mind that the prompts you write to direct your AI models determine how imaginative the AI can be on your behalf.

Following Practical Steps for Idea Generation with AI

A common and useful scenario for using generative AI involves idea generation during a creative brainstorming process. You may instigate the brainstorming session to identify a new product, a customer value proposition, a marketing campaign, or even a broader go-to-market strategy. The extent of ideas that you can generate is limited only by the prompts you articulate and the existing data or examples that you feed into the AI engine. In the following sections, I explain how you can use AI as a copilot when you run a combined human and AI ideation exercise.

Starting with the right prompts

A good starting point for combining human creativity with AI capabilities is to establish a prompt for both parties. Take, for example, a scenario where you want to generate ten advertising concepts for an Apple ad promoting the latest iPhone during the Super Bowl. You can pose this challenge to both the human participants in the room and a generative AI engine such as ChatGPT. Here's what can happen:

>> **The human team:** Draws on their personal experiences and knowledge about Apple and its iPhones to brainstorm ideas during a time frame that you specify. Human understanding — informed by experiences, a sense of taste, and familiarity with what resonates with consumers (especially in the context of Super Bowl ads) — goes into the ideas that the team creates.

>> **ChatGPT:** Generates ten diverse ideas in just a few seconds; some of the ideas, of course, are more compelling than others. *Note:* The richer the information that you provide to the AI, the more robust the ideas it generates. If you include Apple's brand strategy, recent research on the most desired iPhone features, and scripts from Apple's past successful ads, you can significantly enhance the AI's ideas.

REMEMBER

You gather AI results from ChatGPT not to replace human creativity; those results may not match human capabilities. Instead, the real value emerges when the humans involved in the brainstorming session review the AI-generated ideas and select their top three or four favorites from both lists. This shortlist then forms the basis for crafting new, refined prompts, which you can use in subsequent iterations with ChatGPT to further develop and refine the chosen concepts.

This straightforward example illustrates a principle that you can apply to various types of idea-generating exercises. The approach works well, whether you want to focus your efforts on advertising, product feature definition, or strategic planning.

Stepping through an AI-for-ideation exercise

With information from the preceding section in mind, follow these steps when you use generative AI in an idea-generating exercise:

1. **Define the objectives of your ideation session.**

   Clearly define what you want to achieve by using AI-generated ideas. You may be after product innovation, marketing strategies, problem-solving for existing initiatives, or new creative marketing campaigns. As you set the objectives, also establish the boundaries and criteria for the ideas that you want, including

- *Feasibility:* How much time and effort can you spend on a resulting project?

- *Target audience:* Are you going after existing customers or branching out to a new target audience?

- *Budget constraints:* Do you have unlimited funds, or have they been established by previous projects?

Setting objectives and boundaries is always a good business practice, but it's all the more important in the context of AI because you may have to face an even more divergent set of ideas than you do without AI input.

2. **Select the right AI tool(s) for your stated objectives.**

Choose an appropriate AI model based on what you want to accomplish with your ideas. Depending on your needs, choose an AI model that specializes in idea generation in the format that fits your goals, such as

- ChatGPT (http://chat.openai.com) for text-based ideas

- DALL-E (http://openai.com/dall-e) for visual concepts

- Stable Diffusion (http://stability.ai/stablediffusion) and Runway (www.runwayml.com) for multi-modal idea generation

In some cases, you may want to use a combination of tools — starting with ChatGPT, and then taking the results into an image- or video-based tool after that. Doing this allows you to use each tool for what it is best at.

3. **Prepare and input data for your ideation session.**

Compile data that's relevant to your objective. Examples include market trends, consumer behavior data, previous campaign results, competitor dynamics, and previous product launches. Provide the AI with as much context as possible to guide its idea generation process. As I note in the preceding section, the more quality data that you input, the better the potential outcomes.

When selecting data for your idea-generating exercise, be careful about sharing sensitive information because it can lead to privacy breaches, data misuse, and potential legal ramifications.

4. **Engage your AI tool to generate ideas.**

Run your initial queries or prompts through the AI tool to start generating ideas. To stress test how strong your prompts are, have your human creative team respond to the same prompts. Doing so can quickly tell you whether you need to make the queries more specific because it will reveal gaps in clarity and precision. Adjusting the queries for the gaps you reveal can help ensure that the AI outputs are relevant and useful.

TIP

When you run your prompts through your AI tool, specifically encourage the AI to generate a plethora of ideas based on different assumptions. Consider the advice about prompt engineering that you can find in Chapter 13 and encourage the AI to respond in the role of a creative director, a product designer, or a futurist, for example.

5. **Refine prompts based on resulting ideas, and then try again.**

   Analyze the ideas generated by the AI for relevance, innovation, creativity, and feasibility. Use feedback loops in which you refine your queries based on initial outputs to guide the AI toward solutions aligned with your intent. And as you do this, consider highlighting the best ideas and asking the AI to generate more like those ideas. The more guidance you give the AI, the better the subsequent outputs are.

6. **Evaluate and select viable ideas.**

   Use your predefined criteria (from Step 1) to evaluate and shortlist the most promising ideas. As you create this list, consider incorporating feedback not just from your creative team, but also from stakeholders in other departments or maybe even consumer groups. As the Wharton professors show in their research (see the sidebar "ChatGPT versus Wharton MBA students," in this chapter), online purchase-intent surveys can provide you with a powerful customer-centric tool for evaluating ideas.

7. **Develop and test your generated ideas.**

   For product ideas, you can develop prototypes. For concepts such as marketing strategies, you can create testable models or campaigns, or take the ideas into your formal campaign briefing or creative development process. In many cases, you can use other AI tools to translate text-based ideas into conceptual drawings, prototypes, or video animations that you can then test through focus groups, pilot runs, or online surveys.

Deciding on AI Ideation Tools to Use

Recently, many AI ideation tools have cropped up. Some of these tools are stand-alone solutions, such as Adobe Firefly (https://firefly.adobe.com/) and Google's AutoDraw (www.autodraw.com); other tools are integrated into broader software suites.

For example, TikTok's Creative Assistant — which launched in September 2023 — is particularly notable. Situated in TikTok's Creative Center (http://ads.tiktok.com/business/creativecenter), this AI-driven virtual assistant offers advertisers a dynamic toolbox for content creation. By tapping into

TikTok-specific creative insights, the Creative Assistant offers relevant suggestions and guidance that facilitate the crafting of compelling and effective content for TikTok campaigns.

Creative Assistant acts as a virtual collaborator, helping you in various facets of content creation, such as

>> Guiding newcomers through best practices on the TikTok platform

>> Displaying and analyzing top-performing ads to aid in creative research

>> Brainstorming ideas and refining scripts collaboratively, especially when you're struggling to develop new ideas

REMEMBER

The Creative Assistant tool augments human creativity, symbolizing the fusion of human ingenuity with AI capabilities. It empowers creators to continually enhance their presence on TikTok through perpetual ideation sessions. But although the Creative Assistant offers suggestions and collaborates in the creation journey, the creator retains absolute control over the materials, having the liberty to use, edit, discard, or redo them, as desired.

You have literally hundreds of AI tools to consider — many of which use ChatGPT as a foundation — and Table 12-1 highlights some notable ones. Although some of the tools in this table are more oriented toward content creation rather than idea generation, they can still play the role of idea generators, too.

TABLE 12-1   **AI Tools for Idea Generation**

Tool	Website	What It Is	What It Does
ContextMinds	www.contextminds.com	A tool that assists in research and idea generation, combining mind-mapping functionality with AI-driven content suggestions	Organizes thoughts and makes connections through relevant articles, papers, and videos related to their topics of interest
HyperWrite	www.hyperwriteai.com	A writing assistant that helps users develop ideas and refine original text	Generates various writing formats such as e-mails or marketing copy
Jasper	www.jasper.ai	A tool that assists in generating written content for various purposes	Crafts compelling narratives and ideas for marketing copy, blog posts, and so on
Pictory	www.pictory.ai	A tool for ideation in video marketing, transforming existing content into engaging, shareable video formats	Creates short videos from long-form content such as webinars or blog posts.

Tool	Website	What It Is	What It Does
Riffusion	www.riffusion.com	A tool that synthesizes music based on AI-generated sound patterns	Experiments with unique soundscapes and auditory branding elements
Runway	www.runwayml.com	A platform for experimenting with machine learning (ML) models in real time	Offers ideation in the realms of design, art, and multimedia, to explore new visual concepts and effects
Stable Diffusion	www.stability.ai	A text-to-image model that allows users to create visual images from textual descriptions	Helps artists, designers, and marketers to rapidly generate diverse and creative visual concepts
Synthesia	www.synthesia.io	A video creation platform that generates high-quality synthetic media and personalized video content	Creates realistic digital avatars and voiceovers, streamlining the video production process
Wondershare EdrawMind	http://edrawmind.wondershare.com	A tool that facilitates organized visual representation of ideas while also helping to generate ideas	Helps create mind maps, flowcharts, and organizational charts to enhance collaborative thinking and planning
Writer	www.writer.com	A writing assistant for businesses that helps create clear, consistent, and brand-aligned content	Assists with grammar, style, and tone to ensure high-quality writing across all company communications

Chapter **13**

Perfecting Prompts for Conversational Interfaces

On November 30th, 2022, OpenAI — an artificial intelligence (AI) research laboratory — launched a beta version of the AI conversational interface named ChatGPT. *ChatGPT* represented a new paradigm for humans interacting with technology, a paradigm anchored in the ability to communicate with a computer by using everyday language (also known as *natural language processing,* NLP) to get detailed, specific responses in real time. ChatGPT quickly became the fastest growing application in history (at the time) with 100 million active users signed up by January 2023.

ChatGPT appeared to have a brain of its own that went beyond chatting and answering simple questions. For example, it could edit e-mails, create travel itineraries, recommend dinner menus, and help users solve math problems, to name just a few tasks. What made ChatGPT even more extraordinary and human-like was the fact that it could remember what a user said earlier in a conversation, which allowed the user to ask follow-up questions to the original query.

ChatGPT expands on the AI conversational interfaces that came before. These old-timers take the form of chatbots on websites, voice assistants such as Alexa and Siri, and virtual assistants such as Google's Virtual Assistant that can help you complete tasks. As a generative AI agent, ChatGPT depends on extraordinarily large data sets and large language models (LLMs; see Chapter 9 for more about using them) to understand context, generate contextually appropriate responses, and properly interpret intent, nuance, and relevance.

Generative AI and conversational interfaces can help streamline marketing efforts because they use their massive data and language modeling resources to assist marketers with practically every major marketing activity. In this chapter, you can find out how you can use generative AI in your marketing research and campaign work, how to create and refine AI prompts that provide constructive interaction with your AI, and what kind of tools you can use to draft your prompts. Arguably, this chapter may help you communicate better with other people, as well as with your AI chatbot!

Reviewing Use Cases for Conversational Interfaces

Regardless of the industry that you work in or your specific job role, this section goes over some *use cases* (specific scenarios in which a user interacts with a piece of technology to achieve a business goal) for conversational interfaces that may help you do your job more smartly and efficiently. This (by no means exhaustive) list may spark your own ideas for how to harness conversational interfaces and apply strong prompt design to make your work life (and maybe your personal life, too) more efficient:

>> **Brainstorming:** Whether you need to write a new tagline for your brand, develop new campaign ideas, or adjust advertising copy, AI can help you brainstorm alternatives. For example, you can prompt your AI by providing your current company tagline and a short criterion (such as "must have four words"), and your AI can generate ten alternative taglines for you in a matter of seconds.

>> **Coding:** AI tools can write example code if you provide detailed instructions about what result you're looking for and the language that you want the tool to use. You can also provide code libraries, dependencies, filenames, and other details. Similarly, you can also paste in existing code and ask the tool to debug that code. In fact, recent tools — such as Devin, from Cognition.ai (www.cognition.ai/blog/introducing-devin) — can now code complete applications for you.

>> **Extracting:** AI tools can help you extract specific pieces of information from a larger body of text — for example, when you're reading a legal contract or need to find a data point in a larger data set. AI can help you extract text or numeric-based data and also transform it into a new format.

>> **Reformatting:** AI tools can help you format text into a more structured layout, including headlines, sections, and tables. Keep in mind, how well it can reformat your text heavily depends on the prompts that you give the tool. *Prompt chaining* (which I cover in the section "Refining and Iterating Strong Prompts," later in this chapter) can really help you provide more specific instructions when you want AI to reformat your text.

>> **Summarizing:** One of the most popular use cases for conversational interfaces is harnessing its intelligence to summarize. You can paste articles, research reports, transcripts, vendor proposals, and other long text formats into ChatGPT or any of the other AI tools, and then ask the AI interface to summarize the content for you.

REMEMBER

By using aspects of prompt creation (the role, task, voice and tone, and format, all of which I cover in the following section), you can specify exactly how you want the content summarized.

>> **Synthesizing:** You can use AI to synthesize several pieces of different texts together to create a new understanding or a fresh perspective of the information in those texts. Keep in mind that you need to use an AI tool (see the section "Using Prompt Design Apps," later in the chapter) that either enables you to upload multiple pieces of text or paste multiple pieces of content into the tool itself.

>> **Writing:** Users often ask AI to write headlines, ad copy, video scripts, blog posts, e-mails, and taglines. See the section "Identifying the AI's task," later in the chapter. You can use the prompt design recommendations in this and other sections to provide specific directions to the AI tool when you use the AI as a writing aid.

GENERATIVE AI AND CONVERSATIONAL INTERFACES

So how does ChatGPT accomplish its seemingly human-like conversational capability? It uses natural language processing (NLP) and machine learning (ML) algorithms to analyze the text input and generates responses based on its large language model (I tell you about large language models in Chapters 5 and 6). And so, ChatGPT can carry on a conversation in a constructive, synchronous, and informative way, dissimilar to any

(continued)

(continued)

chatbot that came before it. In the months after its launch, ChatGPT, along with a few important competitors, embodied the first conversational interface that can adapt to our human communication styles, versus requiring us to learn a specific syntax that the technology could then understand.

Four of the most popular generative AI tools are

- **ChatGPT:** Arguably the poster child of generative AI agents, ChatGPT enables users to have text-based conversations in everyday language. With the launch of GPT-4.0 in 2023, it supports uploading and analyzing spreadsheets and other document formats, which enables it to generate more accurate and context-aware responses. Building on the foundation of GPT-4, ChatGPT Omni (launched in mid-2024) features enhanced multi-modal capabilities, which allow it to process and generate text, images, and other data types seamlessly. This functionality enables ChatGPT Omni to deliver more comprehensive and contextually enriched responses that make the tool exceptionally versatile for a wide range of applications — from detailed text analysis and creative writing to intricate visual descriptions.

- **Gemini:** Previously known as Bard, Google's direct competitor to ChatGPT, Gemini was launched on May 10th, 2023, in 180 countries. Like ChatGPT, it facilitates text-based conversations in everyday language and supports *multi-modal reasoning*, which allows it to process text, images, and audio. Gemini excels in quick information searches, making it a strong research tool. Recent updates include the Gemini 1.5 model, featuring a context window of up to 2 million tokens, enhanced performance in code generation, logical reasoning, and support for file uploads, including spreadsheets and documents, for more contextually informed responses.

- **DALL-E 3:** Developed by OpenAI, the firm behind ChatGPT, DALL-E 3 is an advanced conversational interface for creating realistic images and art from natural language descriptions. This latest version offers improved image quality and coherence, better understanding of complex prompts, and enhanced capabilities for generating intricate and diverse images. DALL-E 3 allows users to refine and adjust images through follow-up prompts in natural language, enabling precise modifications and creative flexibility. It also introduces new features such as *inpainting* (which allows users to edit parts of an image by describing changes in natural language) and support for generating images with specific styles and compositions. It is a powerful tool for both creative and professional applications.

- **Midjourney:** A direct competitor to DALL-E 3, Midjourney also uses natural language text input to create images in response. It offers users the ability to save images at a higher resolution, known as *upscaling*, which provides clearer and more detailed visuals. Although DALL-E 3 excels at editing existing images and fusing them together seamlessly, Midjourney is known for its artistic style and unique image generation capabilities. Midjourney's strength lies in its ability to produce visually stunning and imaginative artworks; it is often favored by artists and designers for its distinct aesthetic qualities.

Writing Strong Prompts to Guide AI Responses

Human beings communicate in a variety of ways and not always as clearly and crisply as they should. ChatGPT may not always understand what you're trying to say (just like human beings sometimes) and may respond with incomplete or completely wrong answers as a result. To take full advantage of all the features that an artificial intelligence (AI) conversational interface (such as ChatGPT) offers, you need to know how to have a conversation with it so that you get accurate and informative answers as quickly as possible without having to do too many follow-up queries. Think of *prompt design* (how you pose the questions that you ask in the conversation with AI) as both an art and a science.

You may have heard the maxim that artificial intelligence is only as good as what you input — which is very true in the context of conversational AI. To get the most out of AI, you need to craft your question (or your *prompt*, to use the parlance of AI) thoughtfully. Focus on syntax elements — such as the tone, format, role, and even type of task — while you come up with questions to ask the AI. To help you understand these aspects of a prompt, the following sections go through each, offering some do's and don'ts, as well as some examples to help you along the way.

Setting the voice and tone

The first choice you have when writing an AI prompt involves deciding what *voice* (such as formal or informal) and *tone* (such as friendly or serious) to use. The tone you use guides the AI in how it responds to you and with what level of detail, so choose a voice and tone based on the results you need. For example, if you need detailed technical information for a research project, you may choose a formal voice and serious tone. Alternatively, if you're seeking a creative idea for a story, an informal voice and friendly tone may be more appropriate.

If you ask the AI a question pertaining to a work situation, you may want to be more formal so that you get a more serious and specific response back. On the other hand, if you're looking to simply get an answer to a general knowledge question, speaking more conversationally may be good enough. The following mini-table list seven types of voices and tones that you can use when writing an AI prompt.

The voice and tone	How You Use It
Conversational	Make the AI sound like it's having a relaxed chat with you.
Lighthearted	When you don't mind the AI injecting humor into the interaction.
Persuasive	The AI can help you make a compelling argument about a specific topic.
Descriptive	The AI adds detail to your own specific questions.
Spartan	The AI responds both specifically and briefly.
Formal	The AI responds in a serious and professional manner.
Firm	The AI responds with confidence.

Here are two prompt examples that explicitly define the voice and tone that you want the AI to use:

>> **Conversational:** Write an e-mail to Tim and ask him whether he can help you design the new product packaging. Use a conversational voice and tone for the e-mail. You're talking to a friend, so use natural language and phrasing.

>> **Professional:** Write ten sentences on the importance of advertising the new product. Use a professional voice and tone. Use marketing industry–specific language and terminology, provide detailed and accurate information, and support your argument with statistics, research, and expert opinions.

Defining a role

The role you ask the AI to play when responding to your query can have a material effect not only on how the AI answers, but also on what information the AI uses to answer the question. By using roles, you can provide the AI with more direction while it determines the best way to answer the questions that you ask it.

TIP

Consider your own role and context when having a conversation with the AI. Unlike in the real world — where another person may immediately know whether you're speaking as a parent, a teacher, an employee, or a coach — you need to explicitly give this information to the AI so that it has the right context and knows how best to respond to you. You can't assume the AI knows who you are! (But it can often make inferences about relationships depending on the content of your prompt.)

Here are some examples of roles that can dramatically alter the response that you get from the AI. To name a role in a prompt, you can say, "Act as a marketer." Or maybe you say something like, "Act as a brand strategist" — or a designer, digital marketing analyst, writer, investigator, researcher, or accountant, for example. With each role you assign, you get a slightly different response to your query.

So in the same way that you think about the tone in which you're asking the question (see the preceding section), determine whether you want to have the conversation with the AI in a specific role. If you do, then mention that role explicitly in your AI prompt.

Here are two prompt examples in which the prompt explicitly defines the role for the AI:

>> **Brand strategist:** Write a blog post explaining the rationale for the new product's name in the role of a brand strategist who works at the company.

>> **Digital marketing analyst:** Write an e-mail requesting additional budget to spend on Facebook advertising in the role of a digital marketing analyst who's promoting the new product.

Identifying the AI's task

You may consider that identifying the task is the most important piece of writing in the AI prompt. When you identify the task, you ask the conversational AI what specifically you want it to accomplish. Although, on the surface, you may think about AI interactions through the lens of answering questions that you may have, AI can actually accomplish much more for you. In fact, through the performance of tasks, you can truly see the immense power of AI conversational interfaces and the magic that ChatGPT has brought into the world.

Some major tasks that AI can handle for you include creating

>> An essay, article, story, summary, or outline

>> Ad copy, a headline, or a product description

>> A blog or social media post

>> A video script

>> SEO keywords

You can even ask the AI to write an entire book outline for you on a particular subject (and yes, as an experiment, I did just that for this book).

REMEMBER

The more explicitly you define the task for the AI, the better a response you get. Keep in mind that the AI can't do everything — but it may tell you if it can't accomplish a specific task. However, if you define the task at hand very specifically, you have the greatest likelihood of the AI helping you in the way you want.

In these two prompt examples, the prompt explicitly defines the task for the AI:

» **Write a product description** for the new product that the business can sell on the website.

» **Write an outline of a marketing campaign** to promote the new product that the business plans to launch soon.

Specifying the format

Chat interfaces — such as ChatGPT, Bard, Perplexity AI, and others — offer several different formats in which you can require the response. Some of these formats include

» Graphs

» HTML

» PDF

» Plain text

» Presentation slides

» Rich text

» Spreadsheets

» Word cloud

» XML

Within text, you can also specify whether you want a concise response, a bullet list, a response in a table format, or a detailed response.

REMEMBER

Not every AI interface tool supports every file format, and not every tool can format the response to your specifications. Some AI interface tools require you to sign up for a premium service to get access to the more sophisticated output formats. Others may not support the more advanced formats at all. But whatever AI tool you use, it tells you if it can't support a specific format that you request.

Here are two prompt examples that explicitly define the format for the AI:

» **Create a PDF** of all the information pertaining to the new product launch.

» **Create a spreadsheet** showing how much money the business needs to spend on the product launch.

Good and Bad Marketing Prompt Design Examples

The following list provides examples of good prompt design (the aspects of which you can read about in the section "Writing Strong Prompts to Guide AI Responses," earlier in this chapter). You can leverage these designs in your job. Keep in mind that the more specific information you can give the AI, the better a response you get back:

>> **Good prompt design #1:** Play the role of a marketer and help us understand how we can ensure a cohesive brand message across different marketing channels for our new product launch. Please provide a concise answer in text format.

>> **Good prompt design #2:** Play the role of an advertising agency executive and discuss the role of influencer marketing within an integrated marketing communication plan for a luxury brand. Please explain your answer in text format, using statistics and research, as appropriate.

>> **Good prompt design #3:** Play the role of a research analyst and describe advanced segmentation techniques that leverage machine learning to better understand high-value customer segments. Please explain your answer in text format, including tables.

>> **Good prompt design #4:** Play the role of a marketing analytics professional and share the best key performance indicators (KPIs) to assess the long-term health and loyalty of our customer base. Please list the KPIs.

Each of the good examples in the preceding list include the role, voice and tone, task, and format syntax elements, as outlined in Table 13-1.

TABLE 13-1 ## Elements of Good Prompt Designs

Prompt	Role	Voice and Tone	Task	Format
1	Marketer	Persuasive	Ensure a cohesive brand message	Text
2	Advertising agency executive	Descriptive	Discuss the role of influencer marketing within an integrated marketing communication plan for a luxury brand	Text
3	Research analyst	Descriptive	Describe advanced segmentation techniques	Text and table
4	Marketing analytics professional	Spartan	Assess long-term health and loyalty of the customer base	Spreadsheet

And Table 13-2 shows you examples of what not to do when writing prompts. They're bad prompts that won't get you useful results.

TABLE 13-2   **Bad Marketing Prompt Designs**

Bad Prompt	What's Wrong	How to Improve It
Components to include for a global marketing strategy.	No role, context, or format.	Include the right syntax and provide either context or specifics around the industry, the company, or the problem at hand.
How much better are male CEOs than female ones?	Huge bias built into the prompt itself.	The AI won't question the underlying assumption itself, so make the question more objective.
What is good marketing?	Too broad a question to get a meaningful response.	Ask a more specific question. Or follow up this mega prompt with more specific prompts.
Write a Google ad for my business.	Too generic.	Include product details, value proposition, and target-market specifics.

Refining and Iterating Strong Prompts

When it comes to refining your prompts and having a multi-part conversation with the AI, keep the strategies outlined in Table 13-3 in mind.

TABLE 13-3   **How to Refine Prompts**

Strategy	What It Does
Start with a clear purpose.	Know what you want to accomplish with your conversation. Use that purpose to start the conversation by creating prompts that quickly drive the AI toward a specific, relevant, and informative conversation.
Encourage more focus.	After the AI returns its first response, probe further with follow-up prompts that push the AI to provide more detail, encouraging specific directions that you consider important while also asking it to discard less relevant directions.
Don't hesitate to push the AI.	The AI may return a rudimentary response that doesn't help you with your task at hand (the clear purpose you defined). In those instances, ask the AI for examples or deeper explanations. Follow-up prompts help focus the AI.
Stay sensitive to the tone, role, and task language.	When you engage in a meaningful conversation with the AI, try to be as consistent as you can in the tone, role, and task that you use when communicating with the AI. You want to avoid confusion and enable the AI to focus on the substance of the conversation. The more you switch between different roles, tasks, and tones in the way you construct your prompts, the more confusing the conversation becomes for the AI.

Strategy	What It Does
Monitor the conversation carefully.	While the conversation progresses, monitor it carefully for inaccuracies, tangents, and misunderstandings. Continue to focus the AI by reminding it of the conversation's purpose, and use subsequent prompts to drive the AI toward greater specificity and clarity.
Use earlier responses to guide future prompts.	Because the AI determines your needs through the course of the conversation, use earlier AI responses to your prompts — for example, by noting the AI's level of detail and clarity — to guide the future prompts that you use.
Explore prompt chaining.	If you can't seem to get the types of responses that you want with your prompts, consider interacting with the AI by using prompt chaining. *Prompt chaining* refers to breaking down the task of into smaller steps and asking the AI-specific, less-inclusive, prompts one step at a time.
Consider using a mega prompt.	Sometimes, starting with a *mega prompt* — the broadest possible question on the topic — and then drilling down, prompt by prompt, into specific branches of the mega prompt can get you the most specific and actionable responses. Keep mega prompts in mind as an alternative approach to prompt chaining.

REMEMBER

Don't get discouraged if the AI doesn't respond with the exact answer that you want immediately. Refining and iterating on the prompts and having a multi-part conversation with the AI gets you stronger answers. The AI can refer to earlier parts of the conversation and even carries short-term memory (depending on the AI tool, it may be up to 75,000 words or more), which makes it even more informed and responsive the more you converse with it.

Fighting AI Bias in Prompt Writing

As I discuss in Chapter 12, you definitely run the risk of encountering *AI hallucination* (where the AI presents made-up facts in a very authoritative fashion) when you rely solely on AI-generated content without verification. But a more fundamental risk is the risk of bias. In a similar fashion to how human beings have biases based on their own individual experiences, so too, do AI tools. These biases can arise from the data used to train them, which may reflect societal biases and inequalities.

Bias in AI develops primarily through two facets:

>> **The data that you feed into the AI model:** Make sure that the data you feed into the AI tools better represents a breadth of topics, people, cultures, societies, and so on, so that you can fight bias in the data itself.

>> **The algorithms that the AI uses:** Algorithms can unintentionally amplify the bias in the data unless the developers code those algorithms very carefully. When you're interacting with an AI and having a multi-part conversation, how you structure your initial prompt and your follow-up ones can alleviate some of the risks in AI bias.

Here are seven recommendations that can help you limit AI bias via prompt writing:

>> **Construct balanced prompts.** It may sound obvious, but if you ask biased questions, you probably get biased responses. So when you're crafting your prompts, try to identify any bias in how you're framing your questions. That self-awareness (asking yourself how someone different from you may frame the questions) can go a long way in preventing bias in your questions and then subsequently in the AI responses.

>> **Try different prompts.** One of the best ways to fight bias in the real world involves seeking multiple perspectives on a subject. In a similar fashion, you can limit the AI bias by using different prompts to ask the same question, and then comparing the various answers that you get.

>> **Deploy bias detection.** Don't absolve yourself of your own responsibility to detect bias in the answers that you receive from the AI. Question the output if an answer seems to reflect bias or inaccuracies, and use follow-up prompts that challenge the response you receive.

>> **Be wary of over-customization.** Some AI tools allow you to customize so that you get results specifically targeted to your situation and needs. However, over-customization can lead to bias — you may create an AI *echo chamber*, meaning the AI tool only tells you what you'd like to hear versus what you should be hearing.

>> **Limit how you use the AI.** Certain content categories and types of prompts lend themselves to bias built into the responses. Steer away from content categories that may have greater risk of bias. For example, conversations that deal with people, race, religion, ethnicity, and gender carry greater risks of bias in both the prompts that you provide and the responses from the AI.

>> **Provide feedback.** If you spot bias in the AI responses that you receive, provide immediate feedback by telling the AI that the response appears biased. Calling out the AI on the bias forces the AI to make a correction in follow-up responses by being more self-aware of its own responses. Also, you can alert the company that supplies the AI tool if you see repeated instances of bias.

TIP

>> **Share your knowledge with others.** Because tools based on generative AI are still relatively new, everyone is still figuring out how best to use them while the tools themselves mature. Share the way that you combat bias in the AI tools with your coworkers and other people around you. You can help others fight AI bias — and you can get valuable tips in return.

Using Prompt Design Apps

If you have sophisticated queries and/or want to maximize all that conversational interfaces have to offer, consider using prompt design apps to help you draft your prompts. The prompt design apps that I discuss in this section can assist you with drafting your more complex prompts. Keep in mind, some of these prompt design apps also serve as marketplaces where you can see prompts written by others. *Note:* In a few instances, to access the prompts, you may need to pay a small fee.

Here are the prompt design apps that I recommend:

>> **Arvin (www.tryarvin.com):** Arvin offers a variety of prompt generators for many different subjects when you click Prompt Library on the main page. These prompt templates require you to add your own specific context to make them useful. Categories include marketing, social media, writing, research, and design.

>> **Chatx.ai (https://chatx.ai/marketplace/):** A public prompt marketplace and generator that works with the ChatGPT, Midjourney, and DALL-E 2 AI tools. Click the Generator button on the main page to access the prompt generator, which asks you what task you want to accomplish and what role you want the AI to play in that task, and then it spits back prompts. It also includes many text and image examples of prompts and the corresponding AI responses.

>> **Coefficient (www.coefficient.io):** From the main page, under the Resources link, choose GPT Prompt Builder from AI tools. You can enter your own text in boxes or choose from a list the task, topic, style, tone, audience, word count, and format of the prompt that you want to create. Coefficient then returns a prompt example that you can copy into your AI platform.

>> **Gemini Help Center (http://support.google.com/gemini):** The Gemini Help Center includes a section on writing prompts that provides tips and examples (click the "Use Gemini" link in the list on the main page). It gives you a rudimentary starting point, but it can help you with the basics.

>> **OpenAI** (`https://help.openai.com/en/collections/3742473-chatgpt`): On the ChatGPT information page (under All Collections ⇨ ChatGPT), type the term *prompt design* into the search text box and press enter. From this page, you can access a range of resources on prompt design from OpenAI, the maker of ChatGPT itself.

>> **PromptBase** (`www.promptbase.com`): In this mature prompt marketplace, you can search prompts across a range of categories, view some for free, buy others, and sell your own advanced prompts.

>> **PromptPerfect** (`http://promptperfect.jina.ai`): Probably the most unique of the prompt generator tools, PromptPerfect uses a freemium model and optimizes prompts for specific AI services. You first choose the AI tool that you use (ChatGPT, Midjourney, DALL-E 2, and so on), enter your original prompt in the text box, and then have the service provide a more refined prompt that you can use with your AI tool. You can optimize a series of prompts, and PromptPerfect works in multiple languages, including German and Spanish.

>> **PromptStorm** (`http://promptstorm.app`): This Chrome extension includes a library of prewritten prompts specifically designed to work with both ChatGPT and Bard. It also allows you to add your own prompts and customize the ones from its library.

IN THIS CHAPTER

» **Creating a hidden object image with AI**

» **Using AI to come up with brand new visuals**

» **Working with AI tools to improve existing images**

» **Making your creative team even better with AI tools**

Chapter **14**

Developing Creative Assets

An exciting dimension of generative artificial intelligence (AI) is its potential use for the development of creative assets in marketing. Artists, graphic designers, marketing agency leaders, marketers of various levels, and even operational executives increasingly use generative AI text-to-image and image-to-image asset creation to augment their presentations. These efforts enhance marketing campaigns and even create new designs and artwork from scratch.

Many creative leaders may argue (and understandably so) that the creative capabilities of generative AI today are no match for what human beings can do. That may be true for now, but the situation is unlikely to remain the case in the years ahead. In 2023 and 2024 alone, generative AI tools such as Adobe Firefly, Midjourney, and Stable Diffusion advanced immensely in their capabilities; for example, by achieving more realistic image generation and offering a more intuitive user interface. These advancements illustrate generative AI's potential as the technology gets more sophisticated.

But even more than the ever-advancing technological progress, the role of generative AI that I briefly discuss in Chapter 8 becomes more powerful when you pair it with human beings who can turbocharge creativity and drive productivity and efficiency. To explain this pairing further in this chapter, I begin by talking about *Where's Waldo?* to demonstrate both the opportunities and the risks involved in using generative AI to augment your creative process.

Trying Out an AI-Generated Where's Waldo? Illustration

In early 2024, an illustrator who uses the handle @oxFramer on the social media platform X (formerly known as Twitter) created a series of *Where's Waldo?* images to showcase both the opportunities and the challenges that occur when you use generative artificial intelligence (AI) to develop creative assets. This illustrator used the original look-and-find children's books by Martin Handford as inspiration, and then used generative AI tools to create his own variations. For those of you who don't know the series, the book consists of detailed, double-page spread illustrations depicting dozens and dozens of people doing a variety of amusing activities in a given setting. Readers are challenged to find a character named Waldo somewhere in the group.

The illustrator (@oxFramer) showed how anyone can quickly use an AI tool to create similar *Where's Waldo?* illustrations. (Check out his creative process on YouTube at www.youtube.com/watch?v=2nYxeZQmcj0.) To do so, you need to provide your AI tools with a detailed description that encapsulates the essence of a *Where's Waldo?* scene. Follow these steps to define such an illustration by providing input to a tool such as DALL-E 3 or Midjourney:

1. **Describe the background that becomes the setting for your illustration.**

   You can specify a vibrant and detailed background, which can be a beach, a cityscape, an office, a medieval scene, a space station, and so on. The more intricate and crowded the scene, the better.

2. **Identify the characters that you need to appear in the illustration.**

   Mention the need for a large number of diverse characters engaged in various activities. They should be dressed in a wide range of costumes performing numerous actions to create a lively, busy scene.

3. **Describe the Waldo-like character that should appear somewhere in the illustration.**

   Note that you want the character subtly placed within the scene, similar to Waldo in the Handford books. This character should be wearing a red-and-white striped shirt but blend in well with the surroundings.

4. **Detail the color and style of the illustration.**

   Indicate the colorfulness and whimsical style that mimics the original *Where's Waldo?* illustrations.

For the AI to successfully generate an image close to your vision, you need to make your description precise and detailed. See the prompt that I created by following the preceding steps to urge DALL-E to generate such an image:

> A vibrant, densely populated beach scene filled with numerous characters engaging in various activities: playing volleyball, sunbathing, building sandcastles, swimming, and so on. The characters are dressed in colorful and diverse beach attire. Include a character resembling Waldo, wearing a red and white striped shirt, blue pants, and a beanie, subtly blended into the scene. The style should be whimsical and cartoonish, with bright colors.

By using the preceding prompt as inspiration (and finding out about effective prompts in Chapter 13), try creating your own *Where's Waldo?* illustration either in DALL-E or Midjourney. Doing so can give you a sense of the possibilities when it comes to using generative AI to develop creative assets of all types.

Exploring an Approach for Creating Visual Assets with AI

To establish objectives and define an approach to developing creative assets by using artificial intelligence (AI) tools, you need to follow a structured process that ensures that your creations align with your product offering and marketing goals, and resonate with your target audience. AI offers exciting possibilities for creative asset development, but it requires careful management across various dimensions — from aligning with brand values and ensuring ethical use to integrating with existing workflows and respecting legal boundaries. Balancing these factors is key to leveraging AI effectively and responsibly.

TIP

You now have access to some emergent AI tools (such as Jasper.ai and Thewordsmith.ai) that enable you to input and store your brand style guide first — before you even begin creating assets. That way, any image that the AI tool creates for you conforms to the style set out in your brand style guide. Furthermore, you don't have to ask your AI tool of choice to create one image at a time. You can have it create several images in one go.

Follow these steps — and carefully document the prompts — to responsibly create and use AI-generated assets:

1. **Define the marketing objective that you're creating assets for.**

For example, you may want to increase brand awareness for a new eco-friendly clothing line. You expect to accomplish this objective by using AI to create visually striking images that highlight the eco-friendly aspects of the clothing.

Best marketing practice: Clearly define the purpose of the creative asset. Do you want to use it for brand awareness, product promotion, social media engagement, lead acquisition, or something else? Your objective can guide the style, composition, and elements of the creative asset.

2. **Understand the target audience that your marketing intends to reach.**

The target audience for your eco-friendly clothing line may be environmentally conscious young adults ages 18 to 35 in suburban settings. And the creative assets for the marketing project can consist of imagery that appeals to this demographic by prompting an AI tool to incorporate relevant themes and settings.

Watch out: Ensure that the AI-generated content reflects your brand's voice and appeals to your target audience. For example, if an AI tool creates a series of edgy and humorous social media posts, but your brand is known for its serious and professional tone, this content may alienate your established customer base. Constantly align AI outputs with your brand guidelines and audience expectations.

3. **Decide on the marketing message or theme that you want your creative assets to support.**

For example, the marketing team may decide that they want to anchor the message in the phrase *Sustainability meets style*. The task in that case would be to have the AI generate visuals that blend natural, replenishable elements (such as bamboo, organic cotton, or recycled materials) with fashionable clothing styles.

Best marketing practice: Ensure that the images align with your brand's visual identity, including colors, typography, and overall style. Consistency helps in building brand recognition. Include details around the brand visual identity in the prompts that you write for the AI tool.

4. **Choose the right AI tools for the data that you have and the expected output.**

You have a range of tools to choose from, so match the tool to your specific task. For example, DALL-E and Midjourney can create unique images from descriptions that you provide and can also use reference images (also known as *image prompting*) to set the style for the image you want created.

Best marketing practice: You can combine AI image creation with other tools, such as photo editing software, for further refinement. In fact, tools such as Adobe Photoshop now include generative AI capabilities that can help you create different skylines or extend a mountain in a different direction, for example.

Watch out: The choice of AI tools and their training data significantly impacts the type and quality of creative output. For example, an AI model trained primarily on classical European art styles may not be suitable for a campaign aiming to reflect contemporary Asian aesthetics. Select tools and models that align with your specific creative goals. And you don't get a shortcut in this exercise: The only way to know which tools are right for you involves experimenting with several.

5. Develop detailed descriptions for your AI to work from.

An example description for the clothing line may be something like *stylish, modern outfit with bamboo fabric texture, set against a background of lush greenery, with a subtle hint of urban skyline.*

Best marketing practice: When using AI tools such as DALL-E or Midjourney the more specific your description, the better the results. Include details about colors, mood, setting, objects, and any text that you want in the image. Flip to the section "Trying Out an AI-Generated Where's Waldo? Illustration," earlier in this chapter, for inspiration.

6. Insert a description that you create in Step 5 (with or without the assistance of an AI application) into your chosen text-to-image tool (such as DALL-E or Midjourney).

Ideally, generate at least four variations that you can then edit further (see Step 7).

7. Make repeated modifications (iterations) to your descriptions, and then review and refine the assets that the tool creates.

Arguably, this step (or series of steps) is the most important. You must evaluate the AI-generated images and adjust the prompts to further enhance and strengthen the output. For example, if an initial created image lacks the vibrancy that you expect, adjust the description that you offer to the AI to include *bright, vivid colors.*

Best marketing practice: AI-generated images may not be perfect on the first try. In fact, they're very rarely perfect on the first try. Fully expect to iterate constantly when you refine the prompts and tweak the creative asset.

REMEMBER

AI is a tool to augment your creativity and efficiency. The combination of AI capabilities and your unique brand perspective can create the most powerful visual content. Arguably, AI is at its best when you combine it with human creativity, versus asking it to do the creation on its own.

8. **Evaluate the created assets against brand standards to ensure quality and consistency.**

Human involvement is critical, especially when evaluating whether the output reflects desired quality and is on brand. Whether you match colors with the brand palette, check the output against other brand images, or use a separate AI tool that can check for brand consistency, you mustn't skip this step.

Watch out: Don't think of AI as a set-and-forget tool. Regular human oversight ensures the quality of AI-generated content. For example, an AI tool may inadvertently use outdated or inappropriate cultural references in marketing materials. Regular reviews by human editors can catch and correct these missteps. In fact, your marketing department and team should have a policy for verifying every new creative asset generated by the AI before that asset goes out into the world.

9. **Optimize the generated assets for various platforms that you intend to use for marketing.**

After you finalize an image, you can use AI tools (such as Canva or Adobe Spark) to help optimize the output for various platforms. For example, AI tools can create square images for Instagram, wider formats for Facebook banners.

Best marketing practice: Different social media platforms have different preferred image sizes and aspect ratios. Customize your images accordingly for optimal display. When you're using an AI tool to create images or even video, you can input the desired output sizes that you need.

Watch out: Smoothly integrate AI tools into existing workflows. For instance, an AI video editing tool that doesn't integrate well with your current video editing software can create more work, instead of streamlining the process. Ensure that any AI tool you adopt fits seamlessly into your existing production pipeline and also has the appropriate import and export capability.

10. **Test the created visual asset's effect on the intended audience and gather feedback.**

Testing the creative output (whether that's a static image or video) by using a focus group or even a small internal audience can help you see whether it resonates positively. Use that feedback to guide the AI tool on further image refinements, as needed.

Best marketing practice: AI offers the flexibility to explore various artistic styles and formats. Experiment with different aesthetics to see what resonates best with your audience.

Watch out: Biases can slip into AI-generated content. If an AI tool consistently generates images of people in stereotypical roles based on gender or race, this output could reflect and perpetuate harmful biases. As I note in Chapter 22, regular audits of AI outputs can help identify and correct these biases.

REMEMBER

Embed legal and ethical compliance in all steps of the process for creating assets with AI tools. In particular

>> When choosing the right AI tool and assessing the output, ensure that the images don't infringe on copyrights and are ethically sound. Check whether the AI tool indemnifies you from potential copyright claims and find out whether your legal team is onboard with the tools and the process that you're using. Check out Chapter 22 for more discussion of legal and ethical compliance.

>> Stay informed about legal aspects of AI, especially in terms of copyright and intellectual property rights. For example, using AI to generate music for a commercial project may raise copyright issues if the AI's training data includes copyrighted music. Ensure that your use of AI respects legal boundaries and intellectual property rights. And although tools such as Adobe Firefly, Microsoft Copilot, and OpenAI's DALL-E offer IP indemnification, still check with your legal team.

Minding the integrity of your customers, data, and teams

Maintain ethical integrity and transparency when you use AI to create customer-facing content. For example, if you use AI to create realistic human images or voices, disclose that these images are AI-generated to avoid misleading your audience about the reality of what they're seeing. With industry efforts to label AI-generated content gathering steam, make sure that you maintain alignments with new developments. I cover more about ethical concerns in Chapter 22.

REMEMBER

If your AI tools use customer data to personalize content, ensure strict adherence to data privacy laws. For example, using AI to personalize e-mail campaigns requires careful handling of customer data in compliance with the General Data Protection Regulation (GDPR) or other relevant privacy regulations. Failure to do so can lead to legal consequences and damage to your brand's reputation. And make sure to involve your legal team in your conversations regarding customer data use.

Invest in training your team to use AI tools effectively. Lack of understanding can lead to your team underutilizing AI capabilities. For example, a content team not fully trained in using an AI copywriting tool may only use it for basic tasks (such as grammar checking) and miss out on its advanced features for generating more sophisticated content (for example, creating personalized marketing copy). Keep in mind that when your team chooses to use an AI tool, it probably means more work, not less, in the short term while they familiarize themselves with the tool's capabilities and integrate the tool into their regular workflow.

REMEMBER

Make sure that your efforts don't rely too heavily on AI; doing so can hinder creativity and innovation. For example, if a graphic design team uses AI exclusively for creating visuals, they may miss out on unique, human-inspired designs. Balance AI use with human creativity to foster innovation. You don't want your brand to flood its marketing channels with bland, plain, and boring content.

TIP

When you're creating images or video by using AI, some of the AI tools available for use come from the companies whose tools you've used for a long time. These tools now include powerful AI functionality to enhance your creative work. Adobe Photoshop is a perfect example of a design tool that now includes some interesting generative AI functionality that you can use with just a little bit of extra training.

Examining an example scenario

Suppose that you're working on a campaign for the eco-friendly clothing line that I introduce in the section "Exploring an Approach for Creating Visual Assets with AI," earlier in this chapter. After defining your objective and understanding your target audience, you may decide that the theme for your marketing campaign is *Urban Nature*. Then, you select Midjourney as your AI tool to create initial designs that will appeal to young adults. You make your descriptions to Midjourney detailed and focus on elements that signify both suburban life and nature. For example, you may describe a bamboo-fabric jacket set against a city park backdrop.

After several iterations to ensure that the images align with your brand's visual identity, you tailor these images for various social media platforms where you plan to present your marketing campaign. Before finalizing, you gather feedback from a focus group or, at the very least, other team members to test that the images resonate well with your target demographic. Lastly, you double-check all legal and ethical aspects of using AI-generated images in your campaign.

Enhancing Existing Creative Assets

Using artificial intelligence (AI) to enhance or edit existing creative assets involves several innovative techniques that have revolutionized the approach to creativity and asset development. AI's role in enhancing and editing creative assets spans a wide array of applications, from restoring and enhancing old media to creating entirely new content.

Current marketers more frequently use AI for editing and enhancing existing images than they do for creating images from scratch. However, I expect that situation to change in the future. Advancements in AI's capabilities don't only save time and reduce manual effort; they represent a paradigm shift in how marketers approach creative work as a blend of human imagination and machine efficiency.

The following sections describe four distinct ways in which you can use AI for modifying your existing creative visuals.

Enhancing and restoring images

AI-infused tools can significantly improve the quality of existing images. Tools such as Photoshop now integrate AI for tasks including upscaling resolution, enhancing details, and restoring old photographs. For example, AI algorithms can analyze a low-resolution image and intelligently fill in details that the original image didn't actually contain, resulting in a high-resolution version. In photo restoration, AI can remove scratches, adjust faded colors, and even reconstruct missing parts of an image. This capability is particularly valuable in preserving historical photographs or rejuvenating old family pictures.

One of my favorite features in Adobe Photoshop is the Sky Replacement functionality, which allows you to change the sky featured in an existing image based on the criteria that you set. The technology behind these tools, not surprisingly, involves neural networks trained on vast data sets of images, enabling the AI to predict and replicate realistic textures and details.

Enhancing and clarifying audio

Similar to its capabilities for image restoration (see the preceding section), AI's audio processing features make it adept at creating, enhancing, and restoring audio recordings. This functionality is especially useful for remastering old music tracks, restoring archival audio recordings, or improving the clarity of voice recordings.

AI algorithms can isolate different audio elements, remove background noise, and even separate voice sounds from music. For instance, AI can take an old mono track and *upmix* it (extract separate tracks) to stereo or surround sound, breathing new life into classic songs. Tools such as Izotope's RX series use machine learning to identify and repair common audio issues — such as clicks, pops, or hisses — that often occur in older recordings. The BMW example that I talk about in the sidebar "Case study: BMW's AI-generated soundtrack," in this chapter, touches on the potential of using AI to create or enhance audio.

Analyzing and editing video

AI is automating time-consuming video-editing tasks such as object removal, color grading, and even *frame interpolation* (creating and inserting new video frames between existing ones), which results in smoother transitions for slow-motion effects. AI tools can automate the process of analyzing and editing videos frame by frame, which can significantly reduce the manual labor involved in video post-production. For example, AI can automatically identify and tag various elements in a video — such as faces, objects, or landscapes — and enable quick editing or effects application.

Adobe's Sensei AI and Blackmagic Design's DaVinci Resolve with its *neural engine*, (I talk about neural technologies in Chapter 5) are examples of AI technologies that empower editors to achieve more in less time, enhancing the overall quality and visual appeal of videos. Simpler AI tools, such as Animoto or Lumen5, also allow you to enter natural language queries into the application and provide guidelines for creating short instructional videos.

Adding and modifying content

You can use AI to modify or create new elements within existing assets. For instance, AI-driven tools such as DALL-E or GPT-4 can generate new visual or textual content that matches the style or theme of existing assets. You can use this functionality to create variations of an ad campaign, generate additional scenes in a video game, or even produce explanatory images for a book.

REMEMBER

The AI models that you use for supplementing assets are trained on vast data sets and can generate highly original and contextually appropriate content. This capability not only speeds up the creative process, but also opens up new avenues for creativity that were previously unimaginable.

CASE STUDY: COCA-COLA'S "MASTERPIECE" CAMPAIGN

In an era when keeping a heritage brand vibrant and relevant is a formidable challenge, Coca-Cola embarked on a journey in 2023 to infuse its timeless appeal with the cutting-edge allure of AI. The objective was clear: To intertwine Coca-Cola's enduring promise of uplifting refreshment with the dynamism of AI, thereby sparking creativity and connection in the fabric of daily life. The campaign hoped to captivate a global audience with its memorable narrative.

To achieve this, Coca-Cola harnessed the power of generative AI, collaborating with OpenAI, Electric Theatre Collective, and Blitzworks to craft an innovative short film titled "Masterpiece." The film presents an eclectic mix of classical and contemporary art from around the globe, all in a museum setting. It weaves a tale where a Coca-Cola bottle journeys through various paintings, ultimately inspiring an art student. This journey is brought to life through a blend of live-action, digital artistry, and AI-driven animation, showcasing the bottle's transformation as it traverses different artistic realms. Notably, the film incorporates Stable Diffusion, OpenAI's DALL-E 2, and GPT-4.0 to generate unique paintings and dialogues, showcasing the seamless integration of AI in creative storytelling.

Not only was the film a shining example of how to use generative AI in asset creation, but its exposure also lifted Coca-Cola's brand metrics, including a 12 percent increase in brand recall, a 9 percent improvement in brand favorability, and a 7 percent rise in purchase intent for the target audience, as highlighted in a survey from the research firm Kantar. The campaign also achieved viral success, amassing millions of views, likes, and comments across social media platforms, and garnering acclaim with accolades such as the Cannes LIONS Grand Prix for Film Craft, among others.

For marketers, this initiative illustrates the boundless possibilities of blending traditional art and creative asset development with AI, offering fresh perspectives on brand storytelling. By leveraging generative AI, Coca-Cola demonstrated how different tools can lead to entirely new creative concepts that stay on brand and produce strong advertising results.

Fine-Tuning Creativity with AI Tools and Techniques

To fine-tune the creation of visual marketing assets by using AI tools, you have to hone your skills in working with those tools. For example, you can improve the effectiveness of the written descriptions that you use as input for the AI created content. You can also streamline your asset production process and employ various tricks to make sure that the assets created grab your customers' attention. The following sections can help you get started in becoming an AI-content creation wiz.

Crafting descriptions for image creation

To get high-quality AI images, you need to craft detailed descriptions. Here are five examples of descriptions provided to an AI tool — each tailored for a different scenario — to give you inspiration for creating your own imagery or video:

>> **Product promotion in lifestyle setting:**

A cozy, modern living room at dusk, with soft ambient lighting. In the center, a sleek, black, smart coffee maker sits on a rustic wooden table. The background shows a comfortable sofa with colorful cushions and a bookshelf filled with books. There's a large window with sheer curtains, showcasing a city skyline at twilight.

>> **Fashion advertisement for a youth brand:**

A vibrant street art backdrop with graffiti, showcasing a diverse group of young adults wearing trendy streetwear. The clothing includes graphic T-shirts, ripped jeans, and colorful sneakers. Each person is striking a dynamic pose, exuding confidence and style. The setting is an urban alleyway, bustling with energy, and the lighting is bright and lively, emphasizing the vivid colors of the clothes and graffiti.

>> **Travel promotion for a tropical destination:**

A breathtaking beach scene at sunset, with a clear view of the ocean meeting the horizon. The sky is a blend of orange, pink, and purple hues. Palm trees gently sway in the foreground, framing a hammock tied between two trees. In the background, there's a glimpse of a luxury over-water bungalow with a thatched roof. The water is crystal clear, and there's a sense of serene beauty and tranquillity. Nobody is around.

>> **Gourmet food advertisement:**

An elegant dining table set outdoors in a lush garden during the day. The table showcases a gourmet spread: a cheese board with an assortment of cheeses, grapes, and nuts; a freshly baked artisanal bread; and a bottle of red wine with two glasses. The background features blooming flowers and greenery, with soft, natural sunlight filtering through the leaves, creating a warm and inviting atmosphere.

» Tech product launch:

A futuristic, minimalist office space with a large, sleek, curved desk. On the desk, there's a cutting-edge silver laptop with a glowing logo. The room has a large glass window revealing a cityscape with high-tech skyscrapers. The lighting is cool and blue, giving a high-tech, innovative vibe. In the foreground, holographic projections display graphs and code, symbolizing advanced technology and innovation.

Automating creative production

Automating the creative production process by using AI involves integrating intelligent tools at various stages of the workflow. This approach can significantly enhance efficiency, spark creativity, and ensure consistency across projects. The following list gives you a detailed explanation of how to use AI tools in the creative production process, with specific examples and recommendations:

» Concept and planning: The first step in any creative asset production is conceptualization and planning. AI tools such as OpenAI's GPT-4 can assist in generating creative concepts and ideas. For example, you can prompt GPT-4 to generate unique storylines, advertising copy, or design concepts based on initial input criteria. This assistance can help you in brainstorming sessions to provide a broad range of ideas and angles that may not be immediately obvious to human marketing teams.

AI-powered project management tools can assist in planning the production timeline, resource allocation, and budgeting by analyzing data from previous projects to predict timelines and potential bottlenecks.

REMEMBER

» Design and asset creation: In the design phase, AI tools such as Adobe Sensei and Autodesk's AI solutions can greatly expedite the process. These tools can automate repetitive tasks such as image resizing, color correction, and basic layout design. For instance, Adobe Sensei can intelligently crop photos, keeping the main subjects in frame, or suggest design layouts in Adobe Spark. Autodesk's AI, on the other hand, can assist in 3D design processes by suggesting optimizations of model structures and automating certain modeling tasks, such as generating textures or refining mesh details.

You can also use AI tools to generate initial design templates or even come up with complete assets. Tools such as DALL-E, Midjourney, or Runway enable users to create visuals and design elements from textual descriptions, which offers a fast and unique way to create custom graphics.

>> **Content development and writing:** For content creation, AI writing assistants such as Jasper, Writer, or TheWordsmith.ai can generate drafts for articles, scripts, or social media posts. These tools use advanced natural language processing (NLP) to create coherent and contextually relevant content based on keywords or short descriptions. Although AI-generated text often requires human editing to add a personal touch or specific brand voice, these tools can save considerable time in the initial drafting phase.

Find out about the type of writing tools (such as Jasper.ai, Writer.ai, Copy.ai and TheWordsmith.ai) that can incorporate your brand style guidelines before generating any content. Also, keep your audience in mind: AI can assist in *language translation* and *localization of content* (see Chapter 17 for more about these topics), ensuring that the creative output is accessible to a global audience.

>> **Editing in video post-production:** During the post-production process for a video asset, AI can significantly streamline the editing process. Tools such as Adobe Premiere Pro's Auto Reframe use AI to automatically adjust the aspect ratio of videos for different platforms. For example, the tools can transition from a widescreen format to a square format for social media.

For audio production, tools such as Descript offer AI-driven transcription and editing, which enables the creators to edit audio files by adjusting the transcribed text. This type of process can dramatically reduce editing time. In photography and image editing, AI tools can automate tasks such as object removal, sky replacement, or style transfer, as offered in Skylum's Luminar.

>> **Review and optimization:** AI-powered analytics tools can analyze audience engagement with creative content and provide insights into what content works and what doesn't. For instance, tools such as Canva's Magic Switch or Google Analytics can offer data-driven recommendations for design adjustments or content tweaks to help you maximize engagement and reach.

Increasingly, tools such as VidMob use AI to analyze all the advertising that you create *longitudinally* (repeatedly over long periods of time) to determine which types of content and what elements in that content produce the best results. The tool then uses those insights to fuel recommendations for adjustments to new content that you create.

When integrating AI into creative production, maintain a balance between automation and human creativity. AI is best used as a tool to augment and assist the creative process, rather than replace it. Have your creators familiarize themselves with a range of AI tools so that they can understand which tools best suit their specific needs. Also, make sure that everyone continuously updates their skills and knowledge about new AI tools and advancements because the field is rapidly evolving.

Tips and tricks for producing attention-grabbing creative assets

Producing attention–grabbing creative assets by using AI requires a multifaceted process that capitalizes on the unique capabilities of AI tools to create content that's not only visually appealing or engaging but also resonates with your target audience. Effective utilization of AI can transform the way you conceptualize, develop, and deliver content:

>> **Customized content:** AI tools such as Adobe Target can personalize content based on user data and preferences. You can see this approach in AI-driven campaigns for online retailers, where images of products are dynamically generated to align with the interests of specific users. Similarly, Google's responsive display ads use AI to test various combinations of headlines, descriptions, and images, optimizing ad performance for different target audiences. This dynamic content adaptation ensures that each user receives the most relevant and engaging experience. Dynamic Yield, Oracle Maxymiser, and Vue.ai are a few of the other tools that provide this content customization.

>> **Design and video:** Specialized tools, such as Stable Diffusion and Runway, enable the creation of unique AI-generated visuals. For instance, a marketing campaign incorporating AI-generated artwork that merges brand elements with distinct artistic styles results in a visually unique and memorable experience. Additionally, AI-powered image enhancement tools, such as Let's Enhance or Adobe Photoshop's AI features, can significantly improve image quality, making your content sharper and more attention-grabbing.

TIP

Visit the Runway website (www.runwayml.com) and check out their suite of tools to see the potential. Their AI tool suite includes tools for text to video, image to image, erase and replace, backdrop remix, remove silence, add color, and green screen creation capabilities.

>> **Video and animation:** Automated video editing tools, such as Lumen5 and Magisto, can convert blog posts or textual content into engaging video content by selecting relevant stock images or video clips, overlaying text, and adding music. Additionally, AI animation tools, such as Synthesia, allow for the creation of custom avatars that can deliver messages in a more personalized and engaging manner, such as creating an AI spokesperson for a brand. Some of these tools aren't free, but they're not expensive either. As I write this book, Lumen5 starts at $19 a month for unlimited usage.

>> **Creative copywriting:** In the domain of copywriting, AI tools such as Jasper, Writer, or Copy.ai can produce a range of styles and tones, tailored to different platforms, brands, and audiences, which enhances the engagement level of ads, social media posts, or product descriptions. Moreover, AI tools

such as CoSchedule's Headline Analyzer can help you craft attention-grabbing headlines, using algorithms to analyze and predict the engagement level of various word choices.

>> **Audio production:** Tools such as AIVA or Amper Music enable the creation of custom music tracks, allowing users to select a mood or style for the AI to generate a unique piece of music. Furthermore, AI voice synthesis tools, such as Descript, offer realistic voiceovers for videos or podcasts, streamlining the production process and providing greater flexibility in content creation.

CASE STUDY: BMW'S AI-GENERATED SOUNDTRACK

BMW, a leading global automotive brand renowned for its commitment to technological innovation, sought a distinctive approach that would resonate with a younger, tech-savvy demographic. The brand identified an opportunity to leverage its association with cutting-edge technology by collaborating with Tomorrowland, the annual electronic music dance festival, to create a unique brand experience that underscores its innovative ethos.

BMW launched Future Record, an AI-driven music platform developed in partnership with Tomorrowland. This platform offered users an interactive experience where they can craft their own AI-generated tracks. By engaging with Future Record, participants were prompted to answer a series of questions regarding their preferences, such as stage name, tempo, mood, and lyrics. The platform then used those inputs to generate a bespoke song that captured the essence of the user's asks. This process, remarkably efficient, produces personalized songs in under a minute, which users were able to share on social platforms.

The Future Record initiative generated over 10,000 unique tracks and garnered more than 20 million impressions on social media. This campaign significantly boosted BMW's brand awareness and fostered deeper engagement and loyalty among BMW and Tomorrowland's audiences.

Future Record served dual purposes: to showcase the potential of using generative AI to create new music and to strengthen BMW's technology credentials. It showed how generative AI can be used not just by one but by thousands of consumers to create new music that in turn reinforced the BMW brand. Furthermore, it hints at the possibilities when you use generative AI to create custom soundtracks for your consumers on a huge scale — forging a stronger and more nuanced connection with them.

Choosing AI Tools for Creating Visual Assets

Using AI to develop or enhance creative assets has become increasingly popular, especially in marketing. Each tool has its unique strengths, and the best choice depends on your specific needs. For example, your priority may be the style of images that you want to create, how easily you can pick up and use the tool that you choose, or whether you can integrate the tool with your existing workflow. Always consider the tool's compatibility with your marketing objectives and brand identity.

TIP

Stay informed about the latest developments in AI tools by industry newsletters, following relevant tech blogs, and participating in professional forums because the technology is rapidly evolving. Specifically, find out about AI image creation tools to leverage new features and capabilities. For example, Apple just launched an AI image tool that lets you make edits by using *natural language querying* (conversational English instructions).

Table 14-1 shows some of the best tools currently available for AI-generated imagery.

TABLE 14-1   AI-Generated Visual Asset Tools

Tool	Website	Description	Benefits
Adobe Photoshop's Neural Filters	www.adobe.com/products/photoshop/neural-filter.html	An add-on to Adobe Creative Suite that allows you to manipulate and transform images.	Easy to incorporate for those already using Adobe Creative Suite.
Artbreeder	www.artbreeder.com	Blend and mutate images to create new visuals; explore variations in design elements and create unique images.	Exploring variations in design elements.
Canva's Magic Write	www.canva.com/magic-write	Generate design layouts and elements based on textual descriptions.	Simplifies the design process for marketers.
DALL-E 3 by OpenAI	www.openai.com/dall-e-3	Generate highly creative and detailed images from textual descriptions.	Generates high quality images and customizations.

(continued)

TABLE 14-1 *(continued)*

Tool	Website	Description	Benefits
Deep Dream Generator	www.deepdreamgenerator.com	Create surreal and abstract image transformations and eye-catching, dream-like images.	Enables artistic image enhancements.
Lumen5	www.lumen5.com	Video-creation tool that uses AI to help turn text content into engaging video material.	Ease of use, accessibility, and time savings.
Midjourney	www.midjourney.com	Generates images from natural language descriptions.	Most easily accessible via Discord, the online community platform.
NightCafe Studio	http://creator.nightcafe.studio	Offers various AI art generation techniques, including neural style transfer (see Chapter 8 for a bit about this technique) and text-to-image generation.	User-friendly and versatile.
Runway	www.runwayml.com	A user-friendly platform for creating AI-generated images and videos.	Allows experimentation with different AI models without deep technical knowledge.
Stability AI's Stable Diffusion	www.stability.ai/stable-image	AI-powered open source large language model (LLM) that generates digital images based on textual descriptions.	Good for high quality image generation with lots of details.
VanceAI	www.vanceai.com	AI-powered image editing tools, including image upscaling, denoising, and restoration.	Useful for improving the quality of existing images or graphics.

Chapter 15

Search Engine Optimization (SEO) in the AI Era

O ver the last two decades, advancements in Internet search algorithms kept the search and browse paradigm at the heart of the Internet for billions around the world. Traditional search engines, of which Google is the behemoth, serve up a list of links in response to a user's keyword query. The search engines retrieve results based on their indexing of the content available on the Internet and organize the lists of links that they come up with in an order that reflects the content's applicability to the user's inputs.

To take advantage of search engine functionality, companies establish teams to harness the potential of search to acquire customers by writing and optimizing online content that search engines recognize as directly related to user queries. The goal is to have users presented with links (via online search) that match their queries so that they click the links, visit the company website, and make product purchases. You want to design content pages that rank high in the order of search results against commonly entered search terms. And when a company succeeds in reaching this goal, it can attract large audiences to its products or services.

Creating online content that the search engines can easily read and that Google (for example) ranks highly costs less than running paid advertising online. The practice of crafting website content to make it search engine friendly is called *search engine optimization* (SEO), which is a critical part of the digital marketing playbook. However, the traditional approach to SEO may be changing with the increased use of artificial intelligence (AI) to create and optimize the content, on the one hand, and the shift toward AI services such as ChatGPT and Perplexity on the other. These AI services bypass the search engines to give users answers to their queries directly in their results windows. In fact, according to Gartner (a management consulting company), online traffic going to websites directly from search engine results will drop 25 percent by 2026 and will be replaced by the use of tools such as ChatGPT, Claude, and Perplexity.

In this chapter, I begin by discussing why and how users are changing the way that they use search engines, what that change means for marketing, and how businesses can adapt their strategies for this change. Although I cover these topics, I also tell you how you can use AI to augment your current SEO efforts — because the move away from search engine dominance isn't an overnight shift, but rather a gradual evolution.

Describing Search Generative Experiences (SGEs)

You can witness the profound impact of generative artificial intelligence (AI) on Internet search through the shift toward more conversational (also known as *natural language*) user interfaces. Users can now engage with search engines in a more natural and human-like manner, asking complex questions or expressing their queries in full sentences, rather than relying on specific keywords.

In turn, AI search engines can synthesize information from multiple sources to provide a comprehensive answer to the question in everyday English, instead of simply listing websites that contain the relevant keywords. This capability to understand and process natural language queries in real time is beginning to transform search engines from impersonal website directories into knowledgeable assistants. Commonly referred to as *search generative experiences* (SGEs), this shift has profound implications not only for how people use the Internet but also for how they create content for it.

When you look toward the future, you can see that the advancements in search algorithms powered by generative AI promise to make the vast expanse of the Internet more accessible and understandable for everyone.

Enhanced interpretation of queries

The advent of generative AI has enabled search algorithms to understand and interpret the intent behind queries with unprecedented depth. This evolution from simple keyword spotting to understanding the context and semantics of user inquiries marks a significant leap forward. As SGE technologies continue to evolve, you can anticipate a shift from information retrieval to knowledge generation, in which search engines synthesize information and provide specific recommendations tailored to users' needs by using the rest of the Internet as raw material for their responses.

REMEMBER

Generative AI models, such as Claude (https://claude.ai/) and OpenAI's GPT-4 (www.openai.com/gpt-4), are trained on vast amounts of data. The scope of the training enables the models to generate responses that provide direct answers, summaries, or even newly written content based on the user's query. Not to be outdone, both Google and Bing also include SGE results at the top of their search engine results pages as of late 2023.

Personalized search results

The use of SGE opens up many possibilities for personalized search experiences. By analyzing the user's past interactions, preferences, and even the context of their current search, AI can tailor the search results more effectively to meet individual needs. This personalization extends beyond filtering and ranking results based on presumed relevance; it involves generating content or answers uniquely suited to the user's query and context. For example, a search for cooking recipes can take into account the user's dietary restrictions, preferred cuisines, and even the ingredients that they have on hand, offering a level of customization that was previously unavailable.

The transition to custom-crafted search results represents a fundamental change in how people can access and interact with online information, potentially transforming the web into a more dynamic, intelligent, and personalized space.

PERPLEXITY PROVIDES A PEAK INTO THE FUTURE

Perplexity AI (www.perplexity.ai) provides a good example of an artificial intelligence (AI)–driven search engine that demonstrates how natural language interfaces are changing the search and browse paradigm of the internet. The search functionality that Perplexity AI offers directly answers users' questions by pulling together information from what it has already gathered by crawling the web. And Perplexity AI uses this information to give clear and relevant answers to the questions (rather than just a list of links). This situation makes searching for information faster and easier, turning what used to be a long process into a quick and straightforward task.

Thanks to its advanced understanding of language, Perplexity AI can understand the context of what you're asking, not just the specific words that you use, so it can provide answers that are much more relevant to what you're actually looking for, simplifying the process that you have to follow in order to find complex information, removing the need to sift through unrelated links. As a result, there's much less ambiguity in your search experience when you use Perplexity AI.

Additionally, Perplexity AI offers a search experience without ads (at least, as of the time I write this book), which means its results aren't influenced by advertisers. This lack of advertiser influence can lead to more unbiased and focused search outcomes. With recent investments and positive feedback from users, AI-driven search engines such as Perplexity AI are beginning to challenge traditional search engines, pushing them toward adopting new standards for delivering search results.

These AI driven solutions, such as Perplexity AI, are search generative experiences (SGEs) to the core because they literally generate answers to your questions using the internet as the raw ingredients for that generation exercise. You can get the most benefit from them if you have a specific query in mind and are looking for one answer, rather than browsing for different alternatives. Although I can't say how solutions such as Perplexity AI will change the way people search the internet in the future or how the solutions will crawl the web and influence search engine optimization (SEO), but you should pay attention to these new innovations as they enter the mainstream.

Strategies for SEO Success in the AI Era

For many search engine optimization (SEO) experts, the integration of artificial intelligence (AI) with the domain of SEO means a necessary return to the fundamentals of what makes successful content that human beings care about and search algorithms reward. Returning to fundamentals requires that you focus on the following strategies and tactics that the team at SEO.ai (www.seo.ai, a company that offers a highly ranked AI SEO writing tool) have emphasized:

>> **Audience focus:** Research your audience and cater specifically to their interests and needs. Tailor content to match their search queries and personas, evidenced by their queries and online habits. This focus can leverage AI's capability to analyze big data for enhanced audience relevance and engagement.

>> **Originality:** Prioritize the creation of unique, research-based content that human beings will care about. Stand out with original studies, surveys, and case studies that offer new data. The goal is to ensure that AI-generated content complements your content, and that your content retains as much value for both users and search engines. This concept may not feel new, but it matters more with the rise of AI-generated content because it is now increasingly challenging to differentiate between human-created and AI-created material.

>> **Structured data:** Implement *structured data* (data that has a standardized format that both software and humans can easily access) so that search engines can easily understand and index your content. This tactic improves your content's visibility to search engines and adapts content for evolving search technologies (such as voice search) to enhance user experience. It's only a matter of time until marketers learn how large language models (LLMs, such as ChatGPT) read websites. When they do, they'll need to adjust their content to be more accessible to those LLMs. What's clear is that companies that have more structured data will win the battle for recognition from search technologies.

>> **Human touch:** Emphasize the human element behind your content. Showcasing real people, emotions, and personal experiences builds trust and connection with your audience, which is an offering that's beyond AI's reach. The human-oriented content — whether it's SEO or any customer-facing content — can continue to successfully carry your message in the future.

>> **Real-time updates:** Focus on freshness and the integration of real-time data to ensure that your content remains relevant and up to date. This approach keeps your content ahead of synthetic data (AI-generated material), which may lack the latest information.

REMEMBER

As the use of generative AI in marketing increases, the future will bring a lot of AI-created content to compete with your own, so keep your messaging up to date so that it stands out and remains relevant.

>> **Domain authority:** Strengthen *domain authority* (a website's quality ranking in Google search) and secure *high-quality backlinks* (other websites linking back to yours). As content saturation increases, these factors become critical for attracting search engines and AI tools that prioritize and trust your content over others. Both practices emphasize the importance of online relationships

and external validation. ***Note:*** In 2023, *The New York Times* brought a lawsuit against OpenAI for crawling its content without permission to train its models because the media publisher knows that its online content is valuable.

>> **Openness and transparency:** This strategy should feel obvious to any marketer, but it bears stating. To win over your audience in the AI era, having engaging content isn't enough. You need to build trust with your consumers by clearly stating your policies on what data you use in your marketing and how you use it. Don't make the mistakes that CNET did (see the sidebar "A CNET saga: When AI slips in," in this chapter).

A CNET SAGA: WHEN AI SLIPS IN

CNET (www.cnet.com), a well-respected technology news website, faced public scrutiny in the spring of 2023 upon revealing that it had been using AI to write numerous articles, notably for its daily mortgage and refinance rate section on its website. Despite being attributed to Justin Jaffe, CNET Money's managing editor, these stories didn't appear on Jaffe's primary author page; instead, they were on a separate page exclusively for mortgage rate stories, raising questions about transparency and authorship.

The controversy intensified when it was reported that CNET had quietly published over 70 articles under the byline "CNET Money Staff" since November 2022, with only a hidden editorial note indicating the use of AI. This lack of clarity extended within CNET, where even staff members were unsure of how the publisher used AI or the workflow surrounding that use, further complicating the issue. This SEO-friendly content ranked high on Google search results and was monetized through affiliate links. This approach, lucrative for CNET, involved creating content on high-intent queries, such as credit card applications, to earn affiliate fees if a user clicked on the links in the article and went to the credit company's website. However, because AI produced these articles without any appropriate disclosures or internal checks, it raised serious concerns about the quality of content.

The ethical concerns were manifold, primarily centered around CNET's initial failure to disclose the use of AI in creating content. This lack of transparency raised significant questions about credibility and the ethical responsibility of media outlets to inform readers about the origins of the content that they consume. Moreover, subsequent investigations revealed instances of factual inaccuracies within the CNET AI-generated articles, highlighting the risks and limitations of relying on AI for content creation. These findings led to a broader conversation on the reliability and ethical use of AI in journalism, emphasizing the need for stringent quality control measures and the development of robust guidelines to govern AI's application in content creation.

The incident catalyzed a shift toward greater transparency, with CNET and other outlets beginning to label AI-generated content clearly. This case study not only illustrates the potential pitfalls of integrating AI into business without adequate disclosures and quality assurance mechanisms, but it also highlights the evolving dialogue about how best to utilize AI in a manner that supports and enhances reader trust.

Enhancing the User Experience with AI

Optimizing your website or mobile web interface for artificial intelligence (AI)–driven search engines requires a focus on enhancing *user experience* (UX) through strategic design and content approaches. By implementing the tips outlined in this section, you can significantly enhance the user experience of your website or mobile web interface. The enhancements, in turn, make these experiences more favorable in the eyes of AI-driven search engines. The goal is to improve your search engine optimization (SEO) rankings and also drive customer engagement, retention, and sales conversions.

Here are five detailed tips for achieving this goal:

>> **Prioritize mobile-first design.** AI search engines recognize the shift toward mobile browsing and heavily favor websites optimized for mobile devices. Creating a responsive design includes

- Adjusting content and layout based on the user's screen size

- Using large, touch-friendly buttons and readable fonts

- Ensuring quick content load times by optimizing images and leveraging modern coding practices

For example, you can use mobile content frameworks such as AMP (Accelerated Mobile Pages) for presenting news articles. This framework is designed to improve loading speed on mobile devices.

>> **Enhance site structure for easy navigation.** A well-organized site structure not only improves usability but also helps AI search engines understand and index your content more effectively. Using *schema markup* to outline the structured data implementation (a strategy presented in the preceding section) on your site can help AI understand the context and content of your pages, improving the chances that your site gets featured in *rich snippets* (the blurbs that the search engines publish at the top of search results pages).

Create a logical hierarchy in your website's architecture, including a clear menu structure and *breadcrumb navigation* (a structure that facilitates navigation by clearly showing users where they are and where they can go next within the website).

TIP

Make each page of your website or mobile interface accessible within a few clicks (no more than four if you can help it) from the home page.

» **Optimize for voice search.** With the rise of AI assistants such as Siri and Google Assistant, optimizing content for voice search is crucial. Incorporate natural language processing (NLP) by including *long-tail keywords* (a phrase made from three to five words) and questions that people are likely to ask as a search prompt in conversational language. And focus on localized SEO by ensuring that your business is listed on Google My Business and other directories because many voice searches are location-based. For instance, include common voice query phrases such as *near me* or *how to* in your content.

» **Improve content relevance and quality.** AI search engines prioritize content that's relevant and offers substantial value to the user. Follow these simple steps to enhance user experience and keep visitors on your website or mobile interface longer:

- Use AI tools to analyze top-performing content in your market niche and identify key topics and questions that your audience is interested in.

- Create comprehensive, well-researched content that addresses these topics and questions.

- Make use of headings, subheadings, and bullet points for better readability.

- Add engaging multimedia content, such as videos and infographics.

» **Leverage AI for personalized user experiences.** Personalization is key to enhancing UX and improving SEO rankings with AI search engines. Use AI to analyze user behavior and preferences to deliver personalized content recommendations, product suggestions, and targeted promotions. (See Chapter 20 for more information on personalizing content and the approach to customers.) Implement chatbots to provide instant assistance and guide users through your website.

As an example, Netflix uses AI algorithms to recommend movies and TV shows based on individuals' viewing habits. This strategy significantly enhances the user experience and encourages longer session durations.

Maximizing Your SEO Efforts

You can incorporate artificial intelligence (AI) tools and techniques into several aspects of your company's search engine optimization (SEO) practices. A holistic approach to this piece of your marketing presence — powered by AI — propels

SEO from mere optimization to a strategic, insight-driven endeavor. Specifically, you can leverage AI for

>> **Keyword and metadata research:** Helps you create content that not only reaches, but also engages, the target audience effectively. When AI helps with your research, SEO strategies can become more aligned with the constantly changing user trends and SEO competitive dynamics where different companies fight to rank higher in the search results pages. (I go into more detail about this form of research in the following section.)

>> **Content development and optimization:** Streamline the creation process and ensure that content aligns with user intent and preferences. Using AI's help, you can improve your content's SEO quality, user engagement, and sales conversion rates (see the section "Automating content optimization," later in this chapter).

>> **The link-building process:** For both your websites and mobile interfaces, adding AI tools to the mix for building links not only makes identifying and securing high-quality backlinks more efficient (as discussed in the section "Building SEO links," later in this chapter) but also ensures that efforts align closely with overall SEO strategy and goals.

>> **Predictive SEO:** Enables marketers to be proactive rather than reactive in their SEO strategies. This approach — engaging predictive AI tools — not only enhances the effectiveness of content and SEO efforts, but also ensures that businesses remain agile and responsive to ever-changing user needs and search engine evolutions. Check out the section "Harnessing predictive SEO," later in this chapter, for all the details.

Streamlining keyword and metadata research

The heart of SEO today involves writing content that includes the appropriate *keywords* and *metadata*, which are signals used by the search engines to determine the rankings of the websites in response to a query. Arguably, those same elements are foundational to create search generative experiences (SGEs), too. (See the section "Describing Search Generative Experiences [SGEs]," earlier in this chapter.) Therefore, you absolutely have to nail the keywords and metadata that you use as a foundation for creating content. Fortunately, AI can help with creating your SGE-ready content.

Integrating AI into keyword and metadata research strengthens SEO practices by making them more dynamic, precise, and user-focused. Here are specific ways that AI can help SEO professionals and marketers, along with insights on implementing these strategies and examples of useful tools:

>> **Predictive analysis for trending keywords:** AI algorithms can analyze search data and social media trends to identify emerging keywords before those keywords become popular with users. This early keyword optimization gives marketers a competitive edge.

Tools such as Google Trends (`http://trends.google.com`) and Semrush's Keyword Magic Tool (`www.semrush.com/features/keyword-magic-tool`) leverage predictive analytics to spot trends. For instance, an AI tool may flag the phrase *sustainable home goods* as an emerging trend. A distinction such as this enables brands to pivot their content focus accordingly and write strong SEO content that responds to that phrase, even before the trend peaks.

>> **Semantic search optimization:** AI's capability to understand the context and intent behind search terms and queries means that SEO isn't just about the keywords anymore. The goal is to create content that genuinely aligns with the context that users are searching for.

Tools such as Clearscope (`www.clearscope.io`) or MarketMuse (`www.marketmuse.com`) analyze top-performing content to recommend semantically related keywords. This approach ensures that content for a search of *best running shoes* encompasses terms such as *lightweight running sneakers* and *durable running footwear,* closely matching user intent.

>> **Personalization of content strategy:** By analyzing user behavior, AI helps tailor keywords and metadata to specific audience segments. Resulting SEO strategies effectively resonate with various audiences and their preferences.

Marketing platforms such as HubSpot (`www.hubspot.com`) or Salesforce Marketing Cloud (`www.salesforce.com/eu/marketing/`) help you create segmented content strategies. For example, AI analysis may reveal a preference for eco-friendly travel options among millennials; that information provides a guide for focusing a travel agency's SEO content on this area.

>> **Automation of keyword and metadata tagging:** Automating the process of tagging content with relevant keywords and metadata saves time and ensures consistency across content. AI-powered SEO tools such as Yoast SEO (`www.yoast.com`) suggest optimal keywords and metadata based on content analysis. When analyzing a blog post about vegan recipes, for instance, an AI tool can automatically suggest adding *plant-based cooking* and *easy vegan meals* as metadata tags.

Automating content optimization

Using AI for automating content development and optimization allows you to fine-tune content to the intended audience and enables precision, personalization, and efficiency in ways previously unattainable by the more traditional writing and publishing content manually.

The following strategies demonstrate how leveraging AI can transform content strategy and delivery:

» **Personalize content.** AI can dissect and understand user data and thus tailor content dynamically, enhancing user engagement significantly. A notable example is Spotify's use of AI to curate personalized playlists, an offering which has been instrumental in boosting user engagement and subscription rates. Tools such as Salesforce's Einstein (www.salesforce.com/products/einstein) can help you customize content across various channels based on user interactions and preferences.

» **Enhance SEO.** AI tools, such as Moz (www.moz.com) and MarketMuse (www.marketmuse.com), can optimize content for search engines, identify gaps in content, and suggest actionable improvements. Users leveraging these insights have reported significant improvements in SERP (search engine results page) rankings and *organic reach* (visibility of content among its desired audience without any paid advertising investments to support it).

» **Streamline content creation.** Automated content generation tools such as OpenAI's GPT-4 (http://openai.com/gpt-4), Writer (https://Writer.com), and Jasper (https://Jasper.ai) can produce draft articles, social media posts, and even e-mail campaigns. This automation can lead to a more efficient content-production process, and marketers have reported significant time savings and increased output without compromising quality.

» **Predict content success:** Platforms such as Optimizely (www.optimizely.com), Contently (www.contently.com), and others use AI to evaluate content against a myriad of performance indicators, predicting success and suggesting optimizations. Such predictive capabilities enable marketers to allocate resources more effectively, prioritizing content with the highest potential for engagement and impact.

» **Optimize for voice search.** As voice search becomes increasingly prevalent, AI tools can help optimize content, focusing on conversational keywords and queries. Integrating voice search optimization into content strategies can capture a growing segment of voice-first users (users who prefer to use voice to search over typing in search terms), enhancing visibility across digital assistants and smart devices.

>> **Improve engagement by using AI chatbots.** Integrating AI-powered chatbots on digital platforms can offer instant support and personalized content recommendations. This functionality not only boosts engagement, but also gathers insights into user preferences, which may inform future content strategies.

Building SEO links

AI technologies have transformed *link building* (meaning the process of acquiring hyperlinks from other websites to your own to improve search engine ranking), a cornerstone of SEO strategy. You can use AI tools to identify link-building opportunities, automate outreach, and evaluate the quality of potential link sources. The following list gives you some specific opportunities that you can use to leverage AI for link building:

>> **Identify link opportunities.** AI tools can scour the Internet to identify high-quality, relevant sites that you can establish as potential *backlinks* (links that you can provide on your own page that go to supportive content). By analyzing content relevance, domain authority, and web traffic, AI can help pinpoint the most beneficial link-building opportunities.

Tools such as Ahrefs (www.ahrefs.com) and Majestic (https://majestic.com/) provide comprehensive databases and AI-driven insights to streamline this process. For instance, you may use Ahrefs to discover authoritative blogs in the niche of *sustainable living* and identify those blogs that have high user engagement but low external links as prime targets for outreach.

>> **Automate outreach for link building.** AI-powered customer relationship management (CRM) and e-mail marketing tools, such as BuzzStream (www.buzzstream.com) or Mailshake (www.mailshake.com), allow you to automate personalized outreach campaigns to potential link partners. These platforms can segment audiences, personalize messages based on the recipient's interests or recent content, and schedule follow-up. These actions increase the efficiency and success rate of link-building efforts.

For example, the ECOgardener company (specializing in eco-friendly gardening tools and supplies) started an automated campaign targeting webmasters of gardening blogs, resulting in a 20 percent positive response rate and several high-quality backlinks.

>> **Evaluate link quality.** Beyond identifying opportunities, AI can assess the quality and potential impact of backlinks. By examining factors such as site relevance, link context, and the historical performance of similar links, AI tools can predict the value of a prospective link.

Semrush's Backlink Audit tool (www.semrush.com/backlink_audit), for example, uses AI to evaluate the *toxicity* of existing backlinks (whether those links are indeed trusted, factual, and useful) and suggest new, high-quality linking opportunities. A digital marketing agency may use this feature to strengthen a client's backlink profile, removing or disavowing low-quality links and focusing on acquiring valuable ones.

>> **Analyze competitors' links.** AI algorithms can analyze competitors' backlink profiles, offering insights into their link-building strategies and revealing untapped linking opportunities. Tools such as Link Explorer by Moz (www.moz.com/link-explorer) analyze thousands of links in seconds, providing detailed reports on where competitors are getting their links and how those links contribute to their SEO performance. By studying these patterns, an SEO strategist can uncover overlooked niches or platforms, such as industry forums, or collaboration opportunities with influencers in related fields.

>> **Predict link performance.** Some AI tools offer predictive analytics that can forecast the potential SEO impact of a new backlink before you acquire that backlink. SEO managers can then prioritize their link-building efforts based on predicted outcomes, focusing resources on the most impactful links. This technology has the potential to significantly optimize the return on investment (ROI) of link-building campaigns by focusing on links that offer the greatest boost to search rankings.

Harnessing predictive SEO

Harnessing *predictive SEO* (the practice of forecasting future search trends and optimizing content proactively) by using AI tools allows you to anticipate changes, adapt strategies in real time, and stay ahead of trends. Predictive SEO uses data analytics, machine learning (ML), and other AI technologies to forecast future trends in user behavior, search demand, and content effectiveness.

Here are specific strategies to effectively implement predictive SEO:

>> **Forecast search trends.** Utilize AI tools to analyze search data and predict future trends, which can give your business a competitive advantage by enabling you to create or update content that meets emerging demands. As I mention in the section "Streamlining keyword and metadata research," earlier in this chapter, Google's AI-powered tool, Google Trends, offers insights into search trend trajectories, helping marketers identify and capitalize on rising queries. For instance, a digital marketing team may use Google Trends to spot an uptick in interest for *home workout equipment* early in each year and develop targeted content before the peak search period.

>> **Optimize content strategy with predictive analysis.** AI platforms such as MarketMuse (www.marketmuse.com) and BrightEdge (www.brightedge.com) use predictive analytics to suggest content topics and optimization strategies that are likely to perform well. These tools analyze historical data and current market trends to recommend content creation and optimization actions. A content manager can leverage MarketMuse to predict the performance of different content themes on their blog, focusing efforts on those predicted to generate the most engagement and traffic.

>> **Improve user experience with predictive user behavior analysis.** AI can analyze user interaction data to predict future behaviors and preferences, enabling websites to tailor experiences to meet anticipated needs. Tools such as Crazy Egg (www.crazyegg.com) provide *heatmapping* (a color-coded representation of data) and visitor insights, predicting areas of a website that will likely attract a lot of attention and suggesting layout or content adjustments accordingly. An e-commerce site may use these insights to redesign product pages, placing high-demand items in areas predicted to draw more visitor focus.

>> **Anticipate the impact of algorithm changes on SEO.** AI-driven SEO tools such as Moz Pro (www.moz.com/products/pro) offer the capability to simulate and predict the impact of search engine algorithm updates on a website's ranking. By analyzing past updates and current website performance, these tools can forecast potential changes in rankings and suggest preemptive optimizations. You may use this feature to tweak your website's content and technical SEO elements in anticipation of a confirmed Google algorithm update, minimizing negative impacts on your site's search visibility.

>> **Implement predictive link-building strategies.** You can also employ AI to forecast the value and potential success of link-building efforts. By using tools such as Semrush (www.semrush.com) — which assesses the quality of potential backlink sources and predicts the impact of these links on SEO — you can prioritize your outreach efforts more effectively. For example, you can identify and focus on acquiring backlinks from domains that have rising authority in niche markets, as predicted by Semrush's analytics.

Knowing the AI Tools to Use with SEO

Each tool listed in Table 15-1 comes with unique capabilities and artificial intelligence (AI)–driven insights. These tools can help you make informed decisions, streamline workflows, and significantly improve the effectiveness of your search engine optimization (SEO) strategies.

TABLE 15-1 AI Tools That Help with SEO

Tool	Website	Uses
Ahrefs	www.ahrefs.com	Predicts keyword trends and analyzes the search landscape
BrightEdge	www.brightedge.com	Provides content performance metrics, recommendations for optimization, and insights into competitive strategies
BuzzSumo	www.buzzsumo.com	Analyzes content across the web for insights into what content performs best for any topic or competitor, and identifies key influencers
Clearscope	www.clearscope.io	Provides keyword and content recommendations for better search engine rankings
Google Trends	http://trends.google.com	Analyzes the popularity of top search queries in Google Search across various regions and languages
MarketMuse	www.marketmuse.com	Offers content planning, creation, and optimization assistance, identifying content gaps and opportunities for improving topical authority
Moz Pro	www.moz.com/products/pro	Offers site audits, keyword research, and backlink analysis, as well as predicting the potential impact of SEO strategies on your site's performance
Semrush	www.semrush.com	Provides keyword research, SEO audits, competitor analysis, and insights to improve SEO, pay-per-click (PPC), and content marketing strategies
SpyFu	www.spyfu.com	Analyzes your competitors' search marketing strategies, offering insights into competitors' keywords, ad variations, and SEO tactics
Surfer SEO	www.surferseo.com	Analyzes and compares your content against top-performing pages in search engine results and offers guidelines to improve content relevance and SEO performance

Chapter **16**

Performing A/B Testing with AI

O f all the Internet companies, Google was the first to popularize *A/B testing*, which is a process that compares the performance of two versions of content or software against each other to determine which is better received by the target audience. Google incorporated this testing into its data-driven experimentation process for its search product. In the year 2000, Google ran its first A/B test to determine the optimal number of search results to display per page. Since then, Google has conducted thousands of A/B tests on various aspects of its search algorithm and on the design of its search pages.

The Google approach to testing its user-facing products has influenced companies across the world to embrace A/B testing as a fundamental tool for determining how to optimize user experience (UX) and business outcomes. In this chapter, I go over the fundamentals of A/B testing and explain how it's becoming even more valuable to businesses in the AI era. I offer definitions, use cases, and a look at some popular tools that enable you to take advantage of AI in an A/B testing situation. Whether you're a marketer, a user-experience professional, or a product-development lead, this chapter can offer you valuable insights and tips for harnessing the best of A/B testing in the AI era.

Examining the Fundamentals of A/B Testing

A/B testing, at its core, is a method used to compare two versions of content — a digital advertisement, web page, app feature, or other company offering — to determine which one performs better in terms of a predefined metric. Metrics may include conversion rate, click-through rate, or any other measurable action that a user may take. The testing involves showing the two versions (A and B) to two similarly sized, randomly selected audiences.

REMEMBER

The fundamental goal of A/B testing is to isolate variables and measure the impact of a single change, while limiting any difference in the versions' performance to the change itself, rather than external factors that may affect the groups. This method relies on statistical analysis to determine whether the observed performance differences are statistically significant, and thereby provide evidence about which version is more effective in achieving the test objectives.

Reviewing the process of A/B testing

A/B testing begins with a hypothesis that proposes a potential outcome of making a specific change. For example, a hypothesis about changing the color of a call-to-action button may propose that the new color will increase user engagement or conversions. This hypothesis forms the basis of the A/B testing and guides what the test measures and how to interpret results.

Designing and executing an A/B test requires the group performing the test to adhere to a strict methodology to ensure that the test results are valid and offer actionable insights. Much of the methodology relies on statistical principles and analysis. If you need more information on these topics, see *Statistics For Dummies*, 2nd Edition, by Deborah J. Rumsey (Wiley) for an overview of the basics. You can use the following steps to guide your A/B testing process:

1. **Establish a meticulous test plan that underpins the validity of the text results.**

   Setting up the test plan includes

   - Creating a test hypothesis that contains a defined change in the content to be tested and a proposed outcome

   - Selecting the right metrics to measure

   - Determining the sample size needed for the test groups to achieve statistical significance

   - Deciding the duration of the test

2. **Identify the two testing groups within the content's target audience.**

   Randomly divide the target audience into two groups (A and B, of a size as noted in the test plan that you create in Step 1), ensuring that each group is representative of the overall population.

   This random assignment of audience members to the test groups helps to mitigate any biases or external variables that can influence the outcome. You should be able to attribute the observed test effects directly to the changes made in the content.

3. **Expose the control group (A) to the original content version and expose the experimental group (B) to the changed version.**

4. **Collect data that's observed throughout the testing period, based on the test plan's predefined metrics established in Step 1.**

   The data collected should demonstrate how each test group interacts with the content version that they see.

5. **Perform statistical analyses on the data collected during the testing period to determine the significance of the observed test results.**

   You can use statistical tools such as the *T-test* or *Z-test*, which can offer insights into whether a significant difference exists between the measured means of two groups. In A/B testing, these tools reflect the metrics — such as conversion rates — that are measured as defined in the test plan created in Step 1. The goal is to determine whether differences occur simply because of chance or are significant enough to be the result of changes made in the content being tested.

A statistically significant result indicates a high probability that the observed differences between groups are real and that you can act confidently upon them. Non-significant results suggest that the change to the tested content version didn't have a meaningful impact on the metrics, that you select to evaluate user behavior.

Use the statistical analyses that you perform as the final step in your A/B testing to make informed decisions that guide whether to adopt a new content version, further refine it, or discard it in favor of trying other content experiments. A rigorous approach to A/B testing and analysis enables your organization to make data-driven decisions about content and optimize offerings in a way that best meets the needs and preferences of its target audience.

Designing and implementing
AI-driven testing

Designing and implementing AI-driven A/B testing (and its derivatives; see the section "Surveying A/B Testing Extensions," later in this chapter) involves a strategic blend of technology, data analysis, and experimental design to ensure the accuracy and relevance of the tests.

Initiating the testing process

You begin the testing process by creating a clear definition of the objective. You may want to increase the conversion rate for a particular shopping cart flow, enhance user engagement to keep customers on your website longer, or improve any other specific metric. After you set your testing objective, your next crucial step is to identify the key variables that can impact your objective.

REMEMBER

When you use AI to drive your testing efforts, identifying variables involves not only selecting the elements to be tested (such as page layout, ad copy, and call-to-action buttons) but also determining the data points (user behaviors, demographic information, interaction histories) that the AI will analyze to predict outcomes and personalize the experience further.

Deploying machine learning models

The next step in your AI-driven testing process involves deploying machine learning (ML) models. Use models that are trained on historical data that can help them understand patterns and predict how changes may influence user behavior.

TIP

Ensure that the data used for model training is comprehensive and cleaned of any biases that may cause skewed outcomes. Chapter 4 gives you more information on verifying the integrity of your data.

Then set up the AI system to dynamically create and serve different variations of the content or design that you're testing to designated segments of the website traffic or ad viewers. You must integrate the setup with robust analytics tools (flip to the section "Gathering AI Tools for A/B Testing," later in this chapter, for details on some useful tools) that measure the performance of each content or design variation against the defined objectives.

The AI models that you deploy continuously learn from the incoming data and can make real-time adjustments to the testing parameters based on what they learn. This adaptive approach can significantly enhance the efficiency of the A/B testing process, but it requires careful monitoring to avoid *overfitting* (which can happen when the models don't accurately incorporate new data into their predictions; see Chapter 8 for more) and to ensure the validity of the test results.

Infusing the testing process with integrity

A critical aspect of AI-driven A/B testing is maintaining the integrity of the testing process. This idea of maintaining integrity comes up the in the section "Reviewing the process of A/B testing," earlier in this chapter.

Here are some aspects to consider when setting up and monitoring your AI-driven testing:

>> **Proper randomization and statistical significance thresholds:** The process to distribute variations among the test subjects ideally is random, which helps to minimize potential selection bias and uphold the statistical validity of the testing. You also must define the duration of the test and the statistical significance threshold required in advance. These parameters help determine when test results are conclusive enough to make informed decisions.

>> **Introduction of unexpected biases:** These biases can skew test outcomes and may result from the data used to train the AI model. You must regularly audit the AI algorithms and the data that they use to identify and mitigate these biases.

>> **Human oversight of testing results:** Although AI can manage and adapt testing in real time, human involvement remains critical. Humans can help interpret the test results, understand the broader context of the testing, and apply what they discover from these test results in a way that aligns with the overall business strategy and user experience goals.

Surveying A/B Testing Extensions

Split testing, multivariate testing, and *multi-page testing* are extensions of A/B testing that provide powerful tools to digital marketers, web designers, and user experience (UX) researchers. These types of tests attempt to optimize website performance by achieving higher conversion rates and improving user engagement through comprehensive analysis of multiple variables. The methodologies take A/B testing beyond the concept of testing a single content change and allow for data-driven decisions that can significantly impact the success of a website or digital marketing campaign.

Generative AI technologies are reshaping the future of website optimization through their use in A/B testing, split testing, multivariate testing, and multi-page testing. These AI tools not only automate and streamline the testing processes, but they also bring a greater depth of analysis and personalization capabilities because of the scope and applicability of the data that they draw from (see Chapter 4 regarding AI's use of data). Your business can use generative AI to craft more engaging, effective, and personalized user experiences that — when tested by using the methodologies described in the following sections — boost conversion rates and user satisfaction.

Taking advantage of split testing

Split testing involves comparing two versions of a web page to see which one performs better on a given conversion goal. The test usually measures user responses, such as number of clicks, completion of a form, or number and type of purchases.

For instance, marketing and sales professionals at an e-commerce site may use split testing to determine whether a red Buy Now button generates more or fewer sales than a green one. In this simple experiment, half of the site's traffic sees the web page that has the red button (Version A), and the other half sees the web page that has the green button (Version B). The split testing team then measures and statistically analyses the performance of each to determine which color of the Buy Now button leads to more conversions.

REMEMBER

Changing the color of a Buy Now button is a simple example, but the split-testing approach is particularly effective for testing significant design or content changes that have limited variables, so that you can directly attribute the results to the changes made. Split testing differs from A/B testing because it often includes multiple variables, compares two fundamentally different content versions or major website path changes (such as how a shopping path flows across many web pages), and generally has the objective of measuring the cumulative impact of a series of changes.

Sales and marketing teams can use AI and generative AI technologies in split testing to automate the creation and evaluation of test variations. Adding AI as a tool can significantly speed up the testing process by suggesting changes that you can apply to the variables being tested, as well as automatically measuring and analyzing the differences in user responses. Using generative AI for testing web page changes has these benefits:

>> **Automation of variations:** AI can automatically generate variations of web page elements — such as headlines or images — based on the best-performing content from similar contexts. This automation not only reduces

the manual effort involved in creating test variations, but also leverages the power of AI to predict which variations are likely to perform best, based on historical data and user behavior patterns.

>> **Variable analysis:** In addition to creating dozens of web page variations (different banners ads, for example) to test, AI can quickly identify which specific designs, colors, and messages resonate most with the target audience to maximize click-through rates and conversions.

Maximizing multivariate testing

Multivariate testing (MVT) takes the concept of A/B testing even further by examining how multiple variables interact with each other; it allows for the simultaneous examination of two or more elements to understand how combinations of changes affect user behavior. For example, an online retailer may conduct an MVT to optimize a product page by testing variations in the headline, product image, and call-to-action button simultaneously.

Here are some characteristics of MVT:

>> **Multilevel results:** The MVT approach can reveal not only which single changed element performs best, it can also show how the changed elements interact with each other to produce the optimal page layout. For example, a product page that has a relatively small headline and large product image may produce more click-throughs or conversions than a page (for that same product) that has a relatively large heading and small product image.

TIP

>> **Larger audience sample size:** If you want to use MVT, you must be certain that the online interface being tested has a significantly larger flow of online traffic than you need for A/B or split testing. That is, MVT testing needs a larger sample in order to achieve statistical significance for each combination of changed elements.

>> **Heavy resource requirements:** Multivariate testing is more complex to create and more resource-intensive to operate than A/B testing. It isn't as simple as split testing (where you test two variations of a page; see the preceding section for discussion of split testing), because it can include several variables that can dynamically influence each other in various ways.

AI's ability to handle complex data analysis particularly enhances MVT because it allows for the efficient processing of the vast amounts of data generated by testing multiple variables simultaneously. For instance, an AI-driven MVT may reveal that a particular combination of page layout, call-to-action button color, and promotional message significantly increases conversion rates for a specific demographic segment of the test's audience.

REMEMBER

AI algorithms can identify patterns and interactions between variables that are too subtle or complex for traditional statistical methods to detect. This capability can enable your businesses to uncover insightful optimization strategies that you may otherwise miss in the plethora of data gathered during the MVT.

Tracing a path with multi-page testing

Multi-page testing (also called *funnel testing*) extends the principles of A/B testing (discussed in the section "Examining the Fundamentals of A/B Testing," earlier in this chapter) and MVT (flip back to the preceding section) to multiple pages across a user's journey on a website. Instead of testing a single element on a page (A/B testing), several variables on a page (multi-variant testing), or even two versions of a page (split testing; see the section "Taking advantage of split testing," earlier in this chapter), multi-page testing evaluates changes across several pages that make up a conversion pathway, which is also known as a *funnel.*

For example, a subscription service may test variations in its sign-up process, from the initial landing page through the checkout process. By analyzing how changes to each step of the funnel (and the web pages involved) affect overall conversion rates, businesses can identify and remove bottlenecks, streamline the user experience, and hopefully achieve their goal of increasing conversions. This type of testing can help you understand the user journey in its entirety, but it requires careful planning and coordination to ensure that changes across pages work harmoniously toward the desired outcome.

You can use AI tools with multi-page testing to

» Track and analyze the user journey across multiple pages in real time.

» Predict and adapt to users' behavior while they move through the funnel toward conversion.

If you employ machine learning (ML) algorithms in your multi-page testing, your websites can dynamically adjust content and page elements to suit individual user preferences. This reworking effectively creates a personalized pathway that promotes the likelihood of the user becoming a customer. For a subscription service, AI can optimize each step of the sign-up process in real time — based on how individual users interact with each page — and offer a highly personalized experience that significantly increases the chances of users' completing the sign-up process.

VARIOUS TESTING METHODOLOGIES IN PRACTICE

In practice, A/B-related testing methodologies can lead to significant improvements in website performance and user satisfaction. Consider the case of a SaaS (software as a service) company that used split testing to optimize its home page. By testing different headlines and *hero images* (the dominant images on the page used to convey the main message or theme), the company found a combination that increased sign-ups by 25 percent. Similarly, an online retailer applying MVT discovered that a specific combination of product image size and placement, as well as a more prominent customer review section, increased sales by 15 percent. And in a multi-page test, a financial services company revamped its loan application process, resulting in a 20 percent increase in completed applications by simplifying forms and adding reassuring security badges at key steps.

These testing methodologies aren't mutually exclusive; you can use them in concert to achieve the most comprehensive insights into user behavior and preferences. By employing split testing, multivariate testing, and multi-page tests, businesses can methodically refine their digital properties, leading to better user experiences, increased engagement, and higher conversion rates. The key to success lies in the careful design of experiments, rigorous statistical analysis, and a commitment to making data-driven decisions that enhance the value provided to users.

Gathering AI Tools for A/B Testing

In the dynamic world of digital optimization, AI-enabled A/B testing tools stand as powerful solutions for enhancing website performance and user engagement. These tools employ machine learning (ML) and predictive analytics to automate test creation, execution, and analysis, allowing for more personalized and effective experiments. Table 16-1 offers a selection of ten AI-driven tools, each designed to cater to various aspects of A/B testing, from simple split tests to complex multivariate experiments and personalized user experience design.

TABLE 16-1   **AI Tools for A/B Testing**

Tool	Website	Types of Testing	What It Does
AB Tasty	www.abtasty.com	A/B testing, split testing, multivariate testing	Allows for experimentation, content personalization, and AI-driven recommendations
Adobe Target	http://business.adobe.com/products/target	A/B testing, multivariate testing	Delivers individualized experiences at scale
Convert	www.convert.com	A/B testing	Suitable for more complex testing scenarios that require high data accuracy
Coveo's Qubit	https://www.coveo.com/en/solutions/ecommerce-search-platform/ab-testing	A/B testing, multivariate testing	AI-driven personalized recommendations, A/B testing, real-time data integration, customizable merchandising rules, plug-and-play strategies
Dynamic Yield	www.dynamicyield.com	A/B testing, multivariate testing	Tailors experiences across web, mobile apps, e-mail, and kiosks
Instapage	www.instapage.com	A/B testing	Focuses on *post-click optimization* to improve the UX after an initial click on an ad
Kameleoon	www.kameleoon.com	A/B testing	Designed for enterprises
Optimizely	www.optimizely.com	A/B testing, multivariate testing	Experiment across websites, mobile apps, and connected devices
Unbounce	www.unbounce.com	A/B testing, smart traffic routing	Automatically routes visitors to the variant where they're most likely to convert, based on their behavior and characteristics
VWO (Visual Website Optimizer)	www.vwo.com	A/B testing, split URL, multivariate testing	A/B testing, personalization, behavioral analytics, progressive feature rollouts, collaborative program management

Chapter **17**

Fine-Tuning Content with Localization and Translation

When crafting consumers' digital experiences, you must keep localization and translation paramount so that you can engage a global audience effectively. In fact, businesses that market in multiple countries can't run effectively without strong localization and translation strategies. Historically, businesses applied these efforts to localizing and translating the company's website content, but they now extend the practice to all digital advertising and many customer relationship management (CRM) programs, too. Artificial intelligence (AI) can play an important role in making the process of localization and translation more efficient and effective.

Consider a multinational e-commerce platform, such as Amazon, which localizes its website for different countries so that it can enhance the shopping experience worldwide. Amazon accomplishes this goal by translating product descriptions, adapting currency and measurement units, and tailoring the user interface to reflect local tastes and legal requirements. Customers expect this localization from every multinational brand that they purchase from. This level of localization not only makes a company accessible but also builds trust and loyalty among users by showing respect for their language and culture.

Leveraging localization and translation activities to adapt your business content ensures that digital advertising, marketing campaigns, products and services, and all communications are relevant and user-friendly across various geographical and linguistic landscapes. In this chapter, I describe underlying principles of cultural awareness, strategies and best practices for using AI in your localization and translation efforts, and the tools that you can find to help you along the way.

Exploiting AI for Localization and Translation

Using artificial intelligence (AI) in your approach to localization efforts can make those efforts more efficient and workable, whether you're a marketer for a small business or a Fortune 500 company. At a basic level, AI-powered translation services, such as Google Translate, can drastically improve the speed and accuracy of translating web content on the fly. These services enable small businesses to reach international markets without the prohibitive costs of traditional translation services.

AI can also tailor digital advertising and marketing based on geographic and linguistic data, allowing companies to run localized campaigns that resonate with the target audience. For instance, Netflix uses AI not only to translate but also to recommend content by analyzing viewing patterns in different regions. This two-pronged approach helps to ensure that its suggestions are culturally relevant and engaging for each unique user base.

Capturing cultural context

Understanding the cultural context of your intended audience is crucial when localizing and translating so that you can create effective digital content — your website copy, social media campaigns, or CRM newsletters, for example. You must ensure that the adapted content not only translates linguistically, but also aligns with local customs, values, and behaviors. Infusing your translations with an attention to culture can significantly impact audience reception and engagement.

For instance, a social media campaign that acknowledges local holidays and traditions can foster a stronger connection with the audience than generic content developed by a marketing team and then translated. Similarly, CRM newsletters that reference local events or consumer habits can draw a tighter connection with the consumer and boost loyalty.

The cultural context encompasses more than just language — it includes humor, idioms, symbols, and societal norms, all of which can vary dramatically from one region to another. Ignoring these elements when localizing content can lead to misunderstandings and offend audiences, or simply result in content that fails to engage its intended audience.

REMEMBER

Don't think only about your marketing content that appears in text. AI tools can assist with subtitling and captioning for video content, too, which can help ensure that your multimedia materials are accessible to a broader audience.

Harnessing multilingual large language models

A relatively recent development in the world of generative AI involves the development of multilingual large language models (LLMs). A multilingual LLM is an advanced AI system designed to understand, generate, and process text across multiple languages. It leverages vast amounts of text data from various languages to learn linguistic patterns, idioms, and cultural nuances, which enables it to perform a wide range of language-related tasks. For example:

>> **For translation activities,** multilingual LLMs can seamlessly convert text from one language to another while maintaining the original meaning, tone, and context. This capability is crucial for businesses and organizations aiming to communicate effectively in a global market, ensuring that business messaging resonates with diverse audiences.

>> **For localization activities,** these models go beyond mere translation, adapting content to align with specific cultural norms and preferences. Multilingual LLMs can localize marketing materials, websites, and software applications to make products and services more accessible and appealing to users worldwide.

Although these tools are still emerging and aren't perfectly primed for marketing use cases, you can still evaluate them in the context of your marketing translation and localization efforts. As with any AI tools, they also require human oversight. Table 17-1 lists LLMs that you may find useful.

TABLE 17-1 **LLMs for Localization and Translation**

Development Company	LLM	What It Is and Does
OpenAI	GPT-4	Understands and generates text in multiple languages, enabling diverse applications, including translation, content creation, and conversation.
Google	mT5 (Multilingual Text-to-Text Transfer Transformer)	An extension of the T5 model, trained on a large multilingual data set, mT5 excels at translation, summarization, and question-answering tasks across languages.
Meta	XLM-R (Cross-lingual Language Model — Roberta)	Improves language understanding across many languages, focusing on tasks such as text classification and sentiment analysis.
Hugging Face	BERT (Bidirectional Encoder Representations from Transformers) Multilingual	Built on Google's BERT architecture, this model supports over 100 languages for tasks such as named-entity recognition and question answering.
Microsoft	Turing Multilingual Language Model	Used in applications such as translation, content moderation, and more efficient search algorithms.

To use ChatGPT (GPT-4) for translation, follow these steps:

1. **Identify the text that you want to translate and indicate the source and target languages.**

   Keep in mind that ChatGPT's capabilities for translation may vary from language to language.

2. **Input the text into ChatGPT and clearly mention the translation request once more by sharing which language you want to translate it to.**

   ChatGPT processes the text by using its understanding of multiple languages to generate a translation that appears immediately below your input.

3. **Review the translation for accuracy.**

   Keep in mind that ChatGPT is a powerful tool, but it may not always match the quality of a professional human translator, especially for complex or nuanced texts.

REMEMBER

If you're a small business marketer, accessing the other multilingual LLMs listed in Table 17-1 is a little more complex. And as with ChatGPT, reviewing the results for accuracy is critical. The models are reliant on the data used to train them, and the data can result in translations that include bias and cultural insensitivities.

Applying AI's capabilities

Advancements in AI technology enable content creators to produce a variety of localized versions of their work more efficiently and to provide a digital experience that feels deeply personalized. For example, you can customize AI-generated visual content to reflect cultural symbols, motifs, and color schemes that appeal to specific audiences.

REMEMBER

Customer expectations have increased dramatically over the last few years, as evidenced by a 2023 Salesforce article titled "What Are Customer Expectations, and How Have They Changed?" — not to spoil it, but subtitled "Customer expectations hit all-time highs." (To access this article, go to www.salesforce.com and enter "customer expectations" in the search text box. The article should pop up in the results.) Customers expect brands to understand them and talk to them on their terms, in ways that they appreciate and relate to. Using AI to effectively translate and localize all forms of content makes the effort required to meet heightened customer expectations much cheaper and quicker to do.

AI tools offer sophisticated solutions that can help your business navigate the cultural complexities and linguistic challenges of localizing and translating your customer-facing content. You can take advantage of these capabilities of AI tools and language models to fine-tune your websites, advertising, and online marketing:

>> **Broad, inclusive data analysis:** AI tools can analyze large data sets to identify cultural trends, preferences, and sensitivities specific to different audience segments. For example, AI-powered content analysis tools can scrutinize social media behavior, search queries, and online discussions across various cultures to glean insights into what content resonates in which regions. Because cultural trends and preferences can shift quickly, AI tools that continuously analyze online communications and train on real-time data are the most valuable. See Chapter 4 for more on AI and data analysis.

>> **Content adaptation for local relevance:** AI can assist in the localization process by identifying and adapting content that must be customized for cultural relevance. These adaptations may include modifying color schemes on a website to match cultural preferences or adjusting the tone and style of a customer relationship management (CRM) newsletter to align with local communication norms.

>> **Language adjustment to retain content essence:** Certain AI models can detect and adapt to subtle linguistic and cultural nuances, a capability that helps ensure that translations maintain the original message's intent, humor, and emotional tone. For instance, if you need to develop copy for a multinational campaign, choose AI tools that can suggest language adjustments to

avoid cultural taboos and embrace local expressions. When you use these tools to translate, they don't literally translate the text word-for-word, but ideally include the local flavor — idioms, for example — that keeps the essence of the communication whole.

REMEMBER

Although scores of AI tools can help you with translation, localization, personalization, and sentiment analysis for all your customer-facing content, having a human eye to look over what the AI engines generate is essential. Sometimes, AI engines get it wrong (less so now than before, but it still happens). You don't want to risk damage to your brand or your relationship with your customers by an AI-generated bad translation or a missed cultural nuance.

TIP

Engage AI tools to help personalize content at scale — for the entire breadth of your business's reach — and enable your marketers to create variations of a campaign that speak directly to the cultural context of each segment of their global audience. AI-powered *transcreation* (a term for adapting content creatively and culturally by using AI to maintain its original intent and emotional impact across languages and cultures) can help create culturally relevant and creative translations of your brand messaging that resonates with local audiences.

Checking out AI tools you can use

In this section, I introduce some specific AI tools that you can find to assist with localization and translation. Tables 17-2 and 17-3 list tools for consumer and for enterprise use, respectively. Neither table offers an exhaustive list, and many other AI localization and translation tools exist, each with their own strengths and weaknesses. Research and compare various tools to find the best fit for your specific needs.

TRANSLATION GONE WRONG

In 2014, KFC's entry into the Chinese market hit a snag when their iconic slogan "Finger Lickin' Good" was incorrectly translated as "Eat Your Fingers Off." This error led to widespread amusement and bewilderment among Chinese consumers, sparking a flurry of social media activity that highlighted the mistranslation. The incident underscored the challenges of accurately conveying brand messages across languages and cultures, and it emphasized the importance of meticulous localization to avoid misinterpretations that can alienate potential customers. The translation was literally correct but localized incorrectly. Human oversight is probably the only way that this mistranslation could have been avoided. In this instance, AI tools may not have picked it up because the phrase being translated was an idiom specific to the English language.

TABLE 17-2   **Consumer AI Tools for Translation**

Tool	Website	Features
DeepL	www.deepl.com	A neural machine tool focused on European languages (see Chapter 5 for more information on neural networks)
Google Translate	http://translate.google.com	A free tool that supports over 100 languages and can translate text, speech, and web pages
Microsoft Translator	http://translator.microsoft.com	A cloud-based translation platform that offers text and speech translation, as well as real-time conversation translation
Babelfish	www.babelfish.com	Uses human editors and AI to provide translations in over 75 languages
iTranslate	www.itranslate.com	An app that supports over 40 languages and offers text, voice, and offline translation capabilities
SayHi	www.sayhi.com	A chatbot tool that supports over 100 languages and can translate text, voice, and video calls in real time
Phrase	www.phrase.com	Localization and translation platform featuring automation, AI customization, workflow orchestration, and analytics
Wordbee	www.wordbee.com	A management platform that offers AI-powered translation, localization, and project management tools, as well as a community of translators

TABLE 17-3   **Enterprise AI Tools for Translation**

Tool	Website	Features
Acrolinx	www.acrolinx.com	A content creation and translation management platform that works across multiple languages and channels
RWS Tridion	www.rws.com/content-management/tridion	A content management and translation management platform that offers AI-powered translation, localization, and project management tools
Sitecore	www.sitecore.com	A customer experience platform that offers AI-powered translation and localization capabilities, as well as tools for managing and delivering personalized customer experiences
Drupal	www.drupal.org	An open-source content management platform that offers AI-powered translation and localization capabilities through various modules and integrations

(continued)

TABLE 17-3 *(continued)*

Tool	Website	Features
WordPress	www.wordpress.org	A content management platform that offers various AI-powered translation and localization plug-ins, such as WPML and Polylang
HubSpot	www.hubspot.com	A marketing, sales, and customer service platform that offers AI-powered translation and localization capabilities, as well as tools for managing and delivering personalized customer experiences
Salesforce	www.salesforce.com	A customer relationship management platform that offers AI-powered translation and localization capabilities, as well as tools for managing and delivering personalized customer experiences
IBM Watsonx	www.ibm.com/watsonx	An AI platform that offers various language translation and localization tools, including machine translation, natural language understanding, and natural language generation through its Watson Language Translator
Lilt	http://lilt.com	A platform that uses AI and human editors to provide translations in over 50 languages
Smartcat	www.smartcat.com	A management platform that offers translation, localization, and project management tools
Google Cloud Translation	http://cloud.google.com/translation	A cloud-based translation platform that offers AI-powered translation and localization capabilities, as well as tools for managing and delivering personalized customer experiences

Adopting Core Strategies for Localization

To harness AI effectively for localization and translation, you can adopt several core strategies that ensure your digital content is both accurately translated and also culturally relevant and engaging. Some of these strategies may be more appropriate for larger organizations, but understanding them can help you determine your own language translation strategies, even if you're marketing for a smaller business. Increasingly, you can find companies that cater to small and medium businesses, offering to assist in building functionality to support localization and translation strategies.

Leveraging machine learning

You can leverage machine learning for contextual translation by using these tools and practices:

>> **Training AI models by using domain-specific data:** Customize machine learning models by using industry-specific data sets to improve the accuracy of translations. These data sets can help ensure that your efforts correctly translate technical and professional jargon. You can also use *natural language processing* (NLP), which analyzes and interprets natural language, allowing for more accurate translations and localizations.

REMEMBER

The quality of the data used to train an AI tool directly impacts the quality of the translations it produces. Ensure that the training data is high-quality, relevant, and aligned with your brand's tone and style.

>> **Using neural machine translation (NMT):** Employ *NMT*, which uses neural networking to predict the possibility of a sequence of words, to understand and translate entire sentences or paragraphs at the same time, rather than word-by-word. NMT tools can capture context (see the section "Capturing cultural context," earlier in this chapter) and reduce errors, thus providing more fluid and natural translations.

>> **Implementing post-editing processes:** Use AI to flag translations that may require human review. Combining the efficiency of AI with the nuanced understanding of human translators helps you refine content for local markets.

Adopting AI-driven cultural adaptation tools

Check out AI algorithms, tools, and techniques that can help you customize and personalize your content for the culture of the customers you want to reach:

>> **Analyze cultural preferences with AI.** Analyze local consumer behavior and preferences, allowing for the adaptation of content, images, and design elements to match local tastes.

>> **Deploy sentiment analysis.** Gauge the emotional tone of content and adjust messaging so that it's culturally appropriate and it resonates with the target audience's values and expectations.

>> **Customize content for regional trends.** Dynamically update content based on trending topics, local news, and cultural events, ensuring that the brand remains relevant and engaged with local communities.

Enhancing personalization and localization efficiency

AI tools and systems, by design, can add efficiency to workflows. In the case of localization and translation, the following list highlights areas where AI can strategically streamline processes and learn in real time:

>> **Automating content localization workflows:** Streamline the localization process. Specifically, AI can identify content that needs translation, and also assign tasks and manage workflows to accomplish the translation and reduce time-to-market for localized content.

TIP

Consider implementing a *translation memory system,* which stores previously translated content in a database. You can access this database to retrieve and reuse previously translated content — a practice that can reduce costs and improve efficiency.

>> **Personalizing user experiences at scale:** Tailor digital experiences, including website content, social media, and e-mail marketing. AI can learn to recognize individual user preferences and local cultural norms so that it can enhance content aimed at increasing user engagement and satisfaction.

>> **Continuous learning and improvement:** Learn from user interactions and feedback to continuously improve the quality of translations and the effectiveness of localized content. You can use machine learning (ML) algorithms that train by using large data sets of previously translated content to identify patterns and relationships between languages. Doing so can help ensure that digital experiences remain relevant and compelling over time. In addition, these ML practices can help improve the accuracy of translations and reduce the need for human intervention.

Controlling quality when using AI

Using AI for quality control in localization and translation can help improve accuracy, efficiency, and consistency in your marketing content and campaigns. Here are some tips and tricks for teaming up with AI effectively in your quality-control activities:

>> **Use human post-translation editing.** Although AI-powered translation and localization efforts are highly accurate, you may want to add a human post-translation editing phase to refine the AI's output and ensure it meets the desired level of quality that you want for your localization efforts.

TIP

AI tools can be helpful and efficient, but a human editor should review and polish translations, especially for critical content such as branding materials, taglines, and mission statements.

>> **Integrate your localization and translation tools with other marketing tools.** Real-time localization and translation solutions often integrate with popular marketing tools, such as content management systems (CMSs), customer relationship management (CRM) software, and marketing automation platforms. Making sure that these systems work together adds fluidity and consistency to your marketing content and messages.

>> **Use a hybrid approach.** When I talk about a *hybrid approach* for your localization and translation, I mean combining human translation with machine learning algorithms. Adding human knowledge and experience with languages and cultures to your AI-driven translation efforts can help ensure that the translation is accurate and culturally relevant.

TIP

Combine the strengths of both human translators and AI tools to achieve the best results. AI tools can handle large volumes of content quickly and accurately, and human translators can review and refine the translations to ensure that they meet your brand's standards.

>> **Use a glossary and a style guide.** Basic reference materials — such as a glossary and style guide — can infuse localization and translation output with an extra polished feel. You can create a glossary of technical terms and jargon, as well as a style guide (which specifies formatting, tone, and other style issues), which AI and humans can reference during the translation and review processes. When you share these references across all team members involved in the process, you can help to ensure consistency in translation output.

>> **Monitor and analyze.** Continuously monitor and analyze the performance of the AI-powered localization and translation solutions that you use to identify areas for improvement. If you find that the solution is not meeting your needs, either determine the settings you can adjust to increase the accuracy of your translations or change solutions completely.

Examining Real-Time Localization and Translation Solutions

Real-time localization and translation solutions use artificial intelligence (AI) to translate and localize content in real time. This speedy processing allows businesses to reach new markets and engage with customers of varying languages and cultures immediately when those customers have questions. In the following sections, you can get a look at how real-time localization and translation solutions work, their benefits, and their applications in marketing.

Seeing how real-time solutions work

Real-time localization and translation solutions use AI algorithms that train on vast amounts of data, which include text in multiple languages and content that reveals cultural nuances. For example, the idiom "break a leg" in English would translate into German literally, implying a harmful wish. This type of training enables the AI to learn patterns and relationships between languages so that it generates more accurate translations and localizations.

The foundation for and process of real-time localization and translation involves several phases:

>> **Content analysis:** AI algorithms analyze the source content and identify the most critical elements that require localization or translation. This process, known as *content segmentation,* ensures that the AI translates or localizes only the parts of the content that are required to convey the primary message from the original language to the relevant target audience.

>> **Translation memory:** Memory-based translation, also known as *translation memory,* is a technique that stores previously translated content in a database. When similar content is encountered again, the AI can draw upon this database to produce consistent, high-quality translations, which reduces the need for human intervention. The section "Enhancing personalization and localization efficiency," earlier in this chapter, discusses use of translation memory.

>> **Real-time translation:** The trained AI models, along with natural language processing (NLP) algorithms, enable real-time translation of text, speech, or other forms of communication. In marketing, your business can take advantage of the real-time aspects of AI processing to quickly adapt its content for various regions and languages, ensuring that your messaging reaches a global audience.

>> **Localization:** Localization goes beyond translation, encompassing not only language but also cultural adaptations, formatting, and content optimization for a specific region. AI-powered localization solutions analyze the source content and adapt it to the target culture, considering local preferences, norms, and regulations.

Recognizing the benefits of real-time solutions

Real-time localization and translation solutions enable businesses to reach new markets and engage with their audience in various languages and cultures, with the goal of improving their customers' experience and driving growth and revenue. The benefits of using these solutions are numerous, including

>> **Cost savings:** Reduce or limit the need for human intervention, saving businesses time and money.

>> **Increased efficiency:** Reach new markets and engage with a new customer base quickly.

>> **Improved accuracy:** AI algorithms that train on vast data resources can help ensure that translations are accurate and culturally relevant. This increased accuracy reduces the risk of misunderstandings or miscommunications. When the solutions use translation memory (see the preceding section), the accuracy is further improved.

>> **Enhanced customer experience:** Provide your customers with a more personalized and engaging experience. The goal is to increase customer satisfaction and loyalty.

Applying real-time solutions in marketing

Real-time localization and translation solutions can help your business efficiently and effectively adapt your marketing strategies for a global audience. Here are some of the solutions' numerous applications in marketing:

>> **Website localization:** Localize your business's websites for various markets and customer bases. This localization helps ensure that your online marketing presence is felt globally. And don't forget about search engine optimization (SEO); optimize your translated content for local search engines by using local keywords and phrases to improve visibility and drive organic traffic.

REMEMBER

For websites especially, collaborate with local teams and in-country experts to ensure that your translations are accurate, culturally relevant, and aligned with local preferences.

>> **Content marketing:** Because you can create content in one language and translate it into multiple languages by using real-time localization and translation solutions, you can more quickly produce content that resonates with your target audience, regardless of their language or location.

- **»** **Social media marketing:** Engage with your audience on platforms other than your business's own websites or shopping sites.

- **»** **E-mail marketing:** Connect with your audience on a direct, personal level, regardless of their language or location.

- **»** **Advertising:** Reach your target audience in different markets and languages.

5

Targeting Growth Marketing and Customer Focus with AI

Infuse your performance programs with the efficiency and creativity of AI.

See how AI integrates with e-mail and SMS marketing for better customer acquisition and retention.

Improve customer experience via AI-powered personalization.

Effectively integrate AI into your overall business operations.

Consider the ethical, legal, and privacy concerns of using AI in business and marketing.

Chapter **18**

Applying AI to Performance Marketing

I n the ever-evolving landscape of *performance marketing* (an approach to digital marketing in which advertisers pay only when the desired activities, such as click-throughs or online purchases, occur), artificial intelligence (AI) is a constant. That is, performance marketers use AI to personalize the content shown to each user and target advertising to specific audiences based on their propensity to respond. Increasingly, AI identifies and defines the target audience, administers bidding for ads, provides creative alternatives for ads, and monitors the execution and measurement stages of digital advertising.

Over the last decade, businesses used AI to drive keyword research, enhance bidding and targeting, optimize ad placement, deliver predictive analytics, and assist in fraud detection. Marketers deployed AI for these uses to fine-tune ad campaign types, including social media marketing, display advertising, and search (and mobile) advertising. By and large, the platforms where ads appeared — as well as the relevant publishers and advertising networks — drove how AI was used for digital advertising.

With the dawn of generative AI, marketers expanded AI use to not only automate the creation of headlines and ad copy, but also infuse personalized imagery based on customer-specific information available to the advertising platform, publisher, or advertising partner. These additional automations result in solutions for which the advertisers do little more than set their campaign parameters and budget. They leave the actual administration, content creation, and monitoring of the campaign to the AI engines.

In this chapter, I help you understand the transformation in digital marketing by looking under the hood of the AI-enhanced digital advertising solutions from Google, Meta, Amazon, and TikTok. Marketers can easily access these platform solutions, and together, these platforms account for the vast majority of digital-advertising money spent around the world. In addition to presenting how the solutions work by using AI, this chapter also covers the steps that you can take (as a marketer) to run advertising on those platforms.

Examining Google Performance Max

To truly appreciate the power of AI in the Google advertising platform, consider Google's Performance Max campaigns and how they can help your business's marketing efforts. *Performance Max* is a goal-based campaign type in the Google Ads self-serve advertising platform that allows advertisers to access all of their Google Ads inventory from a single campaign. This inventory can include ads from Google's Search ecosystem (Search results, Maps, Shopping, and so on), as well as from Google Display Network (YouTube, Gmail, and Google Finance, for example).

Google designed Performance Max to specifically complement a keyword-based search campaign that can help identify and convert more users across all of Google's channels. And marketers are increasingly using Performance Max as a replacement for keyword-based search campaigns because it's so effective (and cost-effective) for marketing campaigns.

As a marketer, you can expect to see these advantages when you use Performance Max:

>> **Strong advertising results** that optimize your investments against specific conversion goals and deliver those conversions in real time across all Google advertising platforms. The Performance Max campaign uses data from the advertiser regarding performance measurements — for example, cost-per-acquisition (CPA) and return-on-advertising-spend (ROAS) targets, and specific parameters that help identify the creatives to use — to evaluate effectiveness.

>> **Automated campaign decisions,** including choices of where and how to run your ads in real time. Google AI engines make decisions covering smart bidding, budget optimization, audience choices, creative variations, attribution, and more, all on their own. Again, the AI uses the advertiser's first-party data — such as audience signals that point to what advertising has worked in the past — to strengthen the decision-making. This automation removes the need for detailed participation by a digital marketing team for the brand or by an agency.

Most of the time, the more input that a marketer gives the Performance Max system, the better the results. And Google Performance Max shifts the marketer's emphasis from running the campaigns to providing Google with the right data to run the campaigns itself.

Smart Bidding and asset creation

Google Performance Max integrates *Smart Bidding* (bid strategies that use AI to optimize conversions or conversion values in any transaction) with *advanced attribution technology* (a marketing strategy that evaluates which points on a customer's journey work or don't work for conversion). These strategies working together ensure that your campaign uses all Google features to determine auction bids that are most likely to achieve your business objectives. AI helps this determination happen in real time.

Another notable feature of Performance Max involves automatically created assets, which you can set at the campaign level to have AI create additional assets for your campaign. As a marketer, you can activate the setting to create assets when you set up the campaign at the get-go. Performance Max will create alternatives to your own assets and test the alternatives to determine whether they perform better (driving more cost-effective results) than the core assets that you may have shared. Features like automatically created assets become available in campaign settings when accounts participate in the beta.

Performance Max leverages Google AI not only to refine bids' content and placements for optimal conversion or conversion value, but also to offer account-level brand safety settings that enable you to specify platforms where you prefer *not* to display your ads. And so, these settings help ensure that your campaign stays in alignment with your brand's standards, values, and marketing focus.

Marketing outreach

Google Performance Max campaigns help you with the scope of your marketing outreach by

>> **Finding more customers:** If you're running a traditional advertising campaign by using Google Search, sooner or later, your search-driven lead volume can go off the rails for a couple of reasons:

- Not enough people search for the terms that you're paying for in your campaign.
- The campaign breaks the budget and becomes too expensive for each incremental user that you attract.

REMEMBER

Performance Max helps you avoid *wrong-volume* situations (situations in which your ad delivery does not match your desired volume of conversions or interactions) and find users across the entire Google ecosystem. This discovery goes beyond the customers that you may have identified yourself by using its AI for real-time insights (into the broad scope of Google users) and pairing these with your own data inputs.

>> **Identifying more valuable customers:** Because Google can leverage the insights it has from tracking the behavior of every user on the Google platform across all of its products, it can do a more effective job in identifying which users are most likely to efficiently convert for you. The Google AI engine analyzes billions of interactions with its users (practically every adult in the United States and many other countries). The breadth of the Google reach enables the AI to make more accurate predictions for matching audiences with headline, ad copy, imagery, channels, and ad unit types.

>> **Exposing deeper audience insights:** Performance Max provides marketers with richer, deeper, and more specific audience insights than marketers can discover on their own. Google not only looks across all its platforms to understand consumer behavior but also focuses on understanding how the consumers move between its various platforms and are influenced by specific messages at key moments. This understanding translates into making informed decisions about what creative assets to use, which channels or platform(s) to run on, and what types of advertising to run in the campaign.

Creating your Performance Max campaign

Creating a Google Performance Max campaign involves a series of steps designed to harness the power of Google's AI to drive conversions across Google's entire suite of advertising channels. This approach aims to maximize performance by leveraging Google's machine learning (ML) and automation capabilities. By following these steps (and continually refining your campaign based on performance data), you can achieve your marketing objectives:

1. **Sign into your Google Ads account.**

   You reach your command center for starting and managing your campaigns.

2. Click the + New Campaign button to create a new campaign.

Google Ads then prompts you to choose the Goal — such as sales, leads, or website traffic — that matches your campaign's main objective.

Performance Max campaigns are goal-oriented, so selecting the right objective is crucial.

3. Select Performance Max as your Campaign Type.

Using Performance Max means leveraging advanced ML algorithms, which optimizes your campaign's performance across all of Google's advertising channels and inventory.

4. Set up your campaign parameters.

Fill in the specifics that identify and limit your campaign, including

- *Campaign name:* Give your campaign a descriptive name so that you can easily identify it later.

- *Locations:* Specify where you want your ads to appear, geographically.

- *Languages:* Choose the language(s) that your target audience speaks.

- *Budget and bidding:* Set your daily or total campaign budget and choose your bidding strategy. Google Ads recommends bidding strategies based on your campaign goals. These strategies — such as Target CPA (Cost Per Acquisition) or Maximize Conversions — are designed to automatically adjust your bids in real time to achieve the best possible performance within your specified budget.

- *Ad schedule:* Decide whether you want your ads to run continuously or only during specific hours or days.

5. Define your campaign's audience.

Provide audience signals to guide the AI. You can use data such as customer match lists, website visitors, and app users. Although Performance Max uses Google's AI to target your ads, providing audience signals helps the AI choose the right audience. When using customer match lists, for example, you can upload your own data — e-mail addresses or phone numbers of your existing customers — to create more targeted and personalized ad campaigns.

6. Add the assets that you want to include in your campaign.

Your assets may include

- *Creative elements:* Upload images, logos, videos, headlines, and descriptions that apply to your campaign.

Performance Max campaigns require a variety of asset types to serve ads across different formats and platforms.

- *Final URL expansion:* Decide whether you want to allow Google to dynamically make changes that match your landing page to a user's query for more relevance.

7. **Set up conversion tracking by putting tracking codes on your website or app so that you can measure the consumer actions that you value most.**

   For example, you can measure actual sales, or sign-ups and leads acquired. Tracking this data is crucial for optimizing your campaign.

8. **Review all campaign settings and assets.**

   When you review your campaign, make sure that everything aligns with your marketing objectives and complies with Google Ads policies, which you can find by visiting the Google Ads Help Center.

9. **Click the Publish button to launch your campaign.**

10. **Monitor your campaign results by regularly checking your performance metrics and make necessary adjustments to optimize its performance.**

    You can use the insights and data provided by Google Ads in the "Reports" area to make informed decisions about optimizations for targeting, bidding, and creative adjustments.

Exploring Meta Advantage+ Campaigns

What Performance Max is to Google, Advantage+ is to Meta. (See the section "Examining Google Performance Max," earlier in this chapter, for more on this Google offering.) In a similar fashion to Google, Meta groups all its automated ad products and services for marketers together under Meta Advantage+. Through Meta Advantage+, a marketer can buy advertising across all of the Meta platforms at the same time (Facebook, Instagram, WhatsApp, and Messenger) without having to individually create and manually run campaigns in each one.

Meta Advantage+ campaigns take two forms: the Advantage+ app campaigns and Advantage+ shopping campaigns. In the following sections, you can get a look at some features of both types of Meta Advantage+ campaigns. These features and benefits are similar to what Google offers via Performance Max. Both companies use similar AI technology to power their advertising campaigns. *Note:* Because these platforms compete directly for marketers' advertising dollars, they try to match each other capability for capability.

Looking at campaign features

As a marketer, you have to spend less time in the campaign creation process if you let the Meta Advantage+ AI help configure your ads and messages so that you can reach more people in a personalized and cost-effective fashion. Advantage+ features that can help you include

>> **Automated campaign creation and management:** Streamlines the campaign creation process by enabling you to set up campaigns by entering fewer inputs, reducing the complexity of selecting audiences, placements, and ad creative options.

>> **Simplified audience targeting:** Analyzes data and identifies the most effective audience segments for your ads. By simplifying the audience targeting inputs that you need to provide, Advantage+ supplements with its data to help ensure that your campaigns reach the most relevant users without competing for the same audience across different campaigns.

>> **Enhanced ad creative process:** You can upload a variety of advertising creatives — including images, videos, and *Instant Experiences* (a full-screen, interactive ad format that opens after someone taps your ad on a mobile device) — in bulk. The system then automatically tests various combinations of these creative elements with your audience to determine which performs the best. This feature significantly reduces the manual effort involved in ad creation and testing.

>> **Placement optimization:** Automatic placements show your ads across as many places as possible within the Meta ecosystem — Facebook, Instagram, Messenger, and Meta Audience Network. The breadth of ad placement can help zero in on the platform(s) where your ads are likely to perform best. This targeting helps ensure maximum visibility and engagement of customers across the variety of platforms.

>> **Performance optimization:** Machine learning algorithms continually optimize your campaigns and include maximizing app installations, leads, sales, or other customer conversion goals. You can also receive optimized bidding strategies and dynamic adjustments of where and how your ads appear. All adjustments are designed to maximize your return on investment (ROI).

>> **Comprehensive reporting and insights:** Detailed reporting tools enable you to customize how you view your campaign performance. Breakdowns that you see for your marketing campaign can include customer demographics, device types that customers use, placements that customers respond to, and more. These statistics provide you with deep insights that can inform your future optimization and strategy decisions.

Reaping campaign benefits

Creating an Advantage+ campaign through Meta simplifies the advertising process by automating many decisions and instilling other efficiencies that allow you to focus on crafting compelling ad creatives and defining clear marketing objectives. Other benefits of Advantage + campaigns include

>> **Real-time campaign adjustments:** Advantage+ uses AI and machine learning to ensure that campaigns fine-tune in real time (for example, adjusting bids, targeting, and ad placements based on performance data) to achieve the best possible outcomes. The analytical nature of AI technologies can help your campaign adjust to the changing landscape of user behavior and platform dynamics.

>> **Scalability:** Because Advantage+ offers simplified campaign creation and automatic optimization, you can easily scale your marketing efforts across Meta's platforms without significantly increasing workload.

>> **Improved performance:** Advantage+ can improve ad performance, drive customer engagement and conversion rates, and boost return on investment (ROI) by optimizing ad delivery, ad creative, and targeting.

Taking form: App and shopping campaigns

The Meta platform gears a large part of its advertising toward driving app installations on customers' phones. As a result, Meta has a special advertising solution — Advantage+ app campaigns — that helps marketers promote app downloads. In a similar fashion, the Advantage+ shopping campaigns offer benefits to marketers who want to attract consumers interested in buying products and services.

Features of the app campaigns

Advantage+ app campaigns demand fewer inputs from advertisers during the campaign creation process, simplify audience selection, and streamline the management of creative assets. As a marketer, you can use app campaigns to optimize both app installations and app events (such as in-app purchases or user registrations) within a single campaign framework.

Furthermore, Advantage+ app campaigns support Advantage+ catalog ads. These catalog ads — previously referred to as dynamic ads — allow you to craft an ad template that automatically incorporates images and details from your product catalog. This integration helps ensure that your marketing campaign offers customers a more efficient and cohesive advertising experience.

Precise targeting with shopping campaigns

Meta Advantage+ shopping campaigns enable marketers to combine *prospecting* (identifying new customers) with reaching existing customer audiences within a single campaign. Marketers can pull *personalized products* (products most likely to be of interest to a specific user) from their catalog into the advertisement and also access tools that help with customizing the creative content and fine-tuning the target market. The campaign's creative combinations include choosing the right imagery, the headline and ad copy to go with it, and the right call-to-action. The campaign then matches the ad to the *highest value consumer* (the consumer who's most likely to make the most expensive purchase).

And in the same way that Google does (which I talk about in the section "Examining Google Performance Max," earlier in this chapter), Meta applies machine learning to identify and aim for the highest value customers across all the Meta platforms. Meta touts the fact that with Advantage+ shopping campaigns it can automatically test up to 150 creative combinations and deliver the highest-performing ads to the users.

Deriving your Advantage+ campaign

Creating a Meta Advantage+ campaign follows a streamlined process designed to leverage AI that optimizes your ad performance across the Meta family of apps (including Facebook, Instagram, Messenger, and the Meta Audience Network). By following the steps in this section, you can effectively engage your target audience and achieve your advertising goals on Meta's platforms.

Follow these steps to set up your Advantage+ campaign:

1. **Log into your Meta Ads Manager account and click the Create button to start a new campaign.**

2. **Choose your marketing objective from the options provided in the list.**

   Advantage+ campaigns support various objectives, including brand awareness, reach, traffic, engagement, app installs, video views, lead generation, and conversions. Select the objective that best aligns with your campaign goals.

3. **Select the Advantage+ Campaign option from the list.**

   Selecting the Advantage+ option enables you to use automated tools for your campaign.

4. **Configure the settings that name your campaign and control the budget.**

   Enter a name for your campaign that clearly identifies it for future reference. And, depending on the objective that you choose in Step 2, you may see options for optimizing your campaign budget. Decide whether you want to enable this feature, which allows Meta to automatically distribute your budget across ad sets to achieve the best results.

5. **Set up your campaign parameters.**

   You can specify parameters for your Advantage+ campaign by

   - *Defining your target audience:* You can specify basic demographic information such as age, gender, and location. The platform uses its AI to further refine your audience based on who's most likely to respond in accordance with the campaign objective that you specify in Step 2.

   - *Choosing your placements:* Although Advantage+ automatically optimizes ad placements, your Meta Ads Manager account may have options to specify certain preferences, for example, prioritizing mobile devices or excluding specific platforms.

   - *Setting your budget and schedule:* Decide how much you want to spend daily or over the life of your ads and schedule the time frame for when your ads will run.

6. **Outline design characteristics for your campaign ads.**

   You can specify your ads' design characteristics by

   - *Selecting the ad format that you want to use:* Advantage+ supports various ad formats, including single image or video, *carousel* (interactive ads that present multiple images or videos in the same ad), and more.

   - *Uploading your creative assets:* You can upload images, videos, headlines, and descriptions. Advantage+ then tests various combinations of these assets to determine which performs best with your target audience (which you define in Step 5).

   - *Entering the elements that are part of your ad creative:* These elements may include text, a website URL, and call-to-action (CTA) buttons. Make sure that all elements align with your campaign objectives (see Step 2) and audience interests (see Step 5).

7. **Review all settings, parameters, and creative elements that you entered.**

   Reviewing all parts of the campaign before you launch helps to ensure that they all align with your marketing goals and comply with Meta's advertising policies. You can find Meta's advertising policies by visiting the Meta Business Help Center.

8. **Click the Publish button to launch your Advantage+ campaign.**

9. **Monitor your campaign results and make necessary adjustments to optimize your campaign performance.**

After your campaign is live, you can regularly check on its performance data in your Meta Ads Manager account. Although Advantage+ provides features that automatically optimize your campaign (for example, by reallocating the budget to higher-performing ad sets), you must still review its progress and make manual adjustments to your campaign elements. For example, you may find that the performance data reveals that you need to adjust audience targeting, budget, or creative assets.

Inspecting Amazon Ads

The Amazon Ads platform operates a little differently than do the Google or Meta advertising platforms (discussed in the sections "Examining Google Performance Max" and "Exploring Meta Advantage+ Campaigns," respectively, earlier in this chapter) simply because the Amazon advertising is geared toward encouraging consumers to purchase on the Amazon website or mobile app itself. On Google or Meta, ad campaigns take a potential customer to the relevant brand's website or mobile app. Because of this difference, Amazon requires that advertisers register as sellers on its platform, offering products that the advertiser is already selling through Amazon. By being a *closed loop system* (going from advertising to purchasing all on one site), Amazon can provide more sophisticated targeting and data analysis capabilities than the other platforms.

Amazon Ads operates within the vast ecosystem of Amazon's online marketplace and can use the platform's extensive data on consumer preferences and shopping behavior — across a plethora of product types — to help advertisers reach their target audience more effectively. Amazon Ads campaigns are designed to enhance visibility for sellers and brands, which can drive both awareness and sales by placing products in front of consumers who are already in a shopping mindset. The following sections give you an overview of how the Amazon Ads platform works and the various ad formats and targeting mechanisms available.

Meeting the types of Amazon Ads

The Amazon Ads platform offers you ad formats that run the gamut, from ads that promote a single product listing to ads that run on the Amazon website and also on third-party sites. The ad formats that you can create by using Amazon Ads include

>> **Sponsored Products:** These cost-per-click (CPC) ads promote individual product listings on Amazon. Sponsored Products appear in search results and on product detail pages, which helps drive traffic to specific sought-out items.

As an advertiser, you can target these ads based on keywords or product types, making them highly relevant to consumers' search queries or interests.

>> **Sponsored Brands:** Formerly known as Headline Search Ads, Sponsored Brands are also CPC ads that enable brands to promote a custom headline, logo, and up to three products in one ad. These ads appear in more prominent positions — such as at the top of search results — and aim to increase brand awareness and sales for a range of products.

>> **Sponsored Display:** These ads target consumers based on their shopping behavior, including for products they've viewed but haven't purchased through Amazon. Sponsored Display ads can appear not only on Amazon but also on third-party websites and apps to provide advertisers with a broader reach. You can use this ad format to re-engage shoppers, encourage them to revisit products that they have already considered, and expand the reach of the campaign beyond Amazon's platform.

>> **Amazon DSP (demand-side platform):** Amazon DSP enables advertisers to buy display, video, and audio ads *programmatically* (by using algorithms and advertising technology) both on and off the Amazon website. You can use the DSP platform to leverage Amazon's rich shopping and entertainment data and reach audiences across Amazon sites and apps, as well as through its publishing partners and third-party exchanges. Amazon DSP is particularly effective for brand-awareness campaigns.

Zeroing in on targeting mechanisms

Amazon Ads' targeting capabilities are grounded in the platform's deep understanding of consumer shopping patterns, which it feeds into machine learning algorithms that then provide recommendations to the advertisers. Advertisers can target their ads based on the options listed in the following mini-table.

Targeting Option	What It's Based On
Keywords	Search terms that consumers enter
Products	Specific products or categories that are relevant to the advertiser's offering
Interests	Consumers' shopping behaviors and preferences gleaned from their browsing and purchasing history
Demographics	Consumers' demographic information
Custom Audiences	Comprehensive consumer data that identifies *lookalike audiences* (who share characteristics with existing audiences) for DSP ads

Paying and measuring performance

Most Amazon Ads operate on a cost-per-click (CPC) basis, which means that advertisers pay only when a shopper clicks on their ad. This model allows marketers to have tight control over advertising budgets and ensures that the money spent on ads is directly tied to potential customer engagement. Through Amazon DSP (see the section "Meeting the types of Amazon Ads," earlier in this chapter, to get the details), advertisers may also use a *cost-per-thousand-impressions* (CPM) model in which they pay for the visibility of their ads.

As part of the cost of ads, Amazon provides advertisers with a range of tools to measure the performance of their campaigns. These tools include metrics such as *impressions* (how many times an ad appears on users' screens), clicks, conversion rates, and return on advertising spend (ROAS). These insights enable advertisers to optimize their campaigns over time by refining targeting strategies, adjusting bids, and improving ad creatives for better performance.

Creating and running Amazon Ads

Amazon Ads represents a powerful tool for businesses looking to connect with consumers at various stages of their shopping journey, from product awareness and consideration to actual purchase.

Creating an Amazon Ads campaign involves a structured process that enables advertisers to leverage Amazon's vast marketplace and shopper insights for promoting their products. This section gives you a step-by-step guide to setting up your Amazon Ads campaign, focusing on the most common type — Sponsored Products — although the principles apply broadly to other Amazon advertising solutions, such as Sponsored Brands and Sponsored Display.

Follow these steps to set up a campaign in Amazon Ads:

1. **Sign into your Amazon Seller Central or Amazon Advertising console (for a vendor) account.**

    These platforms serve as the command center for your advertising campaigns on Amazon.

2. **In your platform's advertising section, choose the Campaign Manager option.**

3. **In the resulting area, click the Create Campaign button, and then choose the type of campaign that you want to run via Amazon Ads.**

    If you're a beginner with Amazon Ads, consider starting with Sponsored Products because it's a simple and effective format.

4. **Set up your campaign parameters.**

   You can type in the following parameters to identify and limit your campaign:

   - *Campaign Name:* Give your campaign a clear and descriptive name to help you track its performance.
   - *Start and End Dates:* Choose when you want your campaign to start and, if desired, when it should end.
   - *Daily Budget:* Set the amount of money that you can spend on the campaign each day.

REMEMBER

   Choose a budget that reflects your advertising goals (the clicks or other metrics that you're aiming for) and realistically accounts for the competitiveness of your product category so that you don't overspend for unproductive clicks, for example.

5. **Select how you want to target your ads.**

   Amazon offers two main targeting options for a Sponsored Products campaign:

   - *Automatic targeting:* Amazon targets your ads based on the content of your product listing and the queries that shoppers use. Use this option if you're new to Amazon Ads or if you want to cast a wide net to reach a broader audience.
   - *Manual targeting:* You choose keywords or products that you want to target with your ads. This approach offers more control to you, the marketer, and allows you to target specific goals that you have in mind.

6. **Choose the products that you want to advertise from the products that you have for sale on Amazon by selecting them from your product catalog.**

   Selecting products that are competitively priced, have good reviews, and are in stock is a must for maximizing the effectiveness of your ads.

7. **Set your bids, as prompted.**

   Your *bids* are the payment parameters you specify for ads you run on the platform. How much you pay for a click on your Sponsored Products campaign depends on the choices that you make in Step 5:

   - *For automatic targeting:* Set your default bid, which is the maximum amount that you're willing to pay for a click on your ad.
   - *For manual targeting:* Set bids for each keyword or product target that you specify in Step 5. Amazon provides suggested bids based on the competitiveness of the keyword, but you can adjust this amount based on your campaign goals and budget.

8. **Create your ad by taking advantage of product listings or adding additional creative input, depending on your campaign type.**

   Ad creation is based on the type of campaign you're setting up:

   - *Sponsored Products:* Amazon uses your existing product listing as the ad, so before starting your campaign, make sure that your product images and descriptions are high-quality and up to date.

   - *Sponsored Brands and Sponsored Display:* You may need to supply custom ad creatives. If so, follow Amazon's guidelines for image sizes, copy, and branding, which you can find by visiting the Amazon Advertising Support Center.

9. **Verify all the details of your campaign and submit your campaign for Amazon to review by clicking the Submit button in your campaign manager.**

   Amazon reviews your campaign to ensure that it meets all advertising guidelines. This process can take up to 72 hours.

10. **Monitor campaign performance by using the Amazon reporting tools that you can find in your Amazon Ads dashboard and optimize by making campaign adjustments.**

    You can analyze campaign metrics such as impressions, clicks, money spent, and sales to understand your campaign's effectiveness. Use these insights to make informed decisions about how to adjust bids, targeting, or even the product listings themselves for better performance.

Taking Stock of TikTok Advertising

TikTok advertising taps into the platform's dynamic, highly engaging environment to help brands connect with TikTok's vast, diverse audience. With a focus on creativity and authenticity, TikTok ads offer a unique opportunity for advertisers to craft compelling narratives that resonate with users. The following sections offer an overview of how advertising on TikTok works, from ad formats to targeting and measurement.

Following TikTok ad formats

Arguably, TikTok's incredible growth from 2020 on is directly attributable to its ML algorithms and how it makes sure that the right content (and the right advertising) gets in front of the right users to drive highly personalized engagement on a large scale.

TikTok ads come in the following formats:

>> **In-Feed:** Video ads that appear in the TikTok For You feed, among other user content. Similar to a typical TikTok video, users can interact with these ads by liking, commenting, sharing, or following the brand.

>> **Brand Takeover:** Appear immediately when a user opens the TikTok app and provide a full-screen video experience. This format is highly visible and effective for driving brand awareness, and you have the option to link a Brand Takeover ad to a website or TikTok page.

>> **TopView:** Like Brand Takeover ads but less intrusive, TopView ads appear 3 seconds after a user opens the app. They offer up to 60 seconds of full-screen video with sound. You can use this format to capture attention by providing engaging content.

>> **Hashtag Challenge:** Unique to TikTok, these ads invite users to create content around a branded hashtag. Because this ad format solicits user-generated content, it increases engagement and spreads brand awareness organically.

>> **Branded Effects:** Allow advertisers to create custom filters, stickers, and special effects that users can apply in their videos. This interactive format encourages creativity and participation to enhance brand engagement.

Exploring targeting capabilities

TikTok provides a range of targeting options to ensure that ads reach the most relevant audience. The following mini-table lists these options and their bases.

Targeting Option	What It's Based On
Demographics	User age, gender, location, and language
Interests	User interests and interactions, such as content types that they prefer on the TikTok platform
Behaviors	User activity, such as how they interact with content and creators
Custom Audiences	Your customer lists that serve to target existing customers or reach lookalike audiences
Device	User device type, operating system, or other technical specifications

TikTok ad campaign logistics

TikTok advertising stands out for its focus on immersive, interactive content that engages users in a natural and authentic manner. By understanding and leveraging the unique aspects of TikTok's ad ecosystem, advertisers can create successful campaigns that resonate with their target audience, drive engagement, and achieve significant brand impact.

Consider these factors for creating, launching, and optimizing a TikTok ad campaign:

>> **Bidding and budgeting:** TikTok ads operate on a bidding system in which advertisers set their budgets and bid for ad placements. You can choose from various billing methods, including cost per click (CPC), cost per thousand impressions (CPM), or cost per view (CPV) for video views. The platform allows for flexible budgeting options, letting you set daily or total campaign budgets, according to your needs.

>> **Ad creation and launch:** TikTok encourages creativity and authenticity in ad content. The platform helps its potential advertisers with

- *Creative tasks:* Rely on the platform for a range of creative tools and templates to help you (the advertiser) produce ads that resonate with the TikTok community.

- *Testing ads:* You can use TikTok's A/B testing (a method for testing small changes in your content; see Chapter 16) to experiment with ad variations, identify what works best, and optimize your campaigns accordingly.

- *Launch:* After you test your ad's effectiveness and define your target audience, you can launch your campaign to the wide TikTok audience.

>> **Measurement and optimization:** TikTok offers you comprehensive analytics and reporting tools so that you can track the performance of your ads. Metrics such as impressions, clicks, engagement rate, and conversion data help you measure the effectiveness of your campaigns and return on investment (ROI). You must continuously monitor these metrics and optimize your ad campaign (for example, by adjusting targeting or modifying ad creatives) based on the insights that you glean from those metrics.

AI Tools for Performance Marketing

If you're planning to step up your marketing game by using platforms and tools for automation, check out Table 18-1 for a look at some top candidates for using AI to help your efforts.

TABLE 18-1 Marketing Platforms that Use AI

Platform	Website	Description
Acquisio	www.acquisio.com	A bid- and budget-management platform that works across multiple search and social channels, with a focus on local and small business advertisers.
Adobe Marketo Engage	http://business. adobe.com/products/ marketo	A marketing automation platform that personalizes and optimizes campaigns across e-mail, social, and mobile channels.
Albert	www.albert.ai	A tool that automates and optimizes digital ad campaigns across multiple channels, including search, social, and display.
IBM Watsonx	www.ibm.com/watsonx	A platform that personalizes and optimizes campaigns across channels, including e-mail, mobile, and web.
Phrasee	www.phrasee.co	A tool that uses natural language generation to optimize e-mail subject lines, push notifications, digital advertising, and social media copy.
Pixis	www.pixis.ai	A platform for large spenders in digital marketing that creates audiences, develops creatives, and runs digital advertising campaigns.
Salesforce Einstein	www.salesforce.com/ einstein	A set of AI technologies that can personalize and optimize marketing campaigns, including e-mail, social, and mobile.
Skai	www.skai.io	A digital marketing platform that manages and optimizes search, social, and e-commerce campaigns at scale. This company changed its name from Kenshoo.
TextCortex	www.textcortex.com	A content marketing platform that optimizes social media and e-mail campaigns by analyzing and predicting audience engagement.

Chapter **19**

E-mail and SMS Marketing with AI

I n our evolving digital world, e-mail and short messaging service (SMS) marketing have emerged as potent channels of communication that businesses and individuals rely on to connect, inform, and (sometimes) persuade. Many people in the global working population begin their workdays by scanning e-mail and text messages, even before rising from bed. And for marketers, leveraging these channels proves highly effective for guiding consumers through the purchase process or reigniting their engagement with a brand.

This chapter begins by exploring the origins of e-mail and SMS marketing to provide a fundamental understanding of how these technologies emerged as critical marketing tools. You then get a look at AI-enabled tools and the features from e-mail and SMS providers, explore the integration of AI technologies into e-mail and SMS platforms, and discover how the resulting enhanced personalization and engagement strategies empower marketers to craft messages that resonate profoundly with their audience.

And of course, the chapter includes best practices for seamlessly integrating AI into e-mail and SMS marketing strategies and provides a guide to AI tools that you can use for your e-mail and SMS marketing efforts.

Tracking E-mail and SMS Marketing

You can trace the origins of e-mail and SMS marketing back to pivotal moments in technological history that laid the foundation for these powerful communication channels. For e-mail marketing, the timeline is something like this:

>> **1971:** Ray Tomlinson sent the first e-mail from ARPANET (a system that preceded the Internet), which paved the way for electronic mail communication between users that had different network hosts.

>> **The 1990s:** With the commercialization of the Internet, businesses began to recognize the immense potential of e-mails as a marketing tool. Some early attempts to use e-mail for marketing relied on the e-mail recipients to forward the message to other people or resulted in mass unformatted e-mails.

>> **2002:** A significant milestone occurred when the European Union Directive on Privacy and Electronic Communications helped legitimize e-mail marketing by establishing guidelines for privacy, consent, and opt-in subscriptions. These guidelines ushered in an era of more structured and respectful e-mail marketing practices.

And the SMS marketing timeline looks like this:

>> **1992:** The birth of what would become SMS marketing occurred when Neil Papworth sent the first text message — a Merry Christmas greeting — to his colleague's phone.

>> **The early 2000s:** Businesses began to leverage SMS as a marketing channel because of the ubiquity of mobile phone usage and the development of technologies that enabled bulk sending of text messages.

>> **2008:** A seminal moment in SMS marketing history occurred when President Obama's campaign team used SMS messages to announce Joe Biden as his running mate. These text messages showcased the power of SMS to directly reach and engage a vast audience, swiftly and personally.

Recognizing the breadth of use

The transformative potential of e-mail and SMS marketing, with the added focus and impact of AI, has significantly augmented the capabilities and effectiveness of these channels. An Ascend2 study in 2023 (https://www.emarketer.com/content/how-b2b-marketers-take-advantage-of-ai-email-marketing, as quoted in eMarketer) asked U.S. marketers how they plan to leverage AI in the context of e-mail marketing. The study showed the deep interest in using AI to strengthen e-mail marketing efforts and make them more effective. Participants ranked the following categories as opportunity areas:

- **»** Content personalization (50 percent)

- **»** E-mail retargeting (47 percent)

- **»** Subject-line optimization (47 percent)

- **»** Dynamic content generation (44 percent)

- **»** Send-time optimization (44 percent)

- **»** Automated segmentation and targeting (40 percent)

E-mail and SMS marketing have seen widespread adoption across various industries because of their usual cost-effectiveness, extensive reach, and versatility. Retailers use these channels for promotional offers, order confirmations, and customer service communications. The travel industry leverages them for itinerary updates and last-minute deals. And the healthcare sector communicates appointment reminders and health tips. These channels prove invaluable for building customer relationships, enhancing brand loyalty, and driving sales through personalized, targeted messages that reach recipients in the most convenient format.

Personalizing direct message marketing

REMEMBER

Harnessing AI to power e-mail and SMS marketing represents a huge leap in the ability of marketers to personalize, optimize, and measure their campaigns with unprecedented precision. AI transforms these traditional communication channels into highly potent tools for engaging with customers on an individualized level, driving not just increased open and click-through rates, but also enhancing customer satisfaction and fostering greater loyalty.

Over the years, technological advancements have significantly enhanced the sophistication of e-mail and SMS marketing. The integration of artificial intelligence and machine learning algorithms now allows you to personalize messages at scale, optimize send times by using predictive analytics, and automate workflows that respond dynamically to customer interactions. These advancements — combined with a deeper understanding of customer behavior and preferences via other AI technologies — have ensured the continued relevance and effectiveness of e-mail and SMS marketing as direct and engaging communication channels in the digital age.

Best marketing practice: Leverage generative AI tools to create personalized and contextually relevant e-mail and SMS content for each recipient, tailoring the messaging to their preferences and behaviors. For example, employ AI to analyze historical e-mail performance data and generate subject lines that are most likely to catch recipients' attention and drive higher open rates.

Adding the Power of AI to E-mail and SMS Marketing

A primary application of AI in e-mail and SMS marketing lies in the realm of personalization. AI algorithms analyze vast troves of data that sit in the data platforms of companies to reveal the secrets of customer behavior, preferences, and interaction history. AI uses these analyses to craft messages that resonate with individual recipients.

REMEMBER

An e-commerce retailer can leverage AI to send personalized product recommendations via e-mail or SMS based on a customer's previous browsing and purchase history. Netflix, a best-in-class marketer, provides a compelling example of this approach through its use of AI to tailor its e-mail marketing campaigns by sending personalized show and movie recommendations that keep users engaged and likely to return to the platform.

Incorporating predictive analytics to engage customers

AI significantly enhances the optimization of both content and time of delivery for text or e-mail. Through predictive analytics, AI can determine the best time to send messages to each recipient to increase the likelihood that the customer will open and read the message.

Best marketing practice: Use AI to determine the optimal send times for each recipient based on their engagement patterns and online behavior. Called *intelligent send-time optimization,* this practice maximizes the chances of your marketing messages being seen and acted upon.

Additionally, AI-powered *A/B testing* (a method of testing the effectiveness of marketing messaging; see Chapter 16) can automate the process of testing various subject lines, message content, and calls to action. These capabilities can help businesses to rapidly identify the most effective marketing strategies.

Best marketing practice: Use AI to design and execute more effective A/B tests for e-mail and SMS campaigns to automatically identify the best-performing variants for desired outcomes. For example, you can use AI to analyze the performance of various e-mail and SMS content elements (such as images, copy, or layout) and continually optimize them for better engagement.

For example, a marketing team may leverage AI to segment their audience into various groups based on real-time engagement levels and preferences. (Check out Chapter 9 for more about audience segmentation.) The team may then test different messaging strategies for each segment while continuously evaluating and adapting strategies to improve the desired performance metrics (the number of messages opened, for example). AI allows marketers to hyper-personalize e-mail and SMS content by using specific words, phrases, and brand-oriented language that AI analysis determines will resonate well. This personalization can reach not only specific audience segments, but also specific individuals based on analysis of their past behaviors, demographics, or *psychographics* (a classification based on attitudes and other psychological criteria).

REMEMBER

Marketers simply can't cost-effectively do an exceptional level of hyper-personalized messaging manually — or by using any prior technology or tools.

Best marketing practice: Use AI and machine learning algorithms more specifically to analyze customer data and segment audiences based on their predicted interests, behaviors, and likelihood to engage with specific campaigns. Then leverage AI to curate and deliver personalized, relevant content recommendations to customers through e-mail and SMS, based on their interests and preferences.

Tracking metrics and forecasting customer behavior

AI contributes to the sophistication of campaign analytics and insights. Beyond keeping basic metrics, such as message opening and click-through rates, AI tools can track and analyze *customer engagement* (the building of business-to-customer relationships) over time. The goal of these longer-term metrics is to predict future customer behaviors and identify patterns that may not be immediately apparent. Some customer patterns revealed may include

>> **Future click-through rates:** Whether the customer trend to follow a message's call-to-action is increasing or decreasing, for example

>> **A likelihood to purchase:** Whether more or fewer customers are buying

>> **Customer predictability:** How predictably a customer redeems an offer such as a discount or an *upsell item* (an additional or higher-priced item)

>> **Unsubscribing:** A customer's potential to unsubscribe to the marketing messages

AI's deep analytical capability allows marketers to refine their strategies in real time and make data-driven decisions that enhance the effectiveness of their campaigns. An illustrative case is Salesforce's Einstein AI (www.salesforce.com/einstein), which not only predicts the best times to send messages, but also provides insights into customer sentiment and the likelihood of customers engaging with a message, enabling marketers to tailor their follow-ups more strategically.

Best marketing practice: Analyze customer sentiment and feedback by using AI-based natural language processing (NLP) techniques. These techniques then enable targeted follow-up actions and personalized messaging. In addition, AI-driven conversational marketing strategies — which use chatbots and intelligent virtual assistants, for example — can engage customers through personalized, interactive experiences across e-mail and SMS channels.

Infusing e-mail campaigns with AI

By leveraging the creative and automation talents of AI, marketers can create effective, engaging, and customer-centric e-mail campaigns that drive superior results. Here are marketing efforts for which AI can lend a hand:

» **Personalized onboarding campaigns:** Tailor customer onboarding efforts to individual needs and preferences so that you can ensure a welcoming and engaging start for each customer, based on how they came into your ecosystem (through which channel, such as search advertising or sign-up at an event) and what products they're purchasing.

» **Personalized *nurture sequences*:** Develop customized and personalized sequences to guide prospects through the buying journey by offering relevant content and interactions that leverage all the data that exists for those prospects.

» **Automated multi-touch campaigns:** Implement campaigns that automatically engage with prospects across multiple *touchpoints* (points of interaction) so that you can build interest and drive action. Set up A/B tests (see Chapter 16 for more on A/B testing) for different personalized paths before you trigger a multi-touch campaign for all users.

» **Demand-generation workflows:** Craft workflows that strategically generate interest and demand for your products or services among potential customers based on past interactions, *lookalike studies* (analyzing the similarities between individuals or groups to predict behaviors, preferences, or traits), and *value propositions* (offers intended to make your products or services attractive) that resonate the most with your target customers.

- » **Complete e-mail nurtures:** Develop comprehensive e-mail nurturing programs that educate, inform, and move prospects through the sales funnel. Use *predictive churn tools* (which help forecast customers who may end their relationship with a company; see Chapter 11 for more) to determine which users are likely to leak, and then have the tool design more personalized nurturing programs unique to those prospects.

- » **Automated reactivation sequences:** Utilize targeted *sequences* (tailored communication plans personalized to specific customer segments) that you design to re-engage inactive customers or prospects, reigniting interest in your offerings. Harness AI writing to identify the perfect pitch message to reactivate users before you completely lose them.

- » **Sales and account-based marketing (ABM) campaigns:** Execute targeted campaigns aimed at engaging specific high-value accounts, aligning sales and marketing efforts. Focus on accounts that have the greatest propensity to become paying customers.

- » **Product newsletter treatments:** Design newsletters that highlight product features, updates, and benefits that can keep your audience informed and engaged.

- » **Multichannel win-back campaigns:** Initiate campaigns across various channels that aim to win back previous customers by using targeted messages and offers.

Infusing SMS campaigns with AI

The integration of AI technology into SMS marketing strategies helps to unlock the potential for innovation and meaningful connection with audiences. Here are some types of SMS marketing efforts that rely on AI:

- » **Promotional SMS:** Send messages to highlight special offers, sales, and discounts to drive immediate interest and action. Run multivariate testing (see Chapter 16 for information on this type of testing) against specific customer segments.

- » **Transactional SMS:** Communicate important information related to transactions — such as order confirmations, shipping updates, and payment receipts — at times when the users are most likely to respond favorably to them based on previous interactions.

- » **Appointment reminders:** Send reminders for appointments, bookings, and reservations, reducing no-shows and ensuring timely attendance. In a similar fashion, send these reminders when the specific customers are most likely to respond.

- **Feedback requests:** Request customer feedback and surveys to gather valuable insights directly after service or purchase.

- **Customer service:** Provide support and assistance, allowing for quick resolution of inquiries and issues. This offering combines AI chatbot functionality inside the SMS format (phone-based messages).

- **Loyalty program updates:** Inform customers of loyalty program benefits, points balance, and exclusive member-only offers to enhance engagement and retention.

- **Event notifications:** Announce upcoming events, webinars, or workshops, providing all necessary details and registration information.

- **Emergency alerts:** Send urgent updates and alerts to ensure immediate awareness of critical situations or changes.

- **Personalized recommendations:** Share personalized product or service recommendations based on customer preferences and purchase history.

- **Re-engagement:** Reach out to inactive customers by sending messages designed to rekindle interest and encourage re-engagement with your brand.

- **Subscription renewals:** Remind customers of upcoming subscription renewals, highlighting benefits of subscribing and any action needed to continue service.

DAIRY QUEEN CASE STUDY

According to an article from braze (www.braze.com; www.braze.com/customers/american-dairy-queen-case-study), the American Dairy Queen company (ADQ) launched a successful e-mail campaign to expand the reach of their rewards program by converting existing members of the Blizzard Fan Club (to become rewards members) and promote the rewards program through an app download. Here's how they did it:

- **Strategy:** In March 2022, ADQ launched a new mobile app to support its loyalty rewards program. This program marked a strategic pivot towards a cross-channel approach aimed at deepening fan relationships through personalized communication and experiences, fostering habit-forming behaviors among its user base.

- **Engagement tactics:** By 2023, ADQ recalibrated its strategy toward acquiring new fans and driving app downloads to expand the reach of the rewards program. A key initiative involved incentivizing members of the legacy Blizzard

Fan Club to transition to the rewards program. This transition was critical for broadening their engagement base and fostering loyalty within a more integrated digital ecosystem.

- **Experimentation and insight:** In August 2022, ADQ embarked on an A/B testing campaign to gauge the preferences of their Blizzard Fan Club audience. They segmented this audience into four groups, with each segment receiving a distinct welcome offer upon registration for the new rewards program. This methodical approach allowed ADQ to isolate and identify the most compelling offer to motivate sign-ups.

- **Campaign Success and Metrics:** The testing phase highlighted the 85 cent Blizzard Treat as the most effective offer, propelling ADQ to launch a full-scale campaign centered around this offer in April 2023. The campaign's impact was substantial and multifaceted:

  It generated significant revenue and increased rewards program signups and app downloads.

  It achieved a 138 percent boost in revenue relative to the average monthly customer relationship management (CRM) revenue, contributing to 20 percent of the total CRM revenue for the year.

  Loyalty signups surged by 310 percent compared to the typical monthly CRM-attributed signups, representing 37 percent of all CRM-based signups for the year.

  The initial campaign e-mail recorded the highest revenue conversion rate of any e-mail distributed throughout the year.

- **Achieving goals:** This strategic, data-driven campaign enabled ADQ to meet 90 percent of its app download objectives for 2023. Through careful analysis, experimentation, and targeted engagement, ADQ not only enhanced its digital presence but also significantly contributed to its financial and operational goals.

AI-Powered E-mail and SMS Marketing Tools

The AI-powered tools in Table 19-1 take advantage of various AI technologies — including natural language generation (NLG), natural language processing (NLP), machine learning, deep learning, and predictive analytics (see Part 2 for more information about these AI concepts) — to enhance e-mail and SMS marketing efforts through personalization, optimization, and automation.

TABLE 19-1   **AI Tools for E-mail and SMS Marketing**

Tool	Website	What It Does
Persado	www.persado.com	Generates highly personalized and emotionally resonant marketing content, including e-mail subject lines and body copy
Phrasee	www.phrasee.co	Subject line optimization, crafting subject lines that maximize open rates
Zeta Messaging	https://zetaglobal.com/platform/esp/	Creates personalized e-mail and SMS campaigns by analyzing customer data and behavior
Salesforce Einstein	www.salesforce.com/einstein	Offers Einstein Email Insights for optimizing e-mail campaigns and Einstein Engagement Scoring for identifying the best audiences
Drift	www.drift.com	Engage customers through personalized, real-time conversations through e-mail and SMS
Narrato.io	https://narrato.io/	Generates personalized e-mail and SMS content at scale, tailoring the messaging to individual recipients
Brevo	www.brevo.com/	Offers AI-driven e-mail marketing, SMS marketing, and marketing automation with advanced segmentation, content personalization, and optimized send-times
Mailchimp	https://mailchimp.com/	Provides e-mail marketing, SMS marketing, and marketing automation with content optimization and predictive analytics for customer behavior

Best marketing practice: Implement AI-driven analytics tools to gain deeper insights into campaign performance, customer behavior, and opportunities for optimization across e-mail and SMS channels.

Chapter **20**

Diving into Personalized Marketing

This chapter covers the fundamentals of personalization as they relate to business practices and the emerging possibilities for marketers with the advent of generative artificial intelligence (AI). At its core, *personalization* aims to tailor products, services, and experiences to meet individual customer preferences and needs. Before exploring the application of generative AI in personalization, I explain the advantages of personalization and explore core personalization concepts from a customer's perspective. These concepts include understanding the importance of data collection, segmentation, and targeting, as well as the role of predictive analytics and machine learning algorithms in delivering personalized experiences.

Unlocking the value of personalization for a business goes beyond merely customizing marketing messages or product recommendations. It involves creating meaningful connections with customers, fostering loyalty, and driving long-term profitability by taking advantage of data insights that can help deliver relevant and timely content.

Operationalizing personalization (that's a mouthful) by using AI represents a paradigm shift in how businesses approach customer engagement. By harnessing the capabilities of AI-driven algorithms and generative AI to create real-time, custom content, organizations can automate personalized experiences across multiple channels. In this chapter, I explain practical strategies (and best practices) for integrating AI into your existing marketing workflows and offer a look at AI tools that help with these efforts.

Adapting Marketing to Meet Consumer Personalization Preferences

Designing AI-powered personalization systems requires careful planning, strategic thinking, and a deep understanding of both technology and customer behavior. Consumers increasingly expect personalized experiences that resonate with their individual preferences, needs, and behaviors. Their expectations may come partly from a desire for efficiency, convenience, and a deeper connection with brands.

REMEMBER

Personalization can enhance customer satisfaction by making interactions more meaningful and perhaps even timesaving for the customer. The goal of all this personalization is to keep customers and ensure their satisfaction.

Bringing in the past

One key aspect that consumers may seek in personalized shopping or browsing experiences is the integration of their past behaviors and preferences into current interactions. For example, a survey that IT company Accenture conducted found that 91 percent of consumers are more likely to shop with brands that recognize them, remember past purchases, and provide relevant offers and recommendations.

AI plays a pivotal role in fulfilling customer demand for personalization. AI systems can analyze vast amounts of data to uncover patterns and insights, and they use machine learning algorithms to predict customer preferences with high accuracy. For example, online music streaming service Spotify (www.spotify.com) uses AI to create personalized playlists. By analyzing listening habits, Spotify provides users with Made for You playlists, which reflect listeners' musical tastes based on collaborative filtering, natural language processing (NLP), deep learning models, user interaction data, and audio analysis. The goal is to drive *customer engagement* (a relationship that goes beyond the transaction level) and bolster user satisfaction.

Responding in real time or future time

Consumers value real-time personalization that adapts to their immediate context. AI enables this personalization by processing data on-the-fly to deliver content or offers instantly. A notable example is clothing retailer H&M's online store (www2.hm.com), which uses AI to adjust product recommendations based on current shopping trends and individual customer interactions. This real-time personalization provides a dynamic shopping experience that reflects users' immediate preferences.

Best marketing practice: To provide timely and relevant personalized experiences, implement real-time data processing capabilities. AI systems should be able to analyze and act on data while the systems themselves collect it, enabling dynamic adjustments to personalization efforts. For instance, real-time recommendations based on current browsing behavior can significantly enhance user engagement and satisfaction.

Customers also value predictive capabilities that anticipate future needs. Predictive analytics, powered by AI, can forecast future customer preferences and enhance the customer experience by making proactive recommendations. The luxury fashion brand Burberry (www.burberry.com) leverages AI to suggest new arrivals and upcoming trends to customers based on their past purchase history and seasonal shopping trends.

Providing customer service, consistency, and privacy

Consumers expect high levels of personalization in customer service. AI-driven chatbots and virtual assistants use natural language processing (NLP) to provide a tailored customer service experience that mimics interaction with a human assistant. For example, the banking sector has seen significant advancements with AI in customer service. Bank of America's (www.bankofamerica.com) virtual assistant, Erica, uses AI to provide personalized banking advice based on users' spending habits, account balances, and financial goals.

Having a consistent customer experience across the various channels that a business uses for marketing is another expectation. AI helps achieve this omnichannel consistency by integrating data from various *customer touchpoints* (any means or method of customer interaction with a brand) to create a unified customer profile. For instance, the cosmetic company Ulta Beauty (www.ulta.com) uses AI to ensure that the personalization that a customer experiences online is seamlessly integrated with in-store visits to provide a cohesive shopping journey, whether the customer is online or in a physical store.

Consumers see privacy and ethical standards as paramount because of the growing awareness of data security. You must employ AI to address these concerns by implementing robust data security measures and ensuring transparency. According to the 2023 Cisco Consumer Privacy Survey, 46 percent of consumers feel that they can't protect their personal data, primarily because companies are not transparent regarding their data usage practices. In response, companies such as fitness program provider Peloton (www.onepeloton.com) use data responsibly to personalize fitness routines while ensuring that they securely manage users' health data and comply with privacy regulations.

Examining Personalization Concepts

Personalization in digital marketing is the practice of personalizing customer experiences to meet the specific needs and preferences of individual users or audience segments. Its primary goals are to improve *user engagement* (the business-to-customer relationship), customer loyalty, and *conversion* (leading a customer to complete a sale or sign up for a subscription, for example) by providing tailored content that reaches each customer without requiring much effort on that customer's part. The following sections cover key concepts that underpin personalization and contribute to its efficacy for businesses.

Describing elements of personalization

Consumers increasingly expect highly tailored and personalized experiences at every point of their interaction with a business. You can blame Amazon, Netflix, Spotify, Meta, and TikTok for spoiling consumers with this type of relevant content that meets those consumers' needs and desires. And now, consumers expect the same highly personal treatment everywhere.

REMEMBER

From personalized product recommendations to individualized communication, consumers crave seamless interactions that anticipate their needs. In fact, this practice has become the new standard for *customer experience design,* how companies intentionally define and design the optimal experience that they want their customers to have with their products, services, and marketing efforts.

Here are a few basic concepts and mechanisms that businesses employ to achieve a personalized approach to their customers:

>> **Data collection and integration:** Personalization relies on comprehensive customer understanding. It requires data from websites, mobile apps, customer relationship management (CRM) systems, purchase histories,

and third-party sources. Businesses integrate these data sets to create *unified customer profiles* (UCPs; a way to identify your current customers' characteristics), which are essential for accurate and relevant personalization. See Chapter 4 and the section "Institute data management" later in this chapter, for how to work with your customers' data.

» **Segmentation:** Marketers group customers based on shared characteristics such as demographics, behavior, or preferences in a process called *segmentation* (see Chapter 9 for more on this grouping approach). Segmentation enables marketers to craft messages that directly address the specific needs of each customer group that they identify. Increasingly, marketers use AI technologies to automatically generate a huge number of highly personalized consumer segments without the marketers' direct involvement.

» **Predictive analytics and machine learning:** AI machine learning models predict future customer behavior based on historical data, which helps marketers anticipate needs and offer personalized recommendations. Machine learning (ML, covered in Chapter 5) is the technology that businesses use to create consumer segments (discussed in the preceding bullet) that then receive specific marketing messages or experiences.

» **Content personalization:** Businesses tailor digital content to resonate with various audience segments through dynamic website content, personalized e-mails or SMS text messages (see Chapter 19), and customized product recommendations. Historically, content creation efforts served as a bottleneck in delivering personalization because of the time and resources required to produce tailored content. But the capabilities of generative AI have helped relieve that bottleneck by automating content generation and enabling real-time personalization.

» **Omnichannel experience:** Personalization strategies must synchronize across various marketing channels for a consistent customer experience. This synergy ensures that social media interactions align with e-mail offers and website recommendations, for example. And so, any AI segmentation model must deliver the same (omnichannel) experience to the customer across the channels that provide customer access to marketers' messaging.

» **Customer journey mapping:** Analyzing the *customer journey* (the path that a customer follows related to your brand and your products or services) identifies *touchpoints* (points of customer interaction) where personalization can enrich the experience. For example, businesses may identify the need to automate follow-up e-mails after a customer abandons a shopping cart or deliver highly personalized experiences for a customer logged into an app.

>> **Ethical and privacy considerations:** You must comply with data privacy regulations, and transparency in data usage can help foster customer trust. (See Chapter 22 for more on ethics and privacy.)

>> **A/B testing and optimization:** A/B testing (as covered in Chapter 16) provides insights into the most effective personalized messages and recommendations, ensuring that strategies evolve with changing customer preferences.

Recognizing AI's many roles

AI technology and deep learning models transform personalization by enabling more sophisticated recommendations for both marketers and customers. The music streaming service Spotify, for instance, curates unique playlists such as Discover Weekly by analyzing listening history and song attributes so that it can deliver hyper-personalized recommendations. These recommendations adapt over time to reflect changing preferences.

REMEMBER

Recent AI advancements — when combined with fundamental personalization concepts — enable marketers to create nuanced and relevant messaging that enhances customer experience across all *touchpoints* (places, online or offline, where customers interact with your brand). Many personalization solutions then use core AI concepts to assimilate the various data streams that come from these touchpoints.

Here are real-world examples of personalization solutions in which AI technologies can contribute to customer experiences:

>> **Real-time personalization:** Maintains customer engagement. Gatorade (www.gatorade.com), the sports drink company, tracks an athlete's sweat via a patch that the athlete applies before a workout and then scans immediately after to get a unique sweat profile that translates into personalized sports drink recommendations.

>> **Predictive personalization models:** Stitch Fix (www.stitchfix.com), an online personal styling service, uses these machine learning models to predict fashion preferences by examining customer inputted style quizzes, Pinterest boards, and past feedback. These predictions allow the service to match customers with clothing items aligned with those customers' tastes, providing proactive and individualized suggestions that resonate with the customers.

>> **Contextual personalization:** Adapts to a customer's immediate circumstances. Hilton's (www.hilton.com) mobile app provides real-time information for people staying at any of their hotels, such as recommending nearby

restaurants based on the weather or adjusting room service menus depending on the time of day.

>> **Augmented reality (AR):** A powerful tool for immersive, personalized shopping. The furniture and home products giant IKEA (www.ikea.com) has an app that helps users visualize furniture in their homes, simultaneously collecting data on preferences to suggest complementary products that suit their style. Since IKEA Place launched in 2018, other furniture brands such as Pottery Barn (www.potterybarn.com), a high-end home furnishings retailer, have begun to offer similar capabilities.

>> **Dynamic e-mail personalization:** Uses customer behavior data to deliver relevant product offers. Athletic apparel and footwear company Adidas (www.adidas.com) leverages this technology by aligning e-mail content with customers' purchase histories and browsing data, offering tailored shoe designs and apparel that reflect individual tastes and sporting interests.

>> **Behavioral trigger marketing:** Analyzes user behavior to send targeted follow-ups, such as reminders or special offers, when certain actions or inactions are detected so that companies can engage customers at the right moment. Beauty-product online retailer Birchbox (www.birchbox.com) sends recommendations and incentives based on customer engagement, encouraging customers to complete transactions that they showed interest in.

>> **Hyper-personalized loyalty programs:** Starbucks (www.starbucks.com), the ubiquitous chain of coffeehouses, has a loyalty program that integrates with their mobile app, offering rewards and incentives based on each customer's individual buying habits. This program encourages repeat purchases and fosters brand loyalty.

Unlocking the Deeper Value of Personalization with Generative AI

Unlocking the value of personalization in today's business environment requires a strategic approach that leverages the unique capabilities of generative AI. Recent advancements in generative AI have, not surprisingly, made personalization more scalable and accessible than ever before. Businesses can take advantage of these advancements to power increased personalization that hopefully results in more loyal, valuable, and satisfied customers.

Companies can harness generative AI advancements to deliver substantial value. They can

» **Reduce implementation costs by using automation.** Generative AI can automate many personalization processes that previously required significant manual input. For instance, dynamic content generation enables businesses to create personalized e-mails, product recommendations, and website landing pages across channels and customer segments without requiring individual marketers and designers to craft each piece of content. This automation drastically reduces the costs associated with personalized marketing campaigns while ensuring consistency across various *touchpoints* (places, whether online or offline, where customers interact with your brand).

» **Enhance data-driven insights.** Generative AI algorithms, particularly those utilizing deep learning, can analyze vast amounts of data to identify patterns and preferences that humans or traditional analytics methods would find difficult to discern. This capability provides a granular understanding of customer behavior and helps refine customer segmentation models (see Chapter 9 for information on customer segmentation).

» **Create hyper-personalized experiences.** One of the most powerful features of generative AI is its ability to synthesize and generate content that feels genuinely personalized. For instance, AI-driven chatbots can craft personalized responses that address customer queries or concerns with contextually relevant information, fostering a sense of individual attention. To make the most of these capabilities, users must write (or speak) smart prompts that provide the AI with enough context and direction. (See Chapter 13 for information about creating AI prompts.)

» **Optimize cross-channel consistency.** Generative AI ensures that personalization strategies are consistent across all customer touchpoints. By integrating customer data and preferences from different sources — such as customer relationship management (CRM) systems, web analytics, and social media — companies can build unified customer profiles (as noted in section "Describing elements of personalization" earlier in the chapter).

» **Improve return on investment (ROI) through predictive personalization.** Machine learning models can anticipate customer needs before a customer explicitly expresses those needs (or wants). For example, retailers can use predictive models to recommend products that a customer is likely to purchase based on prior purchase behavior and browsing history, leading to higher average order values and increased customer retention rates.

» **Conduct A/B testing and optimize continuously.** Generative AI can rapidly iterate through different personalization strategies by using A/B testing frameworks (see Chapter 16 for more about A/B testing). By analyzing customer response data in real time, businesses can quickly identify the most effective personalized messages and adapt campaigns accordingly.

Making Personalization Operational with AI

To make personalization real by using generative AI, you have to take a comprehensive approach to ensure that your business can effectively leverage data and technology to enhance customer experiences. Most critically, your approach to personalization must recognize that every customer is unique and has their own set of preferences, desires, triggers, and needs. The following sections give you a detailed outline of how to make personalization efforts operational by using AI, with specific steps to execute in a thoughtful way.

Establish clear objectives and metrics

Begin your AI-assisted personalization project by defining precise business goals for your personalization initiatives, which may include enhancing customer engagement, increasing sales conversions, or boosting customer retention. Also, establish the clear metrics required to measure the success of your initiatives. For example, if your aim is to enhance customer engagement, relevant metrics may include *interaction rates* (how many customers you attract), the amount of time the customer spends on your website, and customer feedback scores. After all, you don't want to personalize for the sake of doing so without tying the results to core business objectives.

Follow these steps to define your goals:

1. **Organize workshops that involve your business's key stakeholders to set clear personalization goals.**

   Key stakeholders may include marketers, product leaders, technologists, and customer service teams.

2. **Identify and document specific metrics that align with these goals.**

   You may be able to complete Steps 1 and 2 during the same organizational workshop.

TIP

3. **Create a baseline of current metrics to track improvements over time.**

   Gather and analyze current metrics that you align with your goals in Step 2 so that you can gauge the success of your personalization efforts.

Best marketing practice: Before diving into the technical aspects of personalization for your business, establish clear, measurable goals for your personalization system. These goals should align with overall business goals, such as increasing customer engagement, improving conversion rates, or enhancing customer loyalty. Defining these goals up front helps guide the development of personalization processes and ensure that all efforts are focused on delivering tangible business outcomes.

Institute data management

Personalization starts with the thorough collection and management of data. Gather data from multiple sources. Integrate this data into a centralized system such as a *customer data platform* (CDP, which creates a comprehensive, accessible customer database) or *data lake* (which stores large quantities of data in its native format) to create a unified customer view. When you collect data, do so with the assumption that you must intentionally capture and organize data from every touchpoint with your customers.

To collect and centralize customer data, follow these steps:

1. Identify and catalog all existing and potential data sources relevant to your business.

Your data may come from sources including websites, customer relationship management (CRM) systems, transaction histories, social media, call logs, and transcription notes.

2. Implement a customer data profile to unify and centralize data collection.

A *customer data profile* (a detailed description of an ideal customer) may include demographics, interests and preferences, and typical behaviors. AI technologies can help to create the profile by helping you capture and analyze every single touchpoint that your customers have with your business. (See Chapter 9 for info about how AI helps to develop customer personas.)

3. Maintain data quality through regular cleaning and updating processes.

See Chapter 4 for more information about ensuring data quality for use by AI technologies.

Best marketing practice: High-quality data is the cornerstone of effective personalization. Ensure that data collected from various sources is accurate, up-to-date, and comprehensive. Integrate data from different touchpoints — websites, mobile apps, in-store interactions, and customer service records — into a centralized system. This holistic view of customer data enables more accurate and relevant personalization.

Build detailed customer profiles

Constructing detailed customer profiles involves combining demographic, *psychographic* (classifications based on psychological characteristics), and behavioral data. Generative AI can enrich these profiles by analyzing unstructured data from sources such as social media interactions and customer reviews. These sources provide deeper insights into customer preferences and behaviors.

TIP

Begin your profile-building process by checking with your customer relationship management (CRM) and technology teams about whether they already have a customer data platform (CDP; see the preceding section for more about CDPs).

Follow these steps to build detailed customer profiles:

1. **Enrich customer personal and demographic data with additional attributes.**

   You can accomplish this enrichment by integrating third-party data sources and leveraging machine learning algorithms to predict and fill in missing information. Also, take advantage of AI marketing tools to include data that reveals interests and purchasing behavior, for example. You can also include softer metrics such as browsing behavior, time spent reading product descriptions, and so on.

2. **Use AI algorithms to automate the categorization and segmentation of customers.**

   See Chapter 9 for information about segmenting customers.

3. **Continuously update profiles with new data to reflect changing customer behaviors.**

   You can use AI technologies to help keep your data up to date by automating data collection and validation processes.

Best marketing practice: Move beyond basic demographic customer segmentation to more sophisticated techniques that consider behavioral, psychographic, and contextual factors. AI can analyze these complex data sets to create highly detailed customer segments and profiles. This added depth enables more nuanced and effective personalization strategies that can cater to specific needs and preferences of each segment. In fact, if you have an enterprise version of ChatGPT, you can even ask it to help you with analyzing your internal customer data sets and creating customer segments out of them.

Deploy predictive analytics

Predictive analytics is a powerful tool that allows businesses to anticipate customer needs and preferences. You can train AI machine learning models to forecast outcomes — such as purchase likelihood and *customer churn* (the percentage of customers that a business loses over time; see Chapter 11) — by feeding the models with historical and other customer data. Generative AI can enhance these models by identifying new patterns and trends, which makes predictions more accurate and dynamic.

Follow these steps to deploy predictive analytics by using AI:

1. **Choose suitable machine learning algorithms for predictive modeling.**

   The algorithms that you choose depend on the specific problem you are trying to solve, the nature of your data, and the desired outcome. See Chapter 7 for information about AI and predictions.

2. **Train the AI models that you choose by feeding in historical and real-time data.**

   Providing this data helps ensure accuracy in predictions and recommendations generated by the models. Real-time data can come from sources such as live customer interactions, transaction logs, social media activity, and even IoT sensors.

3. **Implement predictive models across customer touchpoints for real-time personalization.**

   See Chapter 7 for information on predictive models and Chapter 22 for information on maintaining customer privacy while getting personal with your customers.

Best marketing practice: Predictive analytics can anticipate future customer needs and behaviors, allowing businesses to be proactive rather than reactive in their marketing and customer outreach efforts. Train machine learning models on historical data to forecast future actions and enable the creation of personalized offers and content that align with anticipated customer needs. These insights increase the effectiveness of personalization efforts.

Generate personalized content

Generative AI can automate the creation of personalized content to ensure that each customer interaction is relevant and engaging. This approach includes generating tailored e-mails, product recommendations, and website content that resonates with individual preferences.

When personalizing marketing content and messaging, follow these steps:

1. **Use generative AI tools to automate the creation of personalized content.**

   AI is instrumental in collecting and analyzing the data needed to automate marketing content. See Chapter 14 for more information about using AI technologies to develop creative assets that you can use in personalized marketing.

2. **Ensure consistency in messaging across all customer touchpoints.**

   You can safeguard the consistency and validity of marketing messages by implementing centralized content management systems and establishing clear brand guidelines.

3. **Regularly update content to reflect new trends and customer feedback.**

   Maintain updated content by continuously monitoring market trends and actively collecting and analyzing customer feedback. See Chapter 19 to find out how you can incorporate customer feedback and trends in e-mail and SMS (text) marketing, for example.

Best marketing practice: Ensure that your personalization efforts are consistent across all customer interactions. Use an omnichannel approach that integrates personalization across websites, mobile apps, e-mail campaigns, social media, and even in-store interactions. Maintaining consistency in your personalization efforts reinforces the brand message and ensures that customers have a seamless and cohesive experience — regardless of the way in which they interact with the brand.

Test and optimize continuously

To maintain the effectiveness of personalization strategies, continuously test customer responses and optimize messaging. For example, you can implement an *A/B testing framework* (a setup that tests the performance of two versions of content to see which gets a better response) to experiment with content variations and identify the most effective marketing approaches. Generative AI can assist with A/B testing by rapidly generating multiple content variations that feed into the testing framework.

To optimize your marketing messaging based on test results, follow these steps:

1. **Establish an A/B testing framework to compare different testing personalization strategies.**

   A/B testing enables you to systematically evaluate the effectiveness of various marketing approaches by comparing two versions of content or strategies to determine which performs better. Chapter 16 discusses the nuts and bolts of AI-assisted A/B.

2. **Use generative AI to create and test various content variations.**

   Generative AI is a tireless and creative tool for creating and deploying marketing content variations for testing. With a framework in place (as established in Step 1), you can incorporate generative AI to test multiple content variations.

3. **Analyze test results to refine personalization strategies and predictive models.**

   Evaluate the outcomes of your test results and use that information to further customize and personalize your content for specific segments

Best marketing practice: Regularly test and optimize your marketing efforts to maintain the effectiveness of personalization strategies. Use A/B testing and other experimental methods to compare personalization tactics and identify what works best. Analyze the results to make data–driven decisions and refine personalization strategies.

CASE STUDY: MOVINGWALDO

MovingWaldo (www.movingwaldo.com), a digital concierge based in Montreal, Canada, serves as a link between professional movers, service providers, and customers. The company engages with three primary groups:

- A business-to-business (B2B) audience of service vendors
- Real estate agents who recommend their clients to MovingWaldo
- A business-to-consumer (B2C) audience of individuals who are relocating, some of whom speak English and others French

To manage these different groups of clients and potential clients, as of 2023, MovingWaldo sends over 100 targeted e-mails monthly, using AI-powered tools to swiftly segment audiences based on various data points, such as estimated moving dates, referral paths, and whether users visited the French or English version of the MovingWaldo website. The company employs automated A/B testing to effectively time the promotion of vendor services to its consumer audience.

Furthermore, by incorporating marketing automations, MovingWaldo efficiently crafts personalized, data-driven e-mails through predefined customer journeys, enhancing customer conversion at crucial moments and on a large scale.

> The essence of MovingWaldo's strategy lies in its ability to use data integration to communicate personally yet broadly. Advanced AI helps tailor language and tone to distinct audiences, acknowledging that a strategy effective in Toronto may not resonate as well in Montreal, thus ensuring relevance across diverse regions.

Incorporate customer feedback

Incorporate customer feedback into your personalization strategy — both explicit feedback (what you get from direct communication with customers, such as in a survey) and implicit feedback (what you infer from customer behaviors and interactions). Generative AI can analyze the feedback to provide deeper insights (such as identifying emerging trends and sentiment shifts) that help your business continuously refine customer segmentation, profiles, and predictive models.

TIP

Careful customer feedback analysis can help you avoid the risk of creeping out customers by *over-personalizing*, for example by making overly specific recommendations that may feel intrusive.

Follow these steps to incorporate customer feedback into your personalization efforts:

1. **Implement mechanisms to collect explicit customer feedback, such as surveys and reviews.**

   You can offer surveys to customers through follow-up e-mails and give customers an easy way to review products or customer experience directly from your website or shopping page. Collecting this direct, explicit feedback provides insight into the thoughts and opinions of customers who actually take the time to offer them.

2. **Analyze implicit feedback by using AI tools that monitor online interactions and purchase patterns.**

   The goal is to better understand customer behaviors and preferences.

3. **Use the analyzed explicit and implicit feedback to make continuous improvements.**

   Make changes to your segmentation strategy, customer profiles, and AI predictive models based on this feedback analysis.

Best marketing practice: Confirm that the AI system you use is designed to continuously learn and adapt based on new data and user interactions by incorporating automated retraining processes. Regularly update algorithms and models to reflect changing customer behaviors and preferences. Implement feedback loops that allow the system to learn from its successes and failures, continuously improving the accuracy and relevance of personalization efforts.

Ensure compliance and ethical standards

Your marketing personalization processes must adhere to data privacy regulations such as the General Data Protection Regulation (GDPR) and California Consumer Privacy Act (CCPA). Your business must ensure transparent data usage policies — by telling customers how you use their data — and then secure the customers' consent to do so. And as I mention in the preceding section, you also must avoid the creep factor and customer fatigue that can come with over-personalization.

REMEMBER

When you look at infusing your personalization practices with customer privacy and ethical standards, check with colleagues elsewhere in your business for their input. Likely, your legal teams already have policies around GDPR and CCPA.

To instill compliance and ethical standards in your marketing personalization efforts, follow these steps:

1. **Review and comply with relevant data privacy regulations.**

   Find out about regulatory policies that are already in place in your business and incorporate those policies, along with any other measures that your marketing team deems necessary.

2. **Clearly communicate data usage policies and obtain necessary consents from customers.**

   During your customers' interactions with your website, shopping site, and so on, make sure to inform your customers what data you are collecting about them, and why and how your company uses and shares it.

3. **Be strategic about personalization efforts so that you don't overwhelm customers.**

TIP

Although increased personalization can seem like the holy grail for every company and product, it may not always be worth the effort. For some products and services — low-consideration purchases such as toothpaste, for example — customers may not care about personalization because the messaging doesn't meaningfully impact their experience or decision-making.

Best marketing practice: Put ethical considerations at the forefront of AI-powered personalization systems. Ensure that AI algorithms are transparent, fair, and unbiased. Avoid over-personalization that can lead to customer fatigue or your business's perceived creepiness. Respect customer autonomy by providing them with methods for opting out or customizing the level of personalization that they receive. Ethical AI practices not only foster customer trust, but also ensure the long-term sustainability of personalization efforts.

REMEMBER

Maintaining transparency about how your business uses customer data can actually encourage customers to share more information, which in turn supplements the data that you need to fine-tune the personalization process.

Train teams and manage change

Successfully integrating AI-driven personalization into your marketing efforts requires thorough training for marketing teams and a culture of innovation. Train your employees up front on how to use AI tools and work effectively within their roles in the personalization strategy. And along with training, implement change management practices (such as regular workshops, clear communication of benefits, and ongoing support) to address any employee resistance so that you can ensure smooth adoption of AI tools and techniques.

Follow these steps to train and advise your marketing teams on the tools and practices of personalization:

1. **Develop comprehensive training programs centered on AI tools and personalization strategies.**

   Start by identifying use cases where personalization may have the biggest impact and be sure to assess the potential costs of deploying the personalization solutions.

2. **Promote a culture of innovation and collaboration within the organization.**

   Successful programs for promoting an innovative, collaborative culture in your marketing organization include hosting team meetings in which you encourage team members to share not just recent successes but recent failures as well.

3. **Implement change management practices to drive the transition to AI-assisted personalization, and address resistance.**

   Reinforce the training on using AI for personalization by offering continuing education and guidance for its implementation.

Plan for scalability

When your personalization strategies prove successful in your marketing efforts, plan for scalability to handle increasing data volumes and user interactions.

Expand personalization efforts to new channels, products, and markets gradually, and build on successful strategies.

To plan for personalized marketing on a larger scale, follow these steps:

1. **Assess the scalability of existing AI infrastructure and upgrade as necessary.**

   Take a look at the current AI tools and techniques that you use for your personalized marketing campaigns, compare their capabilities with your goals for your ongoing personalization, and update or acquire new technology as needed.

2. **Expand personalization efforts to new channels and markets gradually.**

   To expand gradually, you may identify which marketing channels are performing the least effectively and may be ripe for personalization to improve their performance.

3. **Continuously monitor performance and make iterative improvements to support the growth of your personalized marketing plans.**

   Keep metrics such as customer engagement rates, conversion rates, and customer satisfaction scores. Make changes such as adjusting targeting criteria, refining content strategies, and updating predictive models.

AI Tools to Help with Personalization

Table 20-1 offers some AI tools that can help with personalization, along with brief descriptions of each.

TABLE 20-1 **Tools that Use AI for Personalization**

Tool	Website	Description
Dynamic Yield by Mastercard	www.dynamicyield.com	Creates customer experiences that match content, products, and offers to each customer
Optimizely	www.optimizely.com	Enables A/B testing and personalization, delivering tailored experiences based on real-time data and user interactions
Twilio Segment	www.segment.com	Collects, unifies, and helps companies leverage customer data from various sources to drive marketing programs

Tool	Website	Description
Coveo	www.coveo.com	Analyzes customer behavior and delivers personalized interactions
Blueshift	www.blueshift.com	Combines customer data, predictive intelligence, and multichannel orchestration
Salesforce's Interaction Studio (formerly Evergage)	www.salesforce.com/marketing/personalization	Uses machine learning to deliver individualized experiences based on customer behavior, preferences, and contextual data
Pega Customer Decision Hub	www.pega.com/products/decision-hub	Delivers personalized customer experiences by analyzing data and making optimal decisions across all customer interactions
Lytics	www.lytics.com	Uses machine learning to create unified customer profiles (UCPs)
Acquia Lift	www.acquia.com/drupal/personalization	Integrates with content management software Drupal (www.drupal.org)
Marketo Engage	http://business.adobe.com/products/marketo/adobe-marketo.html	Part of Adobe Experience Cloud; automates and personalizes marketing campaigns
Algolia Recommend	www.algolia.com	Provides personalized product recommendations to enhance user experiences and drive engagement on websites and apps

Chapter **21**

Leading Your Business in the AI Era

very time new transformative technologies emerge, businesses need to reassess how they're organized and how they operate so that they can run their businesses most effectively. With automation through artificial intelligence (AI) taking over certain tasks, reassessing which roles humans should play in your changing organization is critical. This ongoing shift raises important questions about leadership, organization, culture, and how to effectively carry out business tasks that boost productivity and efficiency while also motivating employees to do their best work.

Managing these changes starts with a clear process for integrating AI and its principles into business operations. Integration begins with evaluating your business's current capabilities and determining priority use cases where AI may play a role. From that point, you figure out how AI technologies specifically strengthen those use cases by making them more efficient for your business. In this chapter, I outline a seven-step process to approach the transformation of your business by incorporating AI in a methodical fashion.

Additionally, this chapter delves into how you can directly integrate AI into marketing teams. AI not only alters how you develop marketing strategies but also how you execute those strategies. It is also worth mentioning that AI's role in marketing goes beyond content creation and deployment; it involves providing strategic insights that shape marketing strategies to keep those strategies data-driven and adaptable to evolving market conditions.

Successfully integrating AI into marketing requires broader organizational alignment. Also in this chapter, I show how AI-enhanced marketing operations link to other functions and promote the establishment of a cohesive, informed, and flexible business environment. Whether you work in a large company or a small one, the principles and practices required to maximize the benefits of AI are generally the same. Regardless of company size, you must have a road map to guide you through the initial stages of AI integration when preparing for the longer term and more transformative benefits that you can realize when your company gains an AI-first mindset.

Following Steps for Integrating AI into Your Business

A study late in 2023 by the nonprofit think tank the Conference Board (www.conference-board.org) revealed a striking statistic: 56 percent of employees already leveraged generative AI tools in their day-to-day roles — often unbeknownst to their employers. This statistic underscores a reality that companies can't afford to ignore. Trying to restrict employees from using generative AI is a boneheaded exercise. A cautious wait-and-see approach is, in reality, a wait-and-lose approach because the benefits of using generative AI only increase over time, and waiting puts you behind on reaping these benefits.

REMEMBER

Many companies are nervous about confidential data being shared via ChatGPT or other generative AI tools. Walmart and Amazon have warned employees not to share confidential information in these tools. Chase and Verizon have reportedly blocked employee access to generative AI tools through company computers. Although these short-term responses are understandable, they're not sustainable for the long term. Why? Because people are resourceful and, as the Conference Board study highlights, they'll find ways to harness the power of AI whether or not they're given permission — even if doing so comes with unintentional organizational risks.

With that in mind, I offer an alternative approach: seven steps for leaders to use to integrate AI into their businesses in alignment with their teams' needs. By methodically following these steps, organizations can establish a strong foundation for AI implementations and ensure that the technology supports strategic business goals and delivers real results:

1. **Educate business teams about the benefits and the risks of using AI.**

   Bring in educators, thought leaders, platform partners, agency leaders, and representatives from law firms — whoever it takes to present the facts (and myths) about AI in a methodical, scalable, pragmatic, and solution-oriented fashion. You can't make the education process a one-off exercise; it needs to be a program run over many months.

2. **Give employees an AI sandbox environment to play in.**

   Employees will use AI tools to help them do their jobs better, they just may not tell their leaders about it. So to prevent this subterfuge, you may as well allow employees to use the tools at least in a sandbox environment, where they can experiment and learn without compromising your company's customer and business data.

   WARNING

   Preventing employees from using helpful AI tools sends the message that leaders don't care about employees' productivity or, worse still, don't believe in furthering their employees careers.

3. **Lead from within by involving teams in the logistics of incorporating AI, rather than from the outside by dictating use policies.**

   Leaders should encourage their direct reports and their teams to devise a strategy for incorporating AI into their work. AI impacts each team differently, and those direct reports are best positioned to identify how they can use AI technology and tools to fulfill their job functions.

   TIP

   Urging team leaders to collaborate with colleagues beyond their own function also pays dividends because it fosters cross-functional innovation and ensures a more comprehensive adoption of AI across the organization. Instead of appointing a Chief AI Officer or designating a single individual to take charge, leaders should foster an environment where decisions about changing business practices come from within.

4. **Focus on mission-critical functionality and specific use cases.**

   Identify functions of and uses for AI in your business, and then organize them into categories according to corresponding AI capabilities, tools, and technologies. The head of early-stage venture firm Bloomberg Beta (www.bloombergbeta.com) first introduced these categories to define AI tools and their uses at the Bloomberg Tech Summit in late 2023 (www.bloomberg.com/news/newsletters/2023-10-25/art-has-long-shaped-technology-with-ai-the-roles-reverse). The categories are

   - *Cranes* are technologies that augment human capabilities and give a team member superhuman powers to do its job dramatically better — just like a crane gives a construction worker the ability to lift 1,000-pound steel beams. These use cases can significantly impact a business's output.

Note: Cranes are the most likely to require significant financial and learning curve investment.

A good example of a crane is a new AI-powered data analytics platform that can give marketing teams superhuman capabilities by processing and analyzing vast consumer data sets in real time on their behalf. This computing capability enables predictive analytics and provides input for personalized marketing that can lead to improved business outcomes.

- *Looms* automate entire job activities, the way looms did in the mid-1800s, completely displacing human weavers. Don't deny that loom-type opportunities exist; they do in every function. These AI loom use cases are the most transformative but also the most disruptive to a company, its culture, and employee morale. Leaders should be very careful about how and when they introduce these AI looms.

  An example of a loom is an AI-driven customer service chatbot that automates entire support activities to handle customer inquiries and offer resolutions without human intervention. Although this automation boosts efficiency and cost savings, it may significantly disrupt company culture and employee morale.

- *Slide rules* enhance efficiency for job tasks just like slide rules did for making calculations easier (before the advent of calculators and computing). These use cases aren't transformative, but they can quickly make work easier for employees across the enterprise. Several AI use cases fit into this slide-rule category, and they're relatively easy to implement.

  An example of a slide rule is an AI-powered e-mail sorting tool that enhances efficiency by automatically categorizing and prioritizing e-mails, which makes related task management easier for employees. This quick-to-implement solution simplifies daily workflow without being disruptive.

5. **Finalize a list of the products, tools, and technologies that are essential for the functionalities and use cases that you identify in Step 4.**

   Assess the necessity of involving the chief financial officer (CFO) and chief technology officer (CTO) in the discussions at this point. In practice, the expertise and insights of both these officers can become indispensable. This phase may also involve strategic negotiations with the CTO to incorporate their requirements into the road map for integrating the technology or persuading the legal team to approve the integration of a third-party solution.

6. **Empower the appropriate managers (typically direct reports of the chief executives) to spearhead the implementation of the list of use cases that you create in Step 4.**

Emphasize the importance of having the managers themselves lead the transformation, rather than having changes imposed upon departments by the higher-ups. Encourage these managers to connect with their external advertising and marketing agencies and marketing technology solution providers to explore how those partners can support the process. Numerous technology providers are enhancing their offerings by integrating advanced AI capabilities into their *technology stack* (the collection of technologies used to deliver a fully functioning system).

7. **Regularly assess and measure the progress of AI implementations.**

   Ideally, plan function-wide (across the entire marketing function for example) show-and-tell sessions where each team leader can showcase how they're using AI to improve their work. Present the AI transformation, with its warts and all visible, so that everyone can gain an understanding of each other's experiences. This sharing aspect is of utmost importance to fostering collaboration and continuous improvement.

REMEMBER

Adopting the approach in the preceding step list to assess and measure progress encourages teams to embrace the AI era with an ownership mindset. They're in command — pinpointing opportunities for growth and adaptation — instead of seeing AI as a threat. Venturing into the AI era without the input, participation, and, most critically, leadership of employees at the core can result in a failed attempt.

Building AI Capability within Marketing

The successful integration of AI into marketing (and other business operations) requires a collaborative effort across all levels of an organization. Your business's leaders and their teams — those intimately familiar with the daily operations and challenges — must be the ones to drive this integration. Their motivation, coupled with education and a clear plan, is crucial. Seeing AI not as a competitive threat but as a productivity enabler can unlock unprecedented efficiency and innovation.

Examining the approach of the U.S. federal government

You can take a clue from the initiatives of the U.S. federal government, the nation's largest employer, to systematically integrate and monitor AI technologies in your business.

In early 2024, the U.S. federal government announced rigorous *binding require-ments* (meaning that each agency was required to follow the directive) for the ethi-cal use of artificial intelligence (AI). Key to this directive — outlined in an executive memorandum from the Office of Management and Budget (OMB) — was the implementation of comprehensive safeguards against AI misuse, including thor-ough assessments of AI's societal impacts and measures to prevent algorithmic discrimination, all to be in place by December 1, 2024. You can read ongoing infor-mation about this memorandum by going to www.whitehouse.gov and entering "omb policy ai" in the Search text box. From the list of article titles that appears, select the article from March 28, 2024, titled "Fact Sheet. . .," for example.

To meet these requirements, federal agencies were directed to appoint chief AI officers and establish AI governance boards by May 27, 2024. The agencies charged these appointees and boards with the oversight of AI projects and the enforcement of ethical standards. Additionally, agencies must produce annual inventories that detail AI use cases, focusing on actions taken to address potential risks and pro-tect public rights. You can take a look at their current use cases on the AI.gov website (specifically, http://ai.gov/ai-use-cases). I highlight three of these use cases here:

>> **At airports,** travelers can opt out of TSA facial recognition without delays or losing their place in line.

>> **In the federal healthcare system,** human oversight ensures that AI supports critical diagnostic decisions and maintains equitable access to healthcare services.

>> **For AI in fraud detection** within government services, human oversight reviews significant decisions (such as flagging fraudulent activities or denying services), so that actual people can address any AI-related issues that may have arisen.

Furthermore, the Biden-Harris Administration committed to building AI compe-tency within the federal workforce, targeting the recruitment of at least 100 AI professionals by the summer of 2024. Although businesses (large or small) are very different from the federal government, the binding requirements that the U.S. OMB put in place serve as a guide for how to drive the AI transformation within a business.

Framing your approach to AI in marketing

Marketing leaders can take actions in a similar fashion to the federal govern-ment's approach to implementing and governing the use of AI (see the preceding section). You can rank the following implementation points on a 1-to-5 completion scale (1 is just starting; 5 is completed) to determine where your business and marketing teams stand on their journey to achieving a mature program of AI usage. Leaders using this approach should consider setting dates and milestones around each implementation point.

AI procurement policies

Score (1–5):_____

Establish procurement policies for acquiring AI technologies, as well as engaging with third-party vendors and their AI solutions. When you work with the vendors, incorporate transparency requirements in your *master service agreements* (MSAs; contracts that outline the scope of your relationship with the vendor) and assess these requirements to ensure that the vendors you work with agree to your organization's ethical standards and goals.

REMEMBER

Provide clear direction to both internal teams and external agency partners about which AI tools they can use and how they should manage enterprise information in the context of maintaining data integrity and privacy.

Executive alignment on AI strategy

Score (1–5):_____

You need chief-executive-level collaboration on AI strategies, particularly between the chief marketing officer (CMO), chief technology officer (CTO), and chief financial officer (CFO). A March 24, 2024, *Wall Street Journal* article titled "CFOs Tackle Thorny Calculus on Gen AI: What's the Return on Investment?" (which you can find by searching for the article's title in your favorite search engine) discusses how CFOs are prioritizing generative AI investments but expecting strong returns. The article talks about the need for executive alignment to truly take advantage of this technology. Otherwise, businesses get left in the dust while competitors leapfrog them.

Function-specific AI policies

Score (1–5):_____

Develop clear policies and procedures for incorporating AI into your marketing and customer experience efforts. This point involves collaboration between marketing, legal, and technology functions to establish AI governance structures that are ethical, effective, and compliant with existing laws and guidelines. Keep in mind that these policies also need to be in harmony with corporate-wide policies that may already be in place.

Function-specific use cases

Score (1–5):_____

Identify and develop potential AI use cases within marketing. For this implementation point, experiment with AI and form strategic partnerships between marketing and technology teams to strengthen the use cases. You can take advice from insights and best practices that you find elsewhere in your business's industry. For example, you may access the federal government's inventory of use cases as inspiration, but a more valuable source may be the ideas that surface when you encourage each employee to brainstorm about how AI and specific AI tools can enhance their work.

Progress metrics and assessment frameworks

Score (1–5):_____

Define metrics and frameworks that evaluate the progress of AI integrations. Some of AI's efficiencies may be behind the scenes and visible only through a modern-day equivalent of *time-and-motion studies* (which evaluate the efficiency of a specific business operation) although other efficiencies may be more obvious and visible in existing metrics (the increase in e-mail engagement when you implement AI-driven personalization, for example).

TIP

You can systematically assess and report on the effectiveness of AI initiatives by using methodologies such as the three horizons framework first presented in the book *The Alchemy of Growth,* by Mehrdad Bagai, Stephen Coley, and David White (Basic Books) and discussed by consulting group McKinsey & Company (www.mckinsey.com) in its article "Enduring ideas: The three horizons of growth." (You can search for the article's title on the website to access the article.) Any methodology you use should facilitate making informed decisions about maximizing the results of AI initiatives across product lines, business units, and regions.

Leadership and organizational structure

Score (1–5):_____

Instead of appointing a chief AI marketing officer (although CAIMO does roll off the tongue), designate AI task-force leaders within each sub-function of the marketing teams to spearhead AI efforts. Then establish a governance board that oversees these task forces to ensure alignment and coordination across AI initiatives.

REMEMBER

Task forces within marketing sub-functions can probably inspire and impress their marketing teams at a level beyond what a full-time AI-tsar new-hire can do. Also, with so much of the AI benefits realized behind the scenes, the operators within the teams have the most insight.

Stakeholder protection measures

Score (1–5):_____

Assess whether the company has implemented effective measures to shield customers, employees, partners, and shareholders from any potential risks associated with using AI, including

>> **Algorithmic bias:** Mainly resulting from skewed or limited input data

>> **Deep fakes:** Digital distortion of a person's likeness

>> **Privacy breaches:** Personal information that's lost, stolen, or shared by mistake

These protections also involve collaboration between marketing, legal, risk management, and technology teams. Consider the level of transparency that the company offers about data utilization and whether you've updated your customer-facing data and privacy policies to reflect the nuances of the AI era. (See Chapter 22 for more information about ethics and privacy considerations.)

Talent development

Score (1–5):_____

Begin with investing in *upskilling programs* (which involve training employees to gain new skills) to ensure that your marketing team gains the necessary knowledge and skills to harness the potential of AI in its operations. Leaders owe it to their team members to educate them and set them up for success in the AI era. Engage HR in conversations around upskilling and consider external resources or training services to support this effort. A foundation that instills AI knowledge and skills can help ensure that your marketing team can implement AI effectively over the long term.

Integrating Marketing with the Rest of the Enterprise

Here's the reality: The marketing field has become more complex because of rapidly evolving technologies and changing consumer behavior. As the McKinsey & Company (www.mckinsey.com) article "The power of partnership: How the CEO–CMO relationship can drive outsize growth" emphasizes, many chief executives struggle to even understand key marketing metrics. *Note:* Marketing may be partly to blame for this confusion because the marketers obfuscate some metrics (by using overly complex jargon or inconsistent reporting methods); outsource other metrics to the walled garden experiences provided by online domains such as Meta, TikTok, or Google; and don't do enough to draw the link between marketing measurement and business impact.

Recognizing marketing's vulnerability

REMEMBER

When businesses face downturns and cost-cutting becomes necessary, marketers are often the first to be shown the door. They usually lack exclusive relationships within the distribution channels or the supply chain, and they rarely act as one of the faces of the company to the investor community or the company board of directors. As a result, marketing leaders are easily dispensable when the going gets tough and businesses have to hunker down and cut costs.

And on top of being deemed dispensable, marketing (and perhaps technology) as a business function is most profoundly affected by consumer and digital transformations. Whether it's the rise of the Internet, the transition to mobile communications, the emergence of social media marketing, or consumer trends such as *cord-cutting* (getting rid of landlines and cable TV services, for example), these shifts disrupted the marketing landscape and required marketers to reinvent themselves again and again.

Embracing the AI transformation

Without a doubt, marketers are at a transformative moment (once again) as AI use comes to the forefront. Marketers may find the AI-related changes even more profound, lasting, and potentially career-altering than the previous shifts in communications and customer connections. The following sections offer up five strategies that can help marketers stay ahead of this transformation, and also guide the rest of their business into AI operations in a way that makes marketing roles indispensable.

Transform before you're transformed

Take a step back to propel yourself five steps forward. This strategy may sound frivolous, but at the very least, consider investing the $20 a month for the generative pre-trained transformer GPT-4 and testing it out as a copilot for every part of your professional and personal life. If the tool doesn't meet your expectations, the first question to ask is whether you've fully harnessed its capabilities before pointing fingers at the technology itself. And prepare to immerse yourself in the AI-driven future so that you transform before you get transformed.

Practice, practice, practice

When it comes to your day job, start with GPT-4, but be discerning about where you first direct your attention. The use of AI — even in just the marketing business function — is extensive. It encompasses myriad strategies, tactics, solutions, and vendors for each stage of the marketing process (see Parts 2 through 5 of this book as evidence). If you focus on analytics (for customer operations, as in Part 3, for example), this focus alone could occupy all your time.

If you don't know where to begin your AI practicing, start with the *marketing brief*, an integral document that combines market research, customer insights, business strategies, campaign objectives, channel methods, and branding specifics to steer the creative teams as they develop campaigns. You can

>> **Start by inputting all your customer insights,** market research, and core business strategies into GPT. Consider uploading raw survey and interview transcript data from customer research.

>> **Send GPT out (if research is scant)** so that it can study your consumers, undertake a competitive analysis, and revisit previous campaigns for you.

>> **Seek out GPT's expertise in crafting the marketing brief** and assess the generated content. Refine the brief through several rounds with GPT and monitor its progress.

Adopt asymmetrical networking

AI, which many view as a general-purpose technology that affects many different domains in business, is as impactful, if not more so, than the Industrial Revolution of the 1700s. Merely attending marketing conferences, sitting in on agency briefings, or skimming the occasional AI marketing book (yes, even if it's this one!) won't suffice. I encourage you to shed any reservations, dive in, and be hands-on; read the latest AI research; and understand what the government or governments relevant to your business are doing in relation to AI. Subscribe to the newsletters, attend the hackathons, experiment, and connect with individuals who are leading the charge in the AI revolution — those that you may not typically encounter.

REMEMBER

I understand that this immersion and out-of-character networking can be daunting, perhaps even stirring feelings of insecurity reminiscent of your high school days when faced with an AP class. But you can find out about AI firsthand from the philosophers, founders, designers, technologists, and venture capitalists who are betting the farm on this future with AI. The settings in which you encounter your expanded AI network may not be as plush or well-lit as you're accustomed to, and the catering may leave much to be desired, but you can learn from those who are truly worth learning from. Seek out these people and attach yourself to them.

Cut through the noise and embrace informative AI resources

With most new technology, you often see more hype than reality. In the case of AI, it can't have enough hype. Apart from the hype, though, you still indeed find *noise*, meaning a lot of superficial or misleading information. You could waste more time than you should reading perfunctory articles that don't tell you very much. Instead, here are some pragmatic thinkers in business and academia that you can follow on LinkedIn:

» Mustafa Suleyman, CEO of Microsoft AI (www.microsoft.com/ai) and author of *The Coming Wave* (Crown)

» Fei-Fei Li, professor at Stanford University and author of *The Worlds I See* (Flatiron Books)

» Kai-Fu Lee, CEO of Sinovation Ventures (www.sinovationventures.com) and author of *AI Superpowers* (Harper Business)

» Beena Ammanath, partner at Deloitte (www.deloitte.com) and author of *Trustworthy AI* (Wiley)

» Thomas H. Davenport, professor at Babson College and co-author with Nitin Mittal of *All in on AI* (Harvard Business Review Press)

» Ethan Mollick, professor at the University of Pennsylvania and author of *Co-Intelligence* (Portfolio)

Also, pay attention to the actual innovations coming out of artificial intelligence industry leaders such as OpenAI (www.openai.com), Google AI (http://ai.google.com), Microsoft AI (www.microsoft.com/ai), and others.

TIP

You can also follow some of the rather practical advice coming from consulting groups such as

>> Accenture (www.accenture.com)

>> Boston Consulting Group (BCG; www.bcg.com)

>> Bain & Company (www.bain.com)

>> Deloitte (www.deloitte.com)

>> EY (www.ey.com)

>> Goldman Sachs (https://www.goldmansachs.com/)

>> McKinsey & Company (www.mckinsey.com)

Granted, the consulting firms in the preceding list may more narrowly focus on frameworks, road maps, and building blocks, rather than hands-on implementation and day-to-day operations. But all information about AI in business can help you build a comprehensive understanding. An occasional study from such a firm can provide the perfect ammunition to persuade colleagues in your organization to allocate the necessary resources, time, and support for a deeper exploration into artificial intelligence.

Don't forget about marketing fundamentals

Even with AI, you need to focus on the essence of marketing — building a robust brand, attracting and retaining customers, fostering deep relationships, and enhancing loyalty and engagement. Execute all these tasks in ways that yield measurable results to earn the respect of the entire *C-suite* (your business's chief executives). Maintaining a strong marketing foundation provides the springboard that enables AI to significantly enhance your team's productivity and marketing results.

WARNING

The adage "garbage in, garbage out" is particularly important to follow when it comes to your marketing foundation. Inputting subpar customer data, superfluous brand strategies, and unclear directives into AI yields poor results.

FOCUSING ON THE CRUNCH

Embracing the benefits of the AI era may mean pushing the boundaries of what you expect from your teams and how you partner with the rest of your business. Take for instance one of my favorite brand efforts — Doritos' innovative development of an AI engine designed to identify thousands of variations of crunching sounds made while eating their chips — and not as just a party trick; it plays a strategic role for their gamer consumers. (FoodBev Media has a November 1, 2023, article about this innovation; just go to www.foodbev.com and enter "Silent Doritos" in the Search text box to find it.) They've harnessed the AI capability to mute the crunching noises for gamers who snack on Doritos during multiplayer gaming sessions, calling it Crunch Cancellation. This selective muting ensures that players can enjoy their snack without broadcasting the crunch to teammates during pivotal moments — such as a stealthy assault on an enemy base in *Call of Duty* — when connected by headsets in real time. Now, I'm not sure whether to consider this a marketing effort, a product, or an offering somewhere in between.

Organizing for the Future

In the AI-driven era, marketing functions must not only adapt to new technologies but also redefine roles and workflows to optimize collaboration between human teams and AI copilots. In fact, despite the promise of AI, many companies are struggling to fully harness its potential in every function of their businesses. Surveys of thousands of executives (as reported by McKinsey, www.mckinsey.com/capabilities/quantumblack/our-insights/the-state-of-ai-in-2023-generative-AIs-breakout-year) reveal that less than one-third of respondents' organizations have adopted AI in more than one business function. For most companies as of the time I'm writing, AI initiatives remain limited to ad hoc pilots or isolated experiments within a single business unit.

Shifting culture to adopt AI

One of the drivers limiting AI adoption is organizational inertia and cultural barriers. Leaders often overlook the need to fundamentally restructure their organizations to support AI initiatives effectively. As a *Harvard Business Review* article from July 2019 titled "Building the AI-Powered Organization" (www.hbr.org/2019/07/building-the-ai-powered-organization) highlighted, to drive AI adoption across a business, companies need to transform in three fundamental ways:

>> **Transition from siloed work to interdisciplinary collaboration,** fostering cross-functional teams comprising business, operational, and analytical expertise. This approach ensures that AI initiatives align with broader organizational goals and operational requirements.

>> **Shift decision-making processes** from experience-based, leader-driven approaches to data-driven decision-making at all levels of the organization. You must empower your employees to take advantage of AI algorithms' recommendations, fostering a culture of trust and autonomy.

>> **Embrace agility, experimentation, and adaptability** by fostering a culture that values continuous learning, innovation, and rapid iteration. Organizations should embrace a test-and-learn mentality, viewing mistakes as opportunities for improvement, rather than failures.

REMEMBER

Achieving these shifts requires proactive leadership and organizational preparedness, whether you're a marketing leader or one responsible for broader swathes of a company, large or small. Leaders must invest in cultural transformation, employee education, and overcoming resistance to change.

Adapting organizational structure to embrace AI

Organizational structure plays a crucial role in scaling AI initiatives with various models suited to different organizational contexts, including

>> **Centralized hubs:** These involve a dedicated AI team that centralizes expertise, resources, and infrastructure, ensuring consistent standards and governance across the organization.

>> **Decentralized spokes:** Individual departments or business units develop and deploy AI solutions tailored to their specific needs, fostering innovation and faster implementation.

>> **Hybrid approaches:** A combination of centralized and decentralized models where core AI capabilities are managed centrally, while individual business units customize and deploy AI applications relevant to their functions.

Regardless of the chosen model, successful AI implementation requires collaboration among business, IT, and analytics functions, along with interdisciplinary execution teams tasked with driving AI initiatives. The marketing function is bound to also change as more activities are co-created with artificial intelligence agents. Although it may be difficult to specifically outline how marketing functions will change, one thing is clear: Change is coming.

Chapter **22**

Addressing Ethical, Legal, and Privacy Concerns with AI

I have no doubt that generative artificial intelligence (AI) has the potential to be a more transformative force in business than any single piece of technology in the history of humankind. And, as AI technologies proliferate, they usher in an increasingly complex web of ethical, legal, and privacy concerns that demand scrutiny and responsible handling. In fact, those ethical, privacy, and broader legal concerns have already slowed down the adoption of AI in the business world.

The integration of AI into marketing programs without the appropriate usage guidelines for employees, as well as security protocols for your company and customer data significantly increases the legal risks involved. Businesses have to navigate through these legal concerns carefully, not merely because of a legal obligation but also a moral one. The consequences of missteps when integrating AI and using customer data can deeply impact consumer trust, brand reputation, and your business's image in society.

Establishing robust operating principles for ethical AI use in marketing can help you meet the challenges of securing data and protecting privacy. In this chapter, I help you examine ethical principles that serve as a framework for ensuring that your business designs, deploys, and maintains its AI systems with integrity and transparency. I also present ideas about safekeeping public and private data, protecting copyrights and intellectual property, and keeping related business practices legal and sensitive to the needs of all humans affected by the use of AI.

Operating Principles for Ethical AI

As a part of your business's decision to incorporate AI into its marketing initiatives, creating operating principles for ethical use of AI helps to ensure that the technology serves your company, employees, and customers with integrity. Key aspects of these principles include fairness, accountability, and the safeguarding of consumer privacy. And you must develop these principles so that they're comprehensive, clearly articulated, and implemented consistently across all AI-driven initiatives.

REMEMBER

After a cross-functional task force (ideally) develops the ethical principles and aligns them with the management team, you must train employees across the business about the existence and significance of these principles. This base in ethics is the core that guides the development, deployment, and management of AI systems to ensure that the systems benefit all relevant parties while minimizing potential risks to the business.

The following sections offer detailed information on several important ethical principles. These principles collectively foster an environment where AI serves as a force for good, enhancing marketing efforts without compromising ethical values or consumer trust.

Transparency

Transparency (being open and honest in a business context) is a fundamental principle; it requires that AI systems don't operate like black boxes (which are, by definition, mysterious to their users). Consumers and regulators must be able to understand the decision-making processes of AI — and how the business itself employs these processes. In AI initiatives, transparency may involve providing users with accessible explanations about how their data influences AI decisions — akin to how credit scoring models are required to disclose factors that affect credit scores.

Ensure that your company's AI systems are not only efficient, but also transparent. For instance, a marketing AI that selects which customers receive certain offers should have its selection criteria openly documented and accessible to stakeholders in a business to review and share upon request with consumers. This principle helps in building consumer trust and understanding, and it enables users and regulators to know how and why AI makes decisions.

Accountability

The principle of *accountability* ensures that a clear chain of responsibility exists for AI-driven actions. For instance, when an AI system that your business uses for targeted advertising inadvertently discriminates, the entity using the AI (your marketing department) must be held accountable, not just the developers or the technology itself. You can enforce this principle for your AI-driven marketing initiatives by performing regular audits and compliance checks of the AI systems that you use, like financial audits in corporations. These checks can help verify that your AI systems are operating as intended and that measures are in place to quickly address any deviations from established norms (for example, excluding an entire customer segment from receiving special offers that they should be receiving).

Your business must present a clear line of responsibility for AI's actions and decisions. Establish mechanisms in which your business appoints individuals or teams to take responsibility for monitoring AI's output and ensuring that it adheres to the intended ethical guidelines. For example, if an AI tool misclassifies a customer segment, the assigned monitor should have a clear procedure for addressing the issue and holding the right individuals or groups accountable.

Privacy protection

Privacy protection for consumers is a core ethical principle when using AI, especially given the sensitivity of personal data (names, addresses, purchase history, and so on) often used in marketing. Part of privacy protection involves *data minimization* strategies, in which businesses collect only the data necessary for a defined purpose. Also, systems can use robust data security measures such as *end-to-end encryption* (E2EE; a security method that keeps data safe from third-party access).

Privacy-centric AI deployments can use techniques such as *differential privacy*. These techniques work by slightly altering the data to make it difficult to identify specific individuals within the data set. This practice allows companies to gain valuable insights and perform analyses while ensuring that personal information remains confidential and secure. For instance, a healthcare company can analyze patient data trends without exposing individual patient records. Such approaches not only comply with strict data protection laws, but also reassure consumers that their personal information is secure and handled with care.

REMEMBER

In the era of generative AI, privacy protection is a sensitive concern because consumer groups have begun to wonder whether company functions such as marketing use customer information to train company-specific AI models without those customers' permission. Unfortunately, at the time of writing, laws don't exist about what can and what can't be used to train the AI models.

So if you're a customer interacting with an AI engine belonging to a company, you face a real risk that your interaction and every piece of data that you share with it may be used to train the AI engine to get better at various tasks. If you as a customer are explicitly asked for your permission and grant it, ethical issues are eliminated. But if you aren't or you don't, it can be a significant problem. After all, if customers' data is used without their consent, it violates their privacy rights and can lead to mistrust and reputational damage for the company. Additionally, businesses can experience legal repercussions and penalties if future regulations enforce stricter data protection standards.

Marketing teams must handle consumer data with the utmost care by implementing strategies that prioritize data security and user confidentiality. The strategies may involve advanced encryption methods, secure data storage solutions, and *anonymization techniques* (in which identifying details are removed) to ensure data privacy. Furthermore, companies should adhere to relevant data protection regulations such as the General Data Protection Regulation (GDPR) in Europe or the California Consumer Privacy Act (CCPA) in California, which advocate for strong data privacy practices.

Fairness

The principle of *fairness* in AI necessitates proactive measures to prevent biases in automated decisions and avoid perpetuating discrimination. In this context, fairness includes the diversification of training data sets and the continual testing of AI outputs for bias across different demographic groups. Unfortunately, at the time I'm writing this, many AI tools simply reflect the best and the worst of the public Internet — which constitutes the data that developers use to train AI's large language models (LLMs). Because of this training on Internet data which inherently includes all kinds of biases, these LLMs need to be fine-tuned to take out the bias that therefore gets built into them at the outset.

For example, when an AI model is used to personalize marketing messages, the training data must be representative of diverse consumer demographics (including data from various age groups, ethnicities, and socioeconomic backgrounds, for example) to prevent biases in message targeting. Make regular bias assessments and adjustments in LLMs a standard operational procedure, ensuring that AI-driven marketing is inclusive and equitable.

REMEMBER

Businesses must design, feed, and monitor AI systems with ethics in mind. That is, your company must check for biases that can lead to unfair treatment of individuals based on race, gender, age, or other characteristics. And be sure to include diversity in training data sets and apply algorithmic fairness assessments to prevent discriminatory outcomes. For example, evaluate an AI tool used for targeting ads to ensure that it doesn't inadvertently exclude or favor certain demographic groups for the wrong reasons.

Human-centric AI

The concept of *human-centric AI* advocates that technology should augment human decision-making, not replace it. Following this principle involves designing AI systems that enhance human capabilities and creativity rather than automating jobs out of existence. Although some jobs *will* be automated out of existence (in the same way that certain jobs disappeared with the industrial revolution), other jobs — when performed by AI — may not always yield the same insightful and emotionally impactful of results that you would get with human input.

For instance, AI can assist marketing professionals by providing insights from data analysis that humans can then use to make strategic decisions, rather than having the AI make those decisions autonomously. Such an approach ensures that AI remains a tool under human control and direction, maintaining essential human oversight and ethical alignment in marketing practices. See the section "Implementing oversight mechanisms," later in this chapter, for discussion of how to keep an eye on your AI.

System safety and security

Ensure that the AI systems that you use are secure from cyberthreats and that they function reliably under a wide range of conditions. Companies need to do rigorous testing and validation of AI systems to prevent vulnerabilities that can lead to data breaches or erroneous outputs. Marketing teams should implement robust security protocols and have contingency plans in place for potential AI system failures.

Social responsibility

When companies deploy AI solutions, they should keep in mind the broader implications on society and the environment. Being mindful of these implications involves designing and choosing AI systems that not only enhance efficiency and profitability but also contribute to environmental sustainability. AI systems can address sustainability by minimizing resource consumption, reducing carbon footprints, and fostering social welfare through fair access, reduced biases, and support for community well-being.

For example, in marketing, this responsible design can mean optimizing energy usage in AI data centers or refusing to engage AI in campaigns that promote harmful products or misinformation.

Using All Data Responsibly

Responsible stewardship of data — whether it's private or public — holds a particular significance in the ethical deployment of AI. Marketers are often at the frontline, handling vast amounts of sensitive consumer information that, if misused, could lead to severe privacy breaches and erosion of consumer trust. The ethical use of data involves not only complying with legal frameworks such as GDPR or CCPA (see the section "Privacy protection," earlier in the chapter, where I talk about these requirements), but also embracing practices that ensure your business collects, stores, and uses data in a manner that respects consumer rights and expectations.

Marketing teams depend on private data of three types:

>> **First-party data:** Information that a company collects directly from its customers or users through its own channels, such as websites, apps, or customer interactions. This data is typically highly reliable and relevant because it comes directly from the source.

>> **Second-party data:** Information that is collected by a partner or trusted entity that has a direct relationship with the consumer. This data is shared with your business, often through a direct partnership, and is typically used to enhance customer insights without the need for additional data collection efforts.

>> **Third-party data:** Information collected by entities that do not have a direct relationship with the consumer. This data is aggregated from various sources and sold to businesses for use in marketing, analytics, and other purposes. It often lacks the specificity and accuracy of first- and second-party data but can provide broader market insights.

REMEMBER

Marketers use these data sources to run effective campaigns that reach the right person, at the right time, in the right place, and with the right message. Using these data sets responsibly is critical not only to comply with legal requirements but also to maintain consumer trust and protect individual privacy.

Using private data responsibly

Private data (first- and second-party data, discussed in the preceding section) typically include personal information collected directly from individuals through interactions such as website visits, purchases, or customer service engagements. Here are key components of securely handling private data:

» **Consent management:** Ensure that your business obtains explicit consent from consumers before collecting, processing, or using their data. For instance, a boutique fashion retailer can implement a transparent opt-in system for customers who want to receive personalized offers based on their purchase history or browsing behavior. Make this consent easy to withdraw so that customers have continued control over their information.

» **Data minimization:** Collect only the data that you need for a defined purpose. A health and wellness app, for instance, may collect data about users' fitness activities to provide tailored health tips and recommendations. However, the app should avoid collecting unnecessary information — such as the precise location of a user — if that data is irrelevant to its services.

» **Secure data storage and transmission:** Implement advanced cybersecurity measures, such as encryption and secure access protocols, to protect private data from unauthorized access and breaches. A marketing agency may use end-to-end encryption (E2EE; which denies third-party access) to secure the transmission of campaign data between its servers and client devices, ensuring that sensitive information remains confidential.

The components in the preceding list may sound like good hygiene for data management, but the stakes are higher when you involve AI. Marketing, product, and technology teams may assume that they can readily use existing customer data within the enterprise to train AI models or optimize new algorithms. However, this approach may be misguided if customers haven't consented to having their data used for these emerging applications. *Note:* Given how new many AI tools exist, you probably want to assume that customers *haven't* granted consent!

Using public data responsibly

Public data, which is often referred to as *third-party data,* refers to information that's available to the public, or obtained from public records or third parties that don't have any association with your business. Public data can include census data, public social media posts, or open government data sets. Here's how to use this type of data responsibly:

>> **Avoid de-anonymization:** Even when you use public data sets, take steps to ensure that you don't inadvertently *de-anonymize* (reveal identifying details about) individuals. For example, a real estate marketing company that uses publicly available property records can combine this data with other data sets to improve its market analysis. However, it must ensure that such combinations don't reveal personal identities without consent. For better or worse, detecting identities is much easier to do with AI tools, and therefore companies should be all the more cautious about keeping personal information private.

>> **Practice ethical sourcing:** Source public data ethically by respecting the rights and expectations of the communities involved. A company specializing in economic forecasts may use publicly available employment data from government portals to predict market trends and advise clients on marketing investments. In doing so, they should attribute the data source correctly and ensure its accuracy and relevance. If your business combines third-party data with other private data it has (see the preceding section) and that third-party data wasn't ethically sourced, you may not be able to use the entire data set.

>> **Offer transparency in use:** Be transparent about how your business uses public data in its marketing efforts. For instance, a digital marketing firm can inform its audience that it uses public social media trends to tailor content and ad placements, which provides insights into how this data shapes the firm's marketing strategies.

Practicing responsible data use

You can put into practice some ideas from the preceding sections to responsibly handle any data that you use for marketing. Here are some examples of how specific business sectors can use data responsibly:

>> **Retail sector:** A retailer can use public weather data to plan and promote weather-appropriate products and rely on securely stored private customer data to send targeted promotions based on past purchasing behaviors.

>> **Healthcare marketing:** A healthcare provider can use public health data to identify geographic regions that have increased incidences of certain conditions and use private data from patient interactions (with strict confidentiality and consent) to inform those specific populations about relevant healthcare services.

>> **Event marketing:** A company organizing large-scale events may use public data about local demographics to decide where to host events and look to private data from previous attendees (with those attendees' consent) to personalize event notifications.

By carefully managing both private and public data, with a focus on privacy, security, and ethical use, companies can enhance their marketing efforts while building trust and ensuring compliance with data protection laws. This responsible approach not only safeguards the company and its customers, but also contributes to the integrity and sustainability of its business practices. With AI, you need to manage the use of private and public data even more carefully because the machine learning algorithms may use the data for training purposes and then later to form highly sophisticated recommendations.

THE *NEW YORK TIMES* COPYRIGHT FIGHT WITH OpenAI

The *New York Times* newspaper (www.nytimes.com) filed a lawsuit against OpenAI (www.openai.com; the maker of ChatGPT) in 2023, alleging that the company infringed on the newspaper's copyrights by using its articles to train the ChatGPT language model. The *Times* claimed that OpenAI's AI models challenged the newspaper's role as a reliable source of information because the models could generate near-identical versions of *Times* articles.

OpenAI disputed the lawsuit, stating that the use of copyrighted materials for its technological advancements fell under the purview of fair use. The company emphasized its commitment to collaborating with news organizations and creating new revenue opportunities for the industry. However, the *Times* and other digital media outlets, such as *Raw Story* (www.rawstory.com), *Alternet* (www.alternet.org), and *The Intercept* (www.theintercept.com), all filed separate lawsuits against OpenAI, alleging copyright infringement and demanding the removal of their copyrighted works from the company's training data.

These lawsuits (and there will be many more) highlight the ongoing debate surrounding the use of copyrighted materials to develop AI technologies. Although OpenAI argues that its models don't necessarily contain copied expression from the training data, the media outlets assert that their copyright-protected journalism is the result of human effort and shouldn't be exploited without proper attribution or compensation. The outcome of these legal battles can have significant implications for the development of AI systems because it may impact the availability of high-quality training data and therefore the ability to create unbiased models.

(continued)

(continued)

Marketing and business leaders need to pay attention to these lawsuits because their outcomes will have ramifications for how AI models get trained. (If they're not trained by using high-quality content such as The *New York Times* articles, their outputs will be weak in quality.) These outcomes can also impact data protection policies for companies. Any company's data that's available on the internet, at the time of writing, can be used to train the models — and possibly confidential content that employees input into the AI services like ChatGPT may be, too. That data availability can cause problems for companies when it comes to defending company and customer data.

Fighting Bias in Data and Results

Marketers' responsibility for managing the data that AI uses extends to combating biases in data sets and algorithmic decisions. These biases — if left unchecked — may perpetuate inequality and harm society by reinforcing stereotypes, limiting opportunities for marginalized groups, and creating unfair advantages for certain demographics. Ensuring that AI systems deliver fair and unbiased results requires continuous vigilance and adaptation to make sure that AI marketing output reflects the diverse populations it serves.

You must combat bias in AI model outputs to ensure fairness (see the section "Fairness," earlier in the chapter), enhance accuracy, and uphold ethical standards in marketing and business more broadly.

Here's how companies can address bias by employing actionable methods:

>> **Develop bias-aware algorithms.** Employ or develop AI algorithms designed to minimize bias. For example, you can try out *adversarial debiasing,* in which one model predicts outcomes while another detects biases in the predictions. This model-versus-model technique encourages the primary model to reduce biases in its outputs and promotes fairness in algorithmic decision-making.

>> **Diversify data sources.** Actively incorporate data from a diverse range of sources to minimize biases that may exist if you use limited sources. This approach involves including data from various geographic locations, socioeconomic backgrounds, ages, genders, and ethnicities — particularly in scenarios such as developing national ad campaigns. Diverse sourcing of data can reflect the full spectrum of the population accurately and ensure equitable targeting and message relevance.

>> **Implement inclusive data collection practices.** To avoid excluding under-represented groups, design data collection methods that cater to all potential users. For example, if your marketing function uses a digital app for data collection, optimize the app to function effectively on lower bandwidths (such as 3G) or older mobile platforms (such as Android 6.0) to accommodate users who have limited Internet access or outdated technology.

>> **Incorporate a continuous improvement process.** Establish a continuous feedback loop that allows for updating and improving data and algorithms based on outcomes. This process involves using feedback on AI outputs to make iterative adjustments and help ensure that biases are addressed promptly and continuously.

>> **Instill modeling with transparency.** Maintaining detailed documentation about how data is collected, processed, and used in training AI models enhances transparency (see the section "Transparency," earlier in this chapter). This practice enables stakeholders (such as data scientists, ethicists, and regulators) to understand and critique the methods employed and fosters an environment conducive to identifying and addressing biases more effectively.

>> **Perform regular audits for bias detection.** Regularly review and analyze data sets and AI algorithms for potential biases. Your company may choose to employ statistical methods to examine discrepancies in how various groups are treated or represented by the algorithms. That is, you may analyze customer conversion rates across demographic groups to identify *systematic disadvantages*. You must perform this type of audit because AI engines can develop biases over time when only regular users interact with a service, thus limiting the data collected to just those users.

>> **Provide ethical training and awareness.** Make sure that employees, especially those in data science and marketing, know about the impacts of biased data and the importance of ethical AI practices. Provide workshops, seminars, and ongoing education about reducing biases in AI. This education should emphasize the latest research and methods for fostering inclusivity and fairness.

>> **Use synthetic data to balance data sets.** Generating synthetic data can help represent under-represented groups accurately without compromising privacy. This approach balances the data set by creating realistic, non-real data points and ensuring fair representation across various demographic groups in marketing strategies.

Protecting Copyright and Intellectual Property

In the context of AI in marketing, the protection of copyright and intellectual property becomes very important. As AI systems gain the capability to create synthetic content and replicate complex marketing tasks traditionally performed by humans, the lines between AI-generated and human-created work get blurry.

Protecting copyright and intellectual property (IP) in the age of AI presents unique challenges, particularly as AI systems become increasingly capable of creating content that can potentially infringe on existing copyrights. When you integrate AI into your marketing strategies, you must respect and protect the IP rights of others, while also safeguarding your own creations.

Set up ongoing education and training on IP laws for employees involved in AI development and deployment. Make sure that the training you provide covers the basics of copyright and patent law, as well as more specific issues related to AI and IP rights (which arguably is an emerging field). Holding regular updates and workshops can help ensure that your staff remains aware of the latest developments in IP law and knows how to implement procedures that comply with these laws.

TIP

Taking a proactive approach to educating and involving marketing staff in copyright and IP issues not only helps to prevent inadvertent infringements but also reinforces your company's commitment to ethical and legal business practices.

Avoiding infringement

A primary concern for possible infringement involves the creation of marketing *assets* (imagery, text, video, or even sound) by AI systems, which may inadvertently replicate copyrighted content because the AI models are often trained on large data sets that include copyrighted material. To combat this possibility, companies must implement rigorous checks and balances within their AI systems to ensure that any content generated doesn't violate copyright laws.

For example, when you task an AI system with creating graphics for a marketing campaign, you must also equip the system with technology to compare its creations against a database of copyrighted images. The comparison enables the system to flag potential matches for human review. This process helps prevent copyright infringement and maintains the integrity of the marketing campaign.

Declaring ownership

While AI-generated content becomes more prevalent in marketing campaigns, the question of ownership over AI creations becomes paramount. Companies must clearly define who holds the copyright to AI-generated content — whether it's the company, the developers of the AI, or potentially the AI itself — depending on local laws and regulations.

To address the topic of ownership, establish clear contractual terms with any third-party partners from the outset of any project that involves AI. Make sure that your agreements outline ownership rights and provide for granting usage permissions to avoid legal disputes and ensure that all parties understand their rights and responsibilities.

REMEMBER

When you work with agencies or other third parties, you need to assess who owns the rights to the content creation and address this question of IP rights up front in the legal agreements.

Safeguarding your own creations

Your business must protect its own AI-generated IP. This protection involves securing copyrights for AI-created content, where applicable, and protecting the underlying algorithms and data through patents or trade secrets.

For instance, your company may patent a unique method (developed by your AI) that predicts consumer behavior, or it may choose to keep the algorithm confidential as a trade secret. These protective measures prevent competitors from copying innovative techniques and help your company maintain a competitive edge in the market.

Facing the Deepfake Problem

Deepfakes are synthetic media in which a person's likeness or voice is replaced with someone else's or is artificially produced, making it appear as though they said or did things that they never actually said or did. The technology behind deepfakes has advanced rapidly — thanks to machine learning and generative AI — making it increasingly difficult to distinguish between real and fake content.

The potential for harm from deepfake content is vast. The risks affect

>> **Businesses and brands:** For businesses, deepfakes pose a risk to brand reputation and can lead to financial losses. Fraudulent activities — such as

fake endorsements or misleading advertisements — can undermine trust in the brand's digital communications.

>> **Individuals and families:** Irresponsible people can use deepfakes to create non-consensual pornography, impersonate individuals for fraudulent purposes, or manipulate personal relationships. Any of these activities leads to psychological harm and social disruption.

>> **Society at large:** On a societal level, deepfakes can spread misinformation, interfere with elections, and undermine public trust in media and institutions. Former president Trump was deepfaked in the summer of 2023, which caused widespread confusion as the video falsely depicted him making inflammatory statements that he never actually said. President Biden was deepfaked in January 2024, at the time of the New Hampshire primary, when his voice — impersonated via AI and distributed via robocalls — discouraged Democrats from voting.

Society's approach to deepfakes

The urgency to address the threat of deepfakes can't be overstated because they have the potential to severely undermine public trust, manipulate public opinion, and cause significant harm to individuals and institutions. While society at large and businesses confront this challenge, they must use a multifaceted approach:

>> **Corporate responsibility:** Companies that develop AI and machine learning technologies must prioritize ethical considerations in their work by ensuring that they put safeguards in place to prevent misuse of AI capabilities — including the creation of deepfakes. Microsoft CEO Satya Nadella, upon hearing that a Taylor Swift deepfake may have been created by using Microsoft Designer said, "We must act." (I talk about this deepfake in the sidebar "Taylor Swift and the South China Morning Post get deepfaked," in this chapter.)

>> **Legislation and regulation:** I believe that governments must move quickly (they haven't at the time of writing) to enact stricter laws that address the creation and distribution of deepfakes, with clear penalties for those who misuse generative AI technologies. Legislation should also include laws that protect victims and provide them with legal recourse.

At the time I'm writing this book, various U.S. states have enacted laws regarding data privacy, but no comprehensive federal laws exist for addressing data in the context of AI. Congress seemed to show bipartisan support for such laws with the introduction of the Protecting Consumers from Deceptive AI Act in March 2024, but the deepfake issue may have taken a backseat to other Congressional concerns.

>> **Public awareness and education:** Civil groups, technology companies, the media, and government organizations must raise awareness about the existence and dangers of deepfakes. People need to be educated on how to critically evaluate digital content and recognize potential deepfakes, always verifying the provenance of the content by checking sources and cross-referencing with reputable outlets. Meta announced in February 2024 that it was calling for an industry effort to label AI-generated content, which suggests a move toward greater transparency and accountability.

>> **Technology solutions:** Tech companies need to invest in developing more sophisticated detection tools that can identify and flag deepfake content before it spreads. This detection process includes collaboration between platforms to share information and strategies. These tools can all help:

- *DeepID:* www.deepidentify.ai
- *Sensity:* www.sensity.ai
- *Optic AI or Not:* www.aiornot.com
- *Sentinel:* www.thesentinel.ai

TAYLOR SWIFT AND THE SOUTH CHINA MORNING POST GET DEEPFAKED

In January 2024, a deepfake of Taylor Swift was used to collect consumer data and scam consumers. Taylor Swift's genuine appreciation for Le Creuset cookware, highlighted through her home's decor as shown in a Netflix documentary, contrasted with the fake ads featuring her unauthorized endorsement of the brand's products on Facebook. These ads, part of a broader trend of celebrity-focused scams, utilized AI to create a synthetic version of Swift's voice, falsely claiming she was giving away free cookware sets to anyone who entered their personal information and shipping details. Le Creuset (and Taylor Swift) had nothing to do with the ads.

Another incident provides an example of the ease with which unscrupulous people can produce digital replicas of others for deceptive purposes. As the *South China Morning Post* (www.scmp.com) reported in February 2024, a scammer created highly convincing videos of the newspaper's CFO to scam an employee, instructing that employee to wire $25 million out of the company's bank accounts. This scam happened during a video call where the fraudster had created impersonations of not just the CFO but of several other employees, to make the instructions more believable.

What marketers can do to fight deepfakes

The challenge posed by deepfakes is emblematic of the broader ethical and social dilemmas brought about by rapid deployment of generative AI. By confronting this issue head-on, marketing departments — as well as businesses and society, in general — can mitigate its impact and protect the integrity of brands and each individual. Addressing the threat of deepfakes doesn't just prevent harm (such as misinformation or identity theft); it also helps preserve brand trust, authenticity, and the very fabric of society.

Here are some ways for business marketing functions to tackle the deepfake problem:

>> **Collaborate with social media platforms and tech companies.** Have your marketing team partner with these entities to address deepfake content, including sharing best practices, developing standards for detecting and removing deepfakes, and advocating for platform policies that prevent the spread of AI-generated counterfeit content. Collaboration can also extend to sharing intelligence about new deepfake techniques and coordinating responses to emerging threats, such as whether your advertising is appearing next to deepfakes.

>> **Educate and engage your employees and customers.** Create awareness among your marketing team and your customers about the dangers of deepfakes, explain how to spot fake content (for example, through services such as Optic AI or Not; www.aiornot.com), and encourage them to report suspicious activities. These interactions can help your brand foster a community of vigilant and informed stakeholders.

You also need clear communication channels for reporting deepfakes and a responsive action plan to address concerns. When the *Swifties* (the fandom for musician Taylor Swift) discovered deepfakes released in January 2024 featuring the singer-songwriter, they pushed the hashtag #ProtectTaylorSwift to trend on X. They also flooded other hashtags related to the images with more positive images and videos of her live performances, which made it harder for people to find the deepfakes. Every brand needs its own *Swifties* to aid them. And part of that protection includes having a crisis communication plan in place.

>> **Implement advanced detection technologies.** Invest in cutting-edge technology that can detect deepfakes by using AI and machine learning tools designed to identify inconsistencies or anomalies in videos and images that may not be perceptible to the human eye. Regularly monitoring content associated with your brand or endorsed celebrities can help in early detection of fraudulent materials. Check whether your creative or media agency

partners — or internal technology and legal teams — may have detection technologies already in place.

>> **Leverage digital watermarking and content authentication.** Implement *digital watermarking* (pieces of embedded code that provide copyright information) and other content verification technologies to authenticate genuine brand content. By embedding invisible markers or using *blockchain technology* (that keeps records across linked computers) for digital certificates, brands can help audiences and platforms identify and verify the authenticity of the content that they consume. Push agency, publisher, and platform partners to take proactive measures themselves, such as adopting these technologies and promoting their use across the industry.

>> **Strengthen legal frameworks and copyright protection.** Work with legal teams to ensure that copyright and intellectual property laws related to the brand are enforced vigorously. (See the section "Protecting Copyright and Intellectual Property," earlier in the chapter.) Draft clear contracts that address the unauthorized use of digital likenesses and seek legal remedies against perpetrators of deepfakes. Additionally, understand how the actors and the celebrities your marketing team works with are protected and whether they're susceptible to deepfakes or have been in the past.

Saving Human Beings from Artificial Intelligence

As AI assumes more responsibilities in the marketing function of many businesses, make sure that its use complements, rather than replaces, human input. You must keep this relationship in balance, not only for ethical reasons but also to leverage the unique strengths of both human and machine capabilities. Your marketing initiatives must promote a symbiotic relationship that enhances (rather than diminishes) the human experience in the marketing domain, for example by using AI to handle data analysis and pattern recognition while allowing human marketers to focus on creative strategy and personal customer interactions.

REMEMBER

The evolution of AI use across marketing, business, and society at large raises profound ethical and practical concerns about its impact on human employment and decision-making autonomy. Businesses must take a deliberate and strategic approach when addressing these concerns to ensure that AI enhances human capabilities without supplanting them.

Adopting human-centered AI design

To help save human beings from the potential overreach of AI (no one wants AI running the world!), creators of AI systems must adopt a human-centered approach to AI development. This approach involves putting an emphasis on designing AI systems that augment human abilities and creativity, rather than replacing them.

For instance, business marketing functions can use AI to analyze consumer data, predict trends, run synthetic panels, and execute creative campaigns (see Chapters 6, 7, 9, and 12). But the strategy process — the *insight identification* (identifying unique customer insights that can anchor a creative campaign) and definition of the brand — should remain a human-driven process. Keeping humans in charge at the strategic level ensures that, while providing valuable insights and automations, AI doesn't take away the irreplaceable human touch that's essential for creativity and empathy in marketing.

Establishing clear ethical guidelines for using AI

Businesses must establish and enforce clear ethical guidelines that dictate the limits and uses of AI technology. (See the section "Operating Principles for Ethical AI," earlier in this chapter.) These guidelines should prioritize human safety, rights, and welfare, and clearly define the unacceptable uses of AI.

For example, a firm can implement policies that prohibit the use of AI in making autonomous decisions about employee promotions or customer product renewals. By setting boundaries for how they use AI, companies can prevent the potential for AI to make life-altering decisions that lack human ethical considerations and emotional intelligence.

Continuous learning and skill development

To ensure that employees remain invaluable in a workforce augmented by AI, businesses need to invest in continuous learning and development programs. These programs should focus on skills that AI can't replicate easily, such as strategic thinking, leadership, empathy, and creative problem-solving.

For instance, a marketing function may offer workshops on emotional intelligence and brand storytelling. Understanding these subjects can help employees take advantage of AI-generated data to inform the work that they deliver — for example, compelling marketing narratives that resonate on a human level.

Participating in regulatory compliance and advocacy

Companies should actively participate in shaping the regulatory framework around AI usage. Your business must comply with existing regulations on AI such as those pertaining to data privacy and security (see the section "Privacy protection," earlier in the chapter). But businesses must also advocate for laws that protect jobs and human control in critical decision-making processes. Engaging with government policymakers to support legislation that addresses AI transparency and accountability, and the safeguarding of human jobs, can help mitigate the risks associated with the potential of AI autonomy.

REMEMBER

Companies' involvement with government policy can harness the benefits of AI while ensuring that it serves as an ally to human workers, not a replacement. Some jobs will disappear, like they do with every technological transformation, but others will arise. According to the *Quarterly Journal of Economics* (www.fast company.com/91073170/jobs-that-didnt-exist-1940-wont-exist-2040-automation-study), 6 out of 10 jobs that human beings occupy today didn't exist in 1940. Companies must plan for and manage with sensitivity the transition to new roles and jobs for human beings.

Implementing oversight mechanisms

Implementing robust oversight mechanisms can help businesses monitor and evaluate AI systems continuously. These mechanisms can include *human-in-the-loop* (HITL) systems, where business functions require a human's oversight at certain decision levels. These types of systems help ensure that AI's decisions are continually reviewed and validated by human professionals.

For example, in a digital marketing context, AI may optimize *ad placement* (where the ad appears) and *bidding* (what the marketers pay for the ad) on its own. But human *growth marketers* (who focus on bottom-of-the-funnel performance marketing) would offer the placement strategy and finalize budget decisions. A human in this decision-making position can ensure that the cost and placement of ads align with the company's ethical standards and strategic goals.

ADVOCATING FOR HUMANS FIRST

Nobody better articulated the AI control philosophy than Walmart CEO, Doug McMillon, when he eloquently made the case for having a human-first approach to the development of AI at the Consumer Electronics Show in January 2024. (You can see a recording of his and other presentations at www.youtube.com/watch?v=dNDcwMTzj_8&t=1333s.)

McMillon said,

> *"One path is to completely prioritize technology to maximize what's possible without considering potential implications. The view is that if we can use technology to do something, it's inevitable that it'll happen, so we should just go fast and exploit what's possible. It's a society driven by data and run by increasingly intelligent software. It's a world where technology streamlines operations without much if any concern for the people involved."*

Then when presenting the alternative path, he said,

> *"It's one where the benefits of technology are pursued, but people are considered along the way. It's about our heads and our hearts. The underlying principle is that we should use technology to serve people, not the other way around. This path enables people to do things in more efficient and enjoyable ways."*

And finally bringing it home with the Walmart philosophy,

> *"We love what technology can do, but we're building it in a way that creates better careers at the same time. It creates better customer experiences and a stronger business. No doubt some tasks will go away and some roles will change — and some of them should, like the ones that involve lifting heavy weights or doing repetitive tasks. As that's happening, we're designing new roles that our associates tell us are more enjoyable and satisfying and also often result in higher pay."*

6

The Part of Tens

Chapter **23**

Tens Pitfalls to Avoid When Marketing with AI

As I discuss throughout the book, integrating artificial intelligence (AI) into marketing holds the promise of transforming operations, all the way from strategic planning to evaluating campaign metrics, and everything in between. But be aware that you must avoid specific pitfalls to unlock the full potential of AI across these marketing domains. In this chapter, you can find out about ten pitfalls — tied directly to marketing activities — that marketers should avoid.

Ignoring Qualitative Insights

AI shines (is really good) when studying and analyzing extensive quantitative data sets, such as market trends, consumer behavior patterns, and sales performance metrics. AI models offer invaluable data-driven insights for marketers. But relying exclusively on quantitative analysis poses the risk of potentially overlooking the rich, nuanced insights that qualitative data provides. Integrating qualitative research, such as customer interviews, focus groups, and ethnographic studies, enriches understanding of the customer base and offers a comprehensive perspective on customer needs and desires.

In particular, generative AI enables a shortcut in the qualitative realm with the use of synthetic panels. *Synthetic panels*, which are AI-generated groups of virtual participants that you can align with predefined personas, simulate real human qualitative research that you can incorporate into the overall market research (see Chapter 9 for more on synthetic panels).

TIP

Even with the help of generative AI, you must critically review the synthesized research to ensure that it passes the common-sense test and is contextually relevant.

Depending Solely on Generated Personas

AI enables marketers to segment audiences and create customer personas that influence the direction of marketing efforts (see Chapter 9). But if you accept the AI-generated personas without question, you can overlook the fluidity of consumer behavior and miss real-time trends.

To counter the potential risk of over-reliance on personas, marketers should treat personas as initial drafts that are subject to iterative refinement through continuous research, direct customer interactions, and crucial insights drawn from customers' previous interactions with the company's products and services. Integrating data from customer service engagements and analyzing product return patterns are essential for refining AI-created personas.

TIP

Make sure that the scope of AI-generated personas is clear from the beginning — whether you intend them to represent customers of your business, a specific brand in a portfolio of brands, or a particular product. When using AI tools to generate or enhance specific personas, you can easily find that the lines between these three types of personas can blur and limit their effectiveness as a marketing or design basis.

Relying Only on AI for Creative Briefs

AI can streamline the drafting of *creative briefs* (documents that reveal the strategy and components of a creative project) by compiling data, synthesizing research findings, and performing analyses, which lay the foundational elements for a strong creative brief. In this drafting phase, an overreliance on AI — without human oversight — risks producing briefs that are devoid of sharp insights, creative nuance, and a sophisticated understanding of a brand. (See Chapter 12 for more information about using AI for creative content.) Marketers must not only review but also enrich AI-generated briefs by providing human input to ensure that the output aligns with the brand's identity and fosters emotional resonance with the targeted audience.

REMEMBER

The risk of deficient creative briefs can increase when the AI in use doesn't leverage a large language model (LLM) trained on data from your brand's previous campaigns. In that situation, the model lacks historical context and the capacity to adapt based on previous marketing outcomes.

Bypassing Human Creativity

Employing an AI tool as a *creative director* (responsible for a project's or product's creative vision) to generate ideas through analysis of market trends and data risks dampens the breadth and depth of human creativity. Over-dependence on AI's creative capabilities may yield ideas that lack differentiation (going for the tried-and-true) or fail to capture the dynamic nature of consumer engagement (noting the start of buying trends) while it unfolds in real time.

TIP

View AI-generated ideas as a springboard for creativity, rather than the final outcome. These ideas — without human review — may overlook cultural subtleties and emerging trends in consumer behavior and may unintentionally replicate a competitor's advertising. (See Chapter 12 for more info on using AI to generate ideas and plan campaigns.) These omissions can lead to a creativity vacuum, where unique, resonant ideas are scarce.

Losing Your Brand Voice

Maintaining brand voice and authenticity while using AI requires that marketers take a hands-on approach to mitigate the risk of impersonal, generic outputs that come across as disconnected from the spirit of the brand. To guarantee brand connection in your marketing efforts, establish clear guidelines and frameworks for campaign output by providing the AI model with training data that encompasses the brand messaging architecture, voice/tone guidelines, specific on-brand content samples, and target audience profiles.

WARNING

Be extra careful if you use AI to mine insights, create personas, *and* develop ideas for your campaign. Employing AI for all three activities increases the risks of ending up with undifferentiated outputs. Using AI in marketing requires continuous human evaluation, and you need to send AI-generated drafts of marketing content through a brand review with the brand marketing team to validate the content's alignment with brand guidelines.

You can best use AI to generate initial ideas and develop draft content but leave the final polishing and personalization of marketing materials to human creators who can infuse the content with authenticity, cultural references, and brand language that the customers recognize. See Chapters 12 and 17 for ideas about creating marketing materials and campaigns by using AI.

Neglecting Emerging Media Channels

You need to balance AI's data-driven recommendations with human insight for media planning that also takes advantage of emerging channels and newer ad placements. Although AI models optimize based on mature historical data sets for more traditional media, their inherent limitations mean that AI may overlook newer channels — such as connected TVs, podcasting, influencer marketing, and even the Metaverse — which have limited past data that you can provide to AI so that it can accurately capture those media's full potential.

TIP

To prevent this limited view of media outlets, actively monitor industry trends, shifts in customer behavior, and ad-tech advancements such as *dynamic creative optimization* (DCO), which uses AI to automatically tailor ad content in real time based on user behavior and preferences. You can begin by allocating test budgets for data-acquiring pilot campaigns that test the efficacy of emergent and innovative channels. Then, feed the data that you acquire into AI models to optimize those models for more imaginative media plans. You can also leverage AI's advanced predictive analytics to forecast the potential impact of the emergent channels.

Over-Optimizing for Short-Term Goals

When using AI for performance marketing, cultivate a holistic framework of goals that balances your immediate need for conversions (how much revenue you can drive right now) with leading indicators of customer lifetime value and long-term brand health (such as brand loyalty, customer retention, and overall brand perceptions). You can glean metrics covering a range of goals by using brand awareness surveys, organic search volume measurements, social sentiment analyses, engagement rates, and customer lifetime value projections. (See Chapter 11 for more information on measuring results of your marketing efforts.) Planning your marketing goals to encompass the entire customer journey enables AI to optimize for maximum lifetime value, instead of focusing solely on short-term returns.

Establish and enforce strict guidelines for brand safety and authentic messaging when you use AI for creative automation of your market programs. The goal is to prevent AI-generated outputs from creating damaging inconsistencies or over-emphasis on immediate performance at the risk of brand health.

TIP

Use humans' domain expertise to scrutinize any AI marketing recommendations. This oversight offers a wider brand lens and allows for course corrections if your experts recognize short sighted tactics that risk loss of long-term value or lead to acquiring customers that have an unfavorably high *return rate* (that is, they return a lot of merchandise).

Creeping Customers Out

Striking the right balance between personalization and privacy is paramount when leveraging AI for personalized marketing campaigns. AI's advanced data processing capabilities can enable a deep understanding of individual preferences and behaviors, but over-aggressive personalization tactics can inadvertently violate consumer privacy expectations. You can scare off your customers — fostering distrust and alienation — if they feel that your approach is too directive and pushy. For example, a fine line exists between offering customers occasional ads for products that they seem to prefer and inundating them with suggestions of things to buy multiple times a day.

REMEMBER

Your marketing department must establish clear ethical guidelines and boundaries to avoid creepy or invasive personalization practices, which may damage your brand's reputation and your customer relationships. For example, include full transparency about data collection policies, user-friendly privacy controls, and robust data governance protocols. (See Chapter 22 for more information about ethics and privacy when working with AI.)

Additionally, train your AI personalization models with appropriate contextual guardrails that account for differences in cultural nuances and societal norms around privacy sensitivities. When you deploy them thoughtfully, AI-driven personalization models can delight customers by surfacing relevant offerings that genuinely add value, convenience, and delight — without veering into the uncomfortable territory of creepiness that undermines the very aim of personalization.

Ignoring the Value of the Human Touch

AI-powered customer relationship management (CRM) systems can revolutionize your business's approach to customers and enable unprecedented personalization for their customer journey. However, marketers must recognize that the most impactful, memorable, and loyalty-building customer interactions often stem from authentic human-to-human connections that transcend what AI can deliver alone.

A holistic CRM strategy integrates AI's analytical prowess with human interpersonal skills such as empathy, emotional intelligence, persuasion, and creative problem-solving. AI can automate high-volume, repetitive tasks (notification e-mails about product availability, for example) but also direct high-value opportunities to humans for personalized outreach. Ultimately, leveraging AI to augment, rather than entirely replace, human engagement unlocks CRM systems' full potential for long-term customer loyalty and advocacy.

Retaining a human-in-the-loop component in CRM has the following advantages:

>> **Elevates the impact of customer interactions:** Deploying skilled human beings at pivotal moments, whether in-person or virtually through video-enabled tools, can help your brand when it faces tricky CRM situations such as conflict resolution, consultative selling, and milestone celebrations (such as anniversaries or customer loyalty achievements).

>> **Demonstrates the brand's commitment to personal interactions:** Adding the human touch takes a customer interaction beyond transactional to something more profound. It can instill trust and help solidify the bond a customer feels with your brand.

Relying Solely on AI for ROI Analysis

AI analytics can augment the modern marketer's analytical toolkit as one powerful component, but don't treat it as a solitary black box for complex return on investment (ROI) measurements and strategic decision-making. Relying solely on AI-driven ROI analysis without incorporating contextual insights and real-world market dynamics poses a significant risk of drawing inaccurate or incomplete conclusions about marketing-campaign performance. AI excels at processing vast data sets to uncover granular quantitative trends and patterns, but these algorithms often operate within a data vacuum and fail to account for critical external factors, such as competitive activity, cultural shifts, economic fluctuations, and other social factors.

To gain a comprehensive understanding of marketing ROI, AI's sophisticated computational analyses must be complemented by

>> **Human domain expertise** that can qualitatively assess the interplay between data outputs and actual on-the-ground realities. This oversight can help identify true drivers of success or impediments to campaign effectiveness.

>> **Examination of the data through a multidimensional lens** that includes primary and secondary research, industry reports, voice-of-customer feedback, and cross-functional team insights spanning creative development, channel strategy, brand perception, and sales impact. Only this thorough approach can weed out potentially misleading data and ensure proper interpretation within the appropriate context.

Chapter **24**

Ten Future AI Developments to Watch For

When exploring future artificial intelligence (AI) developments, you'd be wise to work with the assumption that — in our technologically driven future — human imagination may be the only factor limiting our progress. Even if you look just a few years out, you may foresee several AI developments to be mindful of. These AI developments will invariably begin to change the face of marketing when they enter mainstream programs and processes. In this chapter, I present ten AI developments that marketers should anticipate, along with those developments' potential impact on the marketing landscape. Staying abreast of these advancements is crucial for marketers aiming to lead in the AI era.

Quantum Computing–Aided AI

Quantum computing uses quantum-mechanical phenomena (such as superposition and entanglement; see the title *Quantum Physics For Dummies*, 3rd Edition by Andrew Zimmerman Jones [Wiley], for more on these concepts) to perform certain calculations exponentially faster than do classical computers. Quantum computers' potential to process enormous amounts of data in parallel may then massively accelerate AI training (which uses data) and the related inferences that stem from the data-driven training. If quantum computing advances in the way that the current technology field thinks it will, this combination of extraordinary computing power and advanced AI interpretation can likely provide marketers with an immediate, strategic decision-making advantage based on deep and precise data insights.

For marketers, quantum-computer-enhanced AI can potentially enable the analysis of large consumer data sets almost instantaneously. This analysis can then facilitate real-time predictions of market trends, generation of hyper-personalized content across the data set, and optimization of the entire customer journey based on highly granular data insights.

Autonomous Creative Campaigns

Imagine AI systems that go beyond assisting in content creation to spearheading entire marketing campaigns autonomously. Advanced AI has the potential to analyze market data, consumer insights, and past campaign performance to strategically develop comprehensive integrated marketing plans. Based on this analysis, AI could then produce a wide array of creative assets — such as copy, designs, images, and videos — which are all tailored to various specific channels and audiences. See Chapter 14 for information on the influence of AI on creative assets.

In addition, AI may advance to the point that it can autonomously execute the omnichannel campaigns that it develops and gather performance data that it can learn from to continuously optimize campaign targeting, messaging, ad placement, and budgets. Of course, all of this campaign work happens in real time based on *multivariate* (two or more variables) performance data.

This automation sounds like a dream solution for performance marketing (see Chapter 18), bid optimization, budget allocation, and creative refreshes that happen rapidly and maximize a business's return on investment (ROI). In addition, these future marketing systems could adapt strategies, messaging, and creative direction to stay synchronized with rapidly shifting market conditions, consumer trends, and competitor activities.

Cognitive AI Systems for Deep Insights

Advances in artificial general intelligence (AGI) may allow future AI systems to closely mimic and interpret human cognitive capabilities, such as reasoning, abstraction, and contextual understanding across a range of domains. These capabilities then enable the AGI to perform highly sophisticated analyses of complex consumer behaviors, motivations, and emotional responses. The AGI may then develop nuanced and specific psychological profiles of consumers that help businesses get ahead of the curve and drive customer demands based on these profiles.

Some details of how AGI may accomplish these analyses and the effects of doing so include

>> **Consuming massive data resources:** AGI will fuel its analysis and development by ingesting and processing massive volumes of behavioral and conversational data, facial expressions, and *psychographic insights* (classification of people according to their attitude and aspirations, for example).

>> **Combining vast data resources with predictive modeling:** AGI could accurately forecast future consumer needs, desires, and behavioral shifts, even before consumers themselves are consciously aware of them. See Chapter 20 for more about AI's predictive capabilities.

>> **Providing marketing and product teams with the key advantage of foresight:** Potentially, predictive AGI capabilities can enable proactive development of innovative products, services, and marketing campaigns that are precisely tailored to predict and shape customers' continuously evolving, unarticulated needs.

AI-Driven Virtual Reality Experiences

While virtual reality (VR) hardware and software continues advancing (Apple Vision Pro is just the beginning), AI will play a crucial part in creating truly immersive and interactive VR marketing experiences. AI-generated graphics, coupled with *spatial computing* (a concept that combines digital content with the physical world), will simulate highly realistic three-dimensional (3D) virtual environments that replicate real-world places with precise detail, and enable consumers to interact in these virtual worlds. The following mini-table shows how this situation may work.

The AI-Created Environment	How Consumers Interact
A retail store layout	Online shoppers virtually walk through and examine 3D product models from all angles by using natural hand motions. AI voices and animated virtual assistants provide information and guidance to simulate real sales interactions.
An imaginary brandscape	Consumers attend virtual events, gaming opportunities, immersive storytelling, or marketing activities in a *brandscape,* meaning a fanciful virtual world thematically linked to a product and its brand.

The future AI's ability to render realistic physics, respond to user actions seamlessly, and adapt the virtual world in real time can provide customer experiences that include unprecedented levels of interaction and engagement. Done well (and there were several failed efforts in the past such as Google Glass, which aimed to integrate augmented reality into everyday life but failed due to technical limitations, bad usability, and privacy concerns), AI-powered VR can make online shopping more tangible and turn brand marketing into extraordinarily memorable, delightful journeys of discovery.

Neural Interface for Marketing Insights

Advances in neural interfaces and brain-computer integration may eventually lead to direct communication between AI systems and the human brain. For marketing, this brain-machine synergy may enable experimentation in which AI gathers insights by monitoring consumers' neural responses and brain activity patterns while they experience products, services, or advertisements. If it can detect subtle neurological signals that correspond to emotions, desires, and cognitive processes, AI can glean an unprecedented vision of consumer preferences, decision-making drivers, and subconscious psychological reactions — insights practically impossible to articulate through traditional research methods. These insights can allow you to create hyper-targeted product design, positioning, and marketing tailored to individual consumers' deepest predispositions.

AI-Curated Personal Digital Realities

Advanced AI has the potential to securely integrate vast amounts of personal data (interests, behaviors, and preferences) to generate unique *digital realms* (also known as *digital twins*) that offer a virtual representation of the real world that's tailored to specific individuals. This sort of AI can dynamically adapt the entire digital realm experience — from user interfaces and recommended content to virtual environments and interactions. This capability enables marketers to craft hyper-personalized brand narratives and blend them into each consumer's customized digital reality.

WARNING

Although this personalization capacity may make marketing efforts feel seamlessly integrated yet highly impactful — by aligning ads, product recommendations, and brand messaging with a person's *psychographics* (classification according to attitudes, aspirations, and so on), buying habits, and immediate needs and mindset — this extremely personalized targeting may also backfire by distorting the customer's sense of what is real and what isn't! For instance, hyper-targeted ads can create an echo chamber effect, reinforcing biases and limiting exposure to diverse perspectives.

Synthetic Media for Dynamic Content

Advances in generative AI may enable the creation of synthetic media —video, audio, images, and text — that are virtually indistinguishable from human-created content. Machine learning techniques such as diffusion models and transformer architectures (see Chapter 5), can help AI generate highly realistic and coherent synthetic outputs from text prompts or data inputs. In addition, AI may generate synthetic influencers or virtual product ambassadors to further personalize brand messaging.

TIP

As a marketer, keep a close eye on synthetic media creation. If the Sora video-generating product launched by OpenAI in 2024 is any predictor, this AI development may be closer at hand than any of the others in this chapter's top ten list.

When it becomes available, marketers can harness this generative AI capability to dynamically produce personalized content for individuals or very specific consumer segments. From crafting individually tailored video ads and product visualizations to generating custom brand messaging and creative assets, the AI's output will automatically adapt to each viewer's preferences, demographics, and context. And so, future marketers can deliver highly engaging, relevant media assets without the time and cost constraints of manual production.

Predictive World Modeling

By ingesting and processing massive data sets across multiple domains, AI systems have the potential to build sophisticated simulation models that forecast global trends, economic dynamics, political shifts, and broader societal/cultural changes. These predictive models combine machine learning with causal reasoning and game theory to map out how data variables — such as government policies, modern technologies, available resources, and world events — may interact to shape the future.

Illustrating this predictive capability, the CEO of NVIDIA, Jensen Huang, announced in 2024 that meteorologists use NVIDIA chips that have simulation models harnessing generative AI to project weather patterns in Taiwan with unprecedented detail. This implementation shows how AI can create highly accurate predictive models by synthesizing vast amounts of data into complex simulations. The potential applications go beyond just weather forecasting to span numerous domains.

For marketers, access to such AI-powered foresight can provide a strategic advantage. These predictive models can potentially help anticipate upcoming market disruptions, product demand fluctuations, competitor movements, and evolving consumer behaviors well before those changes occur. This longer horizon can enable proactive adaptation of marketing strategies, product road maps, and business models to align with probable future scenarios. Companies will have the opportunity to future-proof offerings and messaging by adjusting to maintain relevance when conditions change.

AI as a Customer Behavior Simulator

Powerful AI systems may soon be able to simulate the behaviors and actions of millions of virtual consumer agents within rich simulated environments. These agent-based models would train on vast data sets to accurately mimic real-world consumer demographics, psychographics, and *decision heuristics* (mental shortcuts that enable quick decision-making). Marketers can then use those virtual environments as massive digital test beds to model the potential impacts of various marketing strategies, product launches, pricing models, or brand messaging before deploying them in the real world.

REMEMBER

By running countless scenarios and observing behaviors of the simulated consumer populations, marketers may identify optimal strategies and refine initiatives based on the scenarios' outcomes. Testing prototype initiatives through AI simulation has the promise of significantly reducing the risks and costs associated with new product rollouts or campaigns by catching potential issues early.

Molecular-Level Product Customization

Looking far into the future, advances in fields such as computational biology and generative AI may enable the customization of products at the molecular level. AI systems may leverage genomic data, biological modeling, and generative chemistry capabilities to design products that precisely adapt to individuals' unique biological characteristics, metabolic processes, and even their fundamental genetic makeup.

With molecular-level customization, marketing may evolve beyond demographic indicators to precisely target solutions optimized for each person's biochemical reality. This biotechnological convergence represents the pinnacle of personalization (and arguably, creepiness!). Imagine products such as personalized pharmaceuticals, *nutraceuticals* (products derived from food sources but with extra health benefits), cosmetics, or even tailored artificial organ designs. Each product could be uniquely engineered down to the molecular compounds that optimally suit an individual customer's physiology, health profile, and genetic predispositions.

Index

lead scoring and, 162–163
LTV and, 162–163
Dynamic Pricing AI, 163
Dynamic Yield, 225, 254, 316

E

Earnix, 163
education, progress
    assessment and, 53
efficiency, 13, 264
ELIZA, 10
e-mail and SMS marketing
    about, 268, 289
    e-mail interactions, 84
    filtering in e-mail, 115
    forecasting customer
        behavior, 293–294
    incorporating predictive
        analytics to engage
        customers, 292–293
    infusing e-mail campaigns with
        AI, 294–295
    infusing SMS campaigns with
        AI, 295–296
    reinforcement learning in, 84
    tools for, 297–298
    tracking, 290–292
    tracking metrics, 293–294
embeddings, as a feature of
    time series analysis, 87
emergency alerts, 296
emerging media channels, 360
emotions, natural language
    processing (NLP) and, 97–98
empirical evidence, lead
    scoring and, 156
employees, educating, 350
encoding, 73
"Enduring Ideas: The three
    horizons of growth," 326
energy sector, predictive
    analytics in, 108

Engage (Adobe Marketo), 288
Enigma machine, 8–9
enterprise data, 68
entertainment industry,
    generative AI in, 120–121
environmental impact,
    as a challenge of
    generative AI, 130
error correction, 73
escape velocity phase, of AI
    incorporation, 57–59
ethical sourcing, 342
ethical standards,
    ensuring, 314–315
ethical training/awareness, 345
ethics
    about, 335–336
    as an element of
        personalization, 304
    as a challenge of generative
        AI, 130–131
    data, 69
    establishing guidelines, 352
    operating principles
        for, 336–340
    in persona
        development, 143–144
    prioritizing, 53
event marketing, responsible
    data use in, 343
event notifications, 296
executive alignment, 325
exit surveys, 172
expert systems, 12, 13–14
expert validation, 143
exploration-exploitation
    dilemma, 84–85
Exploratory Data
    Analysis (EDA), 71
extracting, conversational
    interfaces for, 199
EY, 331

F

fairness, ethical AI and, 338–339
feature extraction, 75
feature learning, used
    by CNNs, 89
features, of time series
    analysis, 87
feedback initiatives, 172
feedback requests, 296
Feedvisor, 163
feelings, sentiment
    analysis and, 100
Fei-Fei Li (author), 330
filtering, 106, 114–117
finance sector, predictive
    analytics in, 107
first-party data, 340
follow-up initiatives, 172
forecasting, 40–41, 241, 293–294
format, specifying for
    prompts, 204
Forwrd, 158
frame interpolation, 220
function-specific AI policies, 325
function-specific use cases, 326
funnel testing, 252
future developments, 365–371
Future Record initiative, 226

G

gamification elements, 171
"garbage in, garbage out," 331
Gartner, 106
Gatorade, 304
Gemini (Google), 120, 129, 200
Gemini Help Center, 209
General Data Protection
    Regulation (GDPR), 69,
    217, 314, 338
generated personas, 358

About the Author

Shiv Singh, with over 25 years of accumulating expertise in marketing and business, has been instrumental in elevating major brands through innovative marketing strategies, customer engagement mechanisms, and data-driven results. As the Chief Marketing & Customer Experience Officer at LendingTree, he oversaw a team of 150 professionals who managed a significant advertising budget and reached over 100 million consumers. His experience spans marketing leadership roles at companies such as the Expedia Group, Visa Inc., and PepsiCo, earning him recognition as a top CMO by *Business Insider* and *Forbes*, among other accolades. He was also inducted into the American Advertising Federation Hall of Achievement in 2016. Beyond corporate leadership, Singh contributes as a board member for United Rentals and as a National Association of Corporate Directors (NACD) Board Leadership Fellow. Shiv is an advisor to Fortune 1000 companies and an investor in the startup ecosystem. He is also co-author with Rohini Luthra of the book *Savvy: Navigating Fake Companies, Fake Leaders and Fake News in the Post-Trust Era*. His work reflects a dedication to generating meaningful impact and innovation within the industry and communities that he engages with. Shiv's first book was *Social Media Marketing For Dummies* (Wiley), which was reprinted four times and translated into several languages.

Dedication

To my wife Rohini and my sons Arjan and Shyam for your endless encouragement and patience through every late-night writing session, soccer game, and family vacation. To my parents, my brother, and my entire family, whose lifelong support and belief in my writing have been invaluable.

Author's Acknowledgments

First and foremost, I'd like to thank Steve Hayes, the executive editor at Wiley Publishing, who has taken two bets on me — first with *Social Media Marketing For Dummies* many years ago and now again with this book, *Marketing with AI For Dummies*. His continued encouragement and advocacy over the years have meant a lot. This book wouldn't be what it is today without the incredible patience, thoughtfulness, and care from Leah Michael, who served as the project editor. It's been an absolute pleasure working with her. Finally, Laura K. Miller, the copy editor, and David Berkowitz, the technical reviewer, both strengthened the book in countless ways with their feedback.

I would also like to acknowledge the following corporate leaders for their formal and informal participation in my research process for this book. Their insights, expertise, and generosity with their time have been invaluable in shaping the book. Additionally, a few of them, although not directly involved in the book itself, have been inspiring influences over many years.

Abe Thomas (Microsoft), Angelique Krembs (A.Team), Bob Lord (IBM), Ben DeCastro (AI Trailblazers), Brad Jakeman (PepsiCo), Carla Hassan (JP Morgan Chase), Dan Kimball (Spectrum), David Jacobs (DoorDash), David Messenger (Trailer Park Group), Deepak Masand (HP), Frank Cooper (Visa), Jill Cress (H&R Block), Kamal Bhandal (Align Technologies), Krista Todd (Gen Digital), Liat Ben Zur (Microsoft), Marisa Thalberg (SeaWorld), Marissa Jarratt (7-Eleven), Mayur Gupta (Kraken), Melanie Huet (Newell Co), Melissa Waters (Upwork), Michael Lacorazza (US Bank), Ricardo Fort (Coca-Cola), Robin Zucker (Codecademy), Sandy Anuras (Panasonic), Shafqat Islam (Optimizely), Steven Wolfe Pereira (TelevisaUnivision), Tara Sharp (Viasat), Tariq Hassan (McDonalds), Veronica Song Gontier (Capital One), and Vineet Mehra (Chime).

Additionally, I extend my gratitude to leaders across the broader marketing and technology ecosystem whose perspectives were invaluable while I researched this book. Adam Schatler (Niantic), Alex Collmer (VidMob), Amit Shah (AI Trailblazers), Andy Pray (Praytell), Angela Mascarenas (Vokal.ai), Bhanu Sharma (Maker.co), Dan Greenberg (Pendium.ai), David Deal (DD Group), Elon Salfati (Venture Studio), Greg Kahn (AI Trailblazers), Jason Wulfsohn (Audience X), Jeff MacDonald (Mekanism), Jeremy Lockhorn (4As), Julie Bernard (Lily.ai), Mark Wagman (MediaLink), Matt Silverman (Swordfish), Matt Weiss (Huge), Max Snow (Yobi), Michael Donnelly (ANA), Michael Kassan (3C Ventures), Noah Brier (Percolate), Patricia Roller (Vidlet), Paul Willmington (Canvas), Pree Rao (Egon Zehnder), Purva Gupta (Lily.ai), Ray Velez (Publicis), Richard Sanderson (Spencer Stuart), Robert Tas (McKinsey), Ryan Detert (Influential), Saneel Radia (Proto), Seth Marlins (Forbes), Shane Ginsberg (MK49), and Tom Allejo (Lipponcott).

All of your contributions have greatly influenced the depth and breadth of this work and my own professional evolution, more broadly. Thank you all.

Publisher's Acknowledgments

Executive Editor: Steve Hayes

Development Editor: Leah Michael

Copy Editor: Laura K. Miller

Technical Editor: David Berkowitz

Production Editor: Tamilmani Varadharaj

Cover Images: © Panther Media GmbH/ Alamy Stock Photo, © Floriana/Getty Images, © Togapix/Getty Images, © Basilico Studio Stock/Getty Images